CALIFORNIA EDITION

EVERYBODY'S GUIDE TO
MUNICIPAL
COURT

BY JUDGE RODERIC DUNCAN

Edited by Attorney Robin Leonard

Illustrated by Mari Stein

NOLO PRESS   BERKELEY

Your responsibility when using a self-help law book

We've done our best to give you useful and accurate information in this book. But laws and procedures change frequently and are subject to differing interpretations. If you want legal advice backed by a guarantee, see a lawyer. If you use this book, it's your responsibility to make sure that the facts and general advice contained in it are applicable to your situation.

Keeping up to date

To keep its books up to date, Nolo Press issues new printings and new editions periodically. New printings reflect minor legal changes and technical corrections. New editions contain major legal changes, major text additions or major reorganizations. To find out if a later printing or edition of any Nolo book is available, call Nolo Press at 510-549-1976 or check the catalog in the *Nolo News*, our quarterly newspaper.

To stay current, follow the "Update" service in the *Nolo News*. You can get the paper free by sending us the registration card in the back of the book. In another effort to help you use Nolo's latest materials, we offer a 25% discount off the purchase of any new Nolo book if you turn in any earlier printing or edition. (See the "Recycle Offer" in the back of the book.)

FIRST EDITION

First Printing	November 1991
BOOK DESIGN	Jackie Mancuso
PRODUCTION	Louis Benainous
COVER DESIGN	Toni Ihara
INDEX	Sayre Van Young
PROOFREADING	Ely Neuman
PRINTING	Delta Lithograph

Duncan, Roderic, 1932-
    Everybody's guide to municipal court / by Roderic Duncan.
      p. cm.
    Includes index.
    ISBN 0-87337-156-9 : $29.95
    1. Municipal courts--California--Popular works. I. Title.
KFC970.Z9D86 1991
347.794'02--dc20
[347.94072]

91-22649
CIP

DEDICATION

Aside from being assigned an understanding judge, a pro per venturing into Municipal Court should hope to encounter a courtroom clerk sympathetic to the problems of a newcomer in a foreign land. In my 16 years as a judge, I've been fortunate to work with many such clerks. This book is dedicated to all of the user-friendly courtroom clerks in this state—in particular, to Municipal Court clerks Barbara Bliefert, Jackie Eklund, Connie Harvey, Mike and Leslye Robey, Mark Montgomery, Suzy Johnston, Bernice Garcia, Mary Trafton-Oxendine and Geny Fabella and to my Superior Court regulars, Nancy Regas, Leo Tungohan and Mary McGlothin.

ACKNOWLEDGEMENTS

The author gratefully acknowledges the assistance of:

Oakland-Piedmont-Emeryville Municipal Court research attorney Rina Hirai, who brought me up to date on the many changes in Municipal Court law and procedures that have taken place since I left the court.

Oakland-Piedmont-Emeryville Municipal Court clerk-administrator Theresa Beltran, civil division chief Sandy Elliott and clerk Mary Trafton-Oxendine, who made helpful suggestions.

Alameda County Law Librarian Cossette Sun, who helped locating resources.

Attorney William D. Gibbs of Oakland, a tort law specialist in, who contributed his expertise, while counseling (not always successfully) that the book not be critical of lawyers.

Frank Hellum, Alameda County Superior Court electronic genius, who was willing—in the middle of the night—to help me through the problems caused by using more than one computer system.

Jake Warner, whose idea it was, Steve Elias,who helped form the concept and Lisa Goldoftas and Robin Leonard, who worked and reworked the manuscript countless times.

All of the members of my family, who encouraged me to struggle back to the word processor to tackle yet another set of revisions suggested by the people named in the last paragraph above.

TABLE OF CONTENTS

chapter 3: Can't We Settle This Somehow?

chapter 4: Picking the Court and Parties

chapter 5: Preparing the Complaint

chapter 6: Filing the Papers

chapter 7: Serving the Papers

chapter 8: Lawsuits from the Defendant's Point of View

chapter 9: If the Defendant Doesn't Respond

chapter 10: Discovery

chapter 11: The Opposition Gets Nasty: Summary Judgment and Other Motions

chapter 12: The Memo to Set for Trial and Arbitration

chapter 13: Preparing for a Trial or Arbitration Hearing

chapter 14: Trial Before a Judge

chapter 15: Trial Before a Jury

chapter 16: After the Trial

chapter 17: Finding a Good Lawyer

appendix of tear-out forms

chapter 1

AN INTRODUCTION TO MUNICIPAL COURT

EVERYBODY'S GUIDE TO MUNICIPAL COURT

This book tells you how to represent yourself—whether you are suing or defending—in the most common types of lawsuits for money damages brought in Municipal Court. (In some small California counties Municipal courts are called "Justice" courts. Although this book uses the term Municipal Court, all the information applies identically to lawsuits brought in Justice courts.) These common types of lawsuits are breach of contract and tort cases. Before deciding whether or not to represent yourself, you should understand what is involved in a Municipal Court case and the advantages and disadvantages of representing yourself. If you are the person bringing the lawsuit, you must also decide:

- if Municipal Court is the appropriate court; and

- if this book covers your particular type of case.

A. What Is a Municipal Court Lawsuit?

A Municipal Court lawsuit begins when a person or a business—called the "plaintiff"—files a formal document—called a "Complaint"—with a Municipal Court clerk. The Complaint identifies:

- the plaintiff

- the defendant—the person or business being sued

- the date the Complaint was filed (this is important if the defendant has a statute of limitations defense—see Chapter 2)

- why the lawsuit was filed

- what the plaintiff wants out of the lawsuit

After the plaintiff files the Complaint, she has a friend, sheriff or professional whose business it is to deliver documents to people (called a "process server") deliver a copy of the Complaint, along with a Summons, to the defendant. (Chapter 7 covers this in detail.) The Summons is a document issued by the court, notifying the defendant that he is being sued.[1] The Summons also notifies the defendant that he has 30 days to contest the lawsuit by filing a written response. Although defendants can file several types of responses, the one that directly responds to the allegations in the Complaint is called an "Answer."

Check-the-box form Complaints that can be used in the breach of contract and tort cases discussed in this book are reproduced, with instructions for their completion, in Chapter 5 and the Appendix. Check-the-box form "Answers" are in Chapter 8 and the Appendix.

If the defendant files no response within the 30-day period, the plaintiff can move ahead to a quick resolution of the lawsuit under what is called "the default judgment procedure." This means that the plaintiff can normally get a judgment by simply asking the court to rule in her favor without having to follow the more complicated legal procedures described in the second half of this book.

If, however, the defendant files an Answer or other written response, the case will progress along a time-worn legal path. Often, the plaintiff and defendant will conduct "discovery," the phase of the lawsuit where the sides seek to find out what evidence the other is relying on. In most Municipal Court cases, discovery is limited

[1]Many people confuse a summons with a subpoena. Subpoenas are used to order someone to appear at a trial or deposition. Subpoenas are discussed in Chapters 10 and 13.

to asking the other side some written questions (called "interrogatories") or asking the other side to answer questions in person (called a "deposition").

Once discovery is over, the court may require the parties to meet and attempt to settle the case. If that is unsuccessful, the case goes on to trial. In the overwhelming majority of cases, the trial takes place before a judge. It is possible, however, for one of the parties (plaintiff or defendant) to force the case to a jury trial. If the losing party believes the judge made a serious error in conducting the trial, he can appeal to the Superior Court.

Because of the backlog of cases in most counties' Municipal Court criminal division, it can take more than a year from the time a case such as yours is filed and served on the defendant to the actual trial. Most cases take much less than a year, but the time your case will take will depend on the following:

- the amount of discovery conducted

- the backlog of cases in your county

- whether a jury trial is requested—a jury takes longer than a trial before a judge; the court expedites shorter cases first

B. Is Municipal Court the Right Court?

If you are a defendant in Municipal Court and you are thinking about defending yourself without a lawyer, you normally have little choice about what court you are in, and can skip ahead the next section. If you are the plaintiff, you need to read this section.

In California Municipal Court, you can sue for any amount from $1 up to $25,000. Depending on the amount of money you are suing for, you should consider two other possible California courts in which to bring your case. These are Small Claims Court and Superior Court.

1. Small Claims Court

The maximum amount you can sue for in California Small Claims Court is $5,000. Technically, Small Claims Court is a division of the Municipal Court. Its advantages are that cases move more quickly through Small Claims Court, and that people who represent themselves are treated much less formally than in Municipal Court. Although you can use either Municipal Court or Small Claims Court for suits of $5,000 or less, we recommend using Small Claims.

California's Small Claims Court

California's Small Claims court limit is somewhat unusual. You can sue for up to $5,000, but only twice in one year. If you need to sue more than twice, you can bring two cases for up to $5,000 and an unlimited number up to $2,500. For help in going to Small Claims court, see *Everybody's Guide to Small Claims Court*, by Ralph Warner (Nolo Press).

Normally lawyers can't appear in Small Claims Court. Also, in Small Claims Court the court clerks do most of the paperwork, there are no formal rules of evidence and judges are more disposed to help people who represent themselves.

Small Claims Court is so advantageous, you may want to use it even if you're case involves more than $5,000—say $6,000 or $7,000. To do this, you must reduce your claim to $5,000. If it is significantly over $5,000, however—say $15,000—it probably makes more sense to learn how to file a lawsuit in regular Municipal Court (called the civil division, as distinguished from the small claims division), which, of course, is what this book is all about.

> **Example:** Your bill for repairing your car after a minor accident is $6,000. Because it will be a lot easier to handle it in Small Claims Court, you scale it back and sue for the $5,000 limit. You are voluntarily giving up $1,000 just to get in the simpler court. But because you will save 25 to 50 hours of your own time and considerable anxiety, giving up the $1,000 makes sense.

There is one disadvantage to filing in Small Claims Court. If you lose, you cannot appeal—a small claims judgment is final against a plaintiff. If you sue in regular Municipal Court, however, and you lose, you can appeal to the Superior Court.[2] Thus, you are taking the risk that the judge hearing the case will render a favorable result. By contrast, if the defendant loses, she can appeal the case in either court. If you win in Small Claims Court and the defendant appeals, however, the case will proceed under informal rules and you can continue to represent yourself.

2. Superior Court

If your claim against a defendant is for more than $25,000 and you don't want to scale it back, your must file your case in Superior Court. Here, plaintiffs and defendants almost always hire lawyers, and the procedures are more complex

---

[2]As covered in Chapter 16, an appeal can be quite expensive and complicated, but in the right case it can be an important avenue in resolving your dispute.

than in Municipal Court. Either side can appeal. If you wish to file in Superior Court, this book is not for you.

C. Can You Represent Yourself?

If you are a competent adult (if you are reading this book and understanding it, you are competent) or a legally emancipated minor, you have the right to bring your own lawsuit or defend yourself if a case is filed against you. Someone who represents herself is referred to as appearing "in propria persona" or "in pro per." (In some states, this is called appearing "in pro se.")

Specifically, you can sue or defend on behalf of:

- yourself as an individual
- a partnership of which you are a partner
- your business, if you are a sole proprietor
- an unincorporated association of which you are a member

You *cannot*, however, represent another person—she must represent herself or hire an attorney to represent her. Thus, you cannot sue or defend on behalf of:

- a corporation (which the law considers to be a person) even if it's a small business in which you own all the stock

- family members (but adults can join you in suing on their own behalf)[3]

- an incapacitated or incompetent person even if you are the court-appointed conservator or guardian

- a minor, even if you are the parent or guardian

- a person for whom you serve as the attorney-in-fact under a durable or regular power of attorney

D. Does This Book Cover Your Type of Lawsuit?

This book is about self-representation in a California Municipal Court. Most people will be able to use it to file or defend a case in Municipal Court. It is important to emphasize, however, that some cases are quite difficult for a person to bring or defend without experienced legal help, and are too complex to cover in this book. Two questions can help you decide where your case falls.

---

[3]There is one exception to this rule. Code of Civil Procedure § 371 lets you defend your spouse if the two of you are sued together and he fails to defend himself.

1. Are You Asking for Money Damages?

This book is designed for lawsuits that are asking for money damages. The principal reason for this is that the court forms that exist to handle money cases are straightforward and easy to explain. In non-money cases, unfortunately, the forms are far more complicated and the legal theories are more difficult to explain.

If you are a plaintiff and plan to ask the court for something other than money damages, or you are a defendant and the plaintiff has requested something other than money damages, you will need to consult a lawyer or do some extensive legal research.

Here is a list of the type of cases I don't cover in this book:

- Criminal cases. All Municipal Court cases are classified as either criminal or civil. Although a criminal case may include a court order to pay money to an injured victim, criminal cases are the business of the District Attorney. Keep in mind, however, that a criminal act (such as an automobile accident involving a drunk driver) may produce both a criminal case and a civil one. In the criminal case, the District Attorney seeks to have the driver sent to jail or fined. In the civil case, the victims of the accident sue the driver for money to compensate them for their injuries.

- Lawsuits to dissolve a partnership, divide up jointly owned land or declare the rightful owner of property.

- Lawsuits to dissolve or annul a marriage, declare the paternity of a child or decide who will have the power to handle the affairs of a child or incompetent person.

- Lawsuits to rewrite (reform) or cancel (rescind) a contract.

- Lawsuits requesting an injunction or temporary restraining order to prevent someone from doing something.

- Lawsuits to evict a tenant.[4]

2. Do You Have a Tort or Breach of Contract Case?

Most Municipal Court requesting money damages fall into one of two categories: tort (injury) or breach of contract cases. The legal principles involved in tort and breach of contract cases were recognized by the courts a long time ago and are now fairly well set. Almost all of these types of cases can be brought in Municipal Court without a lawyer.

a. Tort Cases

This is a broad class of cases in which the plaintiff claims he was injured or damaged as the result of an intentional or careless act of the defendant.

Tort cases all have three basic elements:

- the defendant acted either carelessly or intentionally

- the plaintiff was injured physically, emotionally or both, and/or his property was damaged

- the defendant's act was the direct cause of the plaintiff's injury and/or damage

---

[4]Nolo Press publishes *The Landlord's Law Book: Volume 2, Evictions,* by David Brown, which includes the information and forms necessary to evict a tenant.

Below are several examples of torts. As you read, note that each example contains the three requirements set out. If your situation also has these elements, then you probably have a tort case.

Example 1: Fred, driving in his car, carelessly runs a red light and hits Sue's car in an intersection. The side of Sue's car is smashed and her neck is injured.

Example 2: Janet accidentally drops some fresh produce on the floor in a supermarket. Thirty minutes later Leroy slips and falls on piece of fruit still lying there.

Example 3: Sandy and Leslie are arguing. Sandy grows increasingly angry and suddenly hits Leslie in the face, breaking Leslie's nose.

Example 4: Mike is walking down the street pushing a dolly carrying an expensive piece of computer equipment. A painter working on a building project above the sidewalk drops a bucket of paint that lands on—and ruins—Mike's computer.

Some types of tort cases are more complex than others. This book focuses on the straightforward cases that sensibly can be brought by a pro per plaintiff. This book should not be used for the following types of cases:

- Medical, legal or other professional malpractice—lawsuits against lawyers, doctors or other professionals for negligent treatment. If you paid someone to draft a will, remove your appendix or do your taxes, and she failed to do so, you can sue for breach of contract (discussed in the following section) to get your money back. But if she attempted to do whatever you hired her to do and was negligent in doing it, you can sue her in a tort case called malpractice. These kinds of tort cases are very complex, and usually involve more than $25,000.

- Civil rights or civil liberties—lawsuits involving a deprivation of rights under the constitution or discrimination on account of race, sex, religion or the like.

- Libel and slander—lawsuits requesting damages to compensate a plaintiff because of something injurious the defendant said or wrote about the plaintiff.

- Fraud—lawsuits where a plaintiff claims that a defendant intentionally or carelessly misrepresented or concealed a fact with the intention of deceiving the plaintiff. The misrepresentation must be justifiably relied upon by the plaintiff to her harm. A person who proves that she was defrauded is almost always entitled to punitive damages (see below). Fraud cases are complex and generally require the involvement of a lawyer.

- Emotional distress—lawsuits in which the plaintiff claims that the defendant's negligent or intentional conduct caused the plaintiff emotional upset, but no actual physical harm. This is a fairly new area of the law that involves complicated questions and difficult problems of proof.

- Product liability—lawsuits in which a plaintiff claims that a manufactured item caused physical injury to the plaintiff. If the plaintiff received a defective item, but isn't injured, he can sue for a breach of contract or warranty (see the next section). But if a product malfunctioned and caused the plaintiff physical injury, the matter usually requires a lawyer.

- Exemplary or punitive damage—lawsuits where a plaintiff believes that the outrageous conduct of a defendant entitles the plaintiff to recover damages meant to punish or serve as an example for others. (Chapter 5, Section B.1.f, covers these damages in detail. Be aware that only a very small percentage of people who sue, thinking they were treated outrageously by a defendant, are awarded punitive damages beyond their out-of-pocket losses.)

- Cases in which your auto or homeowner's insurance company has already paid you some money for your damages. In that situation, talk to the company before suing. The company may have negotiated a settlement with the defendant that prevents you from suing.

b. Breach of Contract Cases

Contracts are agreements made between individuals and/or businesses. Many transactions involve contracts, even if no one sat down and prepared any papers. A plaintiff might bring a breach of contract lawsuit if she bought something that wasn't what it was represented to be or hired someone who didn't do what he was supposed to.

In general, your case will involve a breach of contract if a person (or business) failed to perform his end of a binding agreement, thereby causing the other party to the agreement economic loss. Binding agreements come in many forms and include:

- buying or selling goods to be delivered now or in the future

- renting a product, such as an automobile or a rug shampooer

- doing work in exchange for goods or services

- hiring someone to perform services
- borrowing or lending money
- extending credit for goods or services

The contract or agreement can be verbal, written or, in some cases, implied from the circumstances. The issues in most contract cases are whether or not there was a binding agreement and, if so, what it means and whether or not it was broken ("breached" in legalese).

Contracts That Must Be in Writing

Under a law called the "statute of frauds," certain contracts cannot be enforced unless the agreement, or a note or memorandum of it, is in writing and signed by the person you are suing. Thus, if you are a plaintiff and alleging the breach of any one of these kinds of contracts, normally your shouldn't bother to sue unless the contract or a memorandum of it is written down and signed. Otherwise, the defendant will come to court and claim a failure to comply with the statute of frauds, and your case is likely to be dismissed.

There are several ways to get around the statute of frauds, so you may want to consult of lawyer if it appears you might have a statute of frauds problem. You can also consult *Summary of California Law* (9th edition), by Bernard Witkin, at Sections 261-331.

The following contracts are the major types that must be in writing:

- Contracts or leases that cannot be performed within one year, such as a five-year lease
- Contracts for for the sale of goods for the price of $500 or more unless the buyer makes a partial payment, or the goods are delivered, at the time of the sale
- Contracts for the sale of real estate
- Contracts employing a real estate agent
- Contingency fee contracts with a lawyer. A contingency fee contract is one where a lawyer represents you in exchange for a percentage share of what you recover. If you don't win, the lawyer recovers nothing.

Here are some examples of breached contracts.

Example 1: Uncle Walter needed to borrow $10,000 for two months. Audrey loaned it to him on his verbal promise to pay her back. Four months have passed, Uncle Walter hasn't paid and he won't return Audrey's phone calls.

Example 2: Marc paid a plumber $20,000 to install a new bathroom in his storefront. Marc discovers that the plumber hooked up the toilet to the sewer incorrectly. Now the plumber won't fix it unless Marc gives him another $3,000.

Example 3: Sheila owns a clothing store. A supplier convinced her to carry a line of sweaters, and agreed to buy them back if they didn't sell. The sweaters didn't move and now the supplier refuses to buy them back.

Example 4: Chris sold his boat through a classified ad for $19,000. Milt gave him $5,000 down and a written promise to pay the additional $14,000 within ten days. Two weeks later Milt called Chris to say that he lost his job and can't come up with the rest of the money for a while. Milt wants to return the boat, but Chris wants the money.

Example 5: The engine seized up the day after Elaine bought a two-year-old used car from a used car dealer. Elaine's mechanic told her that the engine was shot and that it will cost over $8,000 to replace it and do other necessary work. The used car dealer won't discuss it.

Example 6: Francisco told a salesperson at a computer store that he needed a system to handle a sizeable database and state-of-the-art software. The salesperson talked him out of a national brand that would do the job and instead recommended the house brand for $9,500. Francisco bought it and took it home, only to discover that it can't handle his large database or his specialized software. The store offers to sell Francisco memory enhancements and a larger hard disk, but won't take back the computer and return his money.

Example 7: Ruth runs an import-export business. A year ago she signed a five-year commercial lease when the owner of the building promised he'd put in a loading dock. Ruth is still waiting for the dock. Rather than continue to wait, Ruth builds the dock herself at a cost of $22,000 and sues the owner for the money.

Example 8: Three months ago Art paid a lawyer a "non-refundable" $8,000 retainer to represent him in the purchase of a business. The lawyer talked to Art several times and wrote a few letters, but has otherwise done nothing. Escrow is due to close next week and the lawyer's secretary says he is too busy to talk to Art. Art hires another attorney to represent him and sues the first lawyer for the return of his retainer.

Some Contracts You Might Miss

We enter all sorts of written contracts in our daily life. Even if you don't have a copy of some of them, it that doesn't mean you are not bound by them. Here are some examples:

• credit card agreements

• automobile or truck leases

• insurance policies

• work orders

• invoices a delivery person asks you to sign

---

c. Contract Cases in Which You Should Consult a Lawyer

Two types of breach of contract can could cause you special problems if you tried to bring (or defend) them in Municipal Court yourself. These are cases where:

• a written contract requires that you attempt to mediate a dispute, or resolve it through out-of-court arbitration, before filing a lawsuit. Depending on the terms of the mediation or arbitration, this normally will be a blessing because it can make for a quicker and simpler resolution of your case. But if the arbitration plan doesn't seem fair and you want to avoid it and go directly to court, you will need a lawyer's help.

• the contract is considered illegal under the law, or requires one person to engage in illegal behavior. Most contracts between consenting adults are legal and enforceable; some, however, are not. You will probably need the help of a lawyer if your contract involves one of the following problems.

1. Illegal Interest Rate (Usury)

California has a complicated set of rules, called "usury law," which prohibits interest charges in excess of 10%. The law, however, contains several exceptions, making it difficult to be sure just what transactions this limit applies to. For example, it doesn't apply to banks, loan companies, credit card companies and many merchants, some of whom can charge as much as 30%. Virtually all businesses are aware of the rate they are permitted to charge and it is thus rare to find a business violating the usury law.

In private transactions, however, any agreements to pay more than 10% interest for money or goods intended for personal, family or household purposes is illegal. If you mistakenly loaned money to a friend or relative and charged interest over 10%, don't accept any payment for the interest and offer to rewrite the contract at 10%. If you don't and you sue to collect, you'll be entitled to a judgment for the principal (the amount you loaned) only. If the borrower paid you any interest, she can sue and ask for a penalty of triple the amount of the interest already paid.

2. Gambling and Other Illegal Matters

All gambling, except horse racing and the state lottery, is illegal in California, and lawsuits to collect debts based on gambling are usually unenforceable. If you want to sue on a contract involving gambling or some other criminal activity, consult a lawyer.

3. Services by an Unlicensed Person

The law requires certain people—such as building contractors, architects, real estate agents, real estate brokers and attorneys—to have a license in order to perform their services. If the performer doesn't have the required license, the person receiving the services doesn't have to pay.

The law provides a small exception for building contractors: if the total cost of labor and materials is under $300, the contractor, licensed or not, has the right to be paid. But if the bill is higher and the buyer won't pay, the contractor won't win in court if he didn't have a contractor's license, no matter how beautiful a job he did.

E. The Pros and Cons of Representing Yourself in Municipal Court

If you have a lawsuit that fits in Municipal Court and is within the scope of this book, you still have an important decision to make. Do you want to represent yourself or hire a lawyer? There are pros and cons of each.

How To Find Out Who Has a License

To check whether someone who did work for you is licensed, phone the applicable state licensing bureau. If the number isn't listed below, call the State Department of Consumer Affairs at 916-445-4465.

Accountants	916-920-7121
Architects	916-445-3393
Automotive repair shops	916-366-5023
Chiropractors	916-445-3244
Contractors	916-366-5153
Dentists	916-920-7197
Doctors	916-920-6013
Engineers	916-920-7466
Funeral directors	916-445-2143
Lawyers	415-346-6601
	213-580-5000
Marriage & family counselors	916-445-4933
Nurses	916-322-3350
Optometrists	916-739-4131
Pharmacists	916-445-5014
Podiatrists	916-920-6347
Psychologists	916-920-6383
Social Workers	916-445-4933
Structural pest control (termite) inspectors	916-924-2291
Tax preparers	916-324-4977
Television & appliance repair shops	916-445-4751
Veterinarians	916-920-7662

1. The Up Side of Self-Representation

The main advantage of representing yourself in Municipal Court is that you can save a bucket of money. Assuming you find an attorney you want to hire, that person will charge $100-$200 per hour for meeting with you, talking to you on the phone, attempting to reach a settlement with the other side, studying your case in the library, driving to court, waiting for the case to be called by the judge, as well as actually arguing it for you. And this bill will add up fast, as lawyers rarely bill in less than 15-minute increments. Thus, if your lawyer charges $160 per hour ($40 for 15 minutes), and you call and talk for five minutes, you'll probably be charged $40, not $13.33.

Your bill will probably exceed $1,000 within a very short time, and the total is likely to run to many times that amount. And even if you win your case, the American legal system rarely provides that a winning party's attorneys fees get paid by the losing party.[5]

> **Example:** You win a case against your brother-in-law for the $12,000 he borrowed from you. You hired a lawyer, who charged $3,000 for her services. To make matters worse, she will expect to be paid pronto even though it will probably take years to collect your judgment from your sister's bum of a husband. Had you served as your own lawyer and won the case, the victory would have been $3,000 sweeter.

Lawyers in what are sometimes called "accident cases" (known by lawyers as

---

[5]Some contracts include a provision that if the party that drew up the contract sues the other party and wins, she is entitled to have her attorneys fees paid by the loser. Such a provision is perfectly valid. Under Civil Code § 1717, however, such a provision governs both parties. Thus, if a contract with a creditor says that if he sues you for payment and wins, he is entitled to attorneys fees, if you sue him and win, you can get attorneys fees as well.

"personal injury cases") don't charge by the hour. Instead, they normally receive 33% to 50% of any money you recover at the end of the case. These are called contingency agreements. Obviously if you have a legitimate $20,000 claim against someone whose negligent behavior caused you to be injured, the lawyer's share can be big money.

2. The Down Side of Self-Representation

There are disadvantages to representing yourself. I don't want to overemphasize the negative, but you must understand and accept what you are up against.

a. Municipal Court Is Geared Toward Lawyers

Municipal Court was created by and for lawyers, although pro pers are certainly showing up more frequently. Nevertheless, by representing yourself, you are rocking the boat—and boat rockers are often not appreciated.

A Municipal Court judge is an ex-lawyer and may patronize you or, worse, be openly hostile. Other court personnel are socialized to work with lawyers who know the ropes and sometimes resent pro pers. The lawyer representing your opponent may feel it his duty to take advantage of your lack of knowledge about the law. But many judges and court clerks are sympathetic to pro pers and many people like you successfully handle their own cases every day.

b. Representing Yourself Will Take Time

If you are the plaintiff and the defendant doesn't contest the case, you can normally get a default judgment without spending much time. If, however, the defendant contests your case or you are the defendant and plan to defend yourself—and especially if the other side has a lawyer—your case will probably involve a substantial amount of your time. Not only will you have to prepare legal papers, learn court procedures and possibly initiate or respond to discovery, but you'll also find yourself waiting around courtrooms for your case to he heard. When the day and hour finally arrives, the trial could take several days.

If you are the plaintiff, bear in mind that the likelihood of your case being contested is difficult to predict. If the defendant is a businessperson or has applicable insurance, he'll probably fight. If he clearly owes you money and has no legal defense, there is a decent chance he won't oppose you.

c. You'll Need To Rely on Others for Impartial Judgments

A third basic problem you will have if you represent yourself is one I unhappily observe almost every day in court. Most people have difficulty making rational and sensible decisions about tactics and settlement possibilities when their emotions are running high. Most lawyers avoid representing themselves, realizing that their desire to get even with their opponent is likely to interfere with their ability to make sound decisions.

Because going pro per means, by definition, you will face this problem, I recommend that you set up a mechanism to cope with it. Find a mature, knowledgeable person whose advice you will seek and respect each time you must make an important decision in your case.

d. You'll Have To Lay Out the Court Costs

Even if you represent yourself and save money by not hiring a lawyer, you'll face a number of expenses such as filing fees, a fee to serve the papers on the other side and, in some instances, the cost of taking a deposition. In a typical case, these costs can add up to several hundred dollars. Some of the costs can be waived if you qualify as a low income person.

Typical Court Costs

They typical fees for a plaintiff in a $20,000 lawsuit might include:

Filing fee	$150 (Chapter 6)
Process server's fee	30 (Chapter 7)
Deposition cost	250 (Chapter 10)
Photocopying	15
Postage	10
Miscellaneous	50

A defendant can expect to incur similar costs, except that the filing fee will be lower and he won't have to pay a process server.

If you win the case, the court will most likely order the other side to pay your costs. But then you have to collect. If you lose the case, you not only have to pay your costs, but you'll probably be ordered to pay the other side's as well.

DO YOU HAVE A GOOD CASE?

If you are a defendant, most of this chapter isn't directly relevant. You should read Section A. Then you may want to read Sections B and C for help in evaluating the strength of the plaintiff's case, the strength of your case and for help in deciding if you want to file your own case against the plaintiff. After reading Sections A, B and C, jump ahead to Chapter 3.

Before you file a lawsuit in Municipal Court, ask yourself these two questions:

- How good are my chances of winning?
- If I win, will I able to collect?

To help you answer these and the other questions that will come up during your case, the first thing I recommend you do is find a trusted confidant to discuss important issues as they arise.

A. Find a Sounding Board

I call the person who fills this role a "Sounding Board." Choosing the right person is one of the most important things you will do in handling your case.

Your Sounding Board may be a friend, relative or colleague who can help you analyze your situation objectively. He or she should listen critically to your legal theories, as well as to the practical side of your case. You need someone who will treat your views with a little skepticism and ask tough questions.

Your Sounding Board should not be someone who always tends to agree with the your

opinions. Anything short of honest assessments from your Sounding Board will hurt you in the long run.

B. Has the Statute of Limitation Passed?

Laws called "statutes of limitation" govern the number of years in which you must sue after the incident giving rise to the lawsuit occurred. If the statute of limitation has passed, don't bother to sue.

Statutes of limitation differ for different types of cases:

- Injury to your body resulting from an intentional or negligent act—one year
- Damage to your property—three years
- Oral contract—two years from when the contract is broken
- Written contract—four years from when the contract is broken
- Hidden defects in a construction project (such as a home)—10 years after the completion of the project
- Claims against government entities—this isn't a formal statute of limitation, but if you have a claim against a government agency, you must file a special form within six months. (See Chapter 4, Section D.2.)

Several other statutes of limitation are in the Code of Civil Procedure.[1] Few of these will be relevant to your case. In some situations, more than one statute of limitations may apply. For example, if you were hurt in an accident, you

---

[1]See §§ 312-365.

have one year to sue for the physical injuries to your body, and three years to sue for the damage to your property.

The statute of limitation is shorter for an oral contract than for a written one, but most of your contracts are probably at least partially written. The work order you sign at a garage, an IOU, a credit account with a department store and similar transactions all involve written agreements.

Also, the statute of limitation for a breach of contract starts to run on the day the contract was broken, not the day it was written. And if the contract called for installment payments, the statute runs separately for each installment as it becomes due. For example, your written contract calls for a payment on the 15th days of March and September of 1992. The other party fails to pay on March 15, 1992, you can sue on that payment until March 15, 1996. If the other party doesn't make the September 15, 1992 payment, you can bring suit until September 15, 1996.

Determining if the statute of limitation has run can get complicated. If it appears to have elapsed, consult a lawyer. You have probably lost your right to sue; however, on a rare occasion, a lawyer may be able to get around a time restriction.

C. What Is Your Chance of Winning?

An essential step in deciding whether or not to file a lawsuit—or whether or not to defend against one—is to examine your chance of winning. Lawsuits are won by people who have the facts and the law on their side, not by who have the saddest stories. Sometimes nice people are surprised when they lose a case because they

had assumed "the good guy" always wins. Unfortunately, it isn't that simple.

To analyze your chance of winning, decide if:

* your evidence will convince the court to award you damages (or deny the plaintiff her request for damages)
* your evidence is admissible in court so that it can be considered by the judge
* you can prove each fact you are required to prove in your type of lawsuit (usually a contract or tort), if you are a plaintiff

Let's look at each of these.

1. Is Your Evidence Convincing?

First, consult your Sounding Board. Carefully explain the facts of your case (or defense) and the evidence you plan to use to prove them. Ask for an honest assessment. Then urge your Sounding Board to play devil's advocate—that is, to challenge your conclusions and evidence—and to state the other side's case as strongly as he can. Ask your Sounding Board how he would decide the case if he was the judge. Finally, follow your Sounding Board's advice. If your case doesn't look so hot to your wise adviser, it probably won't look any better in court.

Such a review would have been helpful to a couple who appeared before me several years ago. They described how their Volkswagen engine had burst into flame while they were driving down the freeway with their young child in the back seat. They had pulled over quickly and exited safely, but their car was a total loss. They sued the local Volkswagen dealer who had done repairs on the gas lines about two weeks earlier.

After hearing their testimony, I asked if they had had a mechanic examine their ruined car to try to determine the cause of the fire. They hadn't thought it necessary, assuming anyone would conclude that the gas line repair was done incorrectly by the dealer. I was sympathetic and understood how they had came to that conclusion.

Unfortunately, however, their task was to prove to me that the fire had been caused by some negligence of the dealer. Vague probabilities or suppositions aren't enough—they needed some hard evidence that the fire was the dealer's fault. I could declare them the winner only if their evidence led to the conclusion that their theory was more likely to be correct than any other explanation. Because they lacked that sort of evidence, judgment was for the defendant.

Let's hope that a good Sounding Board would have helped this couple see that in their outrage about the fire, they had jumped to a unproven conclusion that couldn't stand on its own in the harsh light of the courtroom. A good Sounding Board would have asked "What makes you think the fire resulted from the repair?" The need for a detailed examination of the burned car by a mechanic would then have been obvious.

2. Is Your Evidence Admissible?

Okay, your evidence is convincing. Now you must figure out if it is admissible. That means that it is the type of evidence the court is legally authorized to hear and consider. The study of evidence is a year-long course at most law schools and, as you will readily understand, I cannot cover it in depth here. But I can summa-

rize the most important principles. This material is discussed in detail in Chapter 13.

Follow these general rules when analyzing your evidence:

Witnesses must have personal knowledge. Unless a witness qualifies as an expert (see next paragraph), a witness must have been present and have personal knowledge of what happened at some significant event in the story of your case to be able to testify in court about those facts. Possible witnesses include you, your friends and your relatives, as well as complete strangers, as long as they have firsthand knowledge. For the most part, people who merely heard about the events from someone else can't testify.

Opinion evidence is allowed infrequently. Generally, only a person with specialized training in a scientific or technical field (called an "expert") can give an opinion in court. But don't despair—all sorts of experts give opinions in court in exchange for a fee. For example, an experienced mechanic would normally qualify to give an opinion about a car repair; similarly, an electrician could testify about a wiring installation. In some fields, college professors frequently give helpful testimony or know of other experts who may be able to help you.

 For a good review of many fields of expert testimony, see *California Expert Witness Guide*, published by the California Continuing Education of the Bar (CEB), and available at most law libraries.

When You Need an Expert

You won't need an expert in every case. But you should consider hiring one if your case involves:

- a car in need of repair
- plumbing, electrical, construction or similar work around the home
- an accident in which skid marks or other markings may indicate negligent or reckless driving.

There are a few areas in which a non-expert can offer an opinion. A non-expert can offer testimony regarding:

- the identity of a person, including descriptive features such as voice or physical traits
- a person's appearance, state of intoxication, health or age
- her own intention, motive or emotion
- the value of her own property or services
- measurements, such as speed, distance or size
- the directions from which sounds came

Written statements are usually not allowed. Generally, you can't use written statements by witnesses. This rule applies to most police reports and even to notarized affidavits and declarations made under penalty of perjury. There is an exception, however. Routine business records may be brought into court by their custodian. Here are some examples:

- A bank officer can bring monthly bank statements into court.
- Rent receipts may be brought to court by a landlord.
- A creditor can introduce business records showing when bills are sent and payments received, as long as the person who supervises the recordkeeping is available to testify.

Photos and other physical objects must be identified by a knowledgeable witness. The photographer need not testify in court as to the contents of the photo or to the process used as long as a witness can state that the photo accurately depicts a particular scene. Other physical objects may be used as evidence as long as a witness can link them to the case from her own personal knowledge.

Impartial witnesses are preferable. An impartial witness who didn't know any of the parties before the event is a more valuable witness than your friends and relatives. If, however, your only testimony is from your spouse and your sister, by all means use them—their testimony is a lot better than nothing.

You can't introduce evidence about a person's character. Evidence showing what a good person you are and what a bad person the other side is is generally not allowed.

3. Can You Prove Each Legally Required Fact?

The final test in assessing your chances of winning is difficult to explain in a book of this type. But keep in mind the following: For every type of lawsuit, a plaintiff must prove a list of required facts (called "elements") in order to win. The elements of lawsuits are what law students study for three years and legal authorities write about endlessly. Sometimes the requirements change as legislatures enact new laws and amend old ones, and courts interpret the laws.

For the simple lawsuits I discuss in this book, I don't believe you must torture yourself over the question of whether or not you can prove each required fact. Instead, read over the descriptions of tort and contract lawsuits in Chapter 1. If your facts seem similar, your major pieces of evidence are admissible and your Sounding Board agrees that you have a solid case, proceed to prepare your suit.

D. Preserve Your Evidence Now

If you've concluded that your evidence is convincing and admissible, it's time to preserve any evidence you might use. Bruises and skid marks lighten in time. Work orders and cash register receipts are often misplaced. Witnesses move and memories fade.

To preserve your evidence, set up some files in a safe place. Make one file for repair bills, another for medical reports and as many more as you need for your different kinds of evidence. I can't emphasize how important this is. Many times I've seen witnesses in court say that they've lost an important document. If they ask for a few more days to search, I usually can't al-

low it. Evidence produced after the trial is over is useless.

Here are some of the things you should put in your files.

Photographs. Try to take pictures as close to the time of an event as possible—before the scene changes. Photos taken later may be used, but only if nothing else is available. Here are some pointers on particular situations:

• If the subject is difficult to photograph, such as a loose rug in a dark hallway, or a botched paint job on the underside of an roof overhang, hire a professional photographer.

• If the condition of a car is important and the car is being held in a garage, go and take a picture before it is repaired or moved.

• If the presence or absence of a sign is important, photograph the scene before it changes. To prove that the photograph was not taken before a particular date, place a copy of that day's newspaper in the picture.

• Use color film to photograph bruises or wounds. If they are changing rapidly, take a picture every day or two and record the date each was taken. If the date the photograph was taken will be important, consider having a friend or—better yet an impartial person—take the picture. Again, to prove that a photograph was not taken before a particular date, place a copy of that day's newspaper in the picture.

Medical evaluation. Seek a medical evaluation of any physical or emotional injury as soon as possible. Begin with your regular physician. If you're getting treatment from a chiropractor or other non-M.D., you still should be evaluated by a medical doctor. Most injury cases are settled with insurance companies who are notoriously skeptical of chiropractors and other alternative healers. If you don't have an M.D., ask your chiropractor or other healer for a referral.

Physical objects. Keep all relevant physical objects. If you are the plaintiff, you will have to prove your damages. You don't want to have to testify that you threw an important piece of evidence into a garbage can. Also, try to keep damaged items in their damaged condition. Where this is impractical—for example, if you need to repair or replace your faulty wiring or car—get at least two written estimates before having the work done.[2] You can use the estimates in settlement negotiations and at any arbitration hearing, and have the persons who gave the estimates testify at trial. If a particular part of the about-to-be repaired item shows the damage, have the mechanic (or other repairperson) save it.

Witnesses. If you know of any witnesses to the event in question, find them and ask them what they saw. Police reports sometimes list witnesses' addresses and phone numbers. (If the witness doesn't have deep roots in the community, try to get the name, address and phone number of some person who will be able to help you locate your witness in the future.) In talking to witnesses, don't put words in their mouths or argue with them, even if you violently disagree with what they say.

If a witness seems helpful, explain how important his testimony is and ask if you can interview him with a video or tape recorder. If the witness doesn't want to be on tape, write down his words on paper and ask him to sign his name. If he refuses to sign ("I don't want to get

---

[2]Some insurance adjusters will tell you they need three estimates and that you must have the work done by the lowest bidder. This simply isn't true.

involved"), an unsigned statement can still be valuable, as long as a third person was present and will testify that it is a true statement of what was said by the witness.

How To Interview a Witness

If a witness agrees to be interviewed and taped, begin the interview by stating the date, where the interview is taking place and who is in the room. Then ask the witness if she understands that she is being recorded.

For the actual interview, start by asking the witness exactly where she was located and what she could see. Then develop the story slowly, moving step by step. Ask questions that bring out the most basic facts. Try to imagine that the story is being told to someone who knows nothing about what happened. Be sure to get explanations of imprecise words. If the witness says the defendant was acting "crazy," ask just what "crazy" means.

Recorded statements of witnesses are not normally allowed in court, but they can be very effective in settlement negotiations and in reminding a witness of what he saw if the case goes to trial. If the witness changes his testimony at trial, the video or tape recording can be played for the judge or jury to show the witness's lack of reliability (called "impeaching the witness").

Pain diary. If you've been physically or emotionally injured—no matter how minor or severe—keep a daily "pain diary." Every few days describe briefly how you feel, whether you are having sleep, mobility or other problems, and any drugs you are taking. This information is nearly impossible to remember accurately months later. Don't lay it on too thick, however. Your opponent will probably eventually see your diary and will try to get it before the judge if you are too melodramatic.

Police reports. Police reports are generally not admissible as evidence in court, but they can help you investigate and settle your case. Insurance adjusters often base their settlement offers on the opinions of investigating police officers. To obtain a police report, visit the applicable police department, sheriff's office or California Highway Patrol office. Ask for a copy of the officer's report. You'll probably have to pay a few dollars for copying charges.

Reading a Police Report

Police reports come in many formats. Study the report carefully; you'll often find a box where the reporting officer gives her opinion as to who might have been at fault for the accident.

The officer's opinion may be indicated by reference to a Vehicle Code section. For instance, if you're identified as "Driver 1" and the other driver is "Driver 2," you may find a column labeled "Driver 2" with the number "22100" in it. 22100 is the Vehicle Code section dealing with unsafe turns. This probably means that the officer thought the other driver was making an unsafe turn at the time of the accident. Sometimes, this information will be in a police report even if the officer didn't issue a ticket. If you don't understand the report, take it back to the police department and ask for help.

If the officer didn't write down a Vehicle Code section, she may still have an opinion about who caused the accident. The opinion probably won't be admissible in court, but it can be persuasive in settlement negotiations. If the police officer doesn't agree with your version, it doesn't necessarily mean you don't have a case. Police officers make mistakes like everyone else. You just have to look elsewhere for your evidence.

Accident reconstruction experts. Accident reconstruction experts investigate accidents on behalf of injured people. If you want to show that a police officer's opinion was wrong or if your accident was complicated, consider consulting an accident reconstruction expert. You can find them in the telephone Yellow Pages for major cities. Some are quite good; others have little real expertise. To find a good one, ask for references (and check them out) and credentials. Make sure you know what the fee is in advance.

Citations to Laws

 Throughout this book I refer to California codes such as the Vehicle Code, the Evidence Code, the Civil Code and the Code of Civil Procedure. These codes collect all the laws in a particular legal subject area. While laws themselves are written and organized into codes by the state Legislature, they are compiled and published by several different private companies, and are available at many general libraries and all law libraries.

Most of the time when I refer to a law (code section), I explain what it says and how you can use it. But sometimes you will need the exact wording of the law. If so, visit a library and ask a librarian for help in locating the appropriate code. When you find it, look up the particular law in the appropriate bound volume. Then, look for the code section in the pamphlet tucked into the back of the book (called a "pocket-part"). The pocketpart will contain any Legislative amendments passed or court interpretations made since the bound volume was published.

These volumes are published in annotated form by private companies such as West and Matthew Bender. Annotated codes contain not only the laws, but also lists of explanatory materials such as court cases, rules of court and law review articles. Up-to-date copies of unannotated codes can be purchased at law book stores for under $20.

In addition to the codes, various court rules will govern your case. Statewide rules are published in a volume called the California Rules of Court. You can find this book at any law library. Also, your local court will have a set of rules that govern just that court. Be sure to review a copy at either the court clerk's office or your local law library.

E. Can You Collect the Judgment if You Win?

When I was a Municipal Court judge, I often felt a little sad after telling some pro per plaintiffs that I was ruling in their favor. Their face would brighten, their eyes would dart around the courtroom nervously, and then they'd ask what seemed to be the next logical question: "When do I get paid?" It was almost as if they thought the courthouse had a window where winning plaintiffs could go and watch a clerk count out the money due. "The sad truth is," I'd say, "you've just finished the easy part of your case. Now you must start the hard part—collecting."

In fact, many judgments are aptly described as "not worth the paper they are printed on." This isn't the court's fault. The legislature has passed many laws to protect people who have little money from losing what is left. These are called "exemptions" and include basic household goods, furnishings, clothing, $1,200 equity in a car, 75% of wages and between $50,000 and $75,000 of equity in a house.[3] For a complete list of exempt property, see *Collect Your Court Judgment*, by Scott, Elias and Goldoftas (Nolo Press).

The point is to ask yourself "can I collect if I win" before you file your case. Don't sue unless you can answer "yes." If you win your case, the judge or jury will decide how much the defendant should pay you. Some defendants pay right away. Some never pay. If the defendant won't pay voluntarily, you can use certain collection techniques to force him to pay.[4] Court judgments last for 10 years in California and can be renewed indefinitely. This means that just because the defendant doesn't have any money or property now doesn't mean that you'll never collect.

---

[3]For a single person, the house exemption in $50,000. For a married couple, it's $75,000. For the elderly or disabled, it's $100,000.

[4]*Collect Your Court Judgment* explains these techniques.

Here are some ideas about collecting from certain defendants.

Large businesses. If the defendant is an airline, department store or other established business, collecting should be no problem. Big corporations normally pay off Municipal Court judgments within a month or two. Although they can appeal any case they lose, they usually don't. The legal fees don't usually justify appealing and paying a judgment of under $25,000 won't break them.

Small businesses. If a small business has a regular store or office where it pays rent, issues paychecks to employees or operates a cash register, collecting probably won't be a big problem. If the business is run by one person who operates informally out of his home, however, you may encounter problems in collecting.

Individuals. People who receive public assistance, Social Security or disability payments, or who have no recognizable assets or bank accounts are difficult to collect from. On the other hand, the following defendants are usually not hard to collect from:

- people with applicable insurance policies—the insurance company pays on their behalf

- wage earners—the sheriff can collect about 25% of their paycheck with some exceptions

- owners of real estate—you can place a lien and either foreclose or get paid when they sell the property

Don't sue to just get even. If you don't care about recovering money and only have a burning desire to "get even" with someone, I'd advise you to not file a lawsuit. Judges treat these cases harshly, and everyone—the plaintiff, defendant and court system—loses. But if court is the only place you can go to right a wrong or stop someone's be-

havior, then file. Remember, however, the ancient Gypsy curse "May you be involved in a lawsuit in which you know you are right."

If the defendant files for bankruptcy. Even if the defendant files for bankruptcy and tries to cancel your judgment, your may still be entitled to collect your court judgment after the bankruptcy case. For instance, debts that arise from drunk driving can't be erased in bankruptcy. Also, court judgments that arise from willful or malicious injury to another or another's property may remain after bankruptcy. And liens on property arising from court judgments remain after bankruptcy, providing you an avenue of collection. Suing someone who declares bankruptcy is covered in Chapter 4, Section D.4.

F. How Much Should You Sue For?

Okay—you have a reasonable chance of winning and you think you can collect. So now the question is "How much should you sue for?" Municipal Court can hear cases from $1 to $25,000. Before you pick an exact amount, take a look at what types of money damages are routinely awarded in breach of contract and torts cases.

 Remember—if your case is under $5,000, you are almost always better off in Small Claims Court. *Everyone's Guide to Small Claims Court*, by Ralph Warner (Nolo Press) can guide you through the process. If your case is worth much more than $25,000, you probably want to be in Superior Court.

1. Tort Cases

If your lawsuit is based on a tort (intentional or careless behavior directly resulting in injury or damage to you or your property), you may be able to recover the following kinds of damages:

Property damage. Legally, property falls into two categories: real property (land and buildings) and personal property (everything else). When I speak of property, I mean both real and personal. You can collect the cost of repairing an item, but if the repair exceeds the market value, you get only the market value. The market value is the property's worth at the time it was damaged, not its replacement cost. For instance, if your car is totaled, use the car's value as reflected in Edmund's Used Car or Kelly Blue Book, not what it is going to cost you to replace it.

Medical bills. Include both the costs you've already incurred and what you expect to incur in the future for your medical treatment for both physical and emotional injuries. These costs might include ambulance charges, emergency room service, hospital costs, X-rays, chiropractors, orthopedists, plastic surgeons and therapists who have helped you recover from your trauma.

Lost wages and benefits. Always request compensation for income you didn't or won't receive. Be sure to include future lost wages if you'll have to take more time off. If you were paid through an insurance or sick leave plan, request compensation for the regular wages you missed because insurance and sick leave payments are benefits to you that should not be a windfall to the defendant.

If you were forced to use up vacation time to recuperate, ask for your lost wages. If you have a dream employer who ignored your absence and paid your regular wages while you missed work, don't ask to be compensated for the time you missed. If you're self-employed, you may need an accountant to help you figure out what you would have earned had you been able to work.

Pain and suffering. Pain and suffering compensates you for your stiff back, the pain you feel when you hobble down the stairs and your general discomfort. It also includes compensation for fright, nervousness, anxiety and apprehension caused by the incident. Be sure to include both past pain and suffering and any you are likely to experience in the future. A typical approach to calculating pain and suffering is to begin by multiplying your medical bills by a factor of three to five. If your pain and suffering is extreme or out the ordinary, increase it from there.

> **Example:** Nick's total medical bills were $4,000. To figure out his initial pain and suffering loss, he multiplies that amount by three. He didn't have any extraordinary pain and suffering and so he asks for $12,000.

This formula is used because pain and suffering is usually loosely related to the amount of an injured person's medical expenses. Insurance companies deny that they use any such formula, but a review of their rewards suggests otherwise. After a quick trip to an emergency room and one follow up appointment with a doctor, most people won't experience much pain and suffering. But if you required an operation and physical therapy, your pain and suffering would likely be much greater.

Other Ways To Estimate Pain and Suffering

Rarely will two experienced personal injury lawyers agree on what a pain and suffering award in a contested court case should be. This is because the lawyers are trying to guess what 12 people on a jury will feel is fair to compensate someone for something difficult to evaluate monetarily.

Pain and suffering awards are obviously subject to the facts of a particular situation. For example, if your medical care was limited to a doctor sewing up a major wound, but you had a lot of pain and a permanent scar, multiplying your medical bills by three to five wouldn't come close to compensating you for your pain and suffering. At the same time, if your injury is minor (such as a sprained wrist), the fact that you visited the doctor 10 times and ran up a big bill shouldn't mean you're entitled to a huge pain and suffering award. In these situations, insurance companies often offer a flat pain and suffering award, such as $1,000 per month while you were recovering.

Good personal injury lawyers often can get juries to make large pain and suffering awards, usually far in excess of what an inexperienced pro per plaintiff can reasonably expect to recover. But the lawyer takes 1/3 to 1/2 of the recovery in exchange. Nevertheless, if you have sustained a serious injury and suffered a high amount of pain, I'd recommend that you at least consult with a lawyer and get her estimate of what you can expect to recover after the lawyer takes her fee.

Were you partially at fault? If you were injured or your property damaged because of the defendant's act, and your carelessness contributed to the injury or damage, your recovery may be reduced proportionately under a legal doctrine known as "comparative negligence." Comparative negligence requires that a person partially at fault gets charged for her share of the blame.

Example: Linda and Jason were in a car accident. The judge rules for Linda, and finds that her damages—auto repair, lost wages, medical bills and pain and suffering—total $10,000. The judge also finds that Jason was only 75% responsible for the accident (he made an unsafe lane change) and that Linda was 25% responsible (she was driving too fast). Thus, Linda's recovery is reduced to $7,500.

2. Breach of Contract Cases

If you're suing because the defendant breached a contract, the amount of your damages will likely be determined by the type of contract involved. Look at the breach of contract categories below and see which type most nearly matches yours.

Unpaid loans. If you loaned someone money and he hasn't paid you back, you're entitled to the unpaid loan amount, plus any interest specified in the contract, not to exceed 10% per year. If you forgot to include interest in your contract, you can recover 10% per year from the time the loan was due.[5]

Example 1: Wayne loaned John $10,000. John signed a promissory note which said nothing about interest. John failed to pay Wayne. Wayne sued for $10,000 plus 10% per year interest from the time the money was due.

Example 2: This time Wayne loaned John $10,000 for two years at 8% interest. When John fails to pay Wayne back, Wayne sues for the $10,000 plus 8% interest from the time the money was loaned.

If the loan was to be paid in installments, you can sue on each installment as it becomes due or wait until all the installments are owed

---

[5]Civil Code § 3289.

and sue then—assuming the statute of limitations hasn't run on the earlier installments. (See Section B, above.) If, however, your loan agreement has an acceleration clause—a provision that if any payment is missed the full amount becomes due immediately—you can "accelerate" the loan and sue on the full amount as soon as the borrower misses a single payment.

Example: Missy loaned Nora $8,000 to be paid back at $200 a month. The agreement contains an acceleration clause; that is, if Nora misses any payment, the balance amount becomes due immediately. Nora made one payment and then misses several. Missy accelerates the loan and sues for the full balance plus interest.

Failure to provide a service. If you had a contract with someone to provide you a service, you can recover for any damages that could have been reasonably predicted. You're certainly entitled to recover any money you've paid out. You can also recover any extra money you paid to get the services elsewhere. In exchange, you must take reasonable steps to minimize your damages.

Example 1: Mac's bathtub pipes spring several leaks and soak his house. Mac calls a plumber and tells him about the extensive damage the water is causing. The plumber promises to be over within 10 minutes. Mac tells him that if he can't make it right away, he will call someone else. The plumber tells Mac not to worry, but then takes 70 minutes to get there. Mac is entitled to any damage that occurred during the 60-minute period, but nothing else. If Mac let the leak to go unrepaired for a week, his recovery would be limited to the damage incurred before he should have realized the plumber was not going to honor his commitment.

Example 2: In August, Ann hired Atlas Roofing to repair her roof at a bargain rate of $4,000. Atlas promised to complete the work by October 1, when rain was expected. On September 25, Atlas called to say it couldn't begin until the end of October. Ann hires Zeus Roofing at $5,000, to begin work on October 5. From October 1 until October 5 she puts a tarp over the holes in her roof. Her damages are the extra $1,000 she paid to Zeus and the cost of putting up the tarp.

Providing defective goods. If you receive defective goods, you can recover your costs to repair or replace as long as you:

- didn't cause the damage by improper use
- follow reasonable terms of any warranty or agreement from the seller about returning the goods for credit or repair. When you buy goods, you often get a brochure telling you what to do if the goods are defective. The law regarding these matters is covered in Chapter 4. Unless there is a brochure that says otherwise, the seller must repair or replace the item within a reasonable time. If he doesn't, you're entitled to your costs of repair or replacement

chapter 3

CAN'T WE SETTLE THIS SOMEHOW?

Before you sue or defend a case in court, stop and consider if there's another way to resolve the matter. As you've probably gathered by now, lawsuits are expensive, stressful and time consuming. If it's possible, it's almost always better to settle than to litigate, even if you have to compromise somewhat in the process. If you are offered a fair settlement, grab it. If you're offered a settlement that's a little less fair but in the ball park, at least consider it. If you wait for the case to develop, you take the chance the other side will discover new facts and reduce or withdraw the offer.

A. Why Would You Want To Settle Out of Court?

As a judge, I have overseen more than a thousand cases, several hundred of which were jury trials. In at least half these cases, one side or the other (and sometimes both) was shocked by the result—it was so far from what they had predicted. Many lawyers have sadly told me of times that they aggressively pushed a case to trial, only to have the outcome (either for the plaintiff or the defendant) be far worse then what it would have been had they accepted the other side's last settlement offer.

By settling, you control the result. It may not be everything you hoped for. It may not even put you back to where you were before you dealt with the other person. But it's predictable.

Also, by settling your case you'll save a lot of time, expense and stress. And if you are the

plaintiff, you're likely to be paid now, not later. This is because there are normally no collection problems in cases that are settled. Having agreed to a decision rather than having it imposed by a court, the defendant rarely resists paying.[1]

B. How Much Are You Willing to Settle for?

Before you can settle your case, you must figure out how much you're willing to accept, or if you're the defendant, how much you're willing to pay.

For plaintiffs. You arrive at the amount by first following the approach in Chapter 2, Section E, on how much to sue for. This is the amount the plaintiff would hope to recover if everything in her suit goes perfectly. In determining how much you'd settle for, scale this back figure in light of the following:

- the possibility you will lose the case
- if you win, your chances of collecting
- the value of your own time, and how much time you're likely to spend litigating and collecting the judgment if you win

---

[1]If you're the plaintiff, you and the defendant reach a settlement and he reneges, you can sue on your original case or sue to enforce the settlement agreement. Suing to enforce the agreement is usually a quick and easy breach of contract case. See *Hastings v. Matlock*, 107 Cal.App.3d 876 (1990).

Example: Stacy's car was damaged and she was hurt in a recent accident. She read Chapter 2, evaluated her case against Gary (the other driver) and felt she could sue for $16,000. Stacy believes the accident was all Gary's fault, but a police report says that Stacy may have made an unsafe lane change. Thus, Stacy deducts 25% from the $16,000. She also realizes that although her claim for time lost from work is entirely justified, it may be questioned because her doctor's notes on her work return date were vague and the doctor has retired and moved away. Stacy cuts her $3,800 lost wages figure in half. She deducts another $2,000 for the time and stress she will save if she settles now. The result is $8,100—her "bottom line" settlement amount.

In considering you're settlement terms, don't think only about receiving money. If the defendant might be very hard to collect from, consider bartering for goods or services—that is, taking something other than cash for what you are owed. For example, if, in the above example, Gary is a house painter, Stacy might consider taking $5,500 and have her house repainted by Gary.

For defendants. Read the material above for plaintiffs. Do your best to figure out what the plaintiff should reasonably be entitled to. Then scale this back after considering the time and trouble the plaintiff will have to go through to sue you successfully. Next, consider if you will be hard to collect from. If you have little property or available cash, the plaintiff should realize that she will have trouble collecting any judgment from you. Subtract some more for the fact that you are making an "all cash offer."

⚠ **Don't pick a settlement amount prematurely.** Deciding on a settlement amount may be premature if you were just injured and the extent of your injuries are unknown, or if your final medical costs or lost wages can't be estimated. But don't

delay indefinitely; you have only the period of the statute of limitations in which to sue. (See Chapter 2.B.)

C. Should You Use a Third Person To Help You Settle?

Some of the best settlements involve a neutral third-person helping the parties resolve their dispute through an alternative dispute resolution (ADR). ADR is usually informal, fast and inexpensive. You are usually not constrained by formal procedural and evidentiary rules. You just tell your story. These are two the main ADR options:

Arbitration. This is the most formal and widely used form of ADR. You and the other side agree to submit your dispute to a neutral third person—often a lawyer or retired judge—and to be bound by the arbitrator's decision. One disadvantage is that you often have to pay the arbitrator's fees in advance, and they can be high, but not as high as paying a lawyer to fight in court. If you win, however, you're frequently refunded the amount.

Mediation. This is the other common type of ADR. You and the other party work with a neutral third party to come up with a solution to your dispute. Mediation is informal, and the mediator does not have the power to impose a decision on you.

A growing number of private organizations offer ADR help. Many are listed in the phone book under the headings "Arbitration" and "Mediation Services." Others are available through community groups, like San Francisco's Community Boards. Also, the National Council of Better Business Bureaus (BBB) operates a nationwide system for settling consumer disputes through arbitration and mediation. BBB arbitration is quite fair, free to consumers and is geared toward operating without lawyers.

If ADR seems like a likely option, suggest it to the other side.

D. Making a Settlement Offer

I'm often asked when the best time to make (or accept) a settlement offer is. The answer is simple: before you sue (or are sued), after you sue (or are sued), during the litigation, just before trial, during the trial or even when the judge is contemplating her decision. (Judges frequently do not make their decisions as soon as a trial is over. Instead, they take the case "under submission" and announce their decision a few days or weeks later.) In short, the best time to settle is anytime you and the other side agree.

1. Offering To Settle Before a Lawsuit Is Filed

Before you file a lawsuit, you can write a nice, straightforward business letter telling the (potential) defendant about your claim and inviting her to settle. It is surprising how few people do this. Most assume that the person or business who has caused them grief is stubborn, stupid, angry, intransigent or crazy (or all five) and that settling is out of the question. Not so. Most people recognize their mistakes and know that it's cheaper to pay for them sooner rather than later. Also, some people worry about having a court judgment on their credit record.

Many retailers and service agencies have people on staff whose only job is to head off lawsuits by settling. If the potential defendant has insurance, you may benefit from the fact that some insurance companies tell their adjusters to settle cases quickly if the plaintiff has no lawyer. They know that if the plaintiff eventually hires a lawyer, defense costs will sky-rocket.

Sending a letter before suing accomplishes three things:

• you let the other side know you're serious about recovering

• you set out what you believe you are entitled to

• you open up a channel of communication

Settlement Negotiating Tips[2]

1. Organize the documents that show your damages. Use a photo-album type notebook to display copies (never the originals) of your bills, photographs, medical reports and other supporting papers. Send it off to the (potential) defendant or his insurance company. This will show the other side that you are not an amateur.

2. Understand the personal dynamics of what is happening. Be polite and cooperative, but not to an excess. In many cases, the other side won't settle—or won't offer to settle for very much—simply because you are insulting or rude. At the same time, the other side isn't going to offer you extra just because you are really nice.

3. In your letter, state your demand. Start at an amount reasonably above your "bottom line" to give yourself room to go lower. But don't go so high that the other side concludes you're hopeless to deal with and refuses to negotiate. At the same time, don't make your first offer too low; it's seldom feasible to raise a demand. Use your Sounding Board for help in picking an opening amount that is reasonable. You will have plenty of chances to lower it, especially if the other side makes a decent counteroffer.

4. Keep cool and don't get bulldozed by a tough negotiator. If your offer is rejected, press the other side to counteroffer for a specific amount. Remember that most first offers are below what someone will ultimately settle for. Your next job is to counter his counteroffer.

5. Don't split the difference. If you demand an amount to settle, sometimes the defendant will offer a lower amount and then propose that you split the difference. Don't agree to it. Treat his split-the-difference number as a new low and propose an amount between that and your original offer.

Don't be concerned that your offer will be used against you later in court. By law, settlement offers (including demands), no matter what the motivation behind making them, cannot be disclosed in court.[3]

Below are two sample settlement (demand) letters. Remember that the amount you request should be at least a little higher than what you'd be willing to settle for. Also, if the defendant is represented by an insurance company, write directly to the insurance company and send a copy to the defendant.

---

[2]An excellent book about the negotiating process is *Getting To Yes*, Harvard Negotiation Project (Penguin Books), available in paperback for under $10.

[3]California Evidence Code § 1152.

Sample Settlement Letter (Breach of Contract)

947 Elm Street
San Rafael, California
January 6, 19__

Brad Caruso
ABC Plumbing Company
456 Market Street
San Anselmo, California

Dear Mr. Caruso:

On December 6, 19__, Sam Jones, who works for you, attempted to repair a leaking pipe at the address shown above. After working for several days, he told he was finished and presented me with a bill for $2,156 for materials and labor. I paid the bill.

On December 14, 19__, the pipe burst where Mr. Jones had repaired it. My basement flooded and many items of furniture were ruined. I contacted you on December 14, and from December 15-17 your employee, Ralph Sanchez, did more work on the pipe.

On December 20, 19__, I hired XYZ Plumbing to inspect the work done by your employees and offer an opinion as to the cause of the burst pipe. XYZ concluded that Mr. Jones did not repair the pipe correctly, and that his negligence caused my damages, as follows:

Cost of first repair	$2,156
XYZ Plumbing's bill	225
Furniture damage	7,500
Materials spent for cleanup	500
Time spent for cleanup	425
Total	$10,806

Please send me a check in that amount. If I do not hear from you within 10 days, I will assume you are not interested in resolving this matter and promptly will file a formal legal action.

Yours very truly,

Joan Wintucket

Sample Settlement Letter (Tort)

8999 Jefferson Blvd.
Canoga Park, California
May 1, 19__

Robert Wong
333 Green Street
Gardenia, California

Dear Mr. Wong:

This letter concerns the automobile accident that occurred at the corner of 9th and Main Streets in Santa Monica on April 11, 19__. I believe the accident was caused by your failing to stop at the stop sign on 9th Street. The police report and several eye witnesses I have contacted confirm this.

As a result of the accident, I suffered a painful sprained spine and missed five days of work. Also, I had substantial pain and trouble sleeping for 13 days. Today I still have occasional twinges of pain between my shoulders. My doctor has indicated this will continue for at least six months.

My damages as a result of the accident were as follows:

Damage to my automobile	$4,987
(see enclosed estimates from two body shops)	
Mercy Hospital emergency room expenses	879
(see enclosed bill)	
Three visits to Albert Condon, M.D.	110
(see enclosed bill)	
Lost wages	750
(see enclosed letter from payroll department)	
Pain and suffering	5,934
Total	$12,660

Please send me a check in that amount or make arrangements to pay it to me within 10 days. If I do not hear from you within that time, I will assume you are not interested in resolving this matter and I will file a legal action.

Sincerely,

Beth Herzog

In writing your letter, your object is to present your version of the facts, state your damages and show a willingness to settle. Don't insult the other side or make remarks about their lousy motives, bad characteristics or outrageous behavior—even if it's true. Few people will settle if they have to take a lot of insults as part of the package.

Also, don't make threats about what you will do if she doesn't send you a check right away. It's okay to say you'll exercise your right to sue if the matter isn't settled within some stated period. But threatening to tell the DMV that the other driver was uninsured or to ask the police to arrest her for a crime is usually illegal.[4] While few District Attorneys would prosecute you for crossing the line, I've seen supposed settlement letters that clearly constituted criminal extortion.[5]

Finally, stick to your statement that you will file a lawsuit if the other person doesn't respond within a certain number of days. Otherwise, the other side will decide you aren't serious.

2. Offering to Settle After a Lawsuit Is Filed

If you've already filed your lawsuit—or if you're a defendant—you can still try to settle, whether or not you tried to before the case was filed. Over 90% of all cases settle before trial. If not right after the papers are filed, then during a deposition, at a court settlement conference or some other time. There usually will come a time when your opponent will want to talk settlement because he realizes his case has more problems than he had thought it had.

Many cases settle right after the legal papers are filed and served on the defendant. This is when the defendant must face the fact that the plaintiff is not just an angry loudmouth who makes empty threats. The defendant has solid evidence of the plaintiff's seriousness and must decide whether to settle or fight in court.

If the defendant is represented by an insurance company, however, the defendant is unlikely to settle right away. Instead, the case will be assigned to an insurance company lawyer who won't be anxious to settle until she has investigated the case. She'll probably conduct some "discovery," most likely by taking the plaintiff's deposition. (See Chapter 10.) If she thinks the plaintiff's case is weak she may even file a motion for summary judgment. (See Chapter 11.)

But, in all cases you should get across to the other side that you are willing to talk settlement at any time. Just because you were far apart during your previous settlement talks shouldn't mean you won't talk again. Judges who see hundreds of settlement conferences know that parties posture a lot during settlement negotiations. Some cases where the parties are thousands of dollars apart one day mysteriously settle the next.

You can talk to the other side without communicating weakness. If you're very far apart, try saying something like "We don't seem to be making much progress here, is there anything to be gained by our talking settlement today?"

---

[4]See Penal Code §§ 518-527.

[5]California Penal Code § 518 defines "extortion" as obtaining something from another person by the wrongful use of fear. Under California Penal Code § 523, sending a threatening letter with the intent to extort money is a crime.

E. Taking Care of the Details

If you and the other side settle, get it in writing and dismiss any lawsuit that had been filed.

1. Getting the Settlement Agreement in Writing

One danger of not getting the settlement in writing is that even the most honest of people remember events differently. I've seen dozens of cases where the parties came to court, announced that their case had settled, and then couldn't agree on what they thought they agreed to.

Any settlement agreement should contain the following elements:

- a brief description of the facts that led to the dispute

- a statement that the parties disagree about those facts or their implications

- a statement of your settlement

The following settlement agreement resolves the dispute between Joan Wintucket and her plumber, Brad Caruso, described above.

Sample Settlement Agreement (Breach of Contract)

Joan Wintucket and Brad Caruso, who does business under the name of ABC Plumbing, agree as follows:

1. On December, 6, 19__, ABC Plumbing ("ABC") did certain plumbing repair work on the home of Joan Wintucket ("Wintucket") at 947 Elm Street, San Rafael. Wintucket paid ABC $2,156 for doing that work.

2. On December 14, 19__, a pipe that ABC worked on burst and caused damage to items in Wintucket's house. Between December 15-17, at no cost to Wintucket, ABC repaired that break.

3. Wintucket contends the damage that occurred on December 14 was caused by poor workmanship of ABC.

4. ABC contends all work done for Wintucket was performed in a competent manner and not the cause of her damage, if any.

5. In order to settle all claims of Wintucket for damages as the result of the incidents referred to above, ABC agrees to pay her $5,000, payable within five days of when Wintucket signs this Agreement.

_____   _____
Joan Wintucket   date

_____   _____
Brad Caruso, ABC Plumbing   date

Here's another settlement agreement. This one is between Robert Wong and Beth Herzog, who were in a car accident.

Sample Settlement Agreement (Tort)

Robert Wong and Beth Herzog agree as follows:

1. On April 11, 19__, Herzog was driving her car south on Main Street in Santa Monica, California;

2. At the same time, Wong was driving his car east on 9th Street in Santa Monica, California;

3. The two automobiles collided at the intersection of Main and 9th, causing damage to both cars and physical injuries to Herzog;

4. Wong contends that the accident was caused by Herzog's negligence;

5. Herzog contends that the accident was caused by Wong's negligence;

6. In order to settle and release the claims of each party against the other for:

a. damage to their automobiles, and

b. personal injury claims including medical bills, lost wages and pain and suffering, already sustained and which may occur in the future;

7. Wong agrees to pay Herzog the sum of $9,250 within five days of when this Agreement is signed by both parties, as a full and complete compromise of all claims between them.

_____   _____
Beth Herzog   date

_____   _____
Robert Wong   date

Optional Release of Future Discovered Damages

California Civil Code § 1542 provides that a general release, like the two above, doesn't apply to claims unknown or unsuspected at the time of the release. For this reason, the party making the payment may insist that the agreement include a clause releasing him from future unknown damages. If you're the party getting paid and aren't sure you won't have future damages, you should think carefully about agreeing to it. Consider using such a release as a bargaining chip. Agree to include it for 10%-20% more than what you would agree otherwise to.

Here's how Herzog and Wong would include such a clause:

"8. The releases recited in this Agreement shall cover all claims under California Civil Code § 1542 and Herzog and Wong hereby waive the provisions of § 1542, which read as follows:

A general release does not extend to claims which the creditor does not know or suspect to exist in his favor at the time of executing the release, which if known by him must have materially affected his settlement with the debtor."

2. Dismissing the Lawsuit

If you settle your case after the lawsuit was filed, the plaintiff (who may be you) must be prepared to file a document dismissing the lawsuit as soon as payment (or all installment payments) is made. California provides a simple form, called a Request for Dismissal, to accomplish this task. A copy of the form in the Appendix; a completed sample is shown below.

982(a)(5)

Name, Address and Telephone No. of Attorney(s)

Space Below for Use of Court Clerk Only

```
Joan Wintucket
947 Elm Street
San Rafael, CA 94000
(415) 555-2388

Plaintiff in Pro Per
```

Attorney(s) for ....

....Municipal...... COURT OF CALIFORNIA, COUNTY OF...Marin..........
(SUPERIOR, MUNICIPAL, or JUSTICE)

....
(Name of Municipal or Justice Court District or of branch court, if any)

Plaintiff(s):

Joan Wintucket

CASE NUMBER

REQUEST FOR DISMISSAL
TYPE OF ACTION

Defendant(s):

Brad Caruso, dba
ABC Plumbing Company

(Abbreviated Title)

☒ Personal Injury, Property Damage and Wrongful Death:
    ☐ Motor Vehicle   ☒ Other : damage to home
☐ Domestic Relations   ☐ Eminent Domain
☐ Other: (Specify) ....

TO THE CLERK: Please dismiss this action as follows: (Check applicable boxes.)
1. ☒ With prejudice   ☐ Without prejudice
2. ☒ Entire action   ☐ Complaint only   ☐ Petition only   ☐ Cross-complaint only
   ☐ Other: (Specify)*

Dated: ..January.17,.1992.................

*If dismissal requested is of specified parties only, of specified causes of action only or of specified cross-complaints only, so state and identify the parties, causes of action or cross-complaints to be dismissed.

~~Attorney(s) for~~ .Plaintiff.in.Pro.Per...........

Joan Wintucket
(Type or print attorney(s) name(s))

TO THE CLERK: Consent to the above dismissal is hereby given.

Dated: ....

**When a cross-complaint (or Response (Marriage) seeking affirmative relief) is on file, the attorney(s) for the cross-complainant (respondent) must sign this consent when required by CCP 581(1), (2) or (5).

Attorney(s) for ....

(Type or print attorney(s) name(s))

(To be completed by clerk)
☐ Dismissal entered as requested on ....
☐ Dismissal entered on ....as to only ....
☐ Dismissal not entered as requested for the following reason(s), and attorney(s) notified on ....

...., Clerk

Dated..   By..., Deputy

Form Adopted by Rule 982 of
The Judicial Council of California
Revised Effective July 1, 1972

REQUEST FOR DISMISSAL

CCP 581, etc.;
Cal. Rules of Court,
Rule 1233

In paragraph 1, you must check "with prejudice" or "without prejudice." Without prejudice means the plaintiff can renew the lawsuit in the future. If you've settled the case, the plaintiff should not be allowed to resume the case; check "with prejudice."

In Paragraph 2, you're asked to check "entire action," "complaint only," "petition only," "cross-complaint only" or "other." If you have fully settled your claims against each other, check "entire action."

The plaintiff must sign and date the first signature line. If the defendant filed a cross-complaint (see Chapter 8), she must sign and date the second signature line.

F. Should a Lawyer Review the Settlement Agreement?

If your suit is more complicated than the two described above, or your settlement is for more than $10,000, consider having your settlement agreement reviewed, or even drawn up, by a lawyer. If neither party has a lawyer, you can hire one and split the cost. If one party has a lawyer who will draft the agreement, the other side should pay for an hour of a different lawyer's time to review it.

The danger with hiring a lawyer to draft your settlement agreement is that many of them will feel some duty to construct a complex document filled with legalese. The *Prairie Home Companion* radio show had a segment entitled "Worst Case Scenario" in which Garrison Keillor would describe an innocent event and another actor would describe the worst possible (and most outlandish) things that could happen as a result. Many lawyers are like that. Asked to draft a simple document when a dispute has already been resolved, some lawyers will include pages of unlikely issues. This can cost a lot and may jeopardize the settlement. So if you hire a lawyer to draft an agreement, spell out exactly what you want.

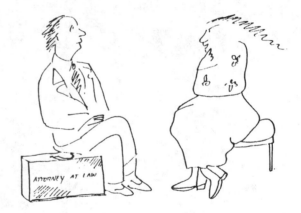

chapter 4

PICKING THE COURT AND PARTIES

If you're a defendant, you can skip this chapter for now even if you plan to file a cross-complaint. Cross-complaints are covered in Chapter 8, and, if necessary, you can come back here after reading that material.

Before you file your lawsuit, you must decide three things

- who will be the plaintiff(s)
- who will be the defendant(s)
- which particular Municipal Court you will sue in

Answering these questions can be straightforward and take only a minute or two of your time. For example, if you're an adult, were in an accident with another adult who lives in the same city you live in and the accident happened in that city while each of you was driving your own car, the decisions are clear. You are the plaintiff, the other driver is the defendant and you sue in the Municipal Court for the city in which you live.

But it's not always so easy. Continuing with the car accident example, you're decisions will be different if either you or the other driver was driving an employer's vehicle when the accident happened or if the accident took place in a city different from where you live.

A. Selecting the Plaintiff(s)

As you know by now, the plaintiff is the person who files the lawsuit. In most situations, this will be you and no one else—remember, as a non-lawyer you can't represent other people. But more than one person can join together to bring a lawsuit. We'll call them co-plaintiffs.

A co-plaintiff must be someone who was injured or damaged in the same incident, accident or business transaction that harmed you. The most common co-plaintiffs are spouses or living together partners who were simultaneously hurt or financially damaged.

You don't want a corporation as your co-plaintiff because corporations must be represented by a lawyer. A partnership is okay, however, because partnerships don't have to be represented by a lawyer as long as they are represented by a partner. In fact, if you run your business as a partnership (Lynn and Lydia's Restaurant)—or as a sole proprietor (Henry's Taco Shop)—and your business was injured, you should name your business as a plaintiff.

Suing In The Name of Your Business

Every sole proprietor, partnership, association or corporation that does business in a name that doesn't include all the real names of the business owners must file a fictitious business name certificate with the county clerk where the business has its principal place of business.[1] If you plan to sue in the name of such a business (remember—corporations must be represented by a lawyer), be sure to file the certificate before you file the lawsuit to avoid any problems. Ask the County Clerk for the certificate form and instructions.

[1]Certain nonprofit organizations are exempt from this law. California Business and Professions Code §§ 17910 and 17911.

Some examples of appropriate co-plaintiffs are:

- you and your passenger if both were injured when your car was hit by another driver

- several tenants who incur damage to their personal belongings when a fire spreads through an apartment house

- you and your spouse if you pay a repairperson to fix a problem in your house and the work is defective

Where co-plaintiffs sue in one lawsuit, each can sue for up to $25,000 if they suffered their damages individually. You and your passenger in your car can each sue up to $25,000, as can the tenants in the apartment building where the fire spread. But the spouses in the above example are limited to $25,000 total, not $25,000 each, as they co-own the house and suffered the damage jointly.

If the lawsuit is based on separate (but similar) incidents, it's not be advisable to try to join them in the same case. Some examples of inappropriate co-plaintiffs are:

- you and a store owner, after your neighbor's wild teenage son splashes your house with paint and then kicks in the window of the store down the street

- you and the family next door, after a door-to-door salesperson defrauds each of you out of $7,500

Now that you know who the plaintiffs will be, write down their names and set that piece of paper aside for later. In Chapter 5, I explain where they go on your court papers.

Each plaintiff must act for himself or herself. If more than one plaintiff files a lawsuit, all plaintiffs must sign the papers and appear in court at the appropriate times. One plaintiff cannot speak for the others.

B. Selecting the Defendant(s)

The defendant is the person, business or governmental entity you sue. It's usually easy to pick out the principal "bad guy"—he's the one who won't pay you, bashed your car or sold you defective merchandise. Often, however, the defendant is more than one person or business. The basic rule in selecting defendants is to name every person, business or agency that is legally responsible for your injury or damage. The reasons are twofold:

- if you win, you can recover from any defendant found responsible

- usually, you can recover the full amount of your judgment from *any* responsible party, no matter how slight that party's contribution to your damages. If one party pays more than his share, he can sue the other defendants to be reimbursed; but that's his problem, not yours.

Example: Alice was hurt in an car accident. She got a judgment against the driver who swerved into her car and knocked it across several lanes, and also against the driver who was speeding on the freeway and smashed into her after her car had come to a stop. Her judgment holds both defendants liable for her medical bills, lost wages, automobile repairs and pain and suffering. She can collect her judgment from either defendant or both.

While you want to sue all defendants responsible for your damages, don't name people who bear no responsibility. First, it is morally not right to do so. You may be a sophisticated person who doesn't get particularly upset if she is sued every once in a while, but many people have never been sued and will be severely disturbed if they are. Don't put them through the process unnecessarily.

Second, a judge can impose a significant penalty on you if you sue someone against whom you have no real claim. After you carefully read the rest of this section, review your decision on whom you want to sue with your Sounding Board. Explain your theory of fault for each potential defendant and follow your Sounding Board's advice.

1. Tort Cases

The general idea in personal injury and property damage (tort) cases is to sue everyone whose careless or intentional behavior contributed even a little bit to the injury or damage.

a. Auto Accidents

If your suit arises out of a vehicular accident, consider suing:

- the driver of the other car
- the parents of the driver of the other car, if the driver was a minor (see Section D.6 below for special rules on suing a minor)
- the owner of the other car—if the owner is married, sue both spouses
- the responsible mechanic, if a mechanical defect possibly contributed to the accident

- the government agency responsible for upkeep of the road, if a road condition or lack of proper signs contributed to the accident
- the employer of the person driving the other car, if the other driver was on the job when the accident happened
- the driver of the car you were riding in, if you were a passenger
- the parents of the driver of the car in which you were a passenger, if the driver was a minor (see Section D.6 below for special rules on suing a minor)
- anybody who entrusted their vehicle to someone who they knew or had reason to know was incompetent, reckless or intoxicated. Entrustment is a theory for holding someone responsible for an accident if he let an incompetent, reckless or intoxicated person use his vehicle. Normally, these persons are a parent, lender of a car or employer. In a few situations, however, a car dealer, the giver of a gift car or a co-owner might be liable for entrustment. If this is your situation and a lawyer is out of the question, you'll need to do some legal research. Check *Summary of California Law* (9th Edition), by Bernard Witkin, §§ 997-1000 and 1025-1040.

b. Slip and Fall Accidents

If you were injured when you fell on a piece of fruit, roll of toilet paper or loaf of bread on the supermarket floor, consider suing:

- the company that operates the store
- the manager
- the employee whose duty it was to sweep it up

• the owner of the building (if there was a defect in the floor covering)

The same general principles apply if you're a letter carrier and you fall because of a toy on a front step or if you're visiting a friend and trip over the afternoon newspaper because the hallway is poorly lit. In these cases, you'd sue the owner of the house or apartment, any manager or supervisor responsible for maintenance and the person who left the toy or paper laying around.

c. Other Accidents

If you were damaged by a painter who, while working above you on a scaffold, drops a can of paint on you as you walk below, consider suing:

• the painting contractor who employed the painter

• the general contractor on the job

• the owner of the building on which the work was being done

• the painter

• the scaffolding company (which perhaps should have provided protection for people on the sidewalk)

• any governmental agency which granted a permit for the work without requiring adequate protection

For other accidents, follow these general principles and sue anyone who is possibly responsible for your damages or injuries.

2. Breach of Contract Cases

In lawsuits for breach of contract, sue the person, business or agency that failed to perform duties required by the contract. If that person was acting in her employment when she breached the contract, sue both the employee and the employer.

a. Breach of Service Contracts

A service contract is one where one person promises to perform a service for another person. Some examples of services are: to play music at your wedding reception; to paint your house; to design a brochure for your new business; and to repair your front porch. The following are the people you'd sue in some common breach of service contract cases:

• If a salesperson falsely represents what the service would accomplish ("Quinn Carpet Cleaner's will remove all these stains on your rugs without any damage"), sue the person who made the false statement.

• If an individual was employed by or represented a business, sue the individual and business to the extent they caused the breach of the contract. For example, if a car garage loosened rather than tightened your brakes and you get into an accident when your car doesn't stop, sue the garage, the mechanic who worked on your car and the shop manager or foreman who gave the orders.

- If the business you hired used a subcontractor or any other additional business you didn't hire yourself, sue both businesses if the second seems partly at fault. For example, if a car dealer you brought your car to for repairs sent your car out to a second garage for some of the work, sue both the dealer and the second garage. Don't sue the second garage, however, if it only replaced a windshield and the problem is with your transmission.

b. Breach of Purchase Contracts

A purchase contract is one where one person sells a product to another. If the product is defective, doesn't do what the seller promised it would do or wasn't delivered as promised, you can sue for a breach of a purchase contract. The following are the people to sue:

- in all cases, sue the business that sold you the item

- if the product was defective in any way, sue the manufacturer of the item

- if you will sue the manufacturer, also sue any middleperson or distributor

- if the item was modified by someone other than the seller or manufacturer, sue that person or business

- if the item was damaged during delivery, sue the delivery company and any business or person who hired the company

- as with service contracts, if an individual was represented or employed by a business, sue

the individual and business to the extent they caused the breach of the contract. For example, if a company vice president orders her salespeople not to deliver goods to you, sue the company and the vice president.

3. Suing a Business

If any of your defendants is a business, you'll have to sue the business itself, and sometimes individuals owning the business. Here's how to proceed.

Individually owned (non-corporate) businesses. Individuals doing business under a fictitious name should be sued in their own name and in the name of the business. For example, if Jeff Taylor owns and operates a store under the name of Seville Row Tailors, your court papers should name both.

Corporations. Both profit and nonprofit corporations should be sued in their correct corporate name as well as any other name they do business under. So if Creamy Dairies, Inc. operates Frosty Ice Cream Stores, sue the company in both names. You normally won't name any shareholders or officers.[2]

Partnerships and unincorporated associations. Partnerships and unincorporated associations should be sued in the name of the business. This could be the last names of the

---

[2]The only time you'd sue a corporation's shareholders or officers is if the corporation is a shell that has little or no assets. In such a case, you might have to "pierce the corporate veil" to try and recover from the individuals who own the company. This is a complicated procedure requiring a lawyer who specializes in business litigation. In the unusual case where you want to sue an officer or director of a nonprofit corporation and the person receives no compensation for the work she does, see Code of Civil Procedure § 425.15. It describes special papers that must be filed with the court before you can sue.

partners (Barney, Barney and Hill) or a fictitious name (Party Time Catering). You may also want to sue some or all of the principal partners or members of the association. If you get a judgment against the individuals, you can try to collect from their assets without the court declaring them responsible for the business's debts. Also, naming the individuals will probably encourage settlement efforts because the named individuals will suddenly realize they may be personally liable for the "business problem."

Unincorporated Associations

An unincorporated association is a group of people who have joined together for a common purpose, but have not formed a corporation or a partnership. The association may work for a nonprofit charitable or social purpose or may carry out a business venture (called a "joint" venture). Associations usually choose a name, select officers and adopt rules or membership requirements. Common unincorporated associations run small labor unions, country or social clubs, neighborhood associations and the like.

4. Finding a Business or Business Owner

Before you can sue a business or business owner, you must know what legal form the business operates under.

Unincorporated businesses (individually owned business, partnerships and unincorporated associations). Remember, these businesses are sued in the name of both the business and some (or all) of the individual owners. The first place to check to find the names of individual owners is the Fictitious Names Index at the County Clerk's office. The Index contains the filings of all the people who have complied with the law requiring business owners who operate under a fictitious name to file a Certificate listing the owner's name and address. Bear in mind that not all business owners comply with this law.[3]

If you come up empty handed after you check the Fictitious Names Index, try the Business Tax Office of the city or county where the business is located or does a substantial business. These taxing agencies aggressively collect taxes from local businesses and usually have up-to-date ownership records. If you are inclined to check here before checking a fictitious business listing, keep in mind that city offices are sometimes poorly run, their records hard to research and they are frequently not prepared to handle requests by pro pers.

If the business is a limited partnership or unincorporated association, the ownership records may be on file with the California Secretary of State. Keep reading.

Corporations. Remember, corporations are normally sued in only the name of the business. To get the name and address of a corporation, call the California Secretary of State Corporate Status Unit (916-445-2900) in Sacramento. All corporations authorized to do business in California must register with the Secretary of State. In addition to telling you the corporation's name and address, the Unit can tell you the corporation's officers and agent for the service of court documents. The agent may be an easy person for you to serve once your court papers have been prepared and filed. (See Chapters 5, 6 and 7.)

---

[3]If, as plaintiff, you want to sue as a business and your business operates under a fictitious name, you must file a Certificate before suing.

To find the name and address of a corporation incorporated outside of California, a large limited partnership or an unincorporated association, call 916-324-6781.

C. Selecting the Right Court

If your principal defendant lives in or does business in California, you should have no problem suing in California. If she lives outside the state but did something that caused you damage or injury in California (for example, she rear-ended you on I5), you can sue here.

If your defendant operates a business out of state, you still may be able to sue it in California. For example, a New York mail order house sent you a catalogue from which you ordered goods. They arrived and were defective. The mail order house won't refund your money. You can sue that company in California because it sent its catalogue into the state for the purpose of doing business in the state.

But where in California do you sue? Each of California's 58 counties has at least one Municipal or Justice Court. Most counties have more than one, each called a "judicial district," which covers a section of the county.[4] Some Municipal Courts even have branches within their judicial districts. You're often faced with choosing among several different Municipal Courts in which to sue.

In general, you can sue in any of the following judicial districts:

- Where any defendant resides—if one defendant lives in Ventura and two live in Santa Barbara, you can sue in either.

- If your case is a tort case, where the injury to persons or property occurred—if the defendant lives in San Diego and the the accident was in Fresno, you can sue in either county.

- If your case is a breach of contract case, where the contract was entered into, was to be performed or was broken.

- If the defendant is a corporation or association, in the county where it has its principal place of business. If the business is located out of state (such as the New York mail order house), any the county in which it does business in California, such as the county in which you live.

- If the business is owned by a partnership or individuals, in any county where the partners or owners live.

---

[4]Los Angeles County, for example, has 25 separate judicial districts. The largest, in the downtown, has over 100 judges and commissioners.

Where Is a Contract Entered Into?

Figuring out where a contract is "entered into" can be tricky. If the contract is entered into face-to-face, it's obvious where it happened. But if it's entered into by mail or over the telephone and the two parties are in different judicial districts, it's not so obvious.

The contract is considered entered into when the last act necessary for its making takes place. This last act is the "acceptance" of an offer. For example, if Jack calls Wendy and offers to buy her dog and Wendy agrees to it, the contract is entered into when Wendy accepts. If an acceptance is by phone, the contract is entered into in the judicial district where the acceptor is. If an acceptance is by mail, the contract is entered into in the district from which the acceptor mails her acceptance.

After reading the above list, write down all the possible counties in which you can sue. If you're not sure what county a particular town or unincorporated area is in, call the town clerk or sheriff's office.

Once you pick the possible counties, you must determine the appropriate judicial district(s) for each county you can sue in. You can determine them by looking at the Government pages of a county's phone book. (Main libraries have phone books for all 58 counties.) Specifically, look under "County Government Offices." Find the heading "Courts" and the subheading "Municipal Courts." Each judicial district will be listed under the subheading.

If you don't know which judicial district is appropriate, call one of the likely courts and explain that you are attempting to determine the right court for filing a lawsuit. If you are using the defendant's residence as the basis for choosing the court, say something like "I want to sue someone who lives in Lynwood. Is this the correct court?" If you are using the place where a tort occurred or a contract was entered into or broken, say "I want to sue someone concerning an incident that happened in Tracy. Is this the correct court?"

Most clerks will answer those questions correctly. If a clerk protests that he's not allowed to give legal advice, change your question slightly and ask "Is the City of Tracy included in your judicial district?" If the judicial district has more than one branch, do the same thing. Now write down each judicial district and branch which is appropriate for your suit. How do you choose among them? Consider the following factors:

Your convenience. Many people choose the court that is closest to where they live or work so they can get there easily when they need to file papers or appear in court.

Convenience of witnesses. If you plan to have witnesses from another area testify, consider their convenience when selecting a court. A witness who must travel 30 miles may be more willing to help you than one who must travel 300 miles. Also, you may have to pay the witnesses' costs.[5]

How fast you can get a trial. In some courts, trials are scheduled within a few months of when you ask for one. Others have a backlog of more than a year. You can get a general idea of how quickly you'll get a trial by contacting a clerk in the judicial district for each court you're considering filing your lawsuit in. I'd suggest visiting, not calling; but if you're considering a court very far away, by all means call. Ask for a ballpark estimate of how long it takes a half-day civil non-jury case to get to trial after a Memo to

[5]Government Code § 68093 allows a witness to request travel fees of $35 per day and $0.20 a mile. In addition, Evidence Code § 1563 allows a witness to request reimbursement for photocopying ($0.10 per page) and clerical costs ($16 per hour).

Set is filed.[6] If the clerk can't help you, ask to speak to a supervisor. As long as you're pleasant, you're likely to get some help. Keep in mind, however, that whatever you're told is only an estimate.

The Consequences of Picking the Wrong Court

If you choose the wrong court, your case won't be thrown out as long as you have a valid ground for suing in California. Technically, every Municipal Court in the state has judicial power anywhere in California over any person or business located in the state, doing business in the state or causing damage or injury in the state. If you flew from California to Chicago and TWA lost your luggage, you can file your suit in any county in California. TWA can ask that the case be transferred to the county where you bought the ticket, flew from or where it has its principal California office.

If you present your papers to a clerk in the Redding Municipal Court to sue a defendant who lives in Orange County regarding an accident that occurred in Fresno, the clerk will take your papers and filing fee, and file the case. Your problems may arise after you serve the defendant; he's likely to file a motion in Redding for a "change of venue" (the place of the trial). Because you filed your case in an inappropriate place, the judge who hears the motion will transfer the case to either Orange County or Fresno.

If the Redding judge decides that your filing in Redding was done in bad faith, she may order you to pay the defendant's attorney fees and costs in filing the motion to transfer. You will also be charged a transfer fee, and you'll have to pay a filing fee in the new court. The sanction and fees together could exceed $650, so try to understand and follow the rules.

---

[6]A Memo to Set is a court form you file with the court when you're ready to be assigned a trial date. It's discussed in detail in Chapter 12.

D. Special Concerns

 Several types of lawsuits or defendants require special treatment before you file your lawsuit. Skim the topics below and read any that apply to your case.

1. Suing Over Defective Goods

If your lawsuit involves a defective product you bought, you will need to understand something about the law of warranty.

a. Breach of Warranty

A warranty is a guarantee that a product will work for a period of time and is fit for the purpose for which it was sold. A warranty can be express (either written or oral) or implied (forced on the manufacturer or retailer by the law). Express written warranties are normally drafted by packs of company lawyers working with green eye shades on their heads deep in the bowels of the corporate headquarters. They mostly state what your rights aren't if you are unhappy with the product. Implied warranties, on the other hand, are not written down—they are imposed on retailers and manufacturers by the law.

A written warranty may be in a little folder that falls out of the box when you open your new coffee maker, or it may be a whole booklet of information that comes with your new car. A written warranty promises that the manufacturer or retailer will try to fix the product if you return it. This is not usually a problem. The problem arises when manufacturer or retailer either denies that there's a defect or tries several times—without success—to make the repair.

Implied warranties fall into two categories:

- Merchantability. This means that a product is fit for the ordinary purposes for which it was designed, and conforms to any statements of fact made on the container or label.

- Fitness. This applies when you tell a seller or manufacturer that the item will be put to a particular use. ("We plan to install this water heater in the basement of a four-story building.") You must also rely on the skill and judgment of the seller to select and furnish suitable goods. ("Which model would you suggest?")

Any implied warranty on the sale of new goods lasts the duration of any express warranty you were given, but no less than 60 days or more than one year. If you received no written warranty, the implied warranty lasts one year on new products. On used products, the implied warranty lasts as long as the express warranty, but no less than 30 days or more than 90.

If you did not receive a written warranty, a seller may attempt to do away with the implied warranty of merchantability by stating that the product is sold "as is" or words to that effect. His words will be unenforceable, however, if you received a written warranty.

Implied warranties apply to anyone who manufactures, distributes or sells consumer goods used, bought or leased for use primarily for personal, family or household purposes, except for:

- clothing
- products intended for consumption (food and drink)
- products used for personal care
- products consumed in household tasks

A rug shampoo solution is not covered, but a rug shampoo machine is. Eye drops aren't, but eye glasses are. Purchases from a corner video store are covered, something bought from your neighbor (assuming he isn't in that business) is not.

If you plan to sue a manufacturer or retailer who refuses to stand behind a product, you need to notify the manufacturer or retailer before filing suit. Send a letter to the manufacturer and retailer describing the product and its failure. Also state when and where the item was purchased. Ask that the product be repaired or replaced. A little assertiveness at the beginning will often solve the problem and eliminate your need to sue. If the product came with a written warranty, follow the procedures described in those materials.

Send the letter by certified mail, return receipt requested, and keep a copy for yourself. I can't tell you how many intelligent people come to court and tell me about the great letter they wrote to the defendant before they sued but forgot to keep a copy of. It helps your credibility with the judge if you have copies of everything you send.

b. Lemon Law

If you've purchased a new car that has a serious problem, or several problems, you must give the manufacturer the opportunity to fix it before suing.[7] In fact, for you to be able to sue under California's lemon law, you must give the manufacturer the opportunity to fix your car four times within either 12,000 miles or a year from the date of delivery. If the manufacturer can't (or if the car has been out of service for 30 days or more within the first year after delivery), the car is considered a lemon.

Follow the instruction in Chapter 5, Section C if you want to file a lawsuit based on the lemon law. At this point, be sure you give the manufacturer (usually through the dealer) the requisite number of opportunities to fix your car during the required miles or time period.

2. Suing the Government

Lawsuits against the Unites States (or any of its agencies) must be filed in federal court and are not within the scope of this book. You can, however, sue a state, county, city, school district or some other non-federal governmental body as long as you first file a special claim with that governmental body within six months after the incident you are suing about occurred. This requirement also applies if you want to sue an employee of a non-federal governmental body for an act (or omission) that occurred within the scope of his public employment.

This means if an employee was doing an activity logically related to his job, file a government claim. If the employee was doing something logically unrelated to his job (such as hiking in the mountains on his vacation), don't file the claim—sue the person and forget about the government. If you're uncertain (the hiking government employee is a park ranger), file a claim, because if you don't, you may lose important rights.

It's not always easy to recognize that an agency responsible for your injury or damage is part of the government. Many government entities—not part of a city or county government—operate hospitals, bus lines, irrigation projects and other services. Because the same type of activity is often carried on by private companies, you may have to ask. Try the Secretary of State's roster of public agencies. If the agency hasn't filed its name, address and board members with the county clerk, you won't be penalized for failing to file a government claim.

All government agencies should have a printed claim form available for your use. If your claim is against the State of California, request a form from the State Board of Control, P.O. Box 3035, Sacramento, CA 95812-3035. If your claims is against a city, county or special district, the claims are normally handled by the clerk to the governing board (such as a county board of supervisors). In a city, its normally the city clerk or the city auditor. A copy of the Alameda County form is below.

---

[7]This is required by California's Lemon Law (the Song-Beverly Consumer Warranty Act, Civil Code § 1790 et seq.).

CLAIM AGAINST THE COUNTY OF ALAMEDA

Clerk, Board of Supervisors
County of Alameda Administration Building
1221 Oak Street, Room 536
Oakland, CA 94612
Phone: (415) 272-6347

1. Claimant's Name (print): Otis Washington

2. Claimant's Address: 12 Evers St., Fremont, CA 94811
         (address)   (city, state and zip code)

         Phone No. 415-555-9022

*3. Total Amount of Claim: $ within the jurisdiction of the
         Municipal Court

4. Address to which notices are to be sent, if different from lines 1 and 2:

    Name (print): _____

    Address or P.O. Box Number: _____

    City, State & Zip Code: _____

5. Date of Accident/Loss: October 18, 1991

6. Location of Accident/Loss: Entrance to Alameda County court house

7. How Did Accident/Loss Occur: As I was entering the court house, the front door opened in a reverse direction, throwing me backwards down the front steps.

8. Describe Injury/Damage/Loss: sprained back, broken elbow, 3 bruised ribs, bruises over entire body, missed work

9. Name of Public Employee(s) Causing Injury/Damage/Loss, If Known: _____
Unknown

10. Itemization of Claim (list items totaling amount set forth above):

    _____ $ _____
    _____ $ _____
    _____ $ _____
    _____ $ _____
    _____ $ _____

         *TOTAL AMOUNT OF CLAIM $ _____

11. Signed by or on behalf of Claimant: _____

12. Dated: January 22, 1992

Please complete four (4) forms, retain one (1) copy for your files, and return the original and two (2) copies to the above address. All attachments must be in triplicate of any estimates, bills, receipts, police reports, etc. which would support your claim.

The claim form asks for your name and address. It also asks for the amount of your claim. Your answer depends on whether you are seeking more or less than $10,000. If your claim is for under that amount, state the precise amount you are asking for. If your claim is for $10,000 or more, say it is "within the jurisdiction of the Municipal Court," meaning it's between $10,000 and $25,000. Finally, the form asks for a description of the event you are making a claim for. Be honest and be sure to include the important dates, locations and the name of the government agency or employee you dealt with. NEVER MAKE ANY ADMISSIONS ABOUT YOUR OWN RESPONSIBILITY FOR THE INCIDENT. If you end up in court, what you say on the form could be used against you.

Once you've prepared the claim form, make several copies. (The form will say how many you need to file.) Make an extra copy for yourself and then file the claim at the office where you picked it up. As long as you're not filing just before the six-month deadline, you can send it by certified mail. Ask the clerk to stamp the date and place where you filed it. Next you must wait. The agency has 45 days to either deny your claim or take no action on it (which is the same as a denial). Agencies almost always deny six-month claims, so you can start working on your lawsuit papers while you are waiting.

 Late filings. You can file a claim against a government agency after the six-month limit if your late filing was because of excusable mistake, inadvertence, surprise or excusable neglect, or if you were a minor or physically or mentally unable to file the claim during the entire six months. But if you missed the filing period, you are in a precarious place and probably need a lawyer's immediate help.

 If you need more help in filing a claim against the government, the *California Government Tort Liability Practice,* by Arvo Van Alstyne (California Continuing Education of the Bar, 1980) is considered the bible in this area. It covers all sorts of claims, not just torts, and is kept up-to-date by separately bound supplements.

3. Suing Someone Who Has Died

When a person dies, someone is frequently appointed to represent her estate. This person is called an "executor" or "administrator." The process of distributing the persons assets is called "probate," and it takes place in the Probate Division of the Superior Court in the county in which the deceased lived. As part of the probate proceedings, the court will issue "letters" to the executor or administrator, usually within 30 days of death. Letters are a legal paper showing that the executor or administrator has authority to represent the estate.

To sue a person who has died (or if the defendant dies while your lawsuit is pending), you sue (or continue the lawsuit through) her estate. You must file a claim with the executor or administrator, usually within four months of the issuance of the letters. You must use a Creditor's Claim Form, which you can obtain from the County Clerk. Instructions on how to file it are on the form.

If the deceased's insurance policy covers the incident you want to sue over, you don't have to file a Creditor's Claim unless the monetary limit of the insurance policy is lower than the amount you are suing for (unlikely in Municipal Court).

If you don't know if the deceased had insurance, file a Creditor's Claim to protect yourself.

The executor or administrator has 30 days to accept or reject your claim and must notify you of his action. If your claim is approved, you don't have to file a lawsuit. If it's rejected, you have three months to sue the estate.

If a defendant has very few assets or has taken steps to pass his property outside of probate, there may be no probate action (and therefore no executor or administrator) after his death. Anyone receiving the deceased's assets is liable for his debts and it is possible to sue those people. You will probably need to hire an attorney.

The rules regarding suits against an estate are covered in California Probate Code §§ 9000 et seq. They are somewhat complicated, and if you appear to have missed a deadline, consult an attorney, preferably one who specializes in probate matters.

4. Suing Someone Who Has Filed for Bankruptcy

If you want to sue someone who has filed for bankruptcy, you may have to rethink your strategy. If you receive a notice from the bankruptcy court, or a letter or phone call from your potential defendant or his attorney stating that he has filed for bankruptcy, do not, under any circumstances, file your lawsuit. If you do, you will be violating the law and could be fined substantially. You should, however, present your claim to the bankruptcy court when you are invited to attend the "meeting of creditors."

If your claim is not satisfied in the bankruptcy court—it probably won't be—there are only a few situations in which you can sue the potential defendant. You can sue if the bankruptcy case is dismissed, if the bankruptcy court gives you permission to sue in Municipal Court (called "lifting the automatic stay") or if the particular debt you want to sue on is not erased ("discharged") by the bankruptcy court. Many debts arising from intentional acts, such as theft, embezzlement or drunk driving, won't necessarily be erased in bankruptcy, but you need to take some steps.

Nolo Press's *Collect Your Court Judgment*, by Scott, Elias and Goldoftas covers what to do when your defendant files for bankruptcy. That discussion applies both before and after you have a judgment.

5. Suing for Libel or Slander

In Chapter 1, I recommended you not sue for libel or slander in pro per. If you nevertheless wish to sue a newspaper, radio station or television station for libel or slander (called a "defamation action"), be aware that before suing, you must serve the publisher or broadcaster with a demand for retraction within 20 days of learning of the defamation.[8]

6. Suing a Minor

You can sue a minor (someone under age 18), but unless she has an insurance policy or some other way to pay you, it's probably not going to be worth the effort.

[8]Civil Code Section 48(a).

a. Breach of Contract Cases

Suing a minor for breach of contract is particularly hard. Minors can back out of most contracts they enter into before they turn 18. All they have to do is notify the other party to the contract before they turn 18 or within a reasonable period afterward that they want out.

This right, however, is not unlimited. A minor can't back out of a contract to pay for things necessary for the support of the minor or her family (such as food, reasonable clothing and housing) if she is not under the care of a parent who is able to provide for her. So if a minor lives away from her parents, or lives with her parents but they live in poverty, the minor can't back out of a contract for necessities.

b. Tort Cases

If a minor is covered by his own or his parents' automobile insurance, collecting a judgment if you win a tort action against the minor may be easy.[9] Even if a minor does not have insurance (or other substantial assets) consider these other possibilities:

• Parents and legal guardians who have custody of a child are responsible up to $10,000 for the willful—but not negligent—misconduct of the child. For instance, if your daughter's 17-year-old boyfriend deliberately plows his car into yours because you insist that they not see each other, his parents are responsible. If he carelessly changes lanes on the freeway and hits you, they are not. The personal injury damage is limited to medical, dental and hospital expenses.[10]

• Parents or legal guardians may be responsible under a law that holds the person who signed a minor's application for a driver's license liable for any damage or injuries caused by the minor's driving, even if caused by his negligence.[11] The maximum liability for physical injuries is $15,000 per person, $30,000 per accident. Maximum property damage liability is $5,000 per accident.[12]

• A parent or legal guardian giving express or implied permission to drive to a licensed or unlicensed minor is liable in the same amounts as the person who signs the license application. In these cases, you sue both the minor and her parents ("Jane Juvenile, a mi-

[9]Because it is illegal to drive without evidence of insurance in California, most people who have insurance will produce evidence of it for you or a police officer at the scene of the accident.

[10]Civil Code § 1714.1.

[11]A minor's application for a driver's license must be signed by his parents if they are living and have custody. If only one parent has custody, she alone may sign. If neither parent is alive or has custody, the application must be signed by the minor's legal guardian or other person having legal custody. Vehicle Code § 17701.

[12]Vehicle Code § 17709.

nor, and David and Mary Juvenile, her parents"). There is no limit to liability if the child was acting as the agent of the signer of the application (such as running an errand to the store) or if the child has a learner's permit and the signer of the application failed to supervise adequately.

If the minor turns 18 while your lawsuit is pending, his parents still remain liable for his acts as a minor.

c. If the Minor Used a Firearm or Shoplifted

If a minor's parents or legal guardian let him have a gun or left him access to a gun and someone is injured, the parent or guardian can be liable up to $30,000 for personal injury per person, not to exceed $60,000 total.[13]

Parents and legal guardians of a minor who has shoplifted something from a store or library can be held jointly responsible with the minor for up to $500 in damages, plus the value of any unreturned merchandise.[14]

d. How To Proceed

If you sue a minor, she will need to have an adult (called a "guardian ad litem") appointed to represent her in court. If you name the minor as a defendant and serve the papers on her parents—any minor over age 12 must be served as

well—they'll most likely ask the court to be appointed guardian ad litem. If they don't (and no one else does), you can ask the court to appoint a guardian ad litem. It's not hard, but it requires drafting several papers. You'll probably need a lawyer, who shouldn't charge more than $250.

7. Dealing With Unknown Defendants

If there's any possibility that you will add yet unknown people as defendants after you investigate the matter a little more thoroughly, you'll want to name "Does." "Does" rhymes with "rows" and is derived from the practice of calling an unknown person "John Doe" or "Jane Doe."

You may want to name a Doe, for example, if an Ajax Construction Company painter drops a can of paint on you, but you haven't been able to learn his name. You would sue the Ajax Construction Company and Doe One. As you conduct discovery (see Chapter 10) and learn the painter's name, you can file an amendment and substitute the correct name for Doe One. For now, just understand that to get a judgment against any particular defendant, you'll eventually need that defendant's name.

If you don't yet know the names of any defendants, you must do some investigating before suing. You can't file a lawsuit and name only Doe defendants.

---

[13]Civil Code § 1714.3.

[14]Penal Code § 490.5.

PREPARING THE COMPLAINT

If you're a defendant, you can skip ahead to Chapter 8.

You're probably anxious to start putting some words to paper. That's what this chapter is all about—creating the first documents you'll need to get your lawsuit moving.

These first documents are the cornerstone of your lawsuit. They'll be referred to constantly by judges and lawyers as your case develops. For this reason, you must take great care in reviewing the material in this chapter, and pay close attention to the sample completed forms included. I've seen otherwise good cases stopped in their tracks because the plaintiff neglected to prepare her initial papers adequately.

A. Drafting a Tort or Contract Complaint

The basic document in which you lay out your lawsuit is called a complaint. Fortunately, for tort and contract cases the complaint is a simple check-the-box form furnished by the court. (Blank copies are in the Appendix and available at the Municipal Court Civil Clerk's office.)

A tort or contract complaint has two parts. The first part contains general information about you and the parties you are suing. The second part consists of attachments describing your "causes of action." A cause of action is a legal theory under which you claim that what happened to you entitles you to relief from the court. Don't worry—later on in this chapter I'll tell you about the possible causes of action for your case.

1. General Tips on Preparing Forms

Remember, your complaint will be studied by every defendant and their insurance company (if relevant). These people will get a preliminary impression of how serious and competent you are. The conclusions they reach may significantly affect the amount of any settlement offer they make. Here are a few tips:

- All papers filed should be typewritten and appear neat. Your typewriter must print in pica. (All standard newer typewriters do.) If you'd rather not type the papers yourself, see Section E, below, on legal typing services.

- To save yourself extra trips to the court house, make several photocopies of each blank form you intend to use before you begin to fill them out. This will let you prepare rough drafts and still have a clean copy to use for the final product.

- You are the plaintiff—always refer to yourself that way. Rather than saying, "I went to the store," say "Plaintiff went to the store." This may feel contrived, but—trust me on this one—it's the way it is done.

- If you run out of space on any printed form, you can finish the information on a plain white sheet of numbered legal paper, called an "Attachment Sheet."

Typing the Attachment Sheet

At the top of each Attachment Sheet, you'll have to type the case's short title, the name of the first (and perhaps only) plaintiff and the first (and perhaps only) defendant. Next, label the page "Attachment," and indicate specifically what you are continuing, such as "Attachment to Cause of Action—Breach of Contract, Item BC-4." Then type your text using double-spacing. Use a new page for each item number you continue. At the bottom of the page, number the pages you're adding to the form.

The Silly World of Legal Paper

As your case progresses, you may have to file papers that are not on pre-printed forms. If so, you must use 8 1/2" x 11" legal paper with a double vertical line on the left side of the page and numbers from 1 to 28 left of the line. The paper, which must be of a least 13-pound weight, is generally available at office supply and stationery stores. We've included one sheet in the Appendix. You can make photocopies and use them.

2. Select the Correct Complaint Form

Depending on what kind of case you have (tort or contract), select the appropriate complaint form:

• Complaint—Personal Injury, Property Damage, Wrongful Death (tort cases); or

• Contract [ ]Complaint [ ]Cross-Complaint (contract cases).

3. The Caption

Regardless of which complaint you chose, the top portion (called "the caption") asks for exactly the same information. To get started, get out the information you prepared in Chapter 4 containing the name(s) of the plaintiff(s), the name(s) of the defendant(s) and the name and address of the court in which you'll be suing.

ATTORNEY OR PARTY WITHOUT ATTORNEY (NAME AND ADDRESS):	TELEPHONE.	FOR COURT USE ONLY
Sam Kim 421 Combes Lane Napa, CA 94559	707-555-1219	

ATTORNEY FOR (NAME) in pro per

Insert name of court, judicial district or branch court, if any, and post office and street address:

Napa County Municipal Court
1125 Third Street
P.O. Box 880
Napa, CA 94559

PLAINTIFF:

Sam Kim, dba Kim's Book Supplies

DEFENDANT:

Jenny Offer, Martin Myotic and April Rain, individually and dba as
ROMMOR Books

[x] DOES 1 TO 5

COMPLAINT—Personal Injury, Property Damage, Wrongful Death

CASE NUMBER:

- [ ] MOTOR VEHICLE
  - [ ] Property Damage
  - [ ] Personal Injury
- [ ] OTHER *(specify):*
  - [ ] Wrongful Death
  - [ ] Other Damages *(specify):*

We'll start in the upper left hand corner.

Attorney or Party Without Attorney (Name and Address): Put your name and the address at which you want to receive mail about the case. Fill in a phone number, including the area code, preferably where you can be reached during the day. Sometimes a clerk may try to reschedule a hearing by phone, so including a number where a message can be left for you will be helpful. If you aren't reachable at a phone number, don't put anything—you don't have to have a phone to file a lawsuit. Also, next to the line that says "Attorney for (Name)," type "in pro per."

Insert name of court, judicial district or branch court, if any, and post office and street address: Type the name, post office box (if applicable) and street address of the court you are using. If you're suing in a branch of a Municipal Court, include the branch name, like this:

Los Angeles Municipal Court
San Pedro Branch Court
505 S. Centre St., Room 202
San Pedro, CA 90731

Justice Courts are handled the same way:

Truckee Justice Court
10870 Donner Pass Road
Truckee, CA 95734

Plaintiff: Fill in your name and the name of any co-plaintiff. If you plan to include your business's name (let's say your name is Michael Smith and you operate a business called Michael's Sandwich Shop), handle it like this: "Michael Smith, dba Michael's Sandwich Shop." Dba stands for "doing business as." Only include your business if it's involved in the lawsuit—and be sure you've filed a fictitious busi-ness name certificate with the County Clerk. (See Chapter 4, Section A.)

Defendant: Fill in the name of the defendants. As with the plaintiff, identify those defendants who are neither adults nor natural persons. Here are some examples:

- Mitchell Davis, a minor
- Axel Construction Company, a corporation (although corporations cannot be pro per plaintiffs, you certainly can sue one)
- Tweedle Associates, a partnership
- John Dee and Frank Dum, partners in Tweedle Associates, a partnership
- Sidney Blue, individually and dba Blue Blood
- the County of Orange, a public entity

For now, skip the "Does 1 to ___" box.

Complaint: This information depends on whether you have a tort or contract case. Leave it blank for now.

Case Number: Leave this blank. The clerk will fill it in when you file your case.

Your Case Number

Once the clerk gives you a case number, be very careful when you type that number on subsequent court papers. An amazing number of documents get filed with the numbers transposed or otherwise wrong. As a result, the documents are placed in the wrong case file and often lost forever.

B. Complaint—Personal Injury, Property Damage, Wrongful Death

 If yours is a contract case, skip ahead to Section C.

Most of the caption box was filled out in Section 3, above. The "complaint" box, however, is still blank. Use these guidelines:

Motor Vehicle: If your case arises out a car or other motor vehicle accident, check this box.

Other (*specify*): Check this box if your case doesn't arise out of a motor vehicle accident. Then specify the type of case. Some possibilities include: "dog bite," "slip and fall," "assault and battery." (An assault is a threat to use force on another person; a battery is the willful and intentional use of force on another person.) Don't stew over the correct choice of words—this is not an especially important decision.

Property Damage: Check this box if you claim damages to your house, yard, car, furniture, child's bicycle or any other item of real or personal property that belongs to you.

Wrongful Death: If you follow my advice, you won't check this box. It's used when you sue because of the death of a close relative. Most wrongful death lawsuits are filed in Superior, not Municipal, Court because you'd normally ask for more than $25,000. If you want to bring a wrongful death lawsuit, consult a lawyer.

Personal Injury: Check this box if you claim an injury to yourself.

Other Damages (*specify*): If you're asking for money for lost wages, medical expenses, lost business profits or for punitive damages (punitive damages are available only if you are suing on an intentional, not negligent, act), check this box and specify which type of damages you're requesting.

Again, don't stew over the exact language. Your lawsuit is ultimately controlled by what you say in the body of the complaint. These boxes are intended to quickly give information about the nature of the case.

Now let's get into the body of the complaint.

1: Skip this for now. You'll come back and enter the number of pages after you complete the complaint and the causes of action.

2: If you and any co-plaintiffs are adult persons, skip Item 2 and go to Item 3 on the next page. If any plaintiff is a business or an organization, continue reading.

2a: Check the first and third boxes if any plaintiff is a member of a partnership or officer of an incorporated association suing on its behalf. (None of the other listed plaintiffs can sue in pro per.) Type in the name of the partnership or association after the first box, and then state whether it is a partnership or association after the third box.

If a second plaintiff is a partnership or association, complete the second paragraph of Item 2a, which is identical to the first. If a third or more plaintiff is a partnership or association, be sure to complete Item 2c.

2b: Check this box if you are suing in the name of your business. If you own a business as a sole proprietor, type your own name after "Plaintiff (*name*)" and the fictitious business name on the next line after "(*specify*)."

If your partnership does business under a fictitious name, type the partnership's name after "Plaintiff (*name*)" and the fictitious business name on the next line after "(*specify*)."

ATTORNEY OR PARTY WITHOUT ATTORNEY (NAME AND ADDRESS):	TELEPHONE:	FOR COURT USE ONLY
Sam Kim 421 Combes Lane Napa, CA 94559	707-555-1219	

ATTORNEY FOR (NAME) in pro per

Insert name of court, judicial district or branch court, if any, and post office and street address:

Napa County Municipal Court
1125 Third Street
P.O. Box 880
Napa, CA 94559

PLAINTIFF:
Sam Kim, dba Kim's Book Supplies

DEFENDANT:
Jenny Offer, Martin Myotic and April Rain, individually and dba as
ROMMOR Books

[X] DOES 1 TO 5

CASE NUMBER:

COMPLAINT—Personal Injury, Property Damage, Wrongful Death

- [ ] MOTOR VEHICLE
  - [X] Property Damage
  - [X] Personal Injury
- [X] OTHER (specify): assault & battery
  - [ ] Wrongful Death
  - [X] Other Damages (specify): medical expenses, lost business profits, punitive damages

1. This pleading, including attachments and exhibits, consists of the following number of pages: 5

2. a. Each plaintiff named above is a competent adult
   - [ ] **Except plaintiff** (name):
     - [ ] a corporation qualified to do business in California
     - [ ] an unincorporated entity (describe):
     - [ ] a public entity (describe):
     - [ ] a minor [ ] an adult
       - [ ] for whom a guardian or conservator of the estate or a guardian ad litem has been appointed
       - [ ] other (specify):
     - [ ] other (specify):

   - [ ] **Except plaintiff** (name):
     - [ ] a corporation qualified to do business in California
     - [ ] an unincorporated entity (describe):
     - [ ] a public entity (describe):
     - [ ] a minor [ ] an adult
       - [ ] for whom a guardian or conservator of the estate or a guardian ad litem has been appointed
       - [ ] other (specify):
     - [ ] other (specify):

   b. [X] Plaintiff (name):
      is doing business under the fictitious name of (specify): Kim's Book Supplies

      and has complied with the fictitious business name laws.
   c. [ ] Information about additional plaintiffs who are not competent adults is shown in Complaint—
      Attachment 2c. *(Continued)*

Form Approved by the
Judicial Council of California
Effective January 1, 1982
Rule 982.1(1)

**COMPLAINT—Personal Injury, Property Damage,
Wrongful Death**

CCP 425.12 C-87

2c: Skip this item unless more than two partnerships or associations are plaintiffs. If there are, you'll have to create an attachment sheet, and enter all the information requested in Item 2a.

Page Two

Short Title: Put the last names (or the business names) of the first (perhaps only) plaintiff and the first (perhaps only) defendant, separated by a "vs.", such as "Brown vs. Black" or "Brown vs. Golden Bear Typing Service."

Case Number: Leave this blank; you won't be able to fill it in until you file your complaint with the court clerk.

3: If all defendants are natural persons, skip all of Item 3.

3a: If any defendant is a partnership, association, corporation or government entity, complete this section. You are given four identical paragraphs. For each defendant that falls into this category, put its name after "Except defendant (name)," and check the applicable sub-box. You'll have to describe an unincorporated entity (simply write "partnership" or "association") and a public entity (such as the "County of Santa Clara"). If more than four defendants fall into this category, continue with Item 3c.

If you are suing one or more individuals who are doing business under a fictitious name, check the appropriate box describing the business type, if you know it. (Usually it's an unincorporated entity.) If you don't know the business form, check the second box.

3b: You need not do anything here.

3c: Skip this item unless more than four partnerships, associations, corporations or government entities are defendants. If there are, create an attachment sheet, and enter all the in-

formation requested in Item 3a for each additional defendant.

3d: Skip this item—it involves a complex legal situation you need not worry about.[1]

4: Check this box if you are suing the State of California, a county, city, school district or other public entity. Otherwise, skip to Item 5.

4a: You should have complied with the claims procedure, discussed in Chapter 4. If you have, check this box.

4b: If you haven't complied with the claims procedure, you should see a lawyer. There are ways to get around it, but they are complex and reliance on them is dangerous.

5: Indicate why you've chosen this court to sue in. (This analysis was covered in Chapter 4, Section C.) You may check more than one box. For example, if you chose the court because a defendant lives in the district, check the first box. If you chose it because a corporate or association defendant has its principal place of business in the district, check the second box. If your personal injury or property damage occurred in this district, check the third box.

If you chose the judicial district because a business defendant does business there, check the "other" box (in addition to the first or second box) and type the reason (for example, "Defendant Box Co. does business in this district").

6: Skip this for now. Later I'll tell you what to do.

---

[1]In the event you are curious, Code of Civil Procedure § 382 allows you to name as a defendant a party that is needed as a plaintiff but has refused to participate in the lawsuit. If this is your situation, you'll need the help of a lawyer. See Chapter 17.

SHORT TITLE:
Kim vs. Offer

CASE NUMBER:

COMPLAINT—Personal Injury, Property Damage, Wrongful Death   Page two

3. a. Each defendant named above is a natural person
   [X] **Except** defendant *(name):*
      ROMMOR Books

      [X] a business organization, form unknown
      [ ] a corporation
      [ ] an unincorporated entity *(describe):*

      [ ] a public entity *(describe):*

      [ ] other *(specify):*

   [ ] **Except** defendant *(name):*

      [ ] a business organization, form unknown
      [ ] a corporation
      [ ] an unincorporated entity *(describe):*

      [ ] a public entity *(describe):*

      [ ] other *(specify):*

   [ ] **Except** defendant *(name):*

      [ ] a business organization, form unknown
      [ ] a corporation
      [ ] an unincorporated entity *(describe):*

      [ ] a public entity *(describe):*

      [ ] other *(specify):*

   [ ] **Except** defendant *(name):*

      [ ] a business organization, form unknown
      [ ] a corporation
      [ ] an unincorporated entity *(describe):*

      [ ] a public entity *(describe):*

      [ ] other *(specify):*

   b. The true names and capacities of defendants sued as Does are unknown to plaintiff.

   c. [ ] Information about additional defendants who are not natural persons is contained in Complaint—Attachment 3c.
   d. [ ] Defendants who are joined pursuant to Code of Civil Procedure section 382 are *(names):*

4. [ ] Plaintiff is required to comply with a claims statute, **and**
   a. [ ] plaintiff has complied with applicable claims statutes, **or**
   b. [ ] plaintiff is excused from complying because *(specify):*

5. This court is the proper court because
   [X] at least one defendant now resides in its jurisdictional area.
   [ ] the principal place of business of a corporation or unincorporated association is in its jurisdictional area.
   [X] injury to person or damage to personal property occurred in its jurisdictional area.
   [X] other *(specify):* defendant ROMMOR Books does business in this district

6. [ ] The following paragraphs of this complaint are alleged on information and belief *(specify paragraph numbers):*

(Continued)   Page two

Page Three

If There's More Than One Plaintiff

If your case involves more than one plaintiff, you must use a different page three for each. You designate each plaintiff's damages and requests by putting a slash mark (/) after the word "plaintiff" in Items 8 and 10, and typing in the name of the particular plaintiff whose damages and requests you're describing above the slash. Each plaintiff must have his or her name at the bottom of his or her page and sign at the signature line.

Short Title: Put exactly what you put at the top of page 2.

Case Number: Leave this blank.

7: Skip this item.

8: Here you check off the various categories of damages you are claiming. Don't specify the amounts.

wage loss: Check if you claim damages for past or future wage loss.

hospital and medical expenses: Check if you claim any of these expenses.

property damage: Check if you claim any physical damage to anything you own, such as your house, yard, car or a camera in the car that broke because of the accident.

loss of use of property: If your car, camera or any other item was in the shop being repaired for any length of time, or you had to do without it while looking for a replacement, check this box.

general damage: This refers to pain and suffering. Anytime someone is physically injured, it is safe to assume he also had pain and suffering, so check the box if you were injured.

Although you can recover for pain and suffering without having a physical injury, such a case is complex and you should consult a lawyer.

loss of earning capacity: If you anticipate a loss of future income because of work you'll miss or because you'll have to take a lower paying job as a result of your injury, check this box.

other damage (*specify*): Check this box if you have any damages not included in one of the other boxes. The most common is punitive or exemplary ("to make an example") damages. You might want to ask for these damages if a defendant acted against you with the intent to cause you injury or with a conscious disregard of your rights or safety. Courts rarely award punitive damages, but it never hurts to ask.

9: This statement is there just to remind you that by using this complaint and filing it in a Municipal or Justice Court, you understand that you are limited to recovering $25,000.

10: Despite the phrase "Plaintiff Prays," this paragraph is not an inquiry into your religious beliefs. It asks you to state what you want out of the lawsuit. (In legalese, that request is called a "prayer.") Check the first box for compensatory damages. Then check the third box for Municipal and Justice Courts. After the "$", insert the total amount of money you are seeking in this suit. You should have arrived at that figure in Chapter 2. Remember—each plaintiff can request up to $25,000, except spouses or co-owners of property who suffered joint damage.

You can insert any number up to $25,000. But be reasonable. If your damages will never exceed $10,000, you may be embarrassed and at a disadvantage later if you put $25,000. In a jury trial, the jury might feel you were being greedy and outrageous. So use some common sense.

SHORT TITLE	CASE NUMBER
Kim vs. Offer	

COMPLAINT—Personal Injury, Property Damage, Wrongful Death (Continued)   Page three

7. ☐ The damages claimed for wrongful death and the relationships of plaintiff to the deceased are
   ☐ listed in Complaint—Attachment 7 ☐ as follows:

8. Plaintiff has suffered
   ☐ wage loss   ☒ loss of use of property
   ☒ hospital and medical expenses   ☒ general damage
   ☒ property damage   ☐ loss of earning capacity
   ☒ other damage *(specify):* lost business profits,
      punitive damages

9. Relief sought in this complaint is within the jurisdiction of this court.

10. PLAINTIFF PRAYS
    For judgment for costs of suit; for such relief as is fair, just, and equitable; and for
    ☒ compensatory damages
       ☐ **(Superior Court)** according to proof.

       ☒ **(Municipal and Justice Court)** in the amount of $ 12,000
    ☒ other *(specify):* punitive damages according to proof.
    Such other relief as the court may deem proper.

11. The following causes of action are attached and the statements above apply to each: *(Each complaint must have
    one or more causes of action attached.)*
    ☐ Motor Vehicle
    ☐ General Negligence
    ☒ Intentional Tort
    ☐ Products Liability
    ☐ Premises Liability
    ☒ Other *(specify):* Exemplary damages

Sam Kim
.... _____ _____
              (Type or print name)   (Signature of plaintiff or attorney)

Rule 982.1(1) (cont'd)   **COMPLAINT**— Personal Injury, Property Damage,   Page three   C-87
                                      Wrongful Death (Continued)   CCP 425.12

State a number that gives you a little room for unforeseen developments, but don't go too far. It is possible to amend your complaint later if it turns out you didn't ask for enough originally.

Check the fourth box. If you're asking for punitive damages, put "punitive damages according to proof" after the "other (specify)." Keep in mind that punitive and exemplary damages combined cannot exceed $25,000 per plaintiff. Also, whether or not you are asking for punitive damages, type "Such other relief as the court may deem proper." Lawyers customarily write this and by putting in your complaint, you will show the other side that you know how to sound like a lawyer.

11: Skip this paragraph for now. You'll fill it out after you prepare your causes of action attachments.

Signature: Type your name above the left dotted line and sign above the solid line on the right.

You've finished your first form. Now you must complete at least one "Cause of Action" attachment to finish the preparation of your Complaint.

1. Tort Causes of Action Forms

As noted earlier, a cause of action is a statement of the legal theory you are using to ask the court for relief. Your Complaint must include at least one cause of action, but certainly can include more. The ones you use will depend on the facts of your case. For instance, if you were in an automobile accident with a defendant who you believe was intentionally trying to run into you, complete both a Motor Vehicle Cause of Action and an Intentional Tort Cause of Action.

 Read only the sections below that pertain to your lawsuit.

a. Motor Vehicle Cause of Action Form

This form must be used if you are suing because of a defendant's negligent use of a motor vehicle (car, truck, van, motorcycle, scooter and the like). Use a separate form for each plaintiff. A completed sample and instructions follow. A blank is in the Appendix.

Short Title: Type exactly what you typed at the top of page 2 of the Complaint.

Case Number: Leave this blank.

_____ Cause of Action—Motor Vehicle: Insert the word "First" in the blank, indicating this is the first attachment to your Complaint.

Page: Add one to the number of the last page you completed and put that number here.

Attachment to: Check "Complaint."

Plaintiff: On the first line, put only one plaintiff's name. If there's more than one plaintiff, complete a separate form for each plaintiff. For each subsequent plaintiff, increase by one the number in the blank preceding the "Cause of Action" and the page number.

MV-1: Type the date and place of the accident here. If you are not sure of the exact date, state something like "on or about April 5, 19__." If the accident didn't occur at an easily identifiable location, such as "the intersection of Third and Market Streets, San Francisco, California," do the best you can, for example, "approximately five miles south of Sea Ranch on State Route 1."

The tort causes of action you can choose among are:

Cause of Action Form	When Used
Motor Vehicle	All car and other motor vehicle accident cases
Premises Liability	If the claim happened on someone's property because of a condition the owner allowed to exist on that property
General Negligence	If defendant acted negligently (carelessly), and the case does not involve motor vehicle, premise liability or defective product
Intentional Tort	If your claim arose out of defendant's intentional, not merely negligent, act
Products Liability	If your claim arose out of a defective product
Exemplary Damages Attachment[2]	If your claim arose out of defendant's intentional, not merely negligent, act

---

[2]This is technically not a cause of action, but the discussion is the same.

SHORT TITLE: Short vs. Merced	CASE NUMBER:

First **CAUSE OF ACTION—Motor Vehicle**   Page _4_
(number)

ATTACHMENT TO [X] Complaint [ ] Cross-Complaint

(Use a separate cause of action form for each cause of action.)

Plaintiff *(name):* Joseph P. Short

MV-1. Plaintiff alleges the acts of defendants were negligent; the acts were the legal (proximate) cause of injuries and damages to plaintiff; the acts occurred
on *(date):* September 12, 1992
at *(place):* the corner of 12th and Main Streets, Needles, California

MV-2. DEFENDANTS
a. [X] The defendants who operated a motor vehicle are *(names):*
Simon Merced and Izzy Axelrod

[ ] Does _____ to _____
b. [ ] The defendants who employed the persons who operated a motor vehicle in the course of their employment are *(names):*

[ ] Does _____ to _____
c. [X] The defendants who owned the motor vehicle which was operated with their permission are *(names):*
Marybeth Merced and Ivan Merced

[X] Does _1_ to _2_
d. [X] The defendants who entrusted the motor vehicle are *(names):*
Marybeth Merced and Ivan Merced

[X] Does _1_ to _2_
e. [ ] The defendants who were the agents and employees of the other defendants and acted within the scope of the agency were *(names):*

[ ] Does _____ to _____
f. [X] The defendants who are liable to plaintiffs for other reasons and the reasons for the liability are
[ ] listed in Attachment MV-2f [X] as follows:

Louise Axelrod and Phoenix Axelrod, the parents of Izzy Axelrod, a minor, by reason of their having signed his application for a driver's license

[ ] Does _____ to _____

Form Approved by the
Judicial Council of California
Effective January 1, 1982
Rule 982.1(2)   **CAUSE OF ACTION—Motor Vehicle**   CCP 425.12 C-88

MV-2: Here you identify the defendants responsible for your damages arising out of a motor vehicle accident.

MV-2a: Check this box and type the full names of all defendants you know or suspect drove the vehicle. Normally there will be just one, but multi-car accidents are not unusual. If you don't know the identity of a driver, check the "Does" box (Doe defendants are covered in Chapter, Section 4.D.7) and name the appropriate number of Does, such as "Does 1 to 2."

MV-2b: If a driver was working on her job at the time of the accident, check this item and type the names of the employers. If you don't know the name of an employer, check the "Does" box and name the appropriate number of Does, such as "Does 3 to 4."

MV-2c: If a driver had permission to borrow someone else's vehicle at the time of the accident, check this box and type the names of the owners. Unless you have facts to the contrary, you can assume permission was granted. The granting could have been expressly stated or implied from the situation. For example, if the owner of a car customarily let his roommates borrow it, his permission to use the car on the day of the accident will be implied. If you don't know the name of an owner, check the "Does" box and name the appropriate number of Does, such as "Does 5 to 6."

MV-2d: Entrustment is a legal theory for holding someone responsible for an accident if that person let an incompetent, reckless or intoxicated person use a vehicle. If you completed Items MV-2b or MV-2c, check this box and list the same information you listed in those items. It's also possible that a car dealer, co-owner or giver of a gift car a might be held responsible for an accident. If you're unsure, refer back to Chapter 4, Section B.1.a. If you don't know the name of someone who entrusted the vehicle, check the "Does" box and name the appropriate number of Does, such as "Does 7 to 8."

MV-2e: In this item, identify any foremen or supervisors of the driver who have an intermediate role in the case. This will be relevant only if the employer doesn't have money or insurance coverage and you identify a foreman or supervisor who does. Because you aren't likely to have this information until after your lawsuit is filed, check the "Does" box and name several Does, such as "Does 9 to 12."

MV-2f: Check this box only if a minor was the driver of a vehicle that contributed to the accident. To sue the parents or legal guardians for signing the minor's driver's license application, check the "as follows" box and write something like: "Bruce and Suzanne O'Brien, the parents of Peter O'Brien, a minor, by reason of their having signed his application for a driver's license." If the minor was unlicensed, check the "as follows" box and write something like "Bruce and Suzanne O'Brien, the parents of Peter O'Brien, a minor who was not licensed to drive."

 The Motor Vehicle cause of action is done; if you have no other tort claims, skip ahead to Section 2.

b. Premises Liability Cause of Action Form

Use this form if you're suing because of an injury due to a condition that existed in a store, home, park or other premises. If more than one plaintiff suffered injuries, use a separate form for each plaintiff.

In general, a defendant is liable for your damage or injury if:

- he failed to warn about or repair a dangerous condition;

- he is aware, or should have been aware, of a concealed or hidden condition not obvious to a normally cautious person involving an unreasonable risk of harm to persons who come on to the property (such as a recently waxed and slippery floor); and

- he should have realized that a person likely to be on the property might come into contact with that condition.

This is true even if the injured person is on the property without permission if the owner or manager of the property could have reasonably anticipated that the injured person would be on the property and exposed to the concealed condition.

In one case, a man was electrocuted when he climbed a Pacific Gas & Electric company pole and attempted to unscrew a bulb that was casting a bright light into his apartment. In the trial, the jury found evidence that PG&E either knew or should have known that he had been unscrewing the bulb in the past and that the high voltage present constituted a high risk of harm. The jury also found that PG&E could have taken several safety precautions. The court upheld the jury's finding that PG&E was negligent.

Similar liability has been found against landlords who fail to keep their rental properties safe and store operators who allow debris to remain on the floor—or even on the sidewalk in front of the store.

A completed sample and instructions follow. A blank form is in the Appendix.

Short Title: Type exactly what you typed at the top of page 2 of the complaint.

Case Number: Leave this blank.

_____ **Cause of Action—Premise Liability:** If this is the first Cause of Action, insert the word "First." If it is the second, use "Second," and so on.

Page: Add one to the number of the last page you completed and put that number here.

Attachment to: Check "Complaint."

Prem.L-1: On the first line, put only one plaintiff's name. If more than one plaintiff was hurt, complete a separate form for each plaintiff. For each subsequent plaintiff, increase by one the number in the blank preceding the "Cause of Action" and the page number. After filling in the plaintiff's name, enter the date of the injury.

Next, the form asks for a description of the premises and the circumstances of injury. Begin your answer with the address of the property where the injury occurred. Normally, a street and city address is sufficient. If the injury occurred in a multi-story building or apartment house, add the apartment or room number.

SHORT TITLE:
Andrews vs. Highrise Management & Associates

CASE NUMBER:

First _____ **CAUSE OF ACTION**—Premises Liability   Page __Four__
     (number)

ATTACHMENT TO [X] Complaint   ☐ Cross-Complaint

(Use a separate cause of action form for each cause of action.)

Prem.L-1. Plaintiff *(name):* Carmen Andrews
          alleges the acts of defendants were the legal (proximate) cause of damages to plaintiff.
          On *(date):* July 4, 1992   plaintiff was injured on the following premises in the following

          fashion *(description of premises and circumstances of injury):*
          Roof of Jackson Square Apartment, 88774 Buena Vista Blvd.,
          Laguna Beach, California; plaintiff was injured when a portion of the
          roof of the apartment building collapsed while plaintiff was
          watching the July 4th fireworks.

Prem.L-2. [X] **Count One—Negligence** The defendants who negligently owned, maintained, managed and operated
           the described premises were *(names):*
           Highrise Management & Associates, Norman Kopp, Albert Harris
           and
           [X] Does __1__ to __5__

Prem.L-3. ☐ **Count Two—Willful Failure to Warn** [Civil Code section 846] The defendant owners who willfully
           or maliciously failed to guard or warn against a dangerous condition, use, structure, or activity were
           (names):

           ☐ Does _____ to _____
           Plaintiff, a recreational user, was ☐ an invited guest   ☐ a paying guest.

Prem.L-4. ☐ **Count Three—Dangerous Condition of Public Property** The defendants who owned public property
           on which a dangerous condition existed were *(names):*

               ☐ Does _____ to _____
           a. ☐ The defendant public entity had ☐ actual ☐ constructive notice of the existence of the
                 dangerous condition in sufficient time prior to the injury to have corrected it.
           b. ☐ The condition was created by employees of the defendant public entity.

Prem.L-5. a. [X] **Allegations about Other Defendants** The defendants who were the agents and employees of the
           other defendants and acted within the scope of the agency were *(names):*

           Felicia McDonald
           [X] Does __6__ to __8__
        b. ☐ The defendants who are liable to plaintiffs for other reasons and the reasons for their liability are
             ☐ described in attachment Prem.L-5.b ☐ as follows *(names):*

Form Approved by the
Judicial Council of California
Effective January 1, 1982   **CAUSE OF ACTION**—Premises Liability   CCP 425.12
Rule 982.1(5)   C-91

Then describe how you were injured, and specifically what the defendant did or did not do that caused your injury. Be concise; try to say what is necessary in 40 words or less. Save the flowery language and the finger pointing for your trial. Also, refer to plaintiffs and defendants in the third person. This may feel contrived, but it's the way it's done. Here are some examples:

"Safeway store, 9356 Market Street, San Jose, California; plaintiff was injured when she slipped and fell as the result of a piece of fruit negligently left on the floor in the produce department."

"Apartment C, 3445 Elm Street, Santa Ana, California; plaintiff was injured when a defective knob on a faucet on the bathroom basin broke while she was turning it."

"Swimming pool, Central Park, Eighth and Park Streets, Long Beach, California; plaintiff was injured when defective diving board collapsed while she was using it normally."

Prem.L-2: Check this box and type the full names of all defendants you know or suspect owned, maintained, managed or operated the property. If you don't know the identity of an owner or manager, check the "Does" box (Doe defendants are covered in Chapter 4.D.7) and name the number of Does as there are unknown identities, such as "Does 1 to 2."

Prem.L-3: California law provides that a person who permits (as opposed to expressly invites) others to use his property for recreational purposes without charge is not liable for injuries to those others unless the owner willfully or maliciously failed to guard or warn

against a dangerous condition, use, structure or activity on the property.[3]

This means you should skip this paragraph if you were not on the premises for recreation. Also skip it if you paid a fee to get on the property or if people are normally charged a fee for entry. Also skip it if you had a specific personal invitation to use the property, as opposed to a general invitation to the public. If none of these apply, check this box and type the names of all of the defendants listed in Item Prem.L-2, including the Doe defendants.

Prem.L-4: Skip this item unless you were using property owned or operated by a government agency. And be sure you've filed a claim for damages with the public agency. (See Chapter 4, Section D.2.)

If the property was owned or operated by a government agency, check this box and type the full names of all defendants who owned the property. If there is possibly an unknown co-owner, check the "Does" box and name the number of Does as there are unknown identities, such as "Does 3 to 4."

Then check paragraph a or b, or possibly both. If you check a, check both actual (the agency actually knew about the dangerous condition) and constructive (the agency should have known about it) to give yourself room to prove either. Even if the agency didn't have actual notice, the court will probably agree that it had constructive notice if a condition existed for a period of time and was obvious enough that a reasonable inspection would have disclosed it.

Prem.L-5a: If any defendants were the agents or employees of the property owner or manager, check this item and type the names of

---

[3]Civil Code § 846.

the agents or employees. Include any foremen or supervisors who had an intermediate role in your getting injured. If a maintenance contractor worked for the owner and he was responsible for your injury, put his name here. If you don't know a name—or if you want to give yourself room in the event a yet-unknown person emerges as responsible for your injury, check the "Does" box and name the number of Does as there are unknown identities, such as "Does 5 to 7."

Prem.L-5b: Leave this blank. The reasons you would add defendants under subparagraph b are beyond the scope of this book.

 The Premise Liability cause of action is done; if you have no other tort claims, skip ahead to Section 2.

c. General Negligence Cause of Action Form

This form is for all careless or negligent acts (as opposed to intentional acts) other than motor vehicle and premises liability accidents. Several samples are listed in Chapter 2; here are a few others:

- A window washer drops soapy water on your car, which eats away the car's finish.

- An owner of a ferocious dog lets it escape from her yard; the dog bites you.

- A restaurant owner serves you spoiled food; you get violently ill.

A completed sample and instructions follow. A blank form is in the Appendix. Use a separate form for each plaintiff.

A Short Course in the Law of Negligence

Negligence cases crowd the dockets of courts throughout the nation. Law students spend months attempting to understand its principles; legal scholars have written thousands of articles on the subject. This "short course" can do no more than give you a glimpse.

Negligence is doing something that a reasonably prudent person would not do, or failing to do something that a reasonably prudent person would do, under similar circumstances. The negligence must cause harm. Negligence also is described as the failure to use ordinary care.

It is the job of the judge (or the jury) to determine what a reasonably prudent person would or would not do under similar circumstances. This mythical person is considered to be neither extraordinarily cautious nor exceptionally skillful.

One test used to help determine if a person was negligent is to ask whether or not a person of ordinary prudence in the same situation with the same knowledge would have anticipated that someone might have been injured as a result of the defendant's action or inaction. If the answer is yes, and the action or inaction could reasonably have been avoided, then the defendant was negligent.

A plaintiff injured because of the defendant's negligent act is entitled to compensation. The act must substantially, not remotely, bring about the injury.

A good case that illustrates the principle of negligence involved a Los Angeles radio station twith a high percentage of teenage listeners. The station had a contest in which a disc jockey drove to certain locations in a conspicuous red car. The station aired clues as to where he was and gave a prize to the first person to find him. One day, as the disc jockey drove about, several cars that were following him got into a pile up. A driver was killed. The station, as well as the drivers of the other cars, were found negligent. The court said it was foreseeable that by broadcasting the contest, teenagers would follow the red car, drive dangerously and cause an accident.

Short Title: Type exactly what you typed at the top of page 2 of the Complaint.

Case Number: Leave this blank.

_____ **Cause of Action—General Negligence:** If this is the first Cause of Action, insert the word "First." If it is the second, use "Second," and so on.

Page: Add one to the number of the last page you completed and put that number here.

Attachment to: Check "Complaint."

GN-1: Put only one plaintiff's name in this blank, and complete a separate form for each plaintiff. For each subsequent plaintiff, increase by one the number in the blank preceding the "Cause of Action" and the page number.

After "defendant (name)" type the full names of all defendants who are in any way responsible for your damage or injury in this cause of action. If other people yet unknown may be responsible for the incident, check the "Does" box (Doe defendants are covered in Chapter 4, Section D.7) and name the number of Does as there are unknown identities, such as "Does 1 to 4."

Next, type the date and place of the accident here. If you are not sure of the exact date, state something like "on or about April 5, 19__." If the accident didn't occur at an easily identifiable location, such as "1800 Main Street, Fresno, California," do the best you can.

Next, the form asks for the reasons for liability. You describe how you or your property were injured, and specifically what the defendant did or did not do that caused the injury. Be concise; try to say what is necessary in 40 words or fewer. Save the flowery language and the finger pointing for your trial. Also, refer to plaintiffs and defendants in the third person. This

may feel contrived, but it's the way it's done. Here are some examples:

"Defendants negligently dropped a bucket of paint on plaintiff's computer causing it to be damaged while plaintiff was pushing the computer across the sidewalk below them."

"Defendants negligently left a gate on their property open and thereby allowed a dangerous German Shepherd dog to come onto plaintiff's property and bite him, which caused injury to plaintiff."

"Defendants negligently prepared an unsanitary meal in their restaurant and served it to plaintiff, who ate it and was thus caused to become violently ill."

You probably see a formula emerging. Each description starts with a recital of something the defendants did negligently. Then the victim (plaintiff) is named. Finally, his injuries or damages are described as having been caused by the defendants' action or inaction. Use this formula to describe a bus driver stopping too sharply causing you to fall to the bus floor or a delivery person running over your toes with her dolly. As long as you mention that the defendants' negligent act caused injury or damage to the plaintiff, you've described the reasons for liability just fine.

 The General Negligence cause of action is done; if you have no other tort claims, skip ahead to Section 2.

SHORT TITLE:	CASE NUMBER:
Andrews vs. Highrise Management & Associates	

Second   **CAUSE OF ACTION—General Negligence**   Page __Five__

(number)

ATTACHMENT TO   ☒ Complaint   ☐ Cross-Complaint

(Use a separate cause of action form for each cause of action.)

GN-1. Plaintiff *(name):* Carmen Andrews

alleges that defendant *(name):*
Highrise Management & Associates, Norman Kopp, Albert Harris and
Felicia McDonald

☒ Does __1__ to __8__

was the legal (proximate) cause of damages to plaintiff. By the following acts or omissions to act, defendant
negligently caused the damage to plaintiff
on *(date):* July 4, 1992
at *(place):* Roof of Jackson Square Apartment building, 88774 Buena Vista
Blvd., Laguna Beach, California
(description of reasons for liability):

Defendants negligently maintained the rooftop of the Jackson Square
Apartment building and thereby allowed a dangerous condition to
exist, which caused injury to plaintiff when she fell through the
roof.

Form Approved by the
Judicial Council of California
Effective January 1, 1982
Rule 982.1(3)   **CAUSE OF ACTION—General Negligence**   CCP 425.12   C-89

d. Intentional Tort Cause of Action Form

Use this form if the defendant intentionally caused you injury or property damage. The law has categorized the various types of intentional torts. The principal categories area

- Battery (a willful and unlawful use of force upon the body of one person by another)
- Conversion (theft—or, more precisely, the intentional and substantial interference with your possession of your personal property)

There are many more intentional torts, such as fraud, defamation (libel and slander), intentional infliction of emotional distress, false imprisonment, malicious prosecution, abuse of process, invasion of privacy, trespass, interference with prospective economic advantage and inducing breach of contract. These are all beyond the scope of this book.[4]

A completed sample and instructions follow. A blank form is in the Appendix. Use a separate form for each plaintiff.

Short Title: Type exactly what you typed at the top of page 2 of the Complaint.

Case Number: Leave this blank.

_____ Cause of Action—Intentional Tort: If this is the first Cause of Action, insert the word "First." If it is the second, use "Second," and so on.

Page: Add one to the number of the last page you completed and put that number here.

Attachment to: Check Complaint."

IT-1: Put only one plaintiff's name in this blank, and complete a separate form for each plaintiff. For each subsequent plaintiff, increase by one the number in the blank preceding the "Cause of Action" and the page number.

After "defendant (name)" type the full names of all defendants who committed an intentional tort that damaged or injured you. If other people yet unknown may be responsible, check the "Does" box (Doe defendants are covered in Chapter 4, Section D.7) and name the number of Does as there are unknown identities, such as "Does 1 to 4."

Next, type the date and place of the incident here. If you are not sure of the exact date, state something like "on or about April 5, 19__." If the accident didn't occur at an easily identifiable location, such as "1800 Main Street, Fresno, California," do the best you can.

---

[4]For a discussion on drafting a complaint for these causes of action, see Section D, below.

SHORT TITLE:
Kim vs. Offer

CASE NUMBER:

_____First_____ **CAUSE OF ACTION**—Intentional Tort   Page ___4___
(number)

ATTACHMENT TO ☒ Complaint ☐ Cross-Complaint

(Use a separate cause of action form for each cause of action.)

IT-1. Plaintiff *(name):* Sam Kim dba Kim's Book Supplies

alleges that defendant *(name):* Jenny Offer, Martin Myotic and April Rain,
individually and dba as ROMMOR Books

☒ Does ___1___ to ___4___

was the legal (proximate) cause of damages to plaintiff. By the following acts or omissions to act, defendant intentionally caused the damage to plaintiff
on *(date):* March 30, 1992
at *(place):* ROMMOR Books, 1125 ½ Third Street, Napa, California

(description of reasons for liability):
Plaintiff entered defendants bookstore carrying a box of bookmarks, bookplates and book jackets for sale. Defendant Offer grabbed plaintiff's box and threw it at plaintiff, hitting him in the face. Plaintiff's glasses shattered and a piece of glass cut his left eye. Plaintiff fell over and sprained his ankle. Furthermore, the bookmarks, bookplates and book jackets contained within plaintiff's box were damaged when defendant Offer threw the box.

As plaintiff tried to leave the store, defendants Myotic and Rain screamed at him "don't ever come back here again" and threw the contents of plaintiff's box at him. Plaintiff was hit in the back several times with bookplates.

Form Approved by the
Judicial Council of California
Effective January 1, 1982
Rule 982.1(4)   **CAUSE OF ACTION**— Intentional Tort   CCP 425.12

Next, the form asks for the reasons for liability. You describe how you or your property were injured, and specifically what the defendant did that caused the injury. Be concise; try to say what is necessary in 40 words or less. Save the flowery language and the finger pointing for your trial. Also, refer to plaintiffs and defendants in the third person. This may feel contrived, but it's the way it's done. Here are some examples:

• "Defendant Robinson approached the table plaintiff was sitting at in a restaurant and intentionally poured water over plaintiff's head and struck plaintiff in the face with his fist, causing her to become unconscious." (Battery)

• "Defendant Robinson came on to plaintiff's property and, without her permission, removed her Hyundai automobile with the intent of interfering with her possession of that automobile. He has not returned it." (Conversion)

 The Intentional Tort cause of action is done; skip ahead to Subsection f.

e.   Products Liability Cause of Action Form

We do not reproduce the check-the-box form for suing a manufacturer, supplier or seller of a defective product that injured your body. Rarely does a pro per handle this type of lawsuit.[5]

---

[5]If you're determined to bring a products liability lawsuit pro per, see *California Forms of Pleading and Practice*, Volume 12A, Part 1. This volume is in major law libraries.

f.   Exemplary Damages Attachment

You use this form when you ask the court to award you damages that punish a defendant or to make her an example to others. You must prove that the defendant acted out of malice, fraud or oppression.[6]

Malice. Conduct intended by the defendant to cause injury to the plaintiff, or conduct carried on by the defendant with a willful and conscious disregard of the rights or safety of the plaintiff.

Oppression. Conduct that subjects the plaintiff to cruel and unjust hardship in conscious disregard of his rights.

Fraud. An intentional misrepresentation, deceit or concealment of a material fact known to the defendant, with the intention the defendant to deprive the plaintiff of property or legal rights, or otherwise causing the plaintiff injury.

⚠️ **Be sure the defendant's conduct fits one of the definitions.**
Complaints seeking exemplary damages for ordinary negligence are not treated seriously. They will hurt you more than help you. In a lawyer's world, you, as a pro per, must look like a reasonable person who was injured and wants just compensation. Separate yourself from the overly aggressive professional litigants who scream for exemplary damages for every minor affront they suffer. After a while, judges recognize these people and have trouble taking them seriously.

A completed sample and instructions follow. A blank form is in the Appendix. Use a separate form for each defendant.

---

[6]These terms are defined at Civil Code § 3293.

SHORT TITLE: Kim vs. Offer	CASE NUMBER:

Exemplary Damages Attachment

Page ___5___

ATTACHMENT TO [x] Complaint [ ] Cross-Complaint

EX-1 As additional damages against defendant (name):

Jenny Offer

Plaintiff alleges defendant was guilty of

[X] malice

[ ] fraud

[ ] oppression

as defined in Civil Code section 3294, and plaintiff should recover, in addition to actual damages, damages to make an example of and to punish defendant.

EX-2. The facts supporting plaintiff's claim are as follows:

As described in plaintiff's First Cause of Action, defendant Offer grabbed plaintiff's box of bookmarks, bookplates and book jackets and threw them at plaintiff. This act caused damage to plaintiff's goods, shattered his eyeglasses, caused glass to cut his eye and caused him to sprain his ankle.

EX-3. The amount of exemplary damages sought is

a. [ ] not shown, pursuant to Code of Civil Procedure section 425.10.

b. [X] $ according to proof

Form Approved by the
Judicial Council of California
Effective January 1, 1982
Rule 982.1(13)

Exemplary Damages Attachment

CCP 425.12

Short Title: Type exactly what you typed at the top of page 2 of the Complaint.

Case Number: Leave this blank.

Page: Add one to the number of the last page you completed and put that number here.

Attachment to: Check "Complaint."

EX-1: After "defendant (name)" type the full name of a defendant who was guilty of malice, fraud and/or oppression. Then check any of the three boxes that apply. For each defendant, complete a separate form and increase by one the page number.

EX-2: Set forth the facts which you claim establish that there was malice, fraud or oppression. Examples of language that might be used in this item are:

"As described in the First Cause of Action, defendant hid in plaintiff's garage and then jumped on him without warning, knocking him to the ground and causing him to become unconscious."

"As described in the First Cause of Action, defendant fraudulently concealed from plaintiff the fact that there was no engine in the automobile he sold to plaintiff and that it was therefore worthless, thus causing plaintiff to be defrauded of the $7,000 he paid to defendant."

EX-3: 3a does not apply to Municipal Court suits, so check 3b. Then insert the words "according to proof." Although the form asks for a specific dollar amount, recent changes in California law prohibit parties from specifying a precise amount here.[7]

---

[7]Civil Code § 3295(e).

2. Cleaning Up the Tort Complaint

Now is the time to fill in the paragraphs you've skipped.

Defendant: Does 1 to ___: Count up your Doe defendants and enter the total.

Complaint Item 1 (total number of pages): Count up your total number of pages—don't forget any attachment sheets—and insert the total.

Complaint Item 6 (the matters you are alleging on information and belief): Here you have to play lawyer for a moment. Read over the factual statements in the complaint and causes of action. If any statement is true, but you can't testify to its contents from your own knowledge (that is, you relied on something someone else told you), the statement is said to have been made "on information and belief." Common information and belief statements include:

- identifying a defendant as the employee or agent of the another
- indicating if a driver had the permission to drive a car

If any statements fit in the category, check this box and type the paragraph number, such as MV-1. If there is more than one cause of action of the same kind (such as Motor Vehicle), be sure to note the paragraph number and the cause of action. Do your best at this, but do not spend a lot of time worrying about it.

Complaint Item 11 (attached causes of action): Check all that are applicable. If you completed an Exemplary Damages Attachment, check the "other" box and specify.

Review all your page numbers and Cause of Action headings. Be sure they are in order.

 You've completed the tort complaint and can skip ahead to Section E.

C. Contract Complaint

You filled out most of the caption in Section 2, above. The "Contract" box is still blank. Check the "Complaint" box.

Now let's get into the body of the complaint. A completed sample and instructions follow. A blank copy is in the Appendix.

1: Skip this for now. You'll come back and enter the number of pages after you complete the Complaint and the causes of action attachments.

2: If all plaintiffs are adults persons, skip item 2. If any plaintiff is a business or an organization, continue reading.

2a: Check the first and third boxes if any plaintiff is a member of a partnership or officer of an incorporated association suing on its behalf. (None of the other listed plaintiffs can sue in pro per.) Then type in the name of the partnership or association after the first box, and state whether it is a partnership or association after the third box.

If a second or more plaintiff is a partnership or association, be sure to complete Item 2c.

2b: Check this box if you are suing in the name of your business and you do business under a fictitious name. If you own a business as a sole proprietor, type your own name after "Plaintiff (*name*)" and the fictitious business name on the next line after "(*specify*)."

If your partnership does business under a fictitious name, type the partnership's name after "Plaintiff (*name*)" and the fictitious business name on the next line after "(*specify*)."

2c: Skip this item unless more than one partnership or association are plaintiffs. If there are, you'll have to create an attachment sheet, and enter all the information requested in Item 2a.

ATTORNEY OR PARTY WITHOUT ATTORNEY (NAME AND ADDRESS):	TELEPHONE:	FOR COURT USE ONLY
Jamie Garcia 82 Southwest Drive San Mateo, CA 94404 ATTORNEY FOR (NAME): in pro per	415 -555-2044	

Insert name of court, judicial district or branch court, if any, and post office and street address:
San Mateo County Municipal Court
Central Branch
800 North Humboldt Street
San Mateo, CA 94401

PLAINTIFF:

Jamie Garcia, dba Flour Power

DEFENDANT:
Anne Warren, individually and dba Anne's Pie Shop

☐ DOES 1 TO _____

CONTRACT ☒ COMPLAINT ☐ CROSS-COMPLAINT	CASE NUMBER:

1. This pleading, including attachments and exhibits, consists of the following number of pages: ___5___

2. a. Each plaintiff named above is a competent adult
   ☐ **Except** plaintiff (name):

      ☐ a corporation qualified to do business in California
      ☐ an unincorporated entity (describe):
      ☐ other (specify):

   b. ☒ Plaintiff (name): Jamie Garcia
      ☒ has complied with the fictitious business name laws and is doing business under the fictitious name
         of (specify): Flour Power
      ☐ has complied with all licensing requirements as a licensed (specify):

   c. ☐ Information about additional plaintiffs who are not competent adults is shown in Complaint—Attachment 2c.
3. a. Each defendant named above is a natural person
      ☒ **Except** defendant (name):   ☐ **Except** defendant (name):
         Anne's Pie Shop
         ☐ a business organization, form unknown   ☐ a business organization, form unknown
         ☐ a corporation   ☐ a corporation
         ☒ an unincorporated entity (describe):   ☐ an unincorporated entity (describe):
            sole proprietorship
         ☐ a public entity (describe):   ☐ a public entity (describe):

         ☐ other (specify):   ☐ other (specify):

   b. The true names and capacities of defendants sued as Does are unknown to plaintiff.
   c. ☐ Information about additional defendants who are not natural persons is contained in Complaint—Attachment 3c.
   d. ☐ Defendants who are joined pursuant to Code of Civil Procedure section 382 are (names):

(Continued)

If this form is used as a cross-complaint, plaintiff means cross-complainant and defendant means cross-defendant.
Form Approved by the
Judicial Council of California
Effective January 1, 1982
Rule 982.1(20)

COMPLAINT—Contract

CCP 425.12   C-96

3: If all defendants are natural persons, skip all of Item 3.

3a: If any defendant is a partnership, association, corporation or government entity, complete this section. You have two identical paragraphs. For each defendant that falls into this category, put its name after "Except defendant (*name*)," and check the applicable sub-box. You'll have to describe an unincorporated entity (simply write "partnership" or "association") and a public entity (such as the "County of Santa Clara"). If more than two defendants fall into this category, continue with Item 3c.

If you are suing one or more individuals who are doing business under a fictitious name, check the appropriate box describing the business type, if you know it. (Usually it's an unincorporated entity.) If you don't know the business form, check the second box.

3b: You need not do anything here.

3c: Skip this item unless more than two partnerships, associations, corporations or government entities are defendants. If there are, you'll have to create an attachment sheet, and enter all the information requested in Item 3a for each additional defendant.

3d: Skip this item—it involves a complex legal situation you need not worry about.[8]

_____

[8]In the event you are curious, Code of Civil Procedure § 382 allows you to name as a defendant a party that is needed as a plaintiff but has refused to participate in the lawsuit. If this is your situation, you'll need the help of a lawyer. See Chapter 17.

Page Two

If There's More Than One Plaintiff

If your case involves more than one plaintiff, you must use a different page two for each. You designate each plaintiff's requests by putting a slash mark (/) after the word "plaintiff" in Item 10, and writing in the name of the particular plaintiff whose requests you're describing above the slash. Each plaintiff must have his or her name at the bottom of "his" or "her" page and sign at the signature line.

Short Title: Put the last names (or the business names) of the first (perhaps only) plaintiff and the first (perhaps only) defendant, separated by a "vs.", such as "Brown vs. Black" or "Brown vs. Golden Bear Typing Service."

Case Number: Leave this blank; you may have to fill it in when you file your Complaint with the court clerk.

4: Check this box if you are suing the State of California, a county, city, school district or other public entity. Otherwise, skip to Item 5.

4a: You should have complied with the claims procedure discussed in Chapter 4. If you have, check this box.

4b: If you haven't complied with the claims procedure you should see a lawyer. There are ways to get around it, but they are complex and reliance on them is dangerous.

5: If you are suing pursuant to either of the listed statutes, you must so indicate. The first, Civil Code § 1812.10, refers to the Unruh Retail Installment Sales Act. It applies if your business sells goods or furnishes services, and you are suing a buyer concerning a retail installment

SHORT TITLE: Garcia vs. Warren	CASE NUMBER:

COMPLAINT—Contract

Page two

4. ☐ Plaintiff is required to comply with a claims statute, and
    a. ☐ plaintiff has complied with applicable claims statutes, or
    b. ☐ plaintiff is excused from complying because (specify):

5. ☐ This action is subject to ☐ Civil Code section 1812.10 ☐ Civil Code section 2984.4.

6. This action is filed in this ☐ county ☒ judicial district because
    a. ☒ a defendant entered into the contract here.
    b. ☒ a defendant lived here when the contract was entered into.
    c. ☒ a defendant lives here now.
    d. ☒ the contract was to be performed here.
    e. ☒ a defendant is a corporation or unincorporated association and its principal place of business is here.
    f. ☐ real property that is the subject of this action is located here.
    g. ☒ other (specify): defendant does business in this district

7. ☐ The following paragraphs of this pleading are alleged on information and belief (specify paragraph numbers):

8. ☐ Other:

9. The following causes of action are attached and the statements above apply to each: (Each complaint must have one or more causes of action attached.)
    ☒ Breach of Contract   ☒ Common Counts
    ☐ Other (specify):

10. PLAINTIFF PRAYS
For judgment for costs of suit; for such relief as is fair, just, and equitable; and for
☒ damages of $ 8,000
☒ interest on the damages ☐ according to proof ☒ at the rate of 6 percent per year
    from (date): April 8, 1992
☐ attorney fees ☐ of $_____ ☐ according to proof.
☐ other (specify):

Jamie Garcia
.... (Type or print name) ....   _____
                                (Signature of plaintiff or attorney)
(If you wish to verify this pleading, affix a verification.)

Page two

contract under which the buyer is required to pay a finance charge.

The second, Civil Code § 2984.4, is the Rees-Levering Motor Vehicle Sales and Finance Act. It applies if your business sells or leases motor vehicles and you are suing a buyer regarding a conditional sales contract.

Businesses that sue under these laws normally use lawyers. Retail installment contracts and motor vehicle sales and leasing are highly regulated areas of the law. If you are suing under either law, check the applicable box and be prepared to show your compliance with these laws when you get to trial. Consider consulting a lawyer for help in preparing your case under the statute, while still representing yourself. (See Chapter 17.)

6: First, check the "judicial district" box. Then check all boxes that describe why you are filing in the particular district.

If a defendant entered into a contract—including buying goods or services—in this district, check a. If a defendant lived in the district when the contract was signed, check b. If a defendant lives in the district now, check c. If services, sales or other terms of the contract were to be performed in the district, check d. If a business defendant (corporation or association) has its principal place of business here, check e.

If your lawsuit has to do with real property that is located in this district, check f. If a business of any type does business in this district (regardless of the location its principal place of business), check g and write "defendant does business in this district" after other (*specify*). If you need help deciding, refer to Chapter 4, Section C.

7: Skip this for now. Later I'll tell you what to do.

8: Skip this.

9: Skip this paragraph for now. You'll fill it out after you prepare your causes of action.

10: Despite the phrase "Plaintiff Prays," this paragraph is not an inquiry into your religious beliefs. It asks you to state what you want out of the lawsuit. (In legalese, that request is called a "prayer.") Check the first box for damages. After the "$," insert the total amount of money you are seeking in this lawsuit. As discussed in Chapter 2, you can recover your out-of-pocket losses that reasonably could have been foreseen by the defendant. If you didn't get what you contracted for, you are entitled to the reasonable costs you incurred in acquiring it elsewhere, as well as any reasonably anticipated incidental expenses.

You're also entitled to interest on your award from the time of the breaking of the contract by the defendant, so check the second box. Check the "according to proof" box unless your agreement specifically provides an interest rate in the event of default. In that case, check the "at the rate of" box and write in the interest rate. After "(date)" put in the earliest date you can reasonably argue the contract was broken.

Skip the rest of the boxes in this item. They only apply if you use a lawyer.

Signature: Type your name above the left dotted line and sign above the solid line on the right.

Although the bottom says you can "affix a verification," there is little to be gained by doing so. A verification is a form in which you swear under penalty of perjury that everything you say in these papers is true. It used to be that if you verified the complaint, the defendant had to verify the answer, but that's no longer the case.

You've finished your first form. Now you must complete at least one "Cause of Action" form to finish the preparation of your complaint.

1. Contract Causes of Action Forms

As noted earlier, a cause of action is a statement of the legal theory you are using to ask the court for relief. Your Complaint must include at least one cause of action, but certainly can include more. The ones you use will depend on the facts of your case. Use as many as apply, even though they ask for a lot of the same information.

 Read only the sections below that pertain to your lawsuit.

a. Breach of Contract Cause of Action Form

A completed Breach of Contract Cause of Action form and instructions follow. A blank copy is in the Appendix. Use this form in every contract action.

Short Title: Type exactly what you typed at the top of page 2 of the Complaint.

Case Number: Leave this blank.

_____ Cause of Action—Breach of Contract: If this is the first cause of action, insert the word "First." If it's the second, use "Second," and so on.

Page: Add one to the number of the last page you completed and put that number here.

Attachment to: Check "Complaint."

BC-1: Put only one plaintiff's name here. If there is more than one plaintiff, decide if you are asking for the same or separate relief from the

court. If you want one sum of money to belong to you jointly, enter both (or all) names here.

If you are seeking separate relief because you were each to receive something different from the contract, then put only one plaintiff's name in this blank, and complete a separate form for each plaintiff. For each subsequent plaintiff, increase by one the number in the blank preceding the "Cause of Action" and the page number.

After "(date)" type the date the contract was made or entered into. This is normally the last date that a party agreed to an oral contract or signed a written one. If you're not sure of the exact date, state something like "on or about April 5, 19__."

Next, check the box that describes the contract. If it was part oral and part written, check both of those boxes. If the contract was neither oral nor written—that is, it was implied because of the past relationship between the parties or by the circumstances—check the "other" box and write the word "implied."

After "(*name parties to agreement*)" list the names of all people (including businesses represented by agents) who were parties to the agreement. This is anyone who agreed—either in writing or orally—to be bound by its terms. If a defendant never orally or in writing agreed to its terms, but acted as if he agreed to them, put his name here also.

Next, you must set forth what the contract said. If the entire agreement is written down, check the box that says a copy of the contract is attached, mark a copy of the contract "Exhibit A," and attach it to this page. Keep the original in a safe place; you may need it later.

The contract causes of action you can choose among are:

Cause of Action Form	When Used
Breach of Contract	All contract cases
Common Counts	All contract cases
Breach of Warranty—Merchantability	Lawsuits against a manufacturer, distributor or seller for a defective product you purchased
Breach of Warranty—Fitness	Lawsuits against a manufacturer, distributor or seller for a defective product you purchased, if at the time of the purchase you told the manufacturer, distributor or seller what particular plans you had for the product

SHORT TITLE:	CASE NUMBER:
Garcia vs. Warren	

_____First_____ **CAUSE OF ACTION—** Breach of Contract   Page _3____
    (number)

ATTACHMENT TO [X] Complaint [ ] Cross-Complaint

(Use a separate cause of action form for each cause of action.)

BC-1. Plaintiff *(name):* Jamie Garcia

        alleges that on or about *(date):* January 8, 1992
        a [X] written [X] oral [ ] other *(specify):*
        agreement was made between *(name parties to agreement):* Jamie Garcia, dba Flour Power and Anne Warren, dba Anne's Pie Shop
        [X] A copy of the agreement is attached as Exhibit A, ~~or~~ (a portion is attached)
        [X] The essential terms of the agreement [ ] are stated in Attachment BC-1 [X] are as follows *(specify):*

Plaintiff delivered to defendant several hundred pounds of flour, baking soda, baking powder, shortening and other wet and dry goods for defendant to use in making pies. The contract called for defendant to pay plaintiff $8,000 for the delivery over a four month period. Payments were to begin 90 days after delivery, or April 8, 1992.

BC-2. On or about *(dates):* April 8, 1992 and at various times thereafter
        defendant breached the agreement by [ ] the acts specified in Attachment BC-2 [X] the following acts
        (specify):

Defendant failed and refused to pay plaintiff anything.

BC-3. Plaintiff has performed all obligations to defendant except those obligations plaintiff was prevented or excused from performing.

BC-4. Plaintiff suffered damages legally (proximately) caused by defendant's breach of the agreement
        [ ] as stated in Attachment BC-4 [X] as follows *(specify):*

$8,000 principal and interest at 6% from April 8, 1992

BC-5. [ ] Plaintiff is entitled to attorney fees by an agreement or a statute
        [ ] of $
        [ ] according to proof.

BC-6. [ ] Other:

Form Approved by the
Judicial Council of California
Effective January 1, 1982
Rule 982.1(21)

CAUSE OF ACTION— Breach of Contract   CCP 425.12   C-97

If your contract is part written and part oral, check the box that says a copy is attached, put a slash (/) after the words "A copy of" and type above the words "a portion of." Also, cross off the word "or" at the end of the line. Mark a copy of the written part as "Exhibit A" and attach it to the page.

If the contract was all or partially oral, check the box "the essential terms of the agreement," and summarize its terms here or on a separate sheet which you designate as BC-1. Be sure to check the appropriate box. Here are some examples of what you might say:

"On or about April 30, 19__, plaintiff loaned defendant $11,000. Defendant agreed to pay back half on June 4, 19__ and half on November 4, 19__ at 4% annual interest compounded monthly."

"Plaintiff paid defendant $17,500 in exchange for defendant's promise to deliver to plaintiff a vintage 1932 Ford Model A Roadster automobile in perfect order, except for the transmission, which had second gear missing."

"Defendant agreed to perform competent legal services to plaintiff regarding plaintiff's proposed purchase of a restaurant business. Plaintiff agreed to pay $125 per hour for defendant's services and defendant agreed to stop performing services and seek a further authorization after she had performed $1,000 worth of services."

"Plaintiff agreed to purchase toys for resale from defendant at prices listed on an agreed upon list. Defendant agreed to deliver the toys promptly upon receiving plaintiff's order and plaintiff agreed to pay defendant within 30 days of being billed. If, in plaintiff's opinion, the toys did not sell well with her customers, she had the right to notify defendant at any time and defen-

dant agreed to pick up the remaining toys and refund any money plaintiff had previously paid defendant."

"For over two years, plaintiff has ordered cosmetics from defendant by telephone. Defendant has delivered them to plaintiff's business without any C.O.D. or delivery charge, with payment due 30 days later. On April 5, 19__, plaintiff placed a similar order with defendant who said nothing about a change in payment or delivery terms."

"In addition to the writing, defendant Brown agreed that if it rained during the week of April 14, 19__, the entire transaction would be cancelled and plaintiff's $15,000 would be returned within ten days."

BC-2: First, write the date the defendant broke the contract. Don't make the common mistake of using the date the contract was entered into. A contract is broken on the date that a party failed to do what she was supposed to do under the agreement. If you loaned Jim money in January and he was to pay you back on April 18 and didn't, April 18 is the day the contract was broken. If he was to pay you back over 6 months—for example, April 18, May 18, June 18, July 18, August 18 and September 18—but never paid a cent, put in the first date it was broken (April 18) and add "and at various times thereafter."

Then set forth how the contract was broken here or on a separate sheet which you mark as BC-2 and attach. Be sure to check the appropriate box. Some examples of what you might say are:

"Defendant failed and refused to pay plaintiff anything."

"The second, third and reverse gears in the automobile that defendant delivered to plaintiff did not work."

"Defendant performed over 50 hours of work for plaintiff in a generally incompetent and unsatisfactory manner and failed to notify plaintiff when total services incurred had reached $5,000."

"Plaintiff notified defendant that the line of toys was not selling well, and that he wished defendant to remove them from his store and refund plaintiff the money he had paid defendant. Defendant failed and refused to remove the toys or refund the money."

"Defendant instructed the delivery company which brought the cosmetics to plaintiff's place of business not to deliver them until plaintiff paid its driver $10,413 for an unmature account receivable plus the cost of the order and delivery charges. Because of an urgent need for the product, plaintiff was forced to pay such an amount to the driver."

BC-3: This statement is there just to remind you that you will eventually have to establish that you performed your part of the bargain.

BC-4: Here you specify exactly how you were damaged either in the space provided or on a separate page which you mark as BC-4 and attach. Be sure to check the appropriate box. Some examples might be:

"$8,000 principal and interest at 4% from June 1, 19__ until paid in full."

"The reasonable cost of the repair of second, third and reverse gears in the amount of $6,250, plus loss of use of the vehicle for three months at a cost of $500 per month."

"$10,789 for sums paid by plaintiff to defendant together with $500 per week for storage of the toys on plaintiff's shelves from March 1, 19__ (when notice was given to defendant) until August 15, 19__ when the toys were picked up by defendant."

"$2,018 for delivery charges and $14,212 for the loss of the use of the remaining funds during the normal maturity period."

BC-5: Skip this. It applies to cases not covered by this book.

BC-6: Skip this. It applies to cases not covered by this book.

b.　Common Counts Cause of Action Form

You'll have to trust me here. This form relates to the way English barristers practiced law 350 years ago. Despite hundreds of subsequent reforms and so-called "simplifications" of the law, this form remains. It probably won't affect the outcome of your lawsuit, but there's a small chance that if a judge decides that your breach of contract cause of action made no sense, the fact that you included this cause of action might save you.

Common counts are stylized sentences that set forth the theory of the case in a historic legal conclusion. The common count does not describe the case in any identifiable way, but it remains because lawyers are familiar with it. If you want more information, see *California Procedure* (3rd Edition), by Bernard Witkin, Volume 4, Section 504, page 538 and the pages that follow. Be sure you have a strong cup of coffee or tea by your side.

A completed sample and instructions follow. A blank copy is in the Appendix. Use this form in every contract action.

SHORT TITLE:	CASE NUMBER:
Garcia vs. Warren	

_____Second_____   **CAUSE OF ACTION—Common Counts**   Page __5__
    (number)

ATTACHMENT TO [X] Complaint [ ] Cross-Complaint

(Use a separate cause of action form for each cause of action.)

CC-1. Plaintiff *(name)*: Jamie Garcia

    alleges that defendant *(name)*: Anne Warren, individually and dba Anne's Pie Shop

    became indebted to [X] plaintiff [ ] other *(name)*:

    a. [ ] within the last four years
        (1) [ ] on an open book account for money due.
        (2) [ ] because an account was stated in writing by and between plaintiff and defendant in which it
            was agreed that defendant was indebted to plaintiff.

    b. [X] within the last [X] two years [ ] four years
        (1) [ ] for money had and received by defendant for the use and benefit of plaintiff.
        (2) [ ] for work, labor, services and materials rendered at the special instance and request of defendant
            and for which defendant promised to pay plaintiff
            [ ] the sum of $
            [ ] the reasonable value.
        (3) [X] for goods, wares, and merchandise sold and delivered to defendant and for which defendant
            promised to pay plaintiff
            [X] the sum of $ 8,000
            [ ] the reasonable value.
        (4) [ ] for money lent by plaintiff to defendant at defendant's request.
        (5) [ ] for money paid, laid out, and expended to or for defendant at defendant's special instance and
            request.
        (6) [ ] other *(specify)*:

CC-2. $ 8,000 _____, which is the reasonable value, is due and unpaid despite plaintiff's demand,
    plus prejudgment interest [ ] according to proof [X] at the rate of ___6___ percent per year
    from *(date)*: April 8, 1992

CC-3. [ ] Plaintiff is entitled to attorney fees by an agreement or a statute
        [ ] of $
        [ ] according to proof.

CC.4. [ ] Other:

Form Approved by the
Judicial Council of California
Effective January 1, 1982
Rule 982.1(22)   **CAUSE OF ACTION—Common Counts**   CCP 425.12

Short Title: Type exactly what you typed at the top of page 2 of the Complaint.

Case Number: Leave this blank.

_____ **Cause of Action—Common Counts:** Insert the word "Second" in the blank, indicating this is the second attachment to your complaint.

Page: Add one to the number of the last page you completed and put that number here.

Attachment to: Check "Complaint."

CC-1: Put only one plaintiff's name here. If there is more than one plaintiff, decide if you are asking for the same or separate relief from the court. If you want one sum of money to belong to you jointly, enter all plaintiffs' names here.

If you are seeking separate relief because you were each to receive something different from the contract, then put only one plaintiff's name in this blank, and complete a separate form for each plaintiff. For each subsequent plaintiff, increase by one the number in the blank preceding the "Cause of Action" and the page number.

For each form you use, type the names of all defendants in the defendant blank. Check the "plaintiff" box after the words "became indebted to."

CC-1a: Check this box if you run a business:

- If the defendant ordered goods or services from you, from time to time, and you recorded a running balance on an account card or in a computer, check box (1).

- If you have had two or more business transactions with the defendant, you sent him a bill for goods or services provided and he didn't object to your bill within a reasonable time, check box (2).

CC-1b: If you didn't check Item CC-1a, check this box. Check either the "two years" box for an oral agreement or the "four years" box for a written agreement. If the agreement is part oral and part written, check "four years." Then check the box that applies:

- If the defendant received some money from you or someone else, which in fairness ought to be paid to you, check (1).

- If you or your employees did work for the defendant and he agreed to pay for the services or materials, check (2). If the defendant agreed to pay a specific sum, check the "sum of $" box and enter the amount. If the defendant agreed to no specific amount, check the "reasonable value" box.

- If you sold and delivered goods to the defendant and he agreed to pay you for them, check (3). If the defendant agreed to pay a specific sum, check the "sum of $" box and enter the amount. If the defendant agreed to no specific amount, check the "reasonable value" box.

- If you loaned the defendant money and he hasn't repaid you, check (4).

Skip boxes (5) and (6).

CC-2: Enter the amount you are claiming in this lawsuit (item 10 on the Complaint), check the second box and specify interest at the rate stated in the contract. If the contract specified no rate, enter 10% per year. Following "(date)" type the date the defendant broke the contract.

CC-3: Skip this. It applies to cases not covered by this book.

CC-4: Skip this. It applies to cases not covered by this book.

 The Breach of Contract and Common Counts causes of action are done; if you have no other contract claims, skip ahead to Section 2.

c. Breach of Warranty Causes of Action

Before suing for breach of an express warranty, you must comply with a notice requirement described in Chapter 4, Section D. If you have done so, and have had no effective response within 30 days, you have the right to sue.[9] Even if you're claiming a breach of an implied warranty, you should comply with the notice requirement.

1. Breach of Express Warranty

If you want to sue for breach of an express warranty, use the breach of contract and common count causes of action forms.

---

[9]The Song-Beverly Consumer Warranty Act, California Civil Code § 1790 et seq., lets you sue a car manufacturer who failed to fix a defect after four tries within either 12,000 miles or a year, or if the car has been out of service for repairs for 30 total days within a year after delivery. Several other laws pertain to warranties, but the Song-Beverly Act is the best for your purposes. It specifies required locations of service facilities and regulates service contracts. It also covers catalog sales, products for disabled persons, appliances and electronics, house trailers, air conditioning systems and leases of consumer goods.

2. Cause of Action—Breach of Warranty (Merchantability)

The California Judicial Council, the body that has created the court forms used in this book, has not prepared one for a cause of action for breach of warranty of merchantability. So we created one, which should work just fine. A completed sample and instructions follow; a blank copy is in the Appendix.

Short Title: Type exactly what you typed at the top of page 2 of the Complaint.

Case Number: Leave this blank.

_____ **Cause of Action—Breach of Warranty (Merchantability):** If this is the first Cause of Action, insert the word "First." If it is the second, use "Second," and so on.

Page: Add one to the number of the last page you completed and put that number here.

Attachment to: Check "Complaint."

BWM-1: Enter the following information here:

- the name of a plaintiff—you must use a different form for each plaintiff requesting separate damages;

- the date you bought the goods;

- the name of the defendants who sold you the goods;

- a description of the goods;

- the retail price you paid; and

- if you have a sales receipt or invoice, check the box, mark a copy of the receipt or invoice "Exhibit BWM-1" and attach a copy to the form.

SHORT TITLE:	CASE NUMBER:
Goodman vs. Hough	

<u>First</u>   **CAUSE OF ACTION**—Breach of Warranty (Merchantability)   Page <u>3</u>
(number)

ATTACHMENT TO   ☒ Complaint   ☐ Cross-Complaint

BWM-1.   Plaintiff *(name):* Jane Goodman

alleges that on or about *(date):* August 12, 1991
defendant(s) *(seller):* Ian Hough, dba Hough's Beds and Brass

sold plaintiff *(quantity and description of goods):* Bedroom furniture consisting of two double beds with brass headboards, one single bed, four dressers two large mirrors, two chairs and an oriental rug

at retail and plaintiff bought such goods from defendant(s) for a price of *(amount):* $ <u>7,200</u>.

☒ A true copy of a memorandum or contract regarding this sale is attached to this Cause of Action as Exhibit BWM-1.

BWM-2.   ☒ On or about *(date):*
defendant(s) *(manufacturer):* Better Bedroom Builders

manufactured such goods for the purpose of their eventual sale to retail buyers.

BWM-3.   ☒ On or about *(date):*
defendant(s) *(distributor):* Does 1-3

acquired such goods from defendant(s) manufacturer and distributed them to defendant(s) seller for eventual retail sale to consumers.

BWM-4.   ☒ In the process, defendant(s) *(name):* Ian Hough, dba Hough's Beds and Brass

appended to such goods a written warranty which is attached to this Cause of Action as Exhibit BWM-4.

BWM-5.   Such retail sale to plaintiff was accompanied separately and individually by the implied warranty that such goods were merchantable by defendant(s) *(name):*
Better Bedromm Builders, Ian Hough, DBA Hough's Beds and Brass and Does 1-3

NP   CAUSE OF ACTION—Breach of Warranty (Merchantability)

SHORT TITLE:	CASE NUMBER:
Goodman vs. Hough	

CAUSE OF ACTION—Breach of Warranty (Merchantability) (continued)   Page 4

BWM-6. Defendant(s) breached their respective warranties implied in the sale in that *(describe)*:
The beds have fallen apart, the dresser drawers stick and the
handles fall off, the mirrors are distorted and one is scratched,
and the chairs and rug smell like mildew

As a result of the breach by defendant(s), plaintiff did not receive merchantable goods as impliedly warranted by
defendant(s).

BWM-7. Plaintiff discovered such breach of warranty on or about *(date)*:
a. ☒ On or about *(date)*: September 3, 1991
plaintiff notified defendant(s) *(name)*: Ian Hough

☒ By letter, a true copy of which is attached to this Cause of Action as Exhibit BWM-7.
☒ Other *(describe)*: by telephone

BWM-8. As a legal result of such breach of the warranty of merchantability by defendant(s), plaintiff has been damaged in the
amount $ 7,450 .

CAUSE OF ACTION—Breach of Warranty (Merchantability)

BWM-2: If the defect may have been caused by the manufacturer, check this paragraph. (Skip the date request.) Type in the name of the manufacturer. If you don't know who that is, use a Doe defendant. If this is your first, type "Doe 1." Otherwise, add one to the number of the last Doe you used.

BWM-3: Use this paragraph if the defect may have been caused by the distributor. (Skip the date request.) If, for some reason, you know the name of the distributor, type it here. More than likely, you'll need to use another Doe defendant.

BWM-4: If you received a written warranty, check the box, mark a copy of the warranty "Exhibit BWM-4" and attach it to the form.

BWM-5: Enter the defendants listed in BWM-2, BWM-3 and BWM-4, including your Doe defendants.

Page Two

Short Title: Tye exactly what you typed on the first page.

Case Number: Leave this blank.

Page: Add one to the previous page.

BWM-6: Describe the defect in the goods. Examples are:

"The transmission will not shift into second, third or reverse gears."

"The printer continually jams, unable to produce any legible pages."

BWM-7: First, fill in the date you discovered the defect. Next, if you notified the defendants of the defect, check box a, type in the date(s) of the notification(s), list the names of the defendants you notified (such as the seller and manufacturer) and check off the box describing your

means of notification. If it was over the phone or in person, check "other" and state the method.

BWM-8: Here you indicate your damages. If the goods have not been satisfactorily repaired, total up your purchase price, the cost you incurred in trying to get the item repaired and the value of your time (at about $10 per hour) in trying to get repairs made and bringing the lawsuit.

If the product is an automobile, there are special requirements the defendants must adhere to in maintaining a service and repair facility.[10] If the defendant acted in a particularly nasty and spiteful way (so that their action could be called "willful" instead of just "negligent") you can ask for twice the amount of your actual damages as a penalty.[11]

3. Cause of Action—Breach of Warranty—Fitness

The California Judicial Council, the body that has created the court forms used in this book, has not prepared one for a cause of action for breach of warranty of fitness. So we created one, which should work just fine. A sample completed form and instructions follow. A blank copy is in the Appendix.

---

[10]See Civil Code § 1793.2.
[11]See Civil Code § 1794.

SHORT TITLE:	CASE NUMBER:
Moran vs. Sagarmatha Dream Co.	

First_____   **CAUSE OF ACTION**—Breach of Warranty (Fitness)   Page _3_

(number)

ATTACHMENT TO   ☒ Complaint   ☐ Cross-Complaint

BWF-1   Plaintiff *(name):* Mae Moran

alleges that on or about *(date):* February 1, 1992
plaintiff required *(quantity and description of goods):*
8000 meters of new static 9mm rope

for the particular purpose of *(describe):*
climbing the south face of Chooyo and the south face of Gyanchung
Kang, two mountains in Nepal

To select and furnish suitable goods for such purpose, plaintiff relied on the skill and judgment of defendant(s) *(name):*

Sagarmatha Dream Co., Obadiah Walters and Does 1-4

BWF-2.   On or about *(date)* February 1, 1992
defendant(s) sold to plaintiff *(quantity and description of goods sold):*

8000 meters of static 9 mm rope

and plaintiff bought such goods from defendant(s), in such reliance, for the amount of *(price paid):* $_8,000_ .

☒ A true copy of the memorandum or contract of the sale is attached to this Cause of Action as Exhibit BWF-2.

BWF-3.   At the time of the retail sale of such goods, defendant(s) had reason to know the particular purpose for which the goods
were required because plaintiff expressly communicated such purposes to defendant(s). Defendant(s) further knew
plaintiff was relying on the skill and judgment of defendant(s) to select and furnish suitable goods; thus there was an
implied warranty that the goods were fit for such purpose.

NP   CAUSE OF ACTION—Breach of Warranty (Fitness)

SHORT TITLE: Moran vs. Sagarmatha Dream Co.	CASE NUMBER:

CAUSE OF ACTION—Breach of Warranty (Fitness) (continued)   Page 4

BWF-4.   Defendant(s) breached such warranty in that plaintiff did not receive suitable goods and such goods were not fit for the particular purpose for which they were required in that *(describe failure)*:

The ropes were needed to climb two steep, technical mountain sides. The ropes were used, had cuts and weak spots. Some ropes were melted together. Many of the ropes broke when we tried to use them.

BWF-5.   Plaintiff discovered such breach of warranty on or about *(date)*: March 15, 1992

   a. [X] On or about *(date)*: March 20, 1992

   plaintiff notified defendant(s) *(name)*: Sagarmatha Dream Co.

     [ ] By letter, a true copy of which is attached to this Cause of Action as Exhibit BWF-5.

     [X] Other *(describe)*: by telephone

BWF-6.   As a result of such breach of warranty of fitness by defendant(s), plaintiff has been damaged in the amount of $ 8,500 .

Short Title: Type exactly what you typed at the top of page 2 of the Complaint.

Case Number: Leave this blank.

_____ Cause of Action—Breach of Warranty (Fitness): If this is the first Cause of Action, insert the word "First." If it is the second, use "Second," and so on.

Page: Add one to the number of the last page you completed and put that number here.

Attachment to: Check "Complaint."

BWF-1: Enter the following information here:

- the name of a plaintiff—you must use a different form for each plaintiff requesting separate damages;
- the date you discussed your special needs;
- a description of the goods;
- a description of your special needs; and
- the names of the defendants to whom you described your needs. Be sure to include Doe defendants if you don't yet have the identities.

BWF-2: Enter the following information here:

- the date you bought the goods;
- a description of the goods;
- the price you paid; and
- if you have a sales receipt or invoice, check the box, mark a copy of the receipt or invoice "Exhibit BWF-2" and attach it to the form.

BWF-3: You don't have to type anything here.

Page Two

Short Title: Tye exactly what you typed on the first page.

Case Number: Leave this blank.

Page: Add one to the previous page.

BWF-4: Describe the defect in the goods. Here's an example:

"The tires on the dune buggy, which I needed for off-road and mountainous riding, punctured when I rode over stone and rocks."

BWF-5: First, fill in the date you discovered the defect. Next, if you notified the defendants of the defect, check box a, type in the dates of the notifications, list the names of the defendants you notified (such as the seller) and check off the box describing your means of notification. If it was over the phone or in person, check "other" and state the method.

BWF-6: Here you indicate your damages. If the goods have not been satisfactorily repaired, total up your purchase price, the cost you incurred in trying to get the item repaired and the value of your time (at about $10 per hour) in trying to get repairs made and bringing the lawsuit.

If the product is an automobile or the defendant acted in a particularly nasty and spiteful way, see the last paragraph of Subsection 2, immediately above.

2. Cleaning Up the Contract Complaint

Now is the time to fill in the paragraphs you've skipped.

Defendant: Does 1 to ____: Count up your Doe defendants and enter the total.

Contract Complaint, Item 1 (total number of pages): Count up your total number of pages—don't forget the attachment sheets—and insert the total.

Contract Complaint, Item 7 (the matters you are alleging on information and belief): Here you have to play lawyer for a moment. Read over the factual statements in the complaint and causes of action. If any statement is true, but you can't testify to its contents from your own knowledge (that is, you relied on something someone else told you), the statement is said to have been made "on information and belief." A common information and belief statement is one identifying a defendant as the employee or agent of the another.

If any statements apply, check this box and type the paragraph number, such as CC-1. If there is more than one cause of action of the same kind (such as Common Counts), be sure to note the paragraph number and the cause of action. Do your best at this, but do not spend a lot of time worrying about it.

Contract Complaint, Item 9 (attached causes of action): Check all that are applicable. If you completed any breach of warranty causes of action, check "other" and specify which ones.

Review all your page numbers and Cause of Action headings. Be sure they are in order.

 You've completed the contract complaint and can skip ahead to Section E.

D. Complaints for Other Types of Lawsuits

To file a lawsuit on grounds other than torts and contracts, you are going to have to do some legal research. Here are the steps I recommend you take:

1. Find a Law Library

Each California county has a law library that is open to the public without charge. These libraries are usually housed at county court houses. In most libraries, you'll find librarians willing and even pleased to give you a hand—as long as you don't ask them to answer legal questions or interpret what you find in the books.

2. Begin Your Legal Research

 If you are not experienced in doing legal research, see *Legal Research: How to Find and Understand the Law*, by Stephen Elias (Nolo Press). This hands-on guide addresses research methods in detail and answers most questions likely to arise in the course of doing research. The book can be purchased through Nolo Press or borrowed from many libraries. Although you probably will want to skip this book and go directly to the books I identify below, I guarantee you it will save you time in the long run to read at least the first five chapters of *Legal Research*.

If you want a guided tour through the basics of legal research, you'll be interested in *Legal Research Made Easy: A Roadmap Through the Law*

Library Maze, a 2-1/2 hour video by Nolo Press and Legal Star Communications.

3. Locate Relevant Books

 You law library will contain a set of books entitled *Cal Practice*, published by Bancroft Whitney. The covers of these books are in three colors and are not to be confused with *California Practice*, an all-black set of books put out by West Publishing. If you find your subject discussed in *Cal Practice*, you'll have all the information you need to prepare an appropriate complaint.

Cal Practice has a General Index volume which you can use to locate information on the subject of your lawsuit.[12] This set is written for lawyers, however, and assumes that no matter how little they about law, they at least know how law is organized. For example, if you're considering suing a newspaper for printing a false story about you, this law is under the index topic of "Libel and Slander."

 Most legal subjects are covered in *Cal Practice* and you should be able to find what you need in there. If you don't, try *California Forms of Pleading and Practice*, published by Matthew Bender. (It has a light blue cover.) The first dozen pages of the General Index contain an overview of the general subjects covered and should be helpful in getting started.

Once you find your subject in *California Forms of Pleading and Practice*, you'll find an in-troduction giving a summary of the law. There's also a research guide referring you to more detailed information in other books. Finally, many subjects include a checklist or a section called "Essential Allegations of Complaint." These lists are extremely helpful in preparing an outline of your case.

4. Choose the Right Form

When you find the right subject area, look at the forms included and choose the one closest to your situation. You may wind up using clauses from more than one form and creating your own—these books contain forms to use in common, but not all, situations. You'll notice that these forms are not like the ones in this book that just need to be checked off. Instead, they contain paragraphs of text you'll have to copy and retype. Don't let that scare you; it may take some time, but it isn't terribly complicated.

These books are used a lot in the library by lawyers who can't afford to buy them themselves; thus, most libraries won't let you check them out. Bring lots of change to the library and be ready to photocopy forms and directions.

5. Prepare the Complaint

After you've gathered your sample forms and directions, you'll have to create your own complaint and type it up to be presented to the court clerk for filing. You need to pay careful attention to the requirements, but if you have some typing experience, you should be able to handle it on your own.

[12]Chapter 4 of Nolo's *Legal Research* book will help you determine where to start looking in the *Cal Practice* index for your subject.

Using a Professional Typing Service

If you want some help in preparing your Complaint, look in the phone book Yellow Pages under "Paralegals, Legal Clinics, Typing Services or Secretarial Services." Many people, especially in large cities, prepare forms for pro per parties. Call one or two and ask what services they offer and at what price.

The people listed under "Paralegals" probably offer their services principally to lawyers, but may be willing to prepare forms for you for a price. The people listed under "Secretarial Services" may include former legal secretaries who lost interest in the nine-to-five routine and began their own businesses.

If you have trouble finding someone, call the National Association of Independent Paralegals, at 800-542-0034.

Gather your pleading paper (that silly paper with the numbers down the left side).

At line 1, in the left corner, type your name, address and phone number single-spaced. Skip a line and then type "In Pro Per," which means you are representing yourself without a lawyer. For each additional plaintiff, repeat the information.

Then skip down to line 8. (If you have more than one plaintiff, you might be below line 8—that's fine.) On the center of the page on two lines, type the name of the court and the county, in all capital letters. You don't need to include the branch of the court or its address.

Move down to line 11 (or just below the court name, if you're already beyond line 11). Here you name the plaintiffs and the defendants. Everything must be kept on the left half of the page. In all capital letters, type the names of the plaintiffs. Then add the word "Plaintiff" or "Plaintiffs" just below and slightly indented. Skip a couple of lines and type "vs." (the abbre-

viation for the word "versus") at the left. Skip another couple of lines and, in all capital letters, type the names of the defendants, plus any "Does" you are suing. Then add the word "Defendant" or "Defendants," as you did with the plaintiffs. Finally, type a line out to the middle of the page.

To the right of the plaintiff's name, type "Case No." Leave it blank for now because you won't get that number until you file your Complaint with the court. On subsequent papers, however, be sure to include it.

In all capitals, immediately under "Case No.," describe the paper you're filing—"Complaint." On subsequent papers, you might type "Motion." On a Complaint, you must also state the nature of the case. Great precision is not necessary. If you are suing on a civil rights violation, type "Complaint—Violation of Civil Rights." If you were improperly fired from your job, type something like "Complaint—Wrongful Termination of Employment."

Now follow the form(s) you've copied from the law library books. Number your paragraphs and follow the instructions in the form book itself. When you get to the end, type your "prayer" (where you ask for money) and sign and date the form.

E. Preparing the Summons

Every Complaint must have a Summons. The Summons is a document that comes from the court (though you have to fill it in for the court) that notifies the defendants that they are being sued and have 30 days to respond in order to contest the case. A completed sample and instructions. A blank copy is in the Appendix.

SUMMONS
(CITACION JUDICIAL)

NOTICE TO DEFENDANT: *(Aviso a Acusado)*

Sagarmatha Dream Co.

FOR COURT USE ONLY
(SOLO PARA USO DE LA CORTE)

YOU ARE BEING SUED BY PLAINTIFF:
(A Ud. le está demandando)

Mae Moran and Harold Aprin

You have *30 CALENDAR DAYS* after this summons is served on you to file a typewritten response at this court.	*Después de que le entreguen esta citación judicial usted tiene un plazo de 30 DIAS CALENDARIOS para presentar una respuesta escrita a máquina en esta corte.*
A letter or phone call will not protect you; your typewritten response must be in proper legal form if you want the court to hear your case.	*Una carta o una llamada telefónica no le ofrecerá protección; su respuesta escrita a máquina tiene que cumplir con las formalidades legales apropiadas si usted quiere que la corte escuche su caso.*
If you do not file your response on time, you may lose the case, and your wages, money and property may be taken without further warning from the court.	*Si usted no presenta su respuesta a tiempo, puede perder el caso, y le pueden quitar su salario, su dinero y otras cosas de su propiedad sin aviso adicional por parte de la corte.*
There are other legal requirements. You may want to call an attorney right away. If you do not know an attorney, you may call an attorney referral service or a legal aid office (listed in the phone book).	*Existen otros requisitos legales. Puede que usted quiera llamar a un abogado inmediatamente. Si no conoce a un abogado, puede llamar a un servicio de referencia de abogados o a una oficina de ayuda legal (vea el directorio telefónico).*

CASE NUMBER: *(Numero del Caso)*

The name and address of the court is: *(El nombre y dirección de la corte es)*

San Francisco Municipal Court
400 Van Ness Avenue
San Francisco, CA 94102

The name, address, and telephone number of plaintiff's attorney, or plaintiff without an attorney, is:
(El nombre, la dirección y el número de teléfono del abogado del demandante, o del demandante que no tiene abogado, es)
Mae Moran
Harold Aprin
3588 Euclid Ave.
San Francisco, CA 94118

DATE:
(Fecha)

Clerk, by _____, Deputy
(Actuario)   *(Delegado)*

[SEAL]

NOTICE TO THE PERSON SERVED: You are served
1. ☐ as an individual defendant.
2. ☐ as the person sued under the fictitious name of *(specify)*:

3. ☒ on behalf of *(specify)*: Sagarmatha Dream Co.

    under: ☒ CCP 416.10 (corporation)   ☐ CCP 416.60 (minor)
            ☐ CCP 416.20 (defunct corporation)   ☐ CCP 416.70 (conservatee)
            ☐ CCP 416.40 (association or partnership)   ☐ CCP 416.90 (individual)
            ☐ other:
4. ☐ by personal delivery on *(date)*:

Form Adopted by Rule 982
Judicial Council of California
982(a)(9) [Rev. January 1, 1984]

(See reverse for Proof of Service)
SUMMONS

CCP 412.20

Under "Notice to Defendant:" type the names of all of the defendants exactly as you typed them on the complaint. Under "You are Being Sued by Plaintiff:" type the names of all of the plaintiffs exactly as you typed them on the Complaint.

Below the bold-faced box, insert the name and address of the court. Use the full name and address, including any branch, as described in Section A2, above. Under the address, put your name, address and phone number just as they appeared on the top of the Complaint form. Leave the Notice to the Person Served and all of page two blank.

F. Preparing a Case Questionnaire

To initiate a lawsuit in a California Municipal Court, you need only prepare and file a Summons and a Complaint. But I recommend that you prepare another form—the Case Questionnaire.

The Case Questionnaire is a four-page form designed to get all the facts out as quickly as possible so as to encourage settlement before trial. It's been around since 1983 but few attorneys are aware of its existence. You are not required to use it, but you should. If you don't use it now, you forever lose the right to do so.

You don't file the Case Questionnaire with the court, but you deliver ("serve" in legalese) it to the defendant with the Summons and Complaint after you file your case. Thus, you should prepare it now. A completed sample and instructions follow. A blank copy is in the Appendix.

Before you start typing, make at least two copies of the blank Case Questionnaire.

At the top of the page, type the following:

- the name and branch of the court;

- the county in which the court is located;

- the names of all the plaintiffs (this must go on all four pages);

- the names of all the defendants (this must go on all four pages);

- the case number—skip this now; you'll get it when you file your Summons and Complaint (this must go on all four pages);

- the name of the requesting party—that's you; and

- the name of the responding party—that's the defendant. If there's more than one, do a separate Case Questionnaire for each.

Once you fill in the top, read the instructions. They explain most of what you need to know to complete the form. In general, you should give the most positive and optimistic view of your case that you can truthfully state. Don't worry about legal language or sounding like a lawyer. Just factually tell your story without exaggeration or insults. Your job is to convince the other side that when you tell the court what happened, you will win.

— DO NOT FILE WITH THE COURT —

— THIS IS NOT AN ANSWER OR RESPONSE TO THE COMPLAINT —

Name of Court: Los Angeles County Municipal Court, Antelope Judicial District

State of California, County of Los Angeles

PLAINTIFF: Beth Wargarten	CASE NUMBER:
DEFENDANT: Salty Products, Inc., Martin DeLong, Does	

CASE QUESTIONNAIRE 1-4

Requesting Party *(name)*: Beth Wargarten

Responding Party *(name)*: Salty Products, Inc.

—INSTRUCTIONS—

1. The purpose of the case questionnaire is to help the parties settle their differences without spending a lot of money. This is accomplished by exchanging information about the case early in the lawsuit. The exchange of case questionnaires may be started only by a plaintiff (or cross-complainant).

2. Instructions for plaintiffs (and cross-complainants)

   a. Under Code of Civil Procedure section 93, a plaintiff (or cross-complainant) *may* serve a *completed* case questionnaire and a blank case questionnaire *with the complaint (or cross-complaint).*

   b. This is the only way you can require defendants (or cross-defendants) to serve you with a completed case questionnaire.

3. Instructions for defendants (and cross-defendants)

   a. If you have been served with a completed case questionnaire by a plaintiff (or cross-complainant), then you *must* fill in the blank case questionnaire. Your completed case questionnaire must be served on the requesting plaintiff (or cross-complainant) *with your answer to the complaint* (or cross-complaint).

   b. THIS IS NOT AN ANSWER OR RESPONSE TO THE COMPLAINT.

4. Instructions for all parties

   a. ALL QUESTIONS REFER TO THE INCIDENT OR AGREEMENT IN THIS LAWSUIT ONLY.

   b. Answer each question. If a question is not applicable, answer "NA."

   c. Your answers are not limited to your personal knowledge, but you are required to furnish all information available to you or anyone acting on your behalf, whether you are a plaintiff, defendant, cross-complainant, or cross-defendant.

   d. Type or *legibly* print your answer below each question. If you cannot completely answer a question in the space provided on the case questionnaire, check the "attachment" box and put the number of the question and the complete answer on an attached sheet of paper. You should *not* put part of an answer on the case questionnaire and part on the attachment. You may put more than one answer on each attached page.

   e. When you have completed the case questionnaire, sign the verification and serve the original.

   f. You may compel compliance with these requirements under Code of Civil Procedure section 2034.

   g. DO NOT FILE THIS CASE QUESTIONNAIRE WITH THE COURT.

(Page one of four)

Form Adopted by Rule 982
Judicial Council of California
982(a)(21) (New July 1, 1983)   **CASE QUESTIONNAIRE**   C-66   CCP 93

— DO NOT FILE WITH THE COURT —

PLAINTIFF: Beth Wargarten

DEFENDANT: Salty Products, Inc., Martin DeLong, Does

CASE NUMBER:

1-4

—QUESTIONS—

1. FOR ALL CASES

a. State your name and street address.

Beth Wargarten
5666 South Starr Boulevard
Los Angeles, CA 90044

b. State your current business name and street address, type of business entity, and your title.

Beth Wargarten   Secretary to the President
Micro Plastics, Inc.
Anaheim, CA 92001

c. Describe in detail your claims or defenses and the facts on which they are based, giving relevant dates.

☐ See attachment for answer number 1c.

On July 17, 1992, at approximately 7:30 am, plaintiff was driving her 1987 Ford Probe westbound on the Santa Monica Freeway, just past the Carson Blvd exit, at approximately 45 mph. A truck owned by defendant Salty Products, Inc. and driven by defendant Martin DeLong changed lanes, striking plaintiff's car on the entire right side. Plaintiff's car spun out of control and came to rest against the center divide.

d. State the name, street address, and telephone number of each person who has knowledge of facts relating to this lawsuit and specify his or her area of knowledge.

☐ See attachment for answer number 1d.

Andy Mumm, 44 Walnut Place, Los Angeles, 213-555-7204
Alice Adams, 1717 Mitten Road, Van Nuys, 818-555-9366
Dr. Roberta Rodriguez, 117 Medical Plaza, Los Angeles, 213-555-8800
Sgt. Anita O'Hara, Calif. Highway Patrol, 1404 Main Drive, Santa
  Monica, 213-555-9999
Elmer Kwong, EK & Children Garage, 3999 Fillmore Ave., Los Angeles,
  213-555-9011

e. Describe each document or photograph that relates to the issues or facts. You are encouraged to attach a copy of each. For each that you have described but not attached, state the name, street address, and telephone number of each person who has it.

☐ See attachment for answer number 1e.

Medical Report and bill of Dr. Roberta Rodriguez
Police Report of Sgt. Anita O'Hara
Estimate, work order and bill from EK's Garage
Photos of automobile
Photos of accident scene
Photos of plaintiff's injuries

9821(a)(21) (New Jan 1, 1983)   **CASE QUESTIONNAIRE**   Page two of four

C-66

PLAINTIFF: Beth Wargarten	CASE NUMBER:
DEFENDANT: Salty Products, Inc., Martin DeLong, Does 1-4	

1. f. Describe each item of physical evidence that relates to the issues and facts, give its location, and state the name, street address, and telephone number of each person who has it.

☐ See attachment for answer number 1f.

Plaintiff's car, 5666 South Starr Blvd, Los Angeles, CA 90044; Beth Wargarten, same address, 213-555-8965

g. State the name and street address of each insurance company and the number of each policy that may cover you in whole or part for the damages claimed.

☐ See attachment for answer number 1g.

Fisherman's Insurance Co., 6200 Highrise Building, Hartford, CT 06111

Policy # 983CV117DF

2. FOR PERSONAL INJURY OR PROPERTY DAMAGE CASES

a. Describe each injury or illness that you received and your present complaints about each.

☐ See attachment for answer number 2a.

Whiplash, bruised knees, chipped kneecap, separated right shoulder, sprained back

b. State the name, street address, and telephone number of each physician, dentist, or other health care provider who treated or examined you, the type of treatment, the dates of treatment, and the charges by each to date.

☐ See attachment for answer number 2b.

Dr. Roberta Rodriguez, 117 Medical Plaza, Los Angeles, CA; 213-555-8800

Dr. Rodriguez treated me for the injuries listed in item 2.a. I saw Dr. Rodrigue on the following dates: 7/17/92, 7/18/92, 7/24/92, 7/31/92, 8/15/92, 9/1/92, 10/1/92, 11/4/92.

The total charges were $4,877

c. Itemize the medical expenses you anticipate in the future.

☐ See attachment for answer number 2c

N/A

d. Itemize your loss of income to date, give the name and street address of each source, and show how the loss is computed.

☐ See attachment for answer number 2d.

N/A

PLAINTIFF:

Beth Wargarten

DEFENDANT: Salty Products, Inc., Martin DeLong, Does 1-4

CASE NUMBER:

2. e. Itemize the loss of income you anticipate in the future, give the name and street address of each source, and show how the loss is computed.

☐ See attachment for answer number 2e.

N/A

f. Itemize your property damage and state the amount or attach an itemized bill or estimate.

☐ See attachment for answer number 2f.

New transmission, new right front tire and wheel shaft, new right front door, painting the right side, replace right rear view mirror

Total bill: $3,891

g. Describe each other item of damage or cost that you claim and state the amount.

☐ See attachment for answer number 2g.

Pain and sufferring: $10,000

3. FOR CASES BASED ON AGREEMENTS

a. In addition to your answer to 1e, state all the terms and give the date of any part of the agreement that is not in writing.

☐ See attachment for answer number 3a.

b. Describe each item of damage or cost you claim, state the amount, and show how it is computed.

☐ See attachment for answer number 3b.

VERIFICATION

I declare under penalty of perjury under the laws of the State of California that the foregoing answers are true and correct.

Date:

. . . . Beth Wargarten . . . .   ▶ _____
                  (TYPED OR PRINTED NAME)   *(SIGNATURE)*

Start by preparing a draft of the form. Before you type your final version, run your answers by your Sounding Board. Ask her if the statements are easily understood and sound like the unvarnished truth. If she thinks something sounds exaggerated or unnecessarily vindictive, make some changes.

Most of the questions are self-explanatory. They can be answered on the form itself, or if you need additional room, on an attachment. I give instructions only for those that are not self-explanatory.

1c: Here are two examples of descriptions of claims:

"At approximately 8:15 p.m. August 15, 19__, plaintiff was driving her 1987 Pontiac Firebird car east on Market Street in Lynwood just west of Ninth Street, at approximately 30 mph. The traffic light in her direction was green. As she entered the intersection of Ninth Street, defendant, who was driving north on Ninth Street at approximately 40 to 50 mph, also entered the intersection. The traffic signal in his direction was red. Defendant depressed his brakes as he entered the intersection, creating four skid marks of approximately 35 feet. Then the front right of his car struck plaintiff's car to the right of the rear passenger side door. The force of the collision caused both cars to spin through the intersection and come to rest against buildings in the area."

"On December 13, 19__, defendant promised plaintiff that for the sum of $10,000, he would place a permanent plaque on the floor of her restaurant commemorating an important event in plaintiff's life. On January 6, 19__, plaintiff paid defendant the $10,000 and accepted defendant's offer. Defendant has since failed and refused to place the plaque."

1d: List every witness you may use. Include eyewitnesses, doctors, police officers, tow truck drivers, repairpeople, payroll person from your job and the like.

1e: Be sure to include contracts, letters, photographs and the like.

1f: Keep in mind that physical evidence is any object—such as a damaged car—or mark—such as a skid mark or mark on the side of a building—or drawing that is relevant.

2. For Personal Injury or Property Damage Cases: These questions should be answered only be used if you are bringing a tort case.

2c-g: Use the calculations you came up with in Chapter 2, Section F.

3. For Cases Based on Agreement: These questions should be answered only if you are bringing a contract case.

Verification and signature: Type your name above the left dotted line and sign above the solid line on the right. Because this form is "verified," you are swearing that what you have said is true. If you've exaggerated—or lied—you could be embarrassed—and possibly discredited—if you have to explain yourself to a judge or jury.

G. Requesting a Waiver of the Filing Fee

When you file your Complaint, you will be required to pay a filing fee, somewhere between $27.50 and $74, depending on the county. There's a second fee for each additional plaintiff.

If you have a very low income, you do not have to pay court fees and costs if you obtain court approval. People currently receiving AFDC, Food Stamps, County Relief, General Relief, General Assistance, SSI or SSP should have no problem qualifying for a fee waiver. You'll need to complete these two easy forms, available from the clerk's office, where you give information about your financial situation and request that fees be waived:

- Application for Waiver of Court Fees and Costs

- Order on Application for Waiver of Court Fees and Costs

By law, you may file your complaint and fee waiver request at the same time, without paying a filing fee. Some clerks may tell you that you'll have to wait a few days for a judge to grant the fee waiver before you can file your papers. If

this happens, be polite but firm. Tell the clerk that you are entitled to file your papers now under Rule 985 of the California Rules of Court. If the clerk still won't file your papers, ask to speak with a supervisor, and give the supervisor the same information.

If you file your documents in person, you may have to take the fee waiver documents to be reviewed and filed by a clerk in a different department or courtroom from the court's filing desk. To find out the procedure, ask the filing clerk where to file fee waiver documents.

Once your fee waiver documents have been filed, the court must decide rule on the request within five days. If the court doesn't deny your request within that time, your fees are automatically waived.

If your request is granted, the court sends you a document so stating. If your fee waiver request is denied, however, the Order on Application for Waiver of Court Fees and Costs will be marked and sent to you and you'll have to pay court fees within 10 days. If you don't get any notification from the court within a week after you file your fee waiver documents, call the clerk to find out whether your fees were waived.

chapter 6

FILING THE PAPERS

You've prepared the Summons and Complaint. Your next step is to file these forms with the court clerk.

A. Call the Clerk's Office

Before you physically visit the clerk's office, call and find out the following:

- If the court has any special local rules. These rules require that you file any additional papers with the Summons and Complaint. (Remember, you don't file the Case Questionnaire.) Most courts don't, but if yours does, you can get a copy of any special forms at the clerk's office. You will probably be able to fill them out by hand when you file your papers.

- How many extra copies of your documents you should bring. As explained in Section B, below, you normally need a copy for each defendant and one for yourself. But some courts, especially if you file in a branch court, require an extra.

- How much the filing fee is. Municipal Court filing fees range from about $27.50 to $74, depending on the county. You can pay in cash or by check in many counties, but some court won't accept checks from pro per plaintiffs. Be sure to ask. If you can't afford the filing fee, you may qualify for a waiver. See Chapter 5, Section G.

- What hours the office is open to the public. Some clerk's offices close for lunch (usually from noon to 1:00 p.m.) and some others close to the public at 4:00 or 4:30 p.m.

B. Photocopy Your Documents

You will need to make photocopies of the documents you've prepared:

- Complaint
- Summons
- Case Questionnaire
- possibly an Application for Waiver of Court Fees and Costs, and the Order on Application for Waiver of Court Fees and Costs.

If a form has printing on both sides. you can make single-sided copies and staple the pages together or, if you have access to the proper equipment, you can make two-sided copies. Here's how many copies to make:

- Complaint: The original gets filed with the court; make one copy for each defendant and two for yourself. Obviously, if the court needs an extra, make one.

- Summons: Make one copy of the Summons for each defendant and two for yourself. Unlike the Complaint, you don't file a Summons when you file the Complaint. Instead, the clerk stamps the Summons, which gets served on the defendants. (See Chapter 7.)

- Case Questionnaire: Make one copy of your completed Questionnaire and one copy of a blank Questionnaire for each defendant. You keep the original. (Make yourself a copy in case you misplace the original.) Don't bring these documents to the clerk's office when you file the Summons and Complaint.

- Application for Waiver of Court Fees and Costs, and Order on Application for Waiver of Court Fees and Costs. If you have a low income and are applying for a fee waiver (see

Chapter 5, Section G): You file the originals with the court. Make two copies of each for yourself.

C. Find the Clerk's Office

The Municipal Court clerk's office is located in the same building as the court. That address is on your Complaint. The civil division—that's the one you want (the other division is the criminal division)—will be combined with the criminal division in small counties. They'll be separated in larger areas.

When you enter the building, look for a directory or information desk. Then locate or ask where the Municipal Court civil division clerk's office is. If you can't find a directory or information desk, look for a court marshal (sheriff) or someone who looks like a lawyer. They'll know where the office is.

Filing the Papers by Mail

It's possible to file the papers by mail. If you do, enclose a note asking the clerk to file the original Complaint, issue the Summons and file-stamp (put the court's stamp, with the date the papers were filed, on the papers) and return to you the extra copies. The clerk will probably file-stamp only one copy. If that happens, make copies of the file-stamped papers and use those when serving the defendants.

Be sure to include a check for the filing fee (or your Application and Order for a Waiver) and a large self-addressed, stamped envelope with enough postage to mail the forms back to you. If your envelope isn't large enough to hold the papers or doesn't have enough postage, the clerk may not mail the papers back to you.

D. File the Papers

When you get to the clerk's office, look for a sign showing where new cases are filed. Be prepared to wait in line a while.

When it's your turn, walk to the counter and immediately tell the clerk that you are a pro per plaintiff filing a new action and that you've never done this before. Often the clerk will become quite helpful. Believe me, this works much better than pretending you are an old experienced litigator who knows the ropes.

Hand the clerk all your documents. Have the original Complaint on top, followed by the copies of the Complaint. Next should be the original Summons and the copies. If you're applying for a fee waiver, those documents should be on the bottom. The clerk will first review the Complaint to see if it meets the requirements for filing.

If the Clerk Rejects Your Forms

It is unlikely this will happen, but if the clerk rejects your forms, be sure you understand exactly what you did wrong. Write down what the clerk tells you and repeat it back. Don't argue with the clerk—establishing a bad relationship at the outset could cause you problems throughout your lawsuit.

If the clerk is hostile and tells you to hire a lawyer, politely ask to talk to the supervisor. You're entitled to represent yourself and to be treated courteously, and most supervising clerks will want to solve any problems that come up.

If you're not applying for a fee waiver, the clerk will ask you to pay the filing fee. You'll get a receipt, which you should keep. If you have requested a fee waiver and you receive SSI or public assistance, the clerk will probably approve the waiver right there. If you don't receive public assistance, a judge must approve your application. The clerk will tell you how to find out the judge's decision.

In the upper right-hand corner of your documents, the clerk will stamp some information on the originals and copies of the Summons and Complaint. Included in this information will be a case number. Then the clerk will sign the original Summons and place the official seal of the court in the lower left corner. Ask the clerk if you can use her stamp to fill in the case number on the copies of the documents where you left it blank. If you forget to do this, you can fill in the numbers by hand later.

In many courts, you'll be handed the stamping device and allowed to place the official court stamp on as many copies as you wish. If you'd prefer not to stand at the desk stamping your papers, you can photocopy the forms with the official court stamp on them. A photocopy of a court stamp is as good as the original itself.

The clerk will hand you back all the copies of the Complaint (unless local rules require her to keep a copy), and the original and copies of the Summons. You may feel strange walking off with the original Summons, but because it is the official notice to the defendant that he has been sued, you keep it. (When he's served, he gets a copy of the Summons.) If a defendant doesn't respond within the time required, you can go back to the court and take a "default." That's when you file the original Summons. Sorry about jumping ahead—this material is covered in Chapters 7 and 9.

If you have gotten this far without a hitch, congratulations! Many new lawyers make several trips to the clerk's office before their first papers pass muster. If you need to fix something, take care of it and file again. You might be able to do this if there's a law library in the same building—some have typewriters and copy machines available for the public. (Be sure to bring some change with you when you file your papers.) Otherwise, you'll have to go back home.

E. Get a Copy of the Court's Fast Track Rules

Before you leave the clerk's office, if you don't already have a copy of the court's "fast track" rules, ask for a copy. The fast track rules, which are different in each court, are designed to speed up litigation. Read them carefully. They provide deadlines for you to move the case through certain stages. For example, some rules provide a specified number of days:

- by which you must file proof of having served the defendant (see Chapter 7)

- for the defendant to file an Answer (see Chapter 8)

- by which you or the defendant must request court to set your case for trial (see Chapter 12)

If you don't comply with the fast track deadlines, you'll probably get a computerized letter from the court ordering you to appear in court and explain why you haven't followed the rules. If you get such a letter, show up, listen to what the judge tells you and follow her instructions. If you don't, your case may be thrown out by the court. The judge might fine you for not following the fast track rules, but more likely, she'll understand that you're a non-lawyer representing yourself in an unfamiliar jungle and will let you off with a warning.

If You're in Los Angeles. The Los Angeles rules require you to attend a status conference with a judge about four months after filing the Complaint. At the conference, the judge sets the various deadlines.

SERVING THE PAPERS

Once you file your papers with the court, you next task is to let the defendant know you have sued him. You do this by serving him with papers. "Serving" means delivering papers to him in one of the methods permitted by law.

The defendant must be served with four papers:

- a copy of the Summons (be sure to keep the original)

- a copy of the Complaint (make sure it has either an original or a photocopy of the court's stamp on it)

- a copy of your completed Case Questionnaire

- a blank Case Questionnaire

A. Completing the Summons

 To prepare to serve the defendant, paper clip together one complete set of the documents (make one set for each defendant), putting the copy of the Summons on top. Before the defendant can actually be served, you must complete the bottom portion of the Summons form. If you have more than one defendant, you must complete a Summons form for each.

Notice to the Person Served:

You are served

1. ___ as an individual defendant.

2. ___ as the person sued under the fictitious name of *(specify):*

3. ___ on behalf of *(specify):*
   under:

   ___ CCP 416.10 (corporation)

   ___ CCP 416.20 (defunct corporation)

   ___ CCP 416.40 (ass'n or partnership)

   ___ CCP 416.60 (minor)

   ___ CCP 416.70 (conservatee)

   ___ CCP.416.90 (individual)

   ___ other:

4. ___ by personal delivery on *(date):*

- Check Box 1 if you are suing an adult person in his own name, such as Jonathan Walton.

- Check Box 2 if you are suing an adult person who does business in a fictitious business name—type the business's fictitious name after "(specify)" or an unknown defendant (see Chapter 4, Section D.7)—type the name and identifying number, such as "Doe 4" after "(specify)."

- Check Box 3 if you are suing a corporation or defunct corporation, an association or partnership, a minor or a person subject to a conservatorship.

   Specify the name of the defendant and check the applicable sub-box.

- Don't check Box 4.

   If you are suing a particular defendant in more than one capacity—such as an individual who does business under a fictitious name, or an officer of a corporation who is being sued as an individual and as the corporation's representative—check all boxes that apply.

B. Selecting a Process Server

Once you've prepared the papers to be delivered to the defendant, you need to select someone to do the actual serving. This person is called a "process server." You have several options, but doing it yourself is not one of them—court papers must be served by someone over age 18 who is not a party to the case.

You can use a friend or a professional process server. You can also use a sheriff or marshal (a person who works as a bailiff in Municipal Court) if the sheriff or marshal's office still provides the service. (Budget cutbacks have forced some of them to eliminate it.) You'll have to pay the sheriff or marshal's office about $20; a professional process server will charge closer to $30.

Even though it's free, I recommend against using a friend. Friends have not been trained in the rules of proper process serving and often make mistakes. In addition, if a dispute arises over whether or not the defendant was served— or served correctly—friends are less likely to be believed than are sheriffs, marshals or professional process servers. Finally, the law presumes that a sheriff, marshal or professional process server's statement that service was correct is true.[1] This law doesn't apply to friends.

I recommend that you hire a professional process server. Not only do professional process servers know the rules of proper service better

---

[1] Evidence Code § 647.

than anyone else, they get paid when they accomplish service and thus will usually work hard to find the defendant and serve him. Sheriffs and marshals have less incentive to complete the task—they're paid by the county regardless of whether or not they serve the defendant. Professional process servers are listed in the telephone Yellow Pages under "Process Serving". Make sure you know the fee before you hire someone.

C. Serving the Summons and Complaint

If you use a sheriff, marshal or professional process server, you don't have to worry about how to actually serve the defendant. That's why you've hired someone to do the job. If you use a friend, however, the rules of proper service are important—though not all that complicated. While you may have seen process servers in the movies or on television act as though they have to touch the defendant with the papers, that is Hollywood hype. In truth, the process server needs only to:

- identify the defendant ("Are you Morton Kaifu?")
- state her purpose ("These are legal documents I am serving on you")
- leave the documents in the presence of the defendant

The process server doesn't have to physically hand the papers to the defendant or see the defendant pick them up. The process server can simply place them on a counter or desk in front of a defendant, leave them under the windshield wiper of a car in which the defendant is sitting or even push them under a door after the process server has identified the defendant as being on the other side.

If the defendant is not a natural adult, your friend will have to follow special rules.

Corporations. All corporations—for profit and nonprofit—must file with the California Secretary of State the names and addresses of their officers and any person who has been designated the agent who accepts legal papers. Your process server can serve the designated agent or any officer or general manager of the corporation. To find out who these people are, see Chapter 4, Section B.4.

Partnerships or unincorporated associations. To serve a partnership or unincorporated association, your process server needs only to serve the papers on any partner, officer or general manager. If this person is being sued in his individual capacity as well, the process server should leave two copies of the papers.

Government agencies. Before suing the government, remember that you must file an administrative claim. (See Chapter 4, Section D.2.) After the claim is rejected and you prepare and file the court papers, your process server can simply deliver them to the clerk of the governing body.

Minors. A minor is served by serving his parent or guardian. If the minor is 12 or older, your process server must also serve the minor personally.

If a defendant is evading service—for example, not answering the door or denying that he is the defendant—there are a few special methods a process server can use to try and serve the defendant. For instance, after several unsuccessful attempts, he can leave the papers with a co-resident at a home or a person in charge of a business and then mail a copy to the defendant.[2] These methods are intricate and should not be attempted by anyone other than a professional process server if at all possible.

Be Sure To Check Your Fast Track Rules

 Your local Municipal Court fast track rules will give you a deadline by which you must complete service after you file the papers. Most limits are either 30 or 60 days. Be sure to comply with the deadline. If you can't, be ready to explain to the court what the problem is.

D. Completing the Proof of Service

Once your process server serves the defendant, she must fill out a form called a "Proof of Service" which describes how and when service was accomplished. A professional process server, sheriff or marshal will complete the form and give it to you.

Your friend will have to complete a Proof of Service as well. She can use the back page of the original Summons. If she served more than one defendant, she must use a separate copy of the back page of the Summons for each defendant served. A completed sample is below; instructions for completion follow. A blank is in the Appendix.

---

[2]Code of Civil Procedure § 415.20.

PROOF OF SERVICE — SUMMONS
(Use separate proof of service for each person served)

1. I served the
   a. [X] summons [X] complaint [ ] amended summons [ ] amended complaint
      [X] completed and blank Case Questionnaires [ ] Other *(specify)*:
   b. on defendant *(name)*: Anne Warren

   c. by serving [X] defendant [ ] other *(name and title or relationship to person served)*:

   d. [X] by delivery [ ] at home [X] at business
      (1) date: December 9, 1992
      (2) time: 2:30 p.m.
      (3) address: Annie's Pie Shop, 1711 Arkansas Lane, San Mateo, California

   e. [ ] by mailing
      (1) date:
      (2) place:

2. Manner of service *(check proper box)*:
   a. [X] **Personal service.** By personally delivering copies. (CCP 415.10)
   b. [ ] **Substituted service on corporation, unincorporated association (including partnership), or public entity.** By leaving, during usual office hours, copies in the office of the person served with the person who apparently was in charge and thereafter mailing (by first-class mail, postage prepaid) copies to the person served at the place where the copies were left. (CCP 415.20(a))
   c. [ ] **Substituted service on natural person, minor, conservatee, or candidate.** By leaving copies at the dwelling house, usual place of abode, or usual place of business of the person served in the presence of a competent member of the household or a person apparently in charge of the office or place of business, at least 18 years of age, who was informed of the general nature of the papers, and thereafter mailing (by first-class mail, postage prepaid) copies to the person served at the place where the copies were left. (CCP 415.20(b)) *(Attach separate declaration or affidavit stating acts relied on to establish reasonable diligence in first attempting personal service.)*
   d. [ ] **Mail and acknowledgment service.** By mailing (by first-class mail or airmail, postage prepaid) copies to the person served, together with two copies of the form of notice and acknowledgment and a return envelope, postage prepaid, addressed to the sender. (CCP 415.30) *(Attach completed acknowledgment of receipt.)*
   e. [ ] **Certified or registered mail service.** By mailing to an address outside California (by first-class mail, postage prepaid, requiring a return receipt) copies to the person served. (CCP 415.40) *(Attach signed return receipt or other evidence of actual delivery to the person served.)*
   f. [ ] Other *(specify code section)*:
      [ ] additional page is attached.

3. The "Notice to the Person Served" (on the summons) was completed as follows (CCP 412.30, 415.10, and 474):
   a. [X] as an individual defendant.
   b. [X] as the person sued under the fictitious name of *(specify)*:
   c. [ ] on behalf of *(specify)*:
      under: [ ] CCP 416.10 (corporation)   [ ] CCP 416.60 (minor)   [ ] other:
             [ ] CCP 416.20 (defunct corporation) [ ] CCP 416.70 (conservatee)
             [ ] CCP 416.40 (association or partnership) [ ] CCP 416.90 (individual)
   d. [ ] by personal delivery on *(date)*:

4. At the time of service I was at least 18 years of age and not a party to this action.

5. Fee for service: $

6. Person serving:
   a. [ ] California sheriff, marshal, or constable.
   b. [ ] Registered California process server.
   c. [ ] Employee or independent contractor of a registered California process server.
   d. [X] Not a registered California process server.
   e. [ ] Exempt from registration under Bus. & Prof. Code 22350(b).

   f. Name, address and telephone number and, if applicable, county of registration and number:

   Wilma Rudolph
   56 Market Street
   Burlingame, California 94400
   415-555-8834

I declare under penalty of perjury under the laws of the State of California that the foregoing is true and correct.

(For California sheriff, marshal, or constable use only)
I certify that the foregoing is true and correct.

Date: December 10, 1992

Date:

▶ _____
(SIGNATURE)

▶ _____
(SIGNATURE)

982(a)(9) [Rev. January 1, 1984]

1a: Check the boxes corresponding to what documents were served—the Summons, Complaint and completed and blank Case Questionnaires.

1b: Fill in the name of the defendant, using the name exactly how it appears in the Complaint. Remember to use a separate form for each defendant served.

1c: If your friend served the defendant, check the first box. Otherwise, check the second box and fill in the name of the person served.

1d: Indicate where and when service occurred.

1e: Skip this. It's for professional process servers, sheriffs and marshals only.

2: Check box 2a. The others are normally used by professional process servers, sheriffs and marshals only.

3: Check the same box(es) that are checked on the front of the Summons for each defendant.

4: She doesn't need to do anything here.

5: Skip this; your friend can't recover a fee.

6: You friend should check box d and fill in her name and address at f.

Date and Signature: Make sure she dates and signs the form in the left date and signature slots.

Once you have the completed Proof of Service—from the sheriff, marshal, professional process server or your friend—make two copies of it. If there's more than one (more than one defendant was served), make two copies of each.

Send the originals and one copy of each proof of service to the court clerk. Ask the clerk to file the original Proof(s) of Service, stamp the copies and return them to you.

E. Serving Other Papers as the Case Proceeds

As the case progresses, you will need to serve other documents on your opponent. This service is much easier than serving the Summons and Complaint—it's all done by mail. Like the personal service of the Summons and Complaint, serving by mail must be done by someone over 18 who is not a party to the lawsuit. You can certainly use a friend, relative or business associate.

To serve papers by mail, your server must prepare a Proof of Service by Mail for each particular document to be sent. In the Proof of Service by Mail, she lists the names and addresses of each party (or each party's attorney, if they have one) to be served. A sample completed Proof of Service by Mail is below. A blank is in the Appendix.

Have your server—after typing up the Proof of Service by Mail—send one set of the documents to each party listed. Then have her sign the Proof of Service by Mail. You should put the completed Proof of Service by Mail into a folder of your lawsuit documents. You don't need to file it with the court.

PARTY WITHOUT ATTORNEY *(My Name and Address)*   MY TELEPHONE NO.

Bonnie Rose   408-555-6290
1406 Silverspoon Circle
San Jose, CA 95100

NAME OF COURT: Santa Clara County Municipal Court
STREET ADDRESS: San Jose Facility
MAILING ADDRESS: 200 W. Hedding St.
CITY AND ZIP CODE: San Jose, CA 95110
BRANCH NAME:

PLAINTIFF:
     Daniel Woods

DEFENDANT: Bonnie Rose, Does 1-5

PROOF OF SERVICE BY MAIL
(CCP Sections 1013a, 2015.5)

CASE NUMBER
RW843-2

I declare that:

1. At the time of service I was at least 18 years of age and not a party to this legal action.

2. I am a resident of or employed in the county where the mailing occurred.

3. My business or residence address is: __1700 Chaplin Parkway, Sunnyvale, CA__

4. I served copies of the following paper(s) in the manner shown:

     a. Papers served [list exact titles of paper(s)]:
         Answer--Personal Injury, Property Damage, Wrongful Death

     b. Manner of service: by placing true copies in a sealed envelope addressed to each person whose name and address is given below and:

         ☐ depositing the envelope in the United States Mail with the postage fully prepaid; or

         ☒ (If deposited at a business:) Placing for collection and mailing following ordinary business practices. I am readily familiar with the business practice for collection and processing of correspondence for mailing with the United States Post Office. The correspondence will be deposited with the United States Post office on the same date as the date of deposit (below) in the ordinary course of business.

         (1) Date of Deposit: __November 5, 1991__

         (2) Place of Deposit (city & state; business address if deposited at a business): __1700 Chaplin Parkway Sunnyvale, CA__

5. I declare under penalty of perjury under the laws of the State of California that the foregoing is true and correct. Executed on __Nov. 5, 1991__ at __Sunnyvale__, California.

Print Name: __Gordon Freed__

_____
[Signature of Person Who Served Papers]

Name and Address of Each Person to Whom Documents Were Mailed:
Milton Upshot, Esq.
4500 Hamilton Building East
Central Plaza
San Jose, CA 95000

☐ _____ Additional names and addresses on reverse.

PROOF OF SERVICE BY MAIL

chapter 8

LAWSUITS FROM THE DEFENDANT'S POINT OF VIEW

Up to now, most of this book has been devoted to considering a lawsuit from the viewpoint of the person suing. If you're being sued, you are surely ready for a sympathetic and understanding word.

Being sued is not fun. You may feel it's unfair for the plaintiff to sue you. Your initial reaction may be rage, followed closely by fear and panic. But remember that all it takes to sue someone is a typewriter and a filing fee (and even the fee can be waived). No government official had to approve the suit for fairness.

Being sued doesn't make you a bad person. Nor does it mean that no one will want to sit next to you on the bus. Most businesspeople know that being sued every so often is a part of life.

A. Initial Steps

When you are sued, your first task is to figure out why you've been sued and what the plaintiff wants. Only when you clearly understand this can you figure out what to do about it. If you have jumped into this book at this chapter, go back and read Chapters 1, 2 and 3. They explain what lawsuits are and how to analyze the papers you were served.

1. Review the Summons

One of the papers that was served on you is called the Summons. Somewhere on that paper, write down the date on which you were served. If you don't remember, call the plaintiff's attorney, or the plaintiff if she doesn't have one, and ask the date you were served. Within 30 days of that date, you must file a formal paper with the

court or, if you need more time, you must make a written agreement with the plaintiff (or her lawyer) extending your time to respond. Fast Track rules (see Chapter 6) adopted by your court may limit the amount of extra time the plaintiff can allow you.

If You're a Plaintiff Who's Received a Cross-Complaint

Sometimes a defendant not only answers a Complaint, but also files her own lawsuit against the plaintiff. This is called a Cross-Complaint. If you're a plaintiff who was served with a cross-complaint, this chapter tells you how to respond. The only difference is that if you were served with the papers by mail (see Chapter 7, Section E), you have 35, not 30, days to respond.

---

2. Review the Complaint

The most important paper served on you is the Complaint, which tells you what the lawsuit is about. The plaintiff can use one of two types of Complaints:

- a simplified fill-in-the-blank form supplied by the court (explained in Chapter 5); or

- a formal document prepared using plain white paper which contains numbers down the left side (called "pleading" paper).

If the plaintiff is represented by a lawyer, you probably received a Complaint on pleading paper. For some reason, lawyers like pleading paper. In either case, here's how to decipher the Complaint:

- If the plaintiff used a fill-in-the-blank form, take a look at Chapter 5 of this book. The paragraphs are explained there.
- If the plaintiff used a numbered pleading-paper Complaint, it will probably be repetitive. This is because the lawyer is trying to fit the lawsuit into a traditional legal format that glories in saying everything several times. Even more confusing will be the lawyer language (legalese). Use an inexpensive legal dictionary if necessary—one good one is *Law Dictionary*, by Steven Gifis (Barrons). If you're still confused, read over Chapter 5, Section C.1.b ("Common Counts").

No matter which kind of Complaint you have, when you get to the end you'll find the plaintiff "praying for" certain relief. In a form Complaint, the prayer is at the end of the form entitled "COMPLAINT," before the Cause of Action forms. In a pleading paper Complaint, the prayer comes at the very end. The prayer is not a religious plea. It's a summary of what the plaintiff is asking for. Usually it's for a sum of money. Don't panic over the number, however. It is often arbitrary and exaggerated, particularly in accident cases where the "prayer" includes a request for pain and suffering. What the plaintiff wants and what a court will award are frequently far apart.

3. Review Your Insurance Policies

It's possible that the lawsuit is covered by your auto, renter's, homeowner's or other type of insurance. So take out your policy and review it.

Check Your Homeowner's or Renter's Policy

If you have homeowner's, renter's or another umbrella liability coverage (they come in various names, but generally agree to protect you from many perils), your insurance company may cover your defense in an amazing number of situations.

Homeowner's policies cover any situation in which you are sued for negligent bodily injury or property damage by another person which doesn't involve a motor vehicle. If someone working at or visiting your home is injured, you are probably covered. If someone claims he was injured as a result of your careless act away from your home, you are probably covered by a homeowner's policy—and even possibly by a renter's policy.

Automobile and other vehicle accidents are usually excluded, however (on the assumption you have automobile insurance), but some homeowner's and renter's policies have covered jet ski accidents. Business incidents usually must be covered by a separate policy or an endorsement on a homeowner's policy.

Most intentional acts are not covered by homeowner's insurance, but it's not always clear whether a particular act was careless or intentional. For example, let's say your house had slide problems but you forgot to tell the buyer before selling the house. The house slips some more and the buyer sues you for fraud. As long as you can convince your insurance company that your concealing the slide problem was due to forgetfulness and was not intentional, the company may agree to defend you.

If it's at all possible that your insurance will cover the case, contact your insurance agent or a claims adjuster immediately. Ask for an appointment and do the following.

Make copies of the papers you were served with, deliver the copies to your agent and have him sign a note acknowledging receipt. Ask if the insurance company will defend you (and therefore file a response within 30 days). The agent may respond in one of three ways. First, the agent may tell you that the company will take care of the matter, but that he can't say so in writing. In this case, you'll have to decide whether or not to trust him. If you don't, you'll have to file the response yourself.

Second, the insurance company may refuse to defend you. If it does, but you think it should, re-read your policy and see what it says the insured (that's you) must do to contest a "denial of coverage." Comply with these provisions. Also, write the company a letter. State that the company has rejected your request for a defense, and that you will defend yourself, seeking reimbursement later. This letter may spur the company to action. And in the mean time, be sure to file your response with the court within 30 days.

If the company still denies coverage, seek some advice on whether or not to pursue a claim against the company further. A good insurance broker not connected with the dispute is likely to have a valuable opinion, and his advice won't cost anything if he thinks you may do business with him in the future. Some lawyers specialize in insurance coverage situations, but the problem is in finding the right lawyer who will charge an affordable fee. (See Chapter 17.)

Third, the insurance company may agree to defend you. If it does, it should give you a letter to that effect. The letter may be one of two kinds.

1. The insurance company agrees that the incident is covered and defends the case. This means it will pay any judgment obtained by the plaintiff within your policy limit.

2. The insurance company agrees to provide your with a lawyer, but won't commit to paying any judgment obtained by the plaintiff. The letter will state that the company will make this

decision as more facts develop. In this situation, meet with the insurance company's lawyer at once. If you are comfortable with her, and she agrees to consult with you and keep you informed about the status of the case, you probably want to accept this defense from the insurance company. But if you are not comfortable with the lawyer and are not convinced she'll keep you informed, consider hiring your own lawyer to work with the insurance company's lawyer and see that you are getting the defense you are entitled to.

4. Consider Settling

When you are sued, you should always consider settling with the plaintiff. Just because the plaintiff "prays" for $25,000 in the complaint doesn't mean he wouldn't accept $5,000 in settlement. Remember—most people use arbitrary and inflated numbers in the Complaint.

One Way To Settle an Expensive Lawsuit Fast

If you don't have the money or energy to fight a battle with the plaintiff, you may want to call the plaintiff's bluff and try to settle fast. One way is to contact a lawyer and find out what it would cost to have one of its attorneys write a letter stating "This firm represents Mr. Evans in this matter and intends to engage in a vigorous defense of the lawsuit you have filed." Some plaintiffs—faced with the prospect of a major battle—will decide to settle for a reasonable sum.

Example: Oliver borrowed $12,000 from Kate, but can't pay her back. Kate sues him for the $12,000, plus interest and the cost of collection. Oliver scrapes together $8,000 and offers that amount to settle the whole thing. Kate accepts, knowing that the costs and delays of a lawsuit make a healthy discount worthwhile. She also realizes that because Oliver is in poor financial shape, having the cash now is preferable to trying to collect a judgment later.

If you want to try and settle the case, read Chapter 3. If you do settle the case, be sure to file (or to have the plaintiff file) a Request for Dismissal. (Also explained in Chapter 3.)

5. Decide Whether or Not To Represent Yourself

The balance of this chapter describes the procedures to follow if you represent yourself in defending the lawsuit. Defending yourself in a court system designed for lawyers can be stressful, time consuming and frequently frustrating. But it can also be rewarding and self-empowering. The pros and cons are covered in Chapter 1.

6. If You Have No Defense

If you decide to represent yourself and you have no defense, you should still take steps to protect your interests. If you can't settle with the plaintiff, prepare and file an Answer (see Section C, below). If you don't, the plaintiff will ask the court to enter a default against you (see Chapter 9) and obtain a judgment that may exceed what the judge would allow if you were present in court giving your side of the story. Also, be sure to attend any court hearings for which you receive notice.

Example: Don borrowed $9,000 from a bank, and is sued for failing to repay it. When Don borrowed the money, he signed a contract letting the bank recover costs and attorney's fees if it had to sue him. At the trial, the bank's lawyer claims that those fees (the lawyer and a collection agency) total $6,000. Don, who filed an answer, is at the trial and protests those amounts as excessive. The judge agrees and sets them at $2,000. Had Don not been in court, it might have cost him $4,000.

Also, if you file an Answer, attend the trial and lose, you can ask the court to let you pay the judgment in monthly payments.[1] In the above example, Don might have been able to convince the judge to let him pay $300 a month. If he didn't, the entire judgment would be payable immediately and the creditor might well have set up a wage garnishment, emptied his bank accounts and placed a lien on his house.

---

[1] Code of Civil Procedure § 85.

B. Ask For More Time

You might need more than 30 days to file your response—for example, discussions with your insurance company (over whether it will defend you) or potential lawyers has taken up most of that time. If so, call the plaintiff (or his lawyer) and ask for a 30-day extension for you to file an Answer. The Fast Track rules explained in Chapter 6 may limit the amount of time he can give you, but he should agree to at least a few extra weeks. If he agrees to extend your time, send a confirming letter immediately.

Sample Letter Confirming Time Extension

September 23, 19__

John Tweedle, Esq.
Tweedle, Dee & Dum
405 14th Street
Oakland, California 97001

re: Solomon vs. Sucherman, case # 890 765

Dear Mr. Tweedle:

This letter is to confirm that you have agreed that I may have until October 19, 19__ to answer or otherwise plead in this case. If you believe this is not our agreement, please contact me immediately.

Sincerely,

Monica Sucherman

If the plaintiff or his lawyer won't agree to an extension of time (most lawyers will), you can apply to the court for an extension. You will need to prepare a form called a "Request and Order for Extension of time to Plead." This is not a fill-in-the blank form but one which you must type on numbered legal paper. (See Chapter 5, Section D.5.) An example is below.

Deliver the form, along with two copies, to the court clerk. Ask when and how you will know whether or not the judge has granted your request. This is usually done without your talking to the judge. Once you get the signed Order back, be sure to keep one copy for your records and send another copy to the plaintiff, or his lawyer if he has one.

C. Prepare an Answer

By filing an Answer, you establish that you contest the case and require the plaintiff to prove her case at trial in order to win.

Sample Request and Order for Extension of Time to Plead

```
 1   MONICA SUCHERMAN
     1818 Euclid Avenue
 2   San Francisco, CA 94111
     415-555-7777
 3
     Defendant In Pro Per
 4

 5

 6

 7

 8               MUNICIPAL COURT OF CALIFORNIA

 9                 COUNTY OF SAN FRANCISCO

10

11   LITTLE PEN SHOPPE,            )        Case No. 4443-9000
                                   )
12   Plaintiff,                    )        REQUEST AND ORDER FOR
                                   )        EXTENSION OF TIME TO
13   vs.                           )        PLEAD
                                   )
14   MONICA SUCHERMAN,             )
                                   )
15   Defendant. _____  )

16

17      Defendant cannot afford to hire a lawyer to represent her in this case and

18   is undertaking the research to represent herself. She needs and requests an

19   additional 20 days to complete the necessary work.

20

21   _____          _____
     Signature                                    Date
22

23                            ORDER

24      It is hereby ordered that defendant may have until_____

25   to answer in this matter.

26

27   _____          _____
     Judge of the Municipal Court                 Date
28
```

Filing a Response Other Than an Answer

The law requires that you "respond" to the complaint within 30 days. Your response does not necessarily have to be an Answer. Lawyers frequently spend hours filing "motion" papers objecting to a Complaint before they ever file an Answer (or at the same time as filing an Answer). This is the litigation game. Usually, all it does is delay the inevitable (filing an Answer if you haven't yet done so) and make the lawyer's wallet thicker. Nevertheless, here are some of the grounds for filing one of those other possible responses:

Wrong state. It's possible that you should have been sued in a state other than California. To raise this defense, you must file a document called a "General Demurrer." If you now live in California, however, you'll gain very little by objecting. The lawsuit may be thrown out and then re-filed in a different state, where it will probably be very inconvenient for you to defend.

Wrong county. It's also possible that you've been sued in the wrong county. (See Chapter 4, Section C.) If so, you can request that the case be moved by filing a Motion To Change Venue when you file your Answer. It's not terribly complicated, but it does require that you compose and type several documents. Unless the county where the suit has been filed is truly inconvenient, it's probably best to ignore the problem.

If it is terribly inconvenient, consider hiring a lawyer to help you prepare a pro per Motion to Change Venue. The lawyer prepares the papers that are filed in your name, and you argue the motion in court without the lawyer. To prepare the forms yourself, see *California Forms of Pleading and Practice*, volume 14, pages 78-116.

Inconvenient county. It's possible to file a Motion for Change of Venue if the county in which the case was filed will be inconvenient for the people who will be called as witnesses in the case. You don't have to file this Motion with the Answer, but be sure to file it soon thereafter. Again, you'll probably be best off having a lawyer draft the Motion for you to file and argue.

Improper service. You may have been served incorrectly with the Summons and Complaint. (See Chapter 7.) For example, the papers may have been shoved under your door when you weren't home. You can contest it by filing a Motion to Quash Service. You'd probably need the help of a lawyer, and normally would accomplish very little—the plaintiff will simply have you served again—most likely on the day you show up in court to fight the initial improper service. Again, it's probably best to ignore the problem.

Legal defects in the Complaint. It's possible to challenge legal defects in a Complaint by filing a Demurrer (the same document you file if the plaintiff sued you in the wrong state) or a Motion to Strike a portion of the prayer (where the plaintiff states what he's asking for) of the Complaint. For example, if the Complaint does not include all of the necessary allegations (such as a statement that you acted negligently), you could file a Demurrer. But this procedure is not worth your time, especially given that even if you're successful, the plaintiff will usually file an Amended Complaint correcting the defect and the case will continue.

 Your Answer should be filed on time. As mentioned above, this is within 30 days of the date you were served with the Summons and Complaint (or whatever extension you arranged). In the unlikely event you file a Demurrer or a Motion to Strike, the court will tell you how long you have to file an Answer. Your Answer will actually be accepted by the clerk anytime up until the plaintiff files a Request To Enter Default (described in Chapter 9), which could be well beyond the 30 days allowed.

If you attempt to file an Answer after the plaintiff has taken your default, the clerk will refuse to accept it and you'll need a lawyer fast to ask the court to "set aside the default." Your right to do this normally expires six months after the default was entered. The decision on your request is in the discretion of the judge, who may not be very sympathetic. Just because you have six months doesn't mean you should wait six months. The longer you wait, the more difficult it is to set aside a default.

1. Examine the Complaint's Causes of Action

The Complaint may be divided into several Causes of Action (First Cause of Action, Second Cause of Action, etc.), each containing numbered paragraphs. These Causes of Action are often different ways of stating the same facts under different legal theories. Sometimes, one Cause of Action incorporates by reference paragraphs from another Cause of Action.

In your Answer, you must state which of the plaintiff's assertions you agree with and which you dispute. You must respond to every paragraph containing an allegation. For each paragraph, your choices will be:

* admit;
* deny;
* deny on information and belief;
* deny because no information; or
* do nothing.

Let's look at them one at a time.

Admit. For each paragraph where you agree absolutely with everything said, write "admit" next to it, such as "Market Street and Van Ness Avenue intersect in the City and County of San Francisco." If you admit a statement, the plaintiff won't have to prove it. Thus, admit only those statements you can't argue about. But don't refuse to admit something obviously true just to make it hard for the plaintiff. Forcing a

plaintiff to prove that Market Street is in San Francisco will anger a judge who is trying to sort out the facts. But if you honestly don't know if a statement is true or you agree with only part of it, don't admit it.

Deny. Write "deny" near each paragraph in which you deny all or part of what was said. For instance, if a paragraph says "Defendant was speeding and driving recklessly on Elm Street" and you agree you were on Elm Street, but deny you were speeding or reckless, deny the whole paragraph.

Deny on information and belief. If you are not sure what the truth is, but you believe the plaintiff's statement is probably more false than true, write "deny on information and belief." For instance, if the plaintiff has alleged that the accident happened at night, but you think—and aren't completely sure—it was in the late afternoon, use this designation.

Deny because no information. If you have no idea whether or not the allegation in a paragraph is true, for example, a paragraph saying that the plaintiff was on the job performing his duties as a delivery person, write "deny because no information."

The distinctions among the different types of denials can be vague. Don't spend a lot of time worrying about which is precisely appropriate. As long as you use one of them, you are protected.

Do nothing. If the Complaint is on pleading paper (not fill-in-the-blank forms) and has more than one Cause of Action, it probably has a paragraph at the beginning of each Cause of Action (other than the first) incorporating paragraphs (often referred to as allegations) from other Causes of Action. It may read something like "plaintiff incorporates paragraphs 1-7 of his

First Cause of Action and makes them a part of this Second Cause of Action." Because you've already responded to the earlier allegations, don't put any designation next to the incorporating paragraphs.

2. Using a Fill-in-the-Blank Form

California provides defendants in Municipal Court with fill-in-the-blank forms that can be used to respond to tort and contract Complaints. (If you don't know what a contract or tort is, see Chapter 4.) You can use these forms even if the plaintiff used a pleading-paper Complaint.

a. Tort Cases

 If you haven't been sued on a tort case, skip ahead to Section 2.b.

To respond to a tort Complaint, use the form "ANSWER—Personal Injury, Property Damage, Wrongful Death." Make several photocopies of the form and fill one in with pencil as a rough draft before you type it. A completed sample and instructions follow. A blank is in the Appendix.

Attorney or Party Without Attorney (Name and Address): Put your name and the address at which you want to receive mail about the case. Include a phone number, preferably where you can be reached during the day. If you aren't reachable at a phone number, don't put anything—you don't have to have a phone to defend a lawsuit. Put "Defendant in pro per" after the line that says "Attorney for (Name):"

Insert name of court, judicial district or branch court, if any, and post office and

street address: Copy this information from the Complaint.

Plaintiff: Fill in the names of the plaintiffs exactly as they appear on the Complaint.

Defendant: Fill in the names of the defendants exactly as they appear on the Complaint, even if your name is misspelled.

Complaint of (name): Check this box and type in the name(s) of the plaintiff(s) whose Complaint you are answering.

Cross-Complaint of (name): Skip this box.

Case Number: Type in the case number that's on the Summons and Complaint. Make sure you type the number correctly.

1: Skip this for now. You'll come back to it.

Defendant or Cross-Defendant (name): Type in your name (spelled correctly, even if the plaintiff spelled it wrong on the Complaint), and if named in the Complaint, the name of your business or partnership. If your spouse is being sued as well, type in both names. Any other defendant should prepare and file a separate Answer.

2: To determine if you are eligible to check this box, look at the end of the Complaint. Does it include a statement called a Verification? A Verification is an optional statement that gives the identity of the person verifying the Complaint (such as the plaintiff, an attorney, a partner in a partnership or an officer of a corporation) and then states that the person has read the Complaint and declares under penalty of perjury that it is true or believed to be true. If the Complaint is not verified, check Item 2.

If the Complaint is verified, you can check Item 2 only if the plaintiff is asking for $1,000 or less.

ATTORNEY OR PARTY WITHOUT ATTORNEY (NAME AND ADDRESS):	TELEPHONE:	FOR COURT USE ONLY

ATTORNEY OR PARTY WITHOUT ATTORNEY (NAME AND ADDRESS):   TELEPHONE:

Bonnie Rose   408-555-6290
1406 Silverspoon Circle
San Jose, CA 95100

ATTORNEY FOR (NAME): defendant in pro per

Insert name of court, judicial district or branch court, if any, and post office and street address:
Santa Clara Municipal Court
San Jose Facility
200 W. Hedding St.
San Jose, CA 95110

PLAINTIFF:
Daniel Woods

DEFENDANT:
Bonnie Rose, Does 1-5

ANSWER—Personal Injury, Property Damage, Wrongful Death
[X] COMPLAINT OF (name): Daniel Wood
[ ] CROSS-COMPLAINT OF (name):

CASE NUMBER:
RW843-2

1. This pleading, including attachments and exhibits, consists of the following number of pages: 2

DEFENDANT OR CROSS-DEFENDANT (name): Bonnie Rose

2. [ ] Generally **denies** each allegation of the **unverified** complaint or cross-complaint.

3. a. [X] DENIES each allegation of the following numbered paragraphs:

8, 10, MV-1, MV-2

b. [X] ADMITS each allegation of the following numbered paragraphs:
1, 5, 11

c. [X] DENIES, ON INFORMATION AND BELIEF, each allegation of the following numbered paragraphs:

2, 3, 4

d. [X] DENIES, BECAUSE OF LACK OF SUFFICIENT INFORMATION OR BELIEF TO ANSWER, each allegation
of the following numbered paragraphs:
6, 7, 9

e. [ ] ADMITS the following allegations and generally denies all other allegations:

(Continued)

Form Approved by the
Judicial Council of California
Effective January 1, 1982
Rule 982.1(15)

**ANSWER—Personal Injury, Property Damage,
Wrongful Death**

CCP 425.12   C-95

SHORT TITLE: CASE NUMBER:
Woods vs. Rose   RW843-2

ANSWER—Personal Injury, Property Damage, Wrongful Death   Page two

f. ☐ DENIES the following allegations and admits all other allegations:

g. ☒ Other *(specify):*

In denying the allegations of the Complaint, above, defendant denies
not only the specific numbers and amounts alleged by plaintiff,
but all other numbers and amounts claimed.

AFFIRMATIVELY ALLEGES AS A DEFENSE

4. ☒ The comparative fault of plaintiff or cross-complainant *(name):*   Daniel Woods
as follows:
Plaintiff's negligence legally contributed to his damages and
injuries in that he ran a stop sign, sped and made an illegal
left turn.

5. ☒ The expiration of the Statute of Limitations as follows:

Plaintiff failed to file this action within one year of his personal
injury.

6. ☐ Other *(specify):*

7. DEFENDANT OR CROSS-DEFENDANT PRAYS
For costs of suit and that plaintiff or cross-complainant take nothing.
☐ Other *(specify):*

Bonnie Rose
(Type or print name)   _____
                                               (Signature of party or attorney)

Page two

3: Here you make use of the the "admit, "deny," "deny on information and belief" and "deny because of no information" notations you made in Section 1, above. If you checked Item 2, above, skip to Item 3e, below.

3a: Check this box if you wrote "deny" for any paragraphs in the Complaint. Next, list the numbers of all the paragraphs you deny. If the Complaint has only one Cause of Action, simply type the corresponding paragraph numbers (for instance, "3, 5, 7 and 9" or "MV-1 and MV-2"). If the Complaint has several Causes of Action, type your answers to each separate Cause of Action (such as "First Cause of Action—paragraphs 3, 5, 6, 7 and 8; Second Cause of Action—paragraphs 1, 2, 5, 7 and 9").

3b: Follow the instructions for Item 3a for all paragraphs next to which you wrote "admit."

3c: Follow the instructions for Item 3a for all paragraphs next to which you wrote "deny on information and belief."

3d: Follow the instructions for Item 3a for all paragraphs next to which you wrote "deny because no information."

3e: Complete this item only if you checked Item 2, the Complaint was not verified *and* you plan to admit at least three of the Complaint paragraphs. In that case, check the box and type the number of each paragraph you admit is true. If the Complaint has only one Cause of Action, simply type the corresponding paragraph numbers (for instance, "3, 5, 7 and 9" or "MV-1 and MV-2"). If the Complaint has several Causes of Action, type your answers to each separate Cause of Action (such as "First Cause of Action—paragraphs 3, 5, 6, 7 and 8; Second Cause of Action—paragraphs 1, 2, 5, 7 and 9").

Page Two

Short Title: Put the last names (or the business names) of the first (perhaps only) plaintiff and the first (perhaps only) defendant, separated by a "vs.", such as "Brown vs. Black" or "Brown vs. Golden Bear Typing Service."

Case Number: Copy it from the Complaint.

3f: Skip this item.

3g: You must check the box and add some silly legal words to cover an ancient legal principle called a "negative pregnant." I could probably invent a humorous story about this name, but I doubt you are much interested in jokes, so just check the box and type "In denying the allegations of the Complaint above, defendant denies not only the specific numbers and amounts alleged by plaintiff, but all other numbers and amounts claimed."[2]

If the Complaint has paragraphs incorporating allegations from other paragraphs, deal with those paragraphs here. Simply type something like "Defendant incorporates her answer to each allegation incorporated in paragraph 1 of the Second and Third Causes of Action."

4, 5 and 6: In these items, you raise any affirmative defenses you have. An affirmative defense goes beyond simply denying the facts and arguments in the plaintiff's Complaint. It sets out new facts and arguments. If you prove your affirmative defense, even if what the plaintiff's Complaint states is true, you will win, or at least reduce the amount the plaintiff is entitled to recover against you.

4: Use this affirmative defense if you believe that the plaintiff was completely or partially at fault concerning the event described in the Complaint. This concept is called comparative fault and is explained in Chapter 2, Section F.1. If it applies, check the box and put in the name of the plaintiff(s) who were at fault. Then describe the fault, with something like "Plaintiff's negligence legally contributed to his damages and injuries in that he:

- "failed to drive with due caution, was speeding and ran a red light."

- "ignored barriers and signs warning all pedestrians that the sidewalk was under construction."

- "knew there was an angry dog on the other side of the gate, but nevertheless opened the gate and walked into the yard."

- "had his head buried in a newspaper while ascending the stairs and failed to see an obvious hazard."

- "placed the ladder on which he was working against an obviously rotten pole."

Don't raise any affirmative defense that is ridiculous. For example, don't allege that a pedestrian who was walking calmly across the street in a crosswalk was somehow partly at fault. If you can't come up with a rational theory of why the plaintiff contributed to the incident, don't say anything.

5: Use this affirmative defense if you believe that the plaintiff didn't file the lawsuit within the time allowed by the law, called the statute of limitations. Chapter 2, Section B, describes the applicable time limits, and if the plaintiff hasn't complied, check the box and describe the problem, such as:

- "Plaintiff failed to file this action within one year of his personal injury."

- "Plaintiff's suit was not filed within three years after his alleged property damage."

6: Check this box only if one or more of the following special defenses applies. Then describe the defense.

Self defense. If the plaintiff claims you deliberately injured him, but believe you were protecting yourself, type something like "At all times and in all of the actions described in the Complaint, defendant was defending himself from plaintiff's unjustified and unprovoked attack."

Assumption of risk. "Assumption of risk" means that before the plaintiff was injured or

---

[2]Negative pregnant is the theory that if you deny that you owe the plaintiff $7,000, you are not denying that you owe him a sum less than $7,000, such as $6,999. To cover the possibility that you're admitting that you owe him anything, I suggest you use this language. If it seems silly, that's because it is.

damaged, she knew (or should have known) that there was a risk of injury or damage and she agreed to be responsible if anything bad happened. Assumption of risk can take place as follows:

- in writing—for example, you asked the plaintiff to housesit and told her about a hazardous bridge in front of your house. She signed a statement acknowledging that you would not responsible if she was injured on the bridge.

- orally—the same as in writing, but done in a conversation

- by implication—for instance, you placed a large sign on the bridge warning that it's dangerous, but the plaintiff walked on it anyway

If you feel that the plaintiff assumed the risk, write "Prior to her alleged injury, plaintiff assumed the risk and responsibility for her injuries:

- "by signing the statement that is attached to this answer as Exhibit A."

- "by orally stating 'I know the bridge is dangerous, but it looks safe to me and I'd like to cross it.'"

- "by reading the sign warning that the bridge was dangerous and voluntarily walking across it."

Worker's compensation remedy. If you are the plaintiff's employer and he sustained his injury while acting within the scope of his employment, check this box and write "Plaintiff's claim is barred by the Worker's Compensation Act." This Act requires an employee injured on the job to take his claim to the state Division of Industrial Accidents, rather than file a lawsuit.

Someone working as an independent contractor, rather than as an employee, is not barred by the Worker's Compensation Act from suing the person who hired him. Also, an employee injured on the job can sue any person other than his employer who may be responsible for his injuries. Because these distinctions are sometime hazy, raise this defense anytime you are sued by an employee unless it is clear that the injury had nothing to do with his job.

Miscellaneous. Several tort suits not covered by this book have rules regarding affirmative defenses. If you are sued for libel, slander, inducing another person to breach a contract or for interfering with another person's prospective advantage, you must raise other defenses. Other defenses to be aware of include:

- plaintiff has signed a release as part of a settlement

- there's another lawsuit pending between these parties over the same matter

- plaintiff is a corporation that has had its corporate powers suspended for not paying taxes

- plaintiff is an out-of-state corporation not qualified to do business in California

 See *California Procedure*, 3rd edition, by Bernard Witkin, Sections 1023-1029.

7: Skip this item.

Now, type your name above the dotted line and sign above the solid line. Also, go back to item 1 and fill in your total number of pages. This will probably be two, but remember to count any attachments, such as a written agreement signed by the plaintiff in which she assumed a risk.

b. Contract Cases

 If you haven't been sued on a contract case, skip ahead to Section 3.

To respond to a contract Complaint, use the form "ANSWER—Contract." Make several photocopies of the form and fill one in with pencil as a rough draft before you type it. A completed sample and instructions are below. A blank copy is in the Appendix.

Top Half of Page 1: Fill in these boxes following the instructions in Section 2a, above.

1: Skip this for now. You'll come back to it.

2: Fill in your name, and if named in the Complaint, the name of your business or partnership. If your spouse is being sued as well, type in both names. Any other defendant should prepare and file a separate Answer.

3a: To determine if you are eligible to check this box, look at the end of the complaint. Does it include a statement called a Verification? A Verification is an optional statement that gives the identity of the person verifying the complaint (such as the plaintiff, an attorney, a partner in a partnership or an officer of a corporation) and then states that the person has read the Complaint and declares under penalty of perjury that it is true or believed to be true. If the Complaint is not verified, check Item 3a.

If the Complaint is verified, you can check Item 3a only if the plaintiff is asking for $1,000 or less.

3b: Check this box. This item is where you make use of the your "admit, "deny," "deny on information and belief" and "deny because of no information" notations.

(1) Find all the paragraphs next to which you wrote "deny." If the Complaint has only one Cause of Action, simply type the corresponding paragraph numbers (for instance, "3, 5, 7 and 9" or "BC-1, BC-3 and BC-4"). If the Complaint has several Causes of Action, type your answers to each separate Cause of Action (such as "First Cause of Action—paragraphs 3, 5, 6, 7 and 8; Second Cause of Action—paragraphs 1, 2, 5, 7 and 9"). Use attachment pages if necessary.

Typing the Attachment Sheet

If you run out of space on any of printed form, you can finish the information on a plain white sheet of numbered legal paper and simply call this paper an "attachment." At the top of each attachment page type the case's short title and case number.

Next, label the page "Attachment," and indicate the Form and Item you are continuing, such as "Attachment to Answer—Contract, Item 3.b.(1)." Then type your text using double-spacing. Use a new page for each item number you continue. At the bottom of the page, number the pages you're adding to the form.

---

(2) Follow the instructions for item (1) for all paragraphs next to which you wrote "deny on information and belief" or "deny because no information."

ATTORNEY OR PARTY WITHOUT ATTORNEY (NAME AND ADDRESS):	TELEPHONE:	FOR COURT USE ONLY

ATTORNEY OR PARTY WITHOUT ATTORNEY (NAME AND ADDRESS): TELEPHONE: 805-555-0862

Joan McCoy
P.O. Box 11178
Santa Barbara, CA 93111

ATTORNEY FOR (NAME): defendant in pro per

Insert name of court, judicial district or branch court, if any, and post office and street address:
Santa Barbara County Municipal Court
118 E. Figueroa St.
Santa Barbara, CA 93101

PLAINTIFF:

A-1 Corporation

DEFENDANT:

Joan McCoy, individually and dba McCoy's, and Does 1-8

ANSWER—Contract

CASE NUMBER: 300045

[X] TO COMPLAINT OF (name): A-1 Corporation
[ ] TO CROSS-COMPLAINT OF (name):

1. This pleading, including attachments and exhibits, consists of the following number of pages: __2__
2. DEFENDANT (name): Joan McCoy, individually and dba McCoy's

answers the complaint or cross-complaint as follows:

3. *Check ONLY ONE of the next two boxes:*
   a. [ ] Defendant generally denies each statement of the complaint or cross-complaint. *(Do not check this box if the verified complaint or cross-complaint demands more than $1,000.)*
   b. [X] Defendant admits that all of the statements of the complaint or cross-complaint are true EXCEPT:
      (1) Defendant claims the following statements are false *(use paragraph numbers or explain):*

      3,4,6,9,10,11

      [ ] Continued on Attachment 3.b.(1).
      (2) Defendant has no information or belief that the following statements are true, so defendant denies them *(use paragraph numbers or explain):*

      5,7,8

      [ ] Continued on Attachment 3.b.(2).
                    (Continued)

If this form is used to answer a cross-complaint, plaintiff means cross-complainant and defendant means cross-defendant.
Form Approved by the
Judicial Council of California
Effective January 1, 1982
Rule 982.1(35)

ANSWER—Contract   CCP 425.12

SHORT TITLE:	CASE NUMBER:
A-1 Corporation vs. McCoy	300045

ANSWER—Contract   Page two

4. ☒ AFFIRMATIVE DEFENSES
Defendant alleges the following additional reasons that plaintiff is not entitled to recover anything:

Plaintiff's lawsuit is barred by Code of Civil Procedure
Section 337.

☐ Continued on Attachment 4.

5. ☒ Other:

In denying the allegations of the Complaint, above, defendant
denies not only the specific numbers and amounts alleged by
plaintiff, but all other numbers and amounts claimed.

6. DEFENDANT PRAYS
   a. that plaintiff take nothing.
   b. ☒ for costs of suit.
   c. ☐ other (specify):

..... Joan McCoy .... _____
         (Type or print name)   (Signature of party or attorney)

Page two

Page Two

Short Title: Put the last names (or the business names) of the first (perhaps only) plaintiff and the first (perhaps only) defendant, separated by a "vs.", such as "Brown vs. Black" or "Brown vs. Golden Bear Typing Service."

Case Number: Copy it from the Complaint.

4: Here you raise any affirmative defenses you have. An affirmative defense goes beyond simply denying the facts and arguments in the plaintiff's Complaint. It sets out new facts and arguments. If you prove your affirmative defense, even if what the plaintiff's Complaint states is true, you will win, or at least reduce the amount the plaintiff is entitled to recover against you. Raise all of the following that apply:

Statute of limitations. Use this affirmative defense if the plaintiff didn't file the lawsuit within the time allowed by the law (called the statute of limitations). Chapter 2, Section B, describes the applicable time limits. If the plaintiff hasn't complied, check the box write:

- "Plaintiff's lawsuit is barred by Code of Civil Procedure Section 337" (written contract); or

- "Plaintiff's lawsuit is barred by Code of Civil Procedure Section 339" (oral contract).

Statute of frauds. Use this affirmative defense if the contract the plaintiff is alleging about should have been in writing but wasn't. (See Chapter 2.) Check this box and write "Plaintiff's claim is barred by the Statute of Frauds—Civil Code Section 1624."

Contract signed because of force, fraud or the pressure of someone in a confidential relationship. Use this affirmative defense if you signed the contract because of the plaintiff's physical force, threats or fraud. Fraud is the intentional lying or concealing of an important fact

in order to induce you into entering the contract. This affirmative defense also applies if someone with whom you have a "confidential" relationship put extreme pressure on you.

A confidential relationship is one between two people who have gained each other's confidences, purport to act with the other's interest in mind and therefore have a duty to act toward each other with good faith and honesty. Spouses, agents and principals, business partners, attorneys and clients, and guardians and wards are in confidential relationships. Car dealers and customers are not.

 These situations are usually complicated and require the help of a lawyer unless you're willing to do considerable legal research. If you are willing, see *California Procedure* (3rd Edition), by Bernard Witkin, Sections 418-429. If you want to at least raise the defense in your Answer, check the box and type something like "The contract that is the subject of this lawsuit is invalid because defendant's agreement to its terms was obtained as a result of plaintiff's threats to injure defendant if he did not sign it."

Mistake of fact. Use this affirmative defense if you signed the contract being mistaken about a material fact. A material fact goes to the core of the contract—for example, you bought a race horse believing it was a one-year old, when in fact the horse was five. It does not include minor terms of the contract.

 This can be complicated and require a lawyer's help unless you want to do some legal research. Again, if you are willing, see *California Procedure* (3rd Edition), Sections 418-429. If you want to at least raise the defense in your Answer, check the box and type something like "The contract that is the subject of this lawsuit is invalid because defendant's agreement to its terms was obtained under a mistake of a material fact in that the parties believed that the horse was a one-year old when in fact the horse was five."

Contracts signed by a minor. Use this affirmative defense if you entered into the contract before you turned 18 and you have since changed your mind. Check the box and type: "At the time defendant entered into the contract alleged by plaintiff, defendant was a minor. Defendant subsequently disaffirmed the contract under Civil Code Section 35."

Before using this defense, read Civil Code §§ 33 through 36 for exceptions which may apply. These exceptions generally bar you from canceling contracts for medical care and for the purchase of items necessary for your support or the support of your family, or contracts relating to show business or sports which have been approved by a court.

Miscellaneous. Several other legal defenses can be raised if they apply, but they involve complicated issues such as the formation of a

contract and are beyond the scope of this book. Some defenses to be aware include:

- plaintiff has signed a release as part of a settlement

- there's another lawsuit pending between these parties over the same matter

- plaintiff is a corporation that has had its corporate powers suspended for not paying taxes

- plaintiff is an out-of-state corporation not qualified to do business in California

 For information, see *California Procedure* (3rd Edition), by Bernard Witkin, Sections 1011-1022.

5: Check the box and add some silly legal words to cover an ancient legal principle called a "negative pregnant." I could probably invent a humorous story about this name, but I doubt you are much interested in jokes so just check the box and type "In denying the allegations of the Complaint above, defendant denies not only the specific numbers and amounts alleged by plaintiff, but all other numbers and amounts claimed."[3]

If the Complaint has paragraphs incorporating allegations from other paragraphs, deal with those paragraphs here. Simply type something like "Defendant incorporates her answer to each allegation incorporated in paragraph 1 of the Second and Third Causes of Action."

6a-c: Check Item 6b.

---

[3]Negative pregnant is the theory that if you deny that you owe the plaintiff $7,000, you are not denying that you owe him a sum less than $7,000, such as $6,999. To cover the possibility that you're admitting that you owe him anything, I suggest you use this language. If it seems silly, that's because it is.

Now, type your name above the dotted line and sign above the solid line. Also, go back to item 1 and fill in your total number of pages. This will probably be two, but remember to count any continuation pages.

3. Answering Other Types of Lawsuits

 If you've been sued on either a contract or tort case, skip ahead to Section D.

No printed forms are provided by the court to answer Municipal Court cases that aren't tort or contract. Discussing the numerous possibilities is beyond the scope of this book. If you are willing to do your own research at a law library, however, you'll have no problem finding sample answers.

To construct an Answer to a Complaint for something other than a contract or tort, first review Chapter 5, Section D. That material advises plaintiffs on how to draft a Complaint for something other than a contract or tort; the research resources and principles for drafting an Answer are the same. Then review Section 2, above, on answering tort and contract complaints. Finally, keep in mind that simply denying the plaintiff's allegations may not be enough. If you have any affirmative defenses, you must raise them when you file your Answer or you will lose them forever.

D. Prepare a Cross-Complaint

A Cross-Complaint allows a defendant to sue a plaintiff. In some cases, a defendant may also use a Cross-Complaint to sue a third person who is not yet a party to the lawsuit. Although a Cross-Complaint is technically an independent legal action, it has the same case number as the original lawsuit and travels with it in the court system to avoid piecemeal disposition of the legal battle.

If your claim "arises out of the same transaction, occurrence or series of transactions or occurrences" as the plaintiff's lawsuit, you must file a Cross-Complaint with your Answer or give up the claim forever. If your claim arises from a different transaction, occurrence or series of transactions or occurrences as the plaintiff's lawsuit, bringing a Cross-Complaint now is optional.

Fortunately, this is a situation where you don't need to mire yourself in technical rules to make a decision. If you have any claim against the plaintiff, law or practicality dictates that you file a Cross-Complaint now.

Example 1: Ted sues Naomi for an automobile accident that she believes was mostly his fault. She was injured in the accident and her car was damaged. She must cross-complain now if she wants to recover for her loss. But if Naomi and Ted were in an accident in March (over which Ted has sued) and another one in June (in which Naomi was injured), Naomi legally does not have to cross-complain now, though as a practical matter she should.

Example 2: Ed sues Ida for the bill she never paid him for repairing her front porch. Ida has a claim against Ed for tearing up her front yard with his truck while he was working on the porch. Ida must cross complain now. If, however, Ida's claim against Ed was for failing to pay back a loan she made him two years ago or for an auto accident that happened six months back, she isn't require to file a Cross-Complaint now, but she might as well.

Preparing a Cross-Complaint is very similar to preparing a Complaint, and so you'll want to read Chapter 5. Fill-in-the-blank court forms are in the Appendix, and completed samples follow. Bear in mind that Cross-Complaints introduce new terminology. The defendant in the original suit who files a Cross-Complaint is now called the "cross-complainant." The original plaintiff against whom the Cross-Complaint is filed is now called the "cross-defendant."

Naming a New Party

With the Cross-Complaint, you can name someone not named by the plaintiff (a "third party") in the lawsuit. For example, assume you were in a car accident and the plaintiff sues only you. You, however, believe the accident was caused by a third car that clipped your rear just before your impact with the plaintiff. You can add this new third party as cross-defendant and proceed as if he had been a party from the start.

The discussions, below, on preparing the tort and contract Cross-Complaint include instructions on adding a third party.

1. Tort Cases

 If you don't want to file a Cross-Complaint involving a tort, skip ahead to Section 2.

To sue on a tort, use the "Cross-Complaint—Personal Injury, Property Damage, Wrongful Death" form. Use this form no matter what type of lawsuit—contract, tort or another—the plaintiff has brought against you. A completed sample and instructions are below. A blank copy is in the Appendix. Use a separate form for each cross-defendant.

Top 2 boxes: Follow the instructions in Section 2a, above.

Short Title: Put the last names (or the business names) of the first (perhaps only) plaintiff and the first (perhaps only) defendant, separated by a "vs.", such as "Brown vs. Black" or "Brown vs. Golden Bear Typing Service."

Cross-Complainant: That's you. If the plaintiff misspelled your name on the Complaint, type it correctly here.

Cross-Defendant: Type the names of all possible cross-defendants. Be sure to identify those cross-defendants who are neither adults nor natural persons. Here are some examples:

- "Mitchell Davis, a minor"
- "Axel Construction Company, a corporation"—although corporations cannot be pro per plaintiffs, you certainly can sue one
- "Tweedle Associates, a partnership"
- "John Dee and Frank Dum, partners in Tweedle Associates partnership"
- "Sidney Blue, dba Blue Blood"
- the County of Orange, a public entity"
- "Does 1, 2, 3 and 4." Doe defendants are people you sue but whose identify you are not sure of. See Chapter 4, Section D.7.

Cross-Complaint: Check all applicable boxes as follows:

Apportionment of Fault: Check if a cross-defendant was partially or totally at fault.

Declaratory Relief: Check if a cross-defendant was partially or totally at fault.

LAWSUITS FROM THE DEFENDANT'S POINT OF VIEW

ATTORNEY OR PARTY WITHOUT ATTORNEY (NAME AND ADDRESS):	TELEPHONE:	FOR COURT USE ONLY

ATTORNEY OR PARTY WITHOUT ATTORNEY (NAME AND ADDRESS): TELEPHONE: 619-555-1290   FOR COURT USE ONLY

Amanda Rice
888 Forest Drive
La Quinta, CA 92000

ATTORNEY FOR (NAME): defendant in pro per

Insert name of court, judicial district or branch court, if any, and post office and street address:

Riverside County Municipal Court
Indio District
82-675 Highway 111
P.O. Box BBB
Indio, CA 92202

SHORT TITLE:

Roloquette vs. Rice

CROSS-COMPLAINANT:

Amanda Rice

CROSS-DEFENDANT:

Cecilia Roloquette, Avis Rental Car Co.

[X] DOES 1 TO __5__

CROSS-COMPLAINT—Personal Injury, Property Damage, Wrongful Death

[X] **Apportionment of Fault**   [X] **Declaratory Relief**
[ ] **Indemnification**   [X] **Other** *(specify):* for damages

CASE NUMBER:

69211C

1. This pleading, including exhibits and attachments, consists of the following number of pages: __5__

CROSS-COMPLAINANT *(name):*

Amanda Rice

SAYS AGAINST CROSS-DEFENDANT *(name):*

Cecilia Roloquette

2. [X] The following causes of action are attached and the statements below apply to each: *(In the attachments plaintiff means cross-complainant and defendant means cross-defendant.)*

[X] Motor Vehicle   [ ] Products Liability
[X] General Negligence   [ ] Premises Liability
[ ] Intentional Tort
[ ] Other *(specify):*

3. a. Each cross-complainant named above is a competent adult
   [ ] **Except** cross-complainant *(name):*

   [ ] a corporation qualified to do business in California
   [ ] an unincorporated entity *(describe):*
   [ ] a public entity *(describe):*
   [ ] a minor [ ] an adult
       [ ] for whom a guardian or conservator of the estate or a guardian ad litem has been appointed
       [ ] other *(specify):*
   [ ] other *(specify):*

   b. [ ] Information about additional cross-complainants who are not competent adults is contained in Cross-Complaint—Attachment 3b.   *(Continued)*

Form Approved by the
Judicial Council of California
Effective January 1, 1982
Rule 982.1(14)

CROSS-COMPLAINT— Personal Injury, Property Damage,
Wrongful Death

CCP 425 12

Indemnification: Skip this, as it involves circumstances beyond the scope of this book.

Other: Check if you are seeking money from this cross-defendant for your injuries or property damages. After checking "Other," type "for damages" after the colon.

Case Number: Type in the case number that's on the Summons and the Complaint.

1: Skip this for now. You'll come back to it.

Cross-Complainant (*name*): Type your name.

Says Against Cross-Defendant (*name*): Type the name of this cross-defendant. (Remember, you must complete a different Cross-Complaint for each cross-defendant.)

2: Check this box if you are seeking money damages from the cross-defendant. Then turn to Chapter 5, Section B.1, for a discussion of tort Causes of Action. Select all Causes of Action that apply. You will complete those forms at Item 9, below.

3: Check the first and third boxes if any cross-complainant is suing as a member of a partnership or officer of an unincorporated association. (None of the other listed cross-complainants can sue in pro per.) Type in the name of the partnership or unincorporated association after the first box, and then state whether it is a partnership or association after the third box. If you need more room, check box b and use an attachment sheet.

Page Two

Short Title: Put the last names (or the business names) of the first (perhaps only) plaintiff and the first (perhaps only) defendant, separated by a "vs.", such as "Brown vs. Black" or "Brown vs. Golden Bear Typing Service."

Case Number: This is the number that's on the Summons and the Complaint.

4: If all cross-defendants are natural persons (adults or minors), skip all of Item 4.

4a: If any cross-defendant is a partnership, association, corporation or government entity, complete this section, which contains two identical paragraphs. For each cross-defendant that falls into this category, put its name after "Except cross-defendant (*name*)," and check the applicable sub-box. You'll have to describe an unincorporated entity (simply write "partnership" or "association") and a public entity (such as the "County of Santa Clara"). If more than two cross-defendants fall into this category, continue with Item 4c.

4b: You need not do anything here.

4c: Skip this item unless more than two partnerships, associations, corporations or government entities are cross-defendants. If there are, create an attachment sheet, and enter all the information requested in Item 4a for each additional cross-defendant.

5: Check this box if you are suing the State of California, a county, city, school district or other public entity.

5a: You should have complied with the claims procedure, discussed in Chapter 4. If you have, check this box.

5b: If you haven't complied with the claims procedure you should see a lawyer. There are ways to get around it, but they are complex and reliance on them is dangerous.

6: Skip this. It is beyond the scope of this book.

SHORT TITLE:	CASE NUMBER
Roloquette vs. Rice	69211C

CROSS-COMPLAINT—Personal Injury, Property Damage, Wrongful Death   *Page two*

4. a. Each cross-defendant named above is a natural person
   - [X] **Except** cross-defendant *(name):*   [ ] **Except** cross-defendant *(name):*

   Avis Rental Car Co.

[ ] a business organization, form unknown	[ ] a business organization, form unknown
[X] a corporation	[ ] a corporation
[ ] an unincorporated entity *(describe):*	[ ] an unincorporated entity *(describe):*
[ ] a public entity *(describe):*	[ ] a public entity *(describe):*
[ ] other *(specify):*	[ ] other *(specify):*

   b. The true names and capacities of cross-defendants sued as Does are unknown to cross-complainant.

   c. [ ] Information about additional cross-defendants who are not natural persons is contained in Cross-Complaint—Attachment 4c.

5. [ ] Cross-complainant is required to comply with a claims statute, **and**
   a. [ ] has complied with applicable claims statutes, **or**
   b. [ ] is excused from complying because *(specify):*

6. [ ] _____ **Cause of Action—Indemnification**
   (number)

   a. I am informed and believe that cross-defendants were the agents, employees, co-venturers, partners, or in some manner agents or principals, or both, for each other and were acting within the course and scope of their agency or employment.

   b. The principal action alleges among other things conduct entitling plaintiff to compensatory damages against me. I contend that I am not liable for events and occurrences described in plaintiff's complaint.

   c. If I am found in some manner responsible to plaintiff or to anyone else as a result of the incidents and occurrences described in plaintiff's complaint, my liability would be based solely upon a derivative form of liability not resulting from my conduct, but only from an obligation imposed upon me by law; therefore, I would be entitled to complete indemnity from each cross-defendant.

7. [X] First _____ **Cause of Action—Apportionment of Fault**
   (number)

   I am informed and believe that each cross-defendant was responsible, in whole or in part, for the injuries, if any, suffered by plaintiff. If I am judged liable to plaintiff, each cross-defendant should be required:

   a. to pay a share of plaintiff's judgment which is in proportion to the comparative negligence of that cross-defendant in causing plaintiff's damages and

   b. to reimburse me for any payments I make to plaintiff in excess of my proportional share of all cross-defendants' negligence.

(Continued)   *Page two*

7: If you believe that this cross-defendant was partially or totally at fault and that she be required to pay for the damages the plaintiff has asked for in the original complaint (or if she is the plaintiff and should be declared at fault), check this box and type in "First" in the blank line.

Page Three

Short Title and Case Number: Enter what you typed on Page Two.

8: If you checked Item 7, check this box and type "Second" in the blank line. Then check the "as follows" box and write "cross-defendant was the legal cause of any injuries and damages sustained by plaintiff and therefore should be responsible for paying any sums recovered in this action by plaintiff."

9: If you or your property was injured, check this box and enter "First" in the blank line if you did not check items 7 and 8, or "Third" if you did. After "(*Specify*)," type "Cross-complainant claims damages as alleged in the attached Cause of Action forms."

Now, return to Chapter 5 and fill out the Cause of Action forms you checked off in Item 2, above. Don't worry about using the terms "cross-complainant" and "cross-defendant" on those forms. As the note at Item 2 states, on the forms consider yourself to the plaintiff and the cross-defendant the defendant. Be careful of your numbering the Causes of Action if you completed Item 7, 8 or 9.

10: If you are asking for damages in Item 9, check the first and third boxes and type an amount up to $25,000 following the third box. If you checked Item 7, above, check the fifth box. If you checked Item 8, checked the sixth box. Don't check any of the others.

Now, type your name above the dotted line and sign above the solid line. Also, go back to item 1 and fill in your total number of pages. Remember to count all Cause of Action forms and their attachments.

SHORT TITLE:	CASE NUMBER:
Roloquette vs. Rice	69211C

CROSS-COMPLAINT— Personal Injury, Property Damage, Wrongful Death (Continued)   Page three

8. [X] ___Second___ **Cause of Action—Declaratory Relief**
      (number)

An actual controversy exists between the parties concerning their respective rights and duties because cross-complainant contends and cross-defendant disputes [ ] as specified in Cross-Complaint—Attachment 8 [X] as follows:

Cross-defendant was the legal cause of any injuries and damages sustained by plaintiff and therefore should be responsible for paying any sums recovered in this action by plaintiff.

9. [X] ___Third___ **Cause of Action—(Specify):**
      (number)

Cross-complainant claims damages as alleged in the attached Cause of Action forms.

10. CROSS-COMPLAINANT PRAYS

For judgment for costs of suit; for such relief as is fair, just, and equitable; and for

[X] compensatory damages
   [ ] (Superior Court) according to proof.
   [X] (Municipal and Justice Court) in the amount of $ 11,544

[ ] total and complete indemnity for any judgments rendered against me.

[X] judgment in a proportionate share from each cross-defendant.

[X] a judicial determination that cross-defendants were the legal cause of any injuries and damages sustained by plaintiff and that cross-defendants indemnify me, either completely or partially, for any sums of money which may be recovered against me by plaintiff.

[ ] other (specify):

___Amanda Rice___   _____
      (Type or print name)   (Signature of cross-complainant or attorney)

Rule 982.1(14) (cont'd)   **CROSS-COMPLAINT—Personal Injury, Property Damage, Wrongful Death (Continued)**   Page three

CCP 425.12   C-94

2. Contract Cases

Here are a few examples of when you might bring a Cross-Complaint in a contract case:

- You're a repairperson sued for doing defective work, but the responsibility lies with a supplier or a subcontractor.

- You're a merchant sued for supplying defective merchandise, but the responsibility lies with the manufacturer or the supplier.

- You borrowed money from your uncle and didn't repay, and now he is suing you. In the meantime, your uncle became indebted to you because he's refused to share the proceeds of a winning lottery ticket you bought together.

To prepare a contract Cross-Complaint, you use the contract Complaint form described in Chapter 5.[4] Follow the instructions in Chapter 5, Sections C.1 and C.2. Bear in mind that on the form, you are the plaintiff and the cross-defendants are the defendants. Make only the following minor changes:

[ ] Complaint [ ] Cross-Complaint: Check the Cross-Complaint box.

Case number: Copy the number from the Summons.

6: Skip this item.

9: Check this only if you are seeking something from the cross-defendant other than that he be responsible for any damages the plaintiff recovers from you. If you check any of these boxes, be sure to complete and attach the appropriate Cause of Action forms.

---

[4]The form states at the very bottom in small print that if the form is used as a Cross-Complaint (rather than a Complaint) plaintiff means cross-complainant (you) and defendant means cross-defendant.

10: Check the first box if you are seeking monetary damages for yourself. If you're asking that a new party cross-defendant be responsible for any damages the plaintiff is awarded, check the "other" box and type: "a judicial determination that defendants are legally responsible for any injuries and damages sustained in this action and a complete or partial indemnification by cross-defendants for any sums of money rendered against me in this action."

3. Prepare Summons if Any Cross-Defendant Is a New Party

If you named a new party to the lawsuit in your Cross-Complaint, fill out a Summons as described in Chapter 5, Section E, with the following changes:

- After the word "Summons" at the top of the page, type "On Cross-Complaint."

- Where it says "Notice to Defendant," put a slash (/) after the "to" and write "Cross-" above the slash.

- Where it says "You Are Being Sued by Plaintiff," cross out "Plaintiff" and type "Cross-Complainant."

- Where it says "name, address and telephone number of plaintiff's attorney or plaintiff without an attorney," cross out the word plaintiff and substitute "cross-complainant."

4. Prepare Case Questionnaire

If you're filing a Cross-Complaint, read Chapter 5, Section F, on the Case Questionnaire. Every plaintiff or cross-complainant should use this excellent tool. Even if the plaintiff may abandon his suit, serve him with a Case Questionnaire now. If you don't serve it with the Cross-Complaint, you lose the right to use it forever.

E. File and Serve the Answer and Cross-Complaint

You should now have the following completed forms ready to go:

- Answer

- Cross-Complaint (if applicable)

- Summons, if you are naming new parties in your Cross-Complaint

- Case Questionnaire, if you are filing a Cross-Complaint

 Your Answer and any Cross-Complaint must be filed with the court within 30 days of the date you were served with a Complaint—or by whatever date you were allowed as a formal extension. If you miss this deadline, the plaintiff has the right to obtain a default against you. (See Chapter 9.)

Photocopy two sets of your documents plus one set for each person named as a plaintiff or cross-defendant. If anyone is named in both capacities, you need only one set of the documents

for that person. To serve the plaintiff, follow the instructions for service by mail in Chapter 7, Section F.

After serving the plaintiff—but within your filing deadline—file your original papers with the court, along with an extra copy for yourself and each new cross-defendant. You'll need to pay a filing fee for the Answer—which ranges from $16.50 to $68 per defendant, depending on the court. If you can't afford the fee, see Chapter 5, Section G.

Most courts accept checks, but some won't—phone ahead. The clerk will file the original Answer and Cross-Complaint, and issue the Summons to be served on any new cross-defendant. The Case Questionnaire is not filed with the court. Instructions for filing documents are in Chapter 6.

Have a copy of the issued Summons, Cross-Complaint and Case Questionnaire personally served on each new cross-defendant, following the instructions in Chapter 7.

F. What Happens Next?

By filing your Answer, you've taken steps to ensure that your side of the dispute will be heard in court. And if you filed a Cross-Complaint, you've preserved your right to possibly recover money. If you're in no particular hurry to resolve this headache called a lawsuit, sit back and see what, if anything, the plaintiff does to move it forward.

An amazing number of lawsuits never progress beyond this spot. Perhaps the plaintiff never expected you to fight back. Maybe she lost interest in the suit. Perhaps a change in her personal life now means that this lawsuit has low priority. Whatever the reason, unless you want a resolution, do nothing.

Dismissing the Case if No One Takes Action

If the plaintiff doesn't take steps to bring the case to trial within your court's fast track limit (see Chapter 6, Section E), the court will dismiss the case. If, somehow, the court never becomes aware that the plaintiff has missed the fast track limit, the court must dismiss the case five years after it was filed. A court will do this on its own or in response to a motion you file.

If you don't want to wait five years, you can file a motion after two years asking the court to dismiss the case if the plaintiff hasn't taken any steps to move the case along. Unlike the five-year motion, which is mandatory, this motion is discretionary with the judge and you'll probably need the help of a lawyer.[5]

Of course, you may want the case to move along, especially if you've filed a Cross-Complaint to recover money. You may also want the case to progress because having a lawsuit filed against you is likely to affect your credit rating. No matter what the reason, you can move the case along by conducting discovery, filing motions and bringing the case to trial. All these procedures are described in this book.

Even if you prefer to sit back, the plaintiff may not let you. He may serve you with discovery requests requiring your response. Or, he may file a Motion for Summary Judgment. Although most of the chapters in this book are written from the plaintiff's perspective, notes from the defendant's viewpoint are in each chapter when applicable.

---

[5]See California Rules of Court, Rules 372 and 373.

chapter 9

IF THE DEFENDANT DOESN'T RESPOND

It's a normal part of the process of going to court (or fighting any battle) to anticipate that your opponent will put up a tough fight. After you've gone through all the rigors described in Chapter 4, 5, 6 and 7, therefore, it will probably be a shock in the defendant doesn't put up a fight. This chapter describes what happens if the defendant fails to file a response within 30 days of service of process, or whatever date you agreed to extend the time to answer.

Defendant Equals Cross-Defendant

If you were the defendant in the original case, and filed a Cross-Complaint against the plaintiff (who is now the cross-defendant) in a case you filed, this chapter applies to you. Just substitute the word "cross-defendant" for the word "defendant" and the word "cross-complainant" for the word "plaintiff."

Sometimes a defendant fails to answer because she can't afford a lawyer and doesn't dare go to court alone. If she has a defense she could have raised, this is a sad commentary on our legal system. The system that supposedly provides everyone a "day in court" too often provides no time in court for the person who can't spare two weeks wages for a lawyer's retainer.

More commonly, however, the defendant doesn't answer because she knows she owes you the money, has no defense and figures that fighting the case will do little good. This is probably a mistake on her part. If she came to court, she could ask the judge to let her pay off the the money she owes on a monthly payment plan. Or could object if you asked for more damages than you were entitled to. But that is the defendant's problem.

A. Taking the Defendant's Default

Once the 30-day response deadline has passed, you can go to the court and ask that judgment be entered for you by the process of "taking the defendant's default." This is a somewhat picky process, but it certainly can be done without a lawyer.

Taking a default involves two steps:

1. You ask the clerk to "enter the default" of the defendant. This means that the clerk writes in the file that the defendant did not file a response to your Complaint on time. Once the default is entered, the defendant can't file a response to your lawsuit. For example, if you had the court clerk enter the defendant's default on April 16, if the defendant tries to file an Answer on April 17, the clerk won't accept it.

2. In most cases, you will have to appear before a judge and ask him to "enter judgment by default."

1. Step One—Entering the Default

 To have the clerk enter the defendant's default, you must complete a two-page, fill-in-the-blanks form.

a. Complete Request for Entry of Default

A sample completed Request for Entry of Default form is below; instructions for completion follow. A blank copy is in the Appendix.

Attorney or Party Without Attorney (*Name and Address*): Copy this from the Complaint.

Insert name of court and name of judicial district and branch court, if any: Copy this from the Complaint.

Plaintiff: Copy this from the Complaint.

Defendant: Copy this from the Complaint.

Request for: You'll check two boxes here.

Entry of Judgment: Check this box, regardless of the type of case involved.

Clerk's Judgment: Check this box if you have a contract case. The clerk can usually enter the judgment for you without you having to appear before a judge. Once you file this form, the clerk should give you a judgment for the amount demanded in your Complaint.[1]

Court Judgment: Check this box if you have a tort or other non-contract case. The judge must personally grant the judgment, which in pro per cases usually means you must appear before the judge.

Case Number: Copy this from the Complaint.

1a: Type the date on which the Complaint was filed with the clerk. The clerk stamped the date in the upper right-hand corner of the Complaint when you filed it.

1b: Type the names of all plaintiffs.

---

[1]Code of Civil Procedure § 585(a).

1c: Check the box and type the names of all named (not Doe) defendants who have missed the 30-day deadline.

1d: If your case is a tort case or other non-contract case, check this box. In contract cases, leave it blank.

1e: If your case is a contract case, check this box and the (2) box below. In tort and other non-contract cases, leave it blank. Leave boxes (1) and (3) blank.

2: If your case is a tort case or other non-contract case, skip ahead to Item 3. If your case is a contract case, read on.

2a: Turn to the prayer, Item 10, of your Complaint. In the first column, enter the dollar amount you requested in your Complaint next to "damages." If the defendant has paid any money since you filed the lawsuit (miracles do happen!), put the amount of the payment in the second column. Enter the balance in the third column.

2b: Put "----" in each of these columns.

2c: Enter the amount of interest to which you are entitled. This must be calculated from the date the contract was broken—not the date it was signed. If the defendant made any payments, you must take this into account when calculating interesting. If your contract provides an interest rate, use that rate unless it violates the usury law. (See Chapter 1, Section D.2.c.1) If the contract is silent (or violates the usury law), use the rate of 10% simple interest per year. List any credits (unlikely) in column two. Enter the balance in the third column.

2d: Turn to Item 5 on the second page of this document and complete it. Then, enter the total costs (item 5e) in the first column. List any credits (again, unlikely), and enter the balance in the third column.

2e: Put "----" in each of these columns unless you consulted—and paid—an attorney to assist you in this lawsuit.

2f: Total up each of the three columns.

2g: Skip this. It applies to eviction cases.

Date and Signature: Fill in the date, type your name above the dotted line and sign above the solid line to the right.

Page Two

Short Title: Copy this from the Complaint.

Case Number: Copy this from the Complaint.

3: Check the first box and all three "is not" boxes unless:

3a: Check the "is" box if you are a businessperson who is suing on a contract that calls for installment payments for goods or services from a retail buyer. If you are, the clerk can only enter the default; you will have to present your papers to a judge to obtain the judgment.

3b: Check the "is" box if you are businessperson who is suing on a conditional sales contract concerning a motor vehicle—where legal ownership of the vehicle remains with the seller until the buyer pays off the full price on time payments. If you are, the clerk can only enter the default; you will have to present your papers to a judge to obtain the judgment.

3c: Check the "is" box if you are businessperson suing for goods, services, loans or extensions of credit intended primarily for personal, family or household use. If you are, the clerk can only enter the default; you will have to present your papers to a judge to obtain the judgment.

4: Before you file this form with the clerk, you must mail a copy of it to the defendant or his lawyer, by first class mail. If you have no address for the defendant or his lawyer, check box a. Otherwise, check box b, and below the (2), type the defendant's address. Be sure to use as exact or current an address as you can. After you mail the form, enter the date in next to (1).

Date and Signature: Fill in the date, type your name above the dotted line and sign above the solid line on the right.

5: Here you list your filing fees and process server's fees, which may be added to the judgment.

5a: Fill in the amount you paid for court filing fees.

5b: Fill in any amounts you paid process servers (including a sheriff or marshal) for serving your court papers.

5c-d: Leave these blank. Ordinarily, you cannot recover what you paid for photocopies, postage paper or other costs associated with your lawsuit.

5e: Add up your listed costs and fill in the total.

5f: Leave this blank.

ATTORNEY OR PARTY WITHOUT ATTORNEY *(Name and Address)*:	TELEPHONE NO.:	FOR COURT USE ONLY
Donna Goodwill 9888 North Broadway Oakland, CA 94610	(510) 555-2001	

ATTORNEY FOR *(Name)*:

Insert name of court and name of judicial district and branch court, if any:

Alameda County Mnuicipal Court, Oakland-Piedmont-Emeryville Judicial District

PLAINTIFF:

Donna Goodwill

DEFENDANT:

Allen Jones

REQUEST FOR (Application)	[X] ENTRY OF DEFAULT [X] CLERK'S JUDGMENT [ ] COURT JUDGMENT	CASE NUMBER: 0051717

1. TO THE CLERK: On the complaint or cross-complaint filed
   a. On *(date)*: March 21, 1992
   b. By *(name)*: Donna Goodwill
   c. [X] Enter default of defendant *(names)*: Allen Jones

   d. [ ] I request a court judgment under CCP 585(b), (c), 989, etc. *(Testimony required. Apply to the clerk for a hearing date, unless the court will enter a judgment on an affidavit under CCP 585(d).)*
   e. [X] Enter clerk's judgment
      (1) [ ] For restitution of the premises only and issue a writ of execution on the judgment. CCP 1174(c) does not apply. (CCP 1169) [ ] Include in the judgment all tenants, subtenants, named claimants, and other occupants of the premises. The Prejudgment Claim of Right to Possession was served in compliance with CCP 415.46.
      (2) [X] Under CCP 585(a). *(Complete the declaration under CCP 585.5 on the reverse (item 3).)*
      (3) [ ] For default previously entered on *(date)*:

2. **Judgment to be entered**

	Amount	Credits Acknowledged	Balance
a. Demand of complaint	$ 9,800	$ -0-	$ 9,800
b. Statement of damages (CCP 425.11) *(superior court only)**			
(1) Special	$ ---	$ ---	$ ---
(2) General	$ ---	$ ---	$ ---
c. Interest	$ 620	$ -0-	$ 620
d. Costs *(see reverse)*	$ 91	$ -0-	$ 91
e. Attorney fees	$ ---	$ ---	$ ---
f. TOTALS	$ 10,511	$ -0-	$ 10,511

   g. **Daily damages** were demanded in complaint at the rate of: $ _____ per day beginning *(date)*:

Date: April 11, 1992

.....Donna Goodwill.....................   ▶
(TYPE OR PRINT NAME)   (SIGNATURE OF PLAINTIFF OR ATTORNEY FOR PLAINTIFF)

* Personal injury or wrongful death actions only.

FOR COURT USE ONLY	(1) [ ] Default entered as requested on *(date)*: (2) [ ] Default NOT entered as requested *(state reason)*: By: _____

(Continued on reverse)

Form Adopted by the Judicial Council of California 982(a)(6) [Rev. September 30, 1991*] — **REQUEST FOR ENTRY OF DEFAULT** (Application to Enter Default) — Code of Civil Procedure, §§ 585-587, 1169 *See note on reverse.

SHORT TITLE:

— Goodwill vs. Jones

CASE NUMBER:

0051717

3. ☒ **DECLARATION UNDER CCP 585.5** *(Required for clerk's judgment under CCP 585(a))*   This action
   a. ☐ is ☒ is not   on a contract or installment sale for goods or services subject to CC 1801, etc. (Unruh Act).
   b. ☐ is ☒ is not   on a conditional sales contract subject to CC 2981, etc. (Rees-Levering Motor Vehicle Sales and Finance Act).
   c. ☐ is ☒ is not   on an obligation for goods, services, loans, or extensions of credit subject to CCP 395(b).

4. **DECLARATION OF MAILING (CCP 587)**   A copy of this Request for Entry of Default was
   a. ☐ **not mailed** to the following defendants whose addresses are **unknown** to plaintiff or plaintiff's attorney *(names)*:

   b. ☒ **mailed** first-class, postage prepaid, in a sealed envelope addressed to each defendant's attorney of record or, if none, to
      each defendant's last known address as follows:
      (1) Mailed on *(date)*: April 11, 1992   (2) To *(specify names and addresses shown on the envelopes)*:

                                                          Allen Jones
                                                          89 Monteca Road
                                                          Oakland, CA 94612

I declare under penalty of perjury under the laws of the State of California that the foregoing items 3 and 4 are true and correct.
Date: April 11, 1992

... Donna Goodwill ....   ▶
(TYPE OR PRINT NAME)   _____
                                                          (SIGNATURE OF DECLARANT)

5. **MEMORANDUM OF COSTS** *(Required if judgment requested)*   **Costs and Disbursements** are as follows (CCP 1033.5):
   a. Clerk's filing fees .... $ 70
   b. Process server's fees .... $ 20
   c. Other *(specify)*: .... $
   d. .... $.
   e. **TOTAL** .... $ 91
   f. ☐ Costs and disbursements are waived.

   I am the attorney, agent, or party who claims these costs. To the best of my knowledge and belief this memorandum of costs
is correct and these costs were necessarily incurred in this case.

   I declare under penalty of perjury under the laws of the State of California that the foregoing is true and correct.
Date: April 11, 1992

.... Donna Goodwill ....   ▶
(TYPE OR PRINT NAME)   _____
                                                          (SIGNATURE OF DECLARANT)

6. ☒ **DECLARATION OF NONMILITARY STATUS**   *(Required for a judgment)*   No defendant named in item 1c of the application
      is in the military service so as to be entitled to the benefits of the Soldiers' and Sailors' Civil Relief Act of 1940 (50 U.S.C.
      Appen. § 501 et seq.).

   I declare under penalty of perjury under the laws of the State of California that the foregoing is true and correct.
Date: April 11, 1992

.... Donna Goodwill ....   ▶
(TYPE OR PRINT NAME)   _____
                                                          (SIGNATURE OF DECLARANT)

**NOTE:* Continued use of form 982(a)(6) (Rev. July 1, 1988) is authorized until June 30, 1992, *except* in unlawful detainer proceedings.

982(a)(6) [Rev. September 30, 1991*]   **REQUEST FOR ENTRY OF DEFAULT**   Page two
                                                       (Application to Enter Default)

Date and Signature: Fill in the date, type your name above the dotted line and sign above the solid line on the right.

6: Here, you or someone with personal knowledge must state that the defendant is not on active military service. If you know the defendant and have never had any indication that he is an active member of the military, check the box. Then date and sign this declaration yourself. If you don't know, ask around. Call the defendant and ask him. Or, ask your process server if he knows. Or pay a visit to one of his neighbors. In any case, the clerk will not enter a default judgment unless this declaration is signed.

If you only want a default—not the actual judgment—at this time, you don't have to complete this section. If the clerk disagrees, ask her to check the Civil Procedures Manual of The Association of Municipal Court Clerks of California, Section 4.50, page 3.

If the defendant is on active military duty and has not responded to your Complaint, the court must appoint an attorney to represent the defendant before the case can proceed.

b. Serve and File Documents

If your case is a contract case, skip ahead to Section 2.

If your case is a tort or other non-contract case, make one copy of the Request for Entry of Default for each defendant, plus an extra copy for your file. Mail a copy of the completed form to each defendant—you can send these yourself. Then gather the following for filing with the clerk:

- the original and one copy of the completed Request for Entry of Default

- the original and one copy of the signed Proof of Service for the Complaint, which may be on the Summons, or a professional process server may have given you a separate form

- the original and one copy of the Summons

- a large self-addressed envelope with sufficient postage for the clerk to return your copies to you

- a letter asking that the default be entered and that endorsed copies of the Request for Entry of Default, Proof of Service and Summons be returned to you

You may want to file the papers in person, so the defendant doesn't beat you to the court house and file his Answer before the default papers arrive in the mail. Also, by filing in person, the clerk can tell you if there are any errors on your Request for Entry of Default and you can fix them right there. If you file in person, you don't need the letter.

2. Step Two—Applying for a Judgment

Read Section a if you have a contract case. Otherwise, read Section b.

a. Contract Cases

As mentioned earlier, in contract cases you can often get your judgment from the court clerk—that is, you don't have to appear before a judge. But in some cases—for example, if the original contract is not available—the clerk won't give you a judgment.

To get the judgment from the clerk, you may have to complete a Judgment form. Call the court clerk's office and ask if the clerk prepares a default judgment on a contract case or if you are expected to do so. You may have to ask to speak to the default clerk.

If you must prepare the Judgment, ask the clerk if the court has a pre-printed form you're required to use. If so, obtain a copy. Otherwise, type up the Judgment on pleading paper—the funny looking legal paper with numbers down the left hand side. A sample completed form is below.

Once you've prepared the Default Judgment, mail a copy of the Request for Entry of Default completed in Step 1 to the defendant and send the following to the clerk:

• the original and one copy of the Request for Entry of Default

• the original and a copy of the Default Judgment, if you were expected to prepare it

• the original of any written contract document, such as a promissory note, work order or signed delivery receipt—the clerk will return it to you

• the original and one copy of the Proof of Service for the Complaint (it may be on the Summons, or a professional process server may have given you a separate form)

• the original and one copy of the Summons

• a large self-addressed envelope with sufficient postage for the clerk to return your copies to you; and

• a letter asking that the default be entered, that a judgment be issued and that endorsed copies of all documents be returned to you

You may want to file the papers in person, so the defendant doesn't beat you to the court house and file his Answer before the default papers arrive in the mail. Also, by filing in person, the clerk can tell you if there are any errors on

your Request for Entry of Default and you can fix them right there. If you file in person, you don't need the letter.

Municipal Court Default Clerks

The Municipal Court default clerk has a very picky job that includes the exercise of a lot of power. In most contract cases, she decides whether or not to issue a judgment if the defendant defaults. Some default clerks delight in finding errors and rejecting judgment requests. Others are happy to help you through the process.

If the default clerk rejects your judgment form, be sure to find out what you need to change. If you don't understand what the clerk is saying, ask to speak to the supervisor. It is usually best to acknowledge your lack of experience and hope that someone will give you a little guidance. Clerks are not allowed to give legal advice, so if you get too pushy, they may simply tell you that your papers are rejected and if you want clarification, see a lawyer.

Sample Default Judgment by Clerk

1	Sanford DeYoung
	1200 Clever Lane
2	Bakersfield, CA 93444
	805-555-8989
3	
	Plaintiff In Pro Per
4	

1 Sanford DeYoung
   1200 Clever Lane
2 Bakersfield, CA 93444
   805-555-8989
3
   Plaintiff In Pro Per
4

5

6

7

8   MUNICIPAL COURT OF CALIFORNIA

9   COUNTY OF SAN BERNANDINO

10.

11 SANFORD DEYOUNG,   )   Case No. MC-18733
)
12 Plaintiff,   )   DEFAULT JUDGMENT
)   BY CLERK
13 vs.   )
)
14 MARGARET WILLIAMS,   )
)
15 Defendant._____)

16   Defendant, Margaret Williams, having had her default entered herein and

17 application for judgment by the clerk having been made by Plaintiff,

18

19   It is hereby adjudged that Plaintiff, Sanford DeYoung, recover from

20 Defendant, Margaret Williams, the sum of $17,000 in damages, $3,400 in interest

21 thereon and $100 in legal costs.

22

23 Judgment entered on _____ (Date).

24

25 Clerk

26 by _____

27

28

b. Tort and Other Cases

Once the court clerk returns your Request for Entry of Default—with the notation at the bottom that the default has been entered—you can proceed to obtain the judgment. You have two choices. First, you can attempt to proceed by mail without appearing before a judge. Second, you can ask the clerk to schedule a hearing date for you to appear (without the defendant) before a judge. Although the second option may require several hours of your time, it's the better approach for a pro per. The judge will probably want to ask you questions; it's much easier and faster if you're there in person.

1. Proceeding Without a Court Appearance

If you choose not to appear before a judge, you must present written evidence to the judge in order for her to issue a judgment in your favor.[2] By this method, you present the evidence in a written declaration and the judge reads it in her office. The major problem is that you're not there for the judge to ask you clarifying questions. If she needs more information, she must mail you her request and wait for your response. Many judges won't make an award for pain and suffering unless you physically appear in court.

Although I don't recommend this approach, I realize that it may be the only practical way for some people to request a judgment. Thus, a sample Declaration is shown below. Type it on pleading (numbered) paper.

Once you complete the Declaration, you're almost ready to apply for the Judgment. But to get the actual Judgment, you may have to prepare a Judgment form. Call the court clerk's of-

fice and ask if the court has a pre-printed form for a Default Judgment on a non-contract case. If the court has a form, get a copy and complete it. Otherwise, type up the Judgment on pleading paper. A sample completed form is below.

Mail the original and one copy of your Declaration with its attachments, along with the original and one copy of the Judgment, to the clerk's office. Enclose a large self-addressed envelope with sufficient postage on it for the copies to be returned to you. And enclose a letter asking that the papers be presented to a judge for review. Then sit back and wait for the judge's decision.

2. Appearing Before a Judge

Once the clerk returns your Request for Entry of Default, call the clerk and ask for a court date in which you can appear before a judge to "prove up"—submit evidence to justify your judgment—your default. You'll be given the date and time on which you must show up at a particular courtroom—perhaps as soon as a week. In some busy counties, however, it may take months.

Before your court date arrives, assemble your written evidence (medical bills, repair bills, doctors' reports and the like) and prepare a brief oral explanation of your case. If you're nervous about going to court, ask the clerk when the judge might be hearing other default cases so you can go and watch in advance of your case.

---

[2]This is authorized by Code of Civil Procedure § 585(d).

Sample Declaration

```
 1   JOSEPH BRANDT
     1800 55th Ave
 2   San Diego, CA 92111
     (619) 555-9900
 3
     Plaintiff in Pro Per
 4

 5

 6

 7

 8                    MUNICIPAL COURT OF CALIFORNIA

 9                    SAN DIEGO JUDICIAL DISTRICT

10

11   JOSEPH BRANDT,              )        CASE NO. 91-44444
                                 )
12   Plaintiff,                  )
                                 )        DECLARATION PURSUANT
13   vs.                         )        TO C.C.P. § 585(d)
                                 )
14   CHRISTINA FLORES,           )
                                 )
15   Defendant. _____)

16

17   Plaintiff, Joseph Brandt, declares as follows:

18      On April 19, 19__, I was driving west on Flower Street in the city of San

19   Diego when the defendant Flores entered Flower Street from Sunnyside Avenue.

20   She ran a stop sign and crashed into the right side of my car. There were no

21   signals or traffic lights controlling my direction of traffic. Ms. Flores was

22   careless and negligent in the way she operated her car.

23      As a result of this accident, I have sustained the following injuries

24   and damages:

25      1. Damage to my car                          $2,567
           (see attached repair bill from ABC Garage)
26

27      2. Car rental while my car was inoperative    $389
           (see attached bill from DEF Rentals)
28
```

1   3. Hospital bills $1,019
    (see attached bills from Doctors' Hospital)

2

3   4. Physician bills $843
    (see attached bills from Dean Dimes, M.D.)

4   5. Lost wages $2,876
    (see payroll statement from Lockheed Corp.)

5

6   6. Pain and suffering $15,000

7   For four days after the accident, I was confined to my bed on the advice of

8   my doctor. I had a badly sprained back and left leg. I was off work and in

9   considerable pain for two weeks; I then returned to work with some difficulty.

10 For two additional months, I continued to have pain and some sleeplessness;

11 then the symptoms gradually subsided.

12   I declare under penalty of perjury under the laws of the state of California

13 that the foregoing is true and correct.

14

15 Signed on June 3, 19__.

16

17

18 _____
    Joseph Brandt

19

20

21

22

23

24

25

26

27

28

Sample Default Judgment by Court

```
 1   JOSEPH BRANDT
     1800 55th Ave
 2   San Diego, CA 92111
     (619) 555-9900
 3
     Plaintiff in Pro Per
 4

 5

 6

 7

 8                    MUNICIPAL COURT OF CALIFORNIA

 9                    SAN DIEGO JUDICIAL DISTRICT

10

11   JOSEPH BRANDT,              )         CASE NO. 91-44444
                                 )
12   Plaintiff,                  )
                                 )         DEFAULT JUDGMENT
13   vs.                         )         BY COURT
                                 )
14   CHRISTINA FLORES,           )
                                 )
15   Defendant._____)

16

17      Defendant, Christina Flores, having had her default entered herein and

18   application for judgment by the court having been made by Plaintiff,

19      It is hereby adjudged that Plaintiff, Joseph Brandt, recover from Defendant,

20   Christina Flores, the sum of $22,591 in damages, $2,269 in interest thereon and

21   $140 in legal costs.

22

23   Judgment entered on _____ (Date).

24

25   by _____
        Judge of the Municipal Court
26

27

28
```

On the day of your hearing, get to the courtroom early. If the judge is already on the bench, quietly take a seat. Assuming the judge is not on the bench yet, check in with the clerk who will be sitting at a table near the front of the courtroom. When your case is called, go forward to the table in front of the judge. Remember to call the judge "your honor" and state that you wish to "prove up" your default.

The judge may ask you questions or listen to your explanation—or may do both. If the judge just tells you to proceed, you should tell the important facts of your case in a form similar to the declaration at the beginning of this section.

Example: Elliot sued the defendant for failure to pay for photographic services Elliot performed. At the default hearing, the judge says "proceed." Elliot replies, "On April 11, the defendant called me at my studio and asked what I would charge to photograph his wedding and produce five albums of 50 photos. I told him the price was $6,500. He hired me. I photographed his wedding and supplied the five albums on May 20. I also gave him a bill for $6,479 on that day. He has not paid me anything."

At the end of your presentation, the judge will probably announce the amount of the judgment awarded to you. The clerk will prepare the judgment for you or give you instructions on how to prepare one yourself, for the judge to sign. If it is your job to prepare the judgment, ask the court for a pre-printed form. Otherwise, use the example in Section 2.b.1, above.

Setting Aside a Judgment

Under some circumstances, a defendant can show up after a default judgment has been entered and ask the court to "set it aside." If the court allows it, the defendant can then file an Answer and contest the case. If the defendant tries to have his default set aside, he has a maximum of six months after its entry to file an application to do so, if he knew about the lawsuit. In addition, he has up to two years to set aside a default judgment if he can prove that he never knew about the case.[3]

To protect yourself from this possibility, after you obtain the judgment, notify the defendant by certified letter, return receipt requested, that judgment has been entered. This prevents him from claiming years later that he never knew about the lawsuit. You may also want to hold off trying to collect on your judgment until six months has expired.

B. Collecting Your Judgment

Once you have a judgment, you must take steps to get paid. Re-read Chapter 2, Section B. First, write to the defendant and send him a copy of the Judgment. Ask him to either pay you immediately or contact you to make arrangements. If he does neither, consult *Collect Your Court Judgment*, by Scott, Elias and Goldoftas (Nolo Press). That book outlines all the steps you need to collect your judgment. If the defendant doesn't pay up, keep in mind that judgments last for ten years and can be renewed for successive ten-year periods.

---

[3]For instance, if you served the complaint using substitute service, it is possible that the defendant never actually learned of your lawsuit.

DISCOVERY

"Discovery" refers to the legal procedures that allow each party to obtain documents, information and a list of expected witnesses from the other. The theory behind discovery is that if each side can find out what cards the other is holding, the parties are more likely to settle before trial. Unfortunately, however, discovery is often used to harass and intimidate the other side or to delay the trial to the point that one party becomes so disgusted, he settles for less than he is entitled to.

Under California law, any information is discoverable if it is relevant to the subject matter of the lawsuit, and it is either admissible as evidence (see Chapter 13, Section A) or reasonably calculated to lead to the discovery of admissible evidence. Also, through discovery you can obtain information such as the monetary limit of any insurance policy the other side has which is related to the lawsuit.

A. Types of Discovery

The discovery methods most often used in Municipal Court are:

Deposition. A proceeding in which a witness or party is asked to answer questions orally under oath at a location away from the court. The questions are asked by the lawyer for each side, or if there is no lawyer, by the party herself. A court reporter is present and prepares a written transcript of the entire proceeding.

Interrogatories. Written questions sent by one party to the other to be be answered in writing under oath.

Request for production of documents or things. A demand from one party to the other to hand over certain defined documents or items for inspecting and copying.

Subpoena duces tecum. An order telling a witness (who is not a plaintiff or defendant) to bring certain documents to a deposition. This procedure can also be used to get documents to a trial.

Requests for admissions. A request from one party to the other to admit or deny certain allegations in the lawsuit.

Other discovery methods used less frequently in Municipal Court include:

Request for physical examination. A request by one party that the other party be examined by a doctor if his health is an issue.

Witness list. A request by one party to the other to turn over the list of witnesses that party plans to use at trial.

B. Discovery Rules and Limits

As noted above, any information admissible as evidence or likely to lead to admissible evidence can be obtained through discovery. Discovery, however, is not an endless fishing expedition. Be sure to read the discovery rules before attending or scheduling a deposition, sending or answering interrogatories, or requesting or responding to admissions.[1]

---

[1]Code of Civil Procedure (C.C.P.) §§ 2025 through 2027 cover depositions; the rules for interrogatories are found in C.C.P. § 2030 and those for requests for admissions are in C.C.P. § 2033. The C.C.P. is available in all law libraries and many large public libraries. It can also be purchased through Nolo Press. (See back of this book.)

Complying With Discovery Rules

As you read the discovery rules, remember they are designed for lawsuits that may involve millions of dollars in the Superior Court. Your suit is for less than $25,000 in the Municipal Court, and so some of the rules may seem unnecessarily detailed. In most cases, if you make a good faith effort to comply with the rules and admit that you are a novice, a judge who may be later called on to review a discovery question will be sympathetic.

A judge, however, may find that rather than searching for admissible evidence, you have unreasonably failed to follow discovery rules or have attempted to use discovery to harass or intimidate your opponent. In that event, she can fine you (perhaps thousands of dollars), order other penalties like prohibiting you from introducing certain evidence or dismiss your lawsuit.

One of the limits on discovery is that it must be completed 30 days before the date of the trial.[2] The biggest limitation on discovery in Municipal Court (this doesn't apply in Superior Court) is the number of questions you can ask the other side. You are limited to a total of 35 questions by way of written interrogatories, requests for production of documents or things, and requests for admissions.[3] If an item is divided into subparts, each inquiry counts as one and your opponent is justified in not answering more than 35 subparts.

For example, if you use one sentence to ask the other party to produce three documents, that counts as three requests. Or, if by way of written interrogatories, the defendant asks you to list, with respect to each place you lived in past 20 years, the address, the names of all persons with whom you resided, the date you moved in and the date you moved out, that's four requests. And if you ask the defendant to admit that he was driving 40 miles an hour and ran a stop light, that's two requests for admissions.

In addition to the 35 requests, each party can take the deposition of one person per case. If you want to make more requests by way of interrogatories, requests for admissions or requests to produce documents or things, or you want to conduct more than one deposition, you will have to formally file a motion before a judge. Keep in mind that judges rarely grant additional discovery, especially in small cases where the expense of lawyers and a court reporter can easily mount into thousands of dollars.

In the next two sections, discovery is discussed from two viewpoints:

- doing discovery to assist your case
- responding to discovery requests made by the other party

---

[2]Code of Civil Procedure § 2024.

[3]See Code of Civil Procedure § 94.

C. Doing Your Own Discovery

My approach throughout this book is to guide you to a quick and simple resolution of your lawsuit. Discovery cuts against that—it complicates and slows down the pace of the litigation. It often gives rise to side battles over the appropriateness of certain questions and whether penalties should be imposed for foot dragging, all of which can require frequent trips to the court in order to argue over esoteric points of discovery law. Lawyers love it. You'll hate it.

Thus, my general advice is to avoid doing your own discovery if possible. If you are the plaintiff (or a cross-complainant), you should have a basic outline of the defendant's defense from his answers to your Case Questionnaire and discovery shouldn't be necessary. What to do if he hasn't answered the Case Questionnaire is covered in Section F, below.

There are, however, a few situations in which conducting limited discovery may be worth your while. If you have no idea what the other party's version of the dispute is, you may want to ask a few interrogatories. This situation may be especially helpful if you are a defendant in a case where the plaintiff did not use a Case Questionnaire.

Also, if your opponent is showing signs of planning to lie about your dispute, a skillfully phrased question during discovery can help you determine which lie she will tell at the trial. This will give you an opportunity to prepare to disprove it.

Example: The defendant states at in her answer to interrogatories that she first saw the plaintiff's car approaching from her left a few seconds before the accident. Several months later, at the trial, she testifies that she never lost sight of the plaintiff after she first saw him approaching from several miles away. The plaintiff might respond to this discrepancy at the trial by asking "were you telling the truth when you answered the interrogatories or are you telling the truth now?"

You can conduct discovery by way of written interrogatories—which are much cheaper than a deposition—but they tend to be less effective. The other side won't answer spontaneously. Because the answers are given in writing, the party answering them has ample time to avoid the question or concoct an answer not damaging to her position.

The sections that follow outline how discovery techniques work.

1. Written Interrogatories

Written interrogatories are the easiest form of discovery for a pro per to undertake. The Appendix contains pre-printed form interrogatories. If you want to serve the other party with interrogatories, make a few photocopies of the form. Review it carefully, and make a list of the questions you want to ask. In a tort case you probably want to ask to many of the questions in Sections 104 to 120.

In a contract case focus on the Section 150 questions. You can add questions if something you want to ask isn't on the form, but remember that along with requests for admissions and requests for production of documents and things, you can't exceed 35 questions.

Once you know what questions you want to ask, fill out the form. Copy the information requested at the top off the Complaint. Check the boxes for the questions you want answered and add any of your own questions—type them onto a piece of pleading (numbered) paper. Then have a friend serve the interrogatories by mail. (See Chapter 7, Section E.)

You don't file the interrogatories with the court unless the other side doesn't respond. That scenario is covered in Section F, below.

2. Request for Production of Documents or Things

If the other side has a document, account, letter, photograph or other tangible item she won't show you voluntarily, you can use discovery to request that it be produced. When the other side gets your request, she must produce the items for you to inspect, copy or photograph. You can also request entry onto land or into a house or building in order to inspect, measure or take a sample.

> **Example:** Wally fell on a slippery painted surface in Grace's store. Wally wants an engineer to conduct some tests to determine just how slippery the surface is. Grace is not being helpful to arrange a time. Wally prepares and sends Grace a Request for Inspection, specifying when he will be there with his engineer.

One good overall discovery strategy is to send your interrogatories, get them back, and then figure out what documents or items you need. The interrogatories can help you narrow the scope and guide you toward objects that go to the very heart of the matter.

For example, if you were rear-ended on the freeway by someone who appeared to have bad

brakes—the police report noted that his brake pedal went to the floor without resistance—you might ask in an interrogatory when and where he last had his brakes inspected by a car repairperson. Then ask him to produce a copy of the work order or invoice for that inspection.

In a dispute with a store owner over a defective product, ask the store to produce the form used to order the item from the manufacturer, the invoice received from the shipper and any notices—including recall or defect notices—received about the item.

The courts have not produced a required form for a production request. Below is a sample you can use. Prepare it on pleading paper.

 Remember that the requests for production, along with interrogatories and requests for admissions, can't exceed 35 in total.

Subpoena Duces Tecum

If you want to obtain documents that are in the custody or control of someone who is not a party to the lawsuit, you must serve that person with a subpoena duces tecum. Using a subpoena duces tecum can be complicated, so I recommend that you hire a paralegal to do the paperwork. Paralegal services can be found in the yellow pages under "Attorneys' Service Bureaus" or "Typing Services." Call and ask if they prepare and serve subpoenas duces tecum.

Sample Request For Production of Documents and Items

```
 1   ALICE MCMANN
     98 Morton Road
 2   Sunnyvale, CA 95000
     408-555-8989
 3
     Defendant In Pro Per
 4

 5

 6

 7

 8                    MUNICIPAL COURT OF CALIFORNIA

 9                      COUNTY OF SANTA CLARA

10

11   CYNTHIA WONG and          )          Case No. SC-90909
     HAROLD WONG,               )
12                             )
     Plaintiffs,                )          REQUEST FOR PRODUCTION
13                             )          OF DOCUMENTS AND OTHER
     vs.                        )          ITEMS
14                             )
     ALICE MCMANN,              )
15                             )
     Defendant._____ )
16
         Pursuant to Code of Civil Procedure § 2031, defendant, Alice McMann, hereby
17
     requests that plaintiffs produce for inspection and copying as follows:
18
     Time: 10:00 a.m.
19
     Date: September 21, 19__
20
     Place: Copy Cat Office, 990 Silver Street, Sunnyvale, California
21
     Documents: (1) work order for repair of 1989 Volkswagen automobile, license
22
     2MUN132 at German Garage June 3, 19__; and (2) cancelled check showing payment
23
     for that work order.
24

25
     _____
26   Alice McMann

27

28
```

3. Request for Admissions

A Request for Admissions is simple enough for a pro per to undertake, but normally in a small case, interrogatories are easier and more practical. The Appendix contains a pre-printed Request for Admissions form. If you want to send one to the other party, photocopy the form. Write down on a piece of paper the requests you want to make. Here are some examples:

Item A:

- "The windshield wipers on your automobile were not in use at the time of your collision with plaintiff's automobile."

- "You did not inspect the contents of the carton containing the A-2550 computer before you removed it from defendant's store."

- "Between 8 a.m. and noon on April, 19__, John Guillory was the employee in charge of sweeping the produce section of your store."

- "You stated on March 19, 19__ words to the effect that you would be able to repay the loan from plaintiff loan within six months."

Requests for Admissions can also help you establish that certain issues have been eliminated from the case because everyone agrees what the facts are. If a party refuses to admit that an issue no longer exists and you prove it in court, a judge can order the other party to pay your costs of proving the non-issue if you so ask.

Item B:

Attach a copy of any important document you want the defendant to admit is genuine.

Remember that along with interrogatories and requests for production of documents and things, you can't exceed 35 requests.

4. Depositions

In a deposition, you pick the date, time and location of the proceeding. You also must hire a court reporter for several hundred dollars to take down the proceeding. Pro pers can schedule the deposition to take place at the court reporter's office. You then must complete a form ("Notice of Deposition" if you're deposing a party; "Subpoena" if you're deposing a witness) and serve it on the person to be deposed. Before the deposition begins, you should prepare a list of questions you will ask.

I don't recommend that you try to take a deposition. While filling out and serving the form, arranging the deposition and preparing the questions are not difficult, conducting a deposition is. It takes lawyers many years to develop the skills to conduct a successful deposition. Many never get good at it.

In addition, an obstructive opposing lawyer will frequently try to turn your deposition into a fiasco. No referee is present to maintain order or insist upon fair conduct. The court reporter simply records what happens. If you're treated unfairly, your only remedy is to file a motion in court and ask the judge to read the transcript and fine the other side.

D. Responding to Discovery

Whether you are a plaintiff or a defendant, if your opponent is represented by a lawyer you will probably be sent discovery requests—sometimes for no other reason than to try to teach you not to mess with the legal system.

1. Notice of Deposition

If you are sent a Notice of Deposition, review it carefully. Depositions are usually conducted at a lawyer's office, and you may be asked to bring relevant documents or tangible objects. The other side must give you at least ten days' notice (15 if the notice was mailed) and can't make you travel more than 150 miles (75 if the deposition won't take place in the county where the lawsuit was filed).

If these distance or time requirements haven't been met, write the other side immediately and explain that you won't be at the deposition because you haven't been given ample notice or are being asked to travel too far. Be sure to keep a copy of your letter.

If you can't make the deposition at the time proposed, call the other side's attorney (or the other side, if she has no lawyer) and try to reschedule. Lawyers usually cooperate in rescheduling depositions. If you arrange a new time, send a letter stating your understanding of the new time. Keep a copy for yourself. If the other side won't cooperate, send her a letter stating that you can't make the deposition (explain

your conflict), that you asked for it to be rescheduled, and that she refused. Be sure to keep a copy.

If the other side goes ahead with the deposition and you don't show up, she'll probably file a motion with the court to "compel" you to appear at a deposition. (See Section F, below.) The court can also fine you for not showing up. But if you had a good reason not to show and hand the judge your letter, the court will probably excuse you for refusing to appear.

If the other side is taking the deposition of a witness other than a party to the case, he must issue a subpoena to get the person to the deposition. You are entitled to (and should) attend.

The purposes of a deposition are to:

- obtain information to help prepare for a settlement or trial
- find out what you or the witness will say at the trial
- trap you or a witness into saying something that will hurt your case or embarrass you at the trial. Within the rules of evidence, relevant portions of a deposition can be—and frequently are—read out loud to the judge or jury during the trial.

a. Preparing for the Deposition

Below are some suggestions on how to behave at a deposition. If the other side is taking your deposition, read that material. These suggestions were prepared by lawyers to instruct their clients. As you'll see from reading the material, not everything will apply to you. But enough will, so study it carefully.

Preparation for a Deposition

These tips can help you prepare for a deposition.

Tell the truth. This is the cardinal rule. Tell the truth even regarding little details that might be embarrassing or seem trivial to you.

Listen to the question carefully. Your job is to answer the question that is asked, not a question you wish had been asked. Concentrate on every word of the question and wait until it's been completely stated before you start to answer.

If you don't hear or understand the question, ask that it be repeated or explained. If the lawyer drops her voice or someone coughs while the question is being stated, and you don't hear it, ask that it be repeated. If the lawyer asks a long or convoluted question, don't answer until you're sure you know what is being asked. If she uses a word you're not familiar with, tell her you don't understand. Don't be embarrassed—it's important that you know what's being asked before you answer.

Answer only the question asked. If the question can be answered with a "yes," "no," "I don't know" or "I don't remember," give that answer. If you want to explain further, keep it short and to the point. Don't make a speech or volunteer information. If the lawyer allows silence after you give an answer, resist the temptation to talk.

Don't guess. If you're pretty sure of an answer, but not positive, say so. If you would have to guess to answer a question, state that you don't know.

Don't argue with your opponent's lawyer. If a question makes you angry, don't argue. Just answer it. By arguing you'll only lose in the long run. Be courteous—but on guard—at all times.

Don't let a lawyer trick you. Your opponent's lawyer may try to trick you into thinking you've given a wrong or stupid answer by asking a question over and over again with slight variations. He may smirk and ask if you REALLY meant what you just said. He's probably just trying to get you to change your answer. Stick to your answer, even if you begin to sound like a broken record.

b. Attending the Deposition

For moral support, you can take your Sounding Board to the deposition and occasionally take short breaks to confer with him. If you whisper during the deposition, a truly obstreperous lawyer representing your opponent might object, claiming that the Sounding Board was practicing law without a license. But if you do all the audible talking and the Sounding Board doesn't make speeches, ignore the objection.

The deposition itself may begin with the other side asking you to agree to "the usual stipulations."[4] These stipulations are no longer necessary because of a change in the law. So it's best to state that you do not agree to anything other than what is provided in the Code of Civil Procedure. Next, the court reporter will administer an oath ("do you swear to tell the truth, the whole truth and nothing but the truth") to you or the witness being deposed.

Then the lawyer who scheduled the deposition takes over. His job is to ask questions. Many are routine and harmless, but some are designed to wear you down or trap you or the witness into an inconsistency. For example, in an automobile accident case, a lawyer might first ask you what you saw when you were 100 yards from the point of impact, 50 yards, 20 yards, ten yards and then five yards. Then he'll ask you what speed you were traveling at each point. Finally, he'll ask how hard you were applying your brake pedal at each point.

You probably won't be able to give a precise answer to his questions. So adopt a standard reply and parrot it over and over if the lawyer tries to wear you down. In the above situation,

---

[4]These stipulations pertain to giving the deposed person a chance to read and correct the deposition, the delivery of the deposition and similar mechanics.

you might say "I can't answer that precise question, but I can tell you that the yellow car appeared from out of the alley going very fast when I was about half a block from the point of impact." If the lawyer gets angry and loud, don't worry about it. Some lawyers think that discovery was created to intimidate people.

What you say in the deposition can be read to the judge or jury during the trial. So if it is at all possible, frame your answer in a positive light. If the lawyer asks, "Ms. Davis, the rain was coming down quite hard at the time of the accident, wasn't it?" A good answer, if it's true, would be, "Yes, it was, but I grew up in Seattle and am very accustomed to driving in the rain and observing what is going on."

If the lawyer asks if you are sure you told the service manager at the car repair shop that your car had stalled in the fast lane at 5:00 p.m., answer "yes, and I remember he said that it sounded like a defective fuel pump that he could fix quickly and easily."

The law provides that you can make several different objections to the questions asked of you or another witness, but it best to limit yourself to the following:

1.   If a question doesn't seem to have anything to do with the issues in your case, say "Objection, the question does not appear to be reasonably calculated to lead to the discovery of admissible evidence."

Objecting to a Deposition Question

As pointed out earlier, a discovery request can seek information related to the lawsuit if it would be either admissible as evidence or is reasonably calculated to lead to admissible evidence. Discovery can also seek the monetary limits of any insurance policy that may cover the lawsuit.

If a deposition question clearly calls for information not within this scope, go ahead and answer it anyway unless it reveals information that is very private. Otherwise, you'll likely have to fight it out in court.

There is, of course, a time to take a stand against irrelevant questions. If your car was totalled while it was parked at a curb and you're asked if you have ever been under a psychiatrist's care, object and refuse to answer it. Or, in a breach of contract case you're asked about the time you shoplifted when you were 17, refuse to answer.

2.   If the lawyer badgers you or the witness, say "Objection, the question calls for material that is unduly intrusive, harassing or embarrassing to the witness. Under the provisions of Evidence Code § 765 and Code of Civil Procedure § 2017, I decline to answer it (or I recommend to the witness that he not answer it)."

Example: Blake is involved in an automobile accident on his way to work in the morning. At his deposition, the lawyer wants to know who he slept with the night before. Blake objects and refuses to answer.

It's a good idea to keep your objections to a minimum so you can get the deposition completed peacefully. If the lawyer asks the same questions over and over, or becomes insulting, bullying or extremely objectionable, warn him that if he does not discontinue these practices, you'll terminate the deposition and leave the premises. If he doesn't stop, state for the court reporter why you are leaving, and leave. The law does not require you to be harassed. If a witness being deposed is harassed, remain at the deposition and make your objections until the witness leaves.

2. Interrogatories

If you are sent interrogatories, you should have little trouble responding. Begin by reading the "Instructions to the Answering Party" on the first page of the form interrogatories in the Appendix. Be careful to observe your time deadline. Even if the other side didn't use form interrogatories, these instructions are helpful. Then write down the number of each interrogatory asked of you on a sheet of paper and write out your answers. Review your answers with your Sounding Board. Finally, use the sample, below, to prepare your answers.

Your answers should be a responsible attempt to give information, not an effort to be cute and avoid the subject. Nor should you give more information than what you've been asked. For instance, if you're a store owner asked how many lawn mowers you sold in May, answer

"nine." Don't say "I sold as many lawn mowers as there were people paying for them." At the same time, don't give the names and addresses of the buyers.

When you've completed the form, have a friend serve (by mail) the answers to the requesting party. (See Chapter 7, Section E.)

Objecting to an Interrogatory

Remember, a discovery request can seek information related to the lawsuit if it is either admissible as evidence or is reasonably calculated to lead to admissible evidence. Discovery can also seek the monetary limits of any insurance policy that may cover the lawsuit.

If an interrogatory clearly calls for information not within this scope—such as events that occurred long ago or private details unrelated to this case—you can object by writing "Plaintiff (or defendant) objects to interrogatory number __ and refuses to answer. It is outside the scope of discovery provided in Code of Civil Procedure § 2017."

Before objecting, talk it over with your Sounding Board. Ask her if the question could be related to the lawsuit. Be imaginative. The judge who may decide the question will be. If the question is at all possibly related, answer it.

Sample Answer to Interrogatories

```
 1   ALICE MCMANN
     98 Morton Road
 2   Sunnyvale, CA 95000
     408-555-8989
 3
     Defendant In Pro Per
 4

 5

 6

 7

 8                    MUNICIPAL COURT OF CALIFORNIA

 9                      COUNTY OF SANTA CLARA

10

11   CYNTHIA WONG and            )        Case No. SC-90909
     HAROLD WONG,                 )
12                                )
     Plaintiffs,                  )
13                                )        DEFENDANT ALICE MCMANN'S
     vs.                          )        ANSWER TO INTERROGATORIES
14                                )        (SET NO.____)
     ALICE MCMANN,                )
15                                )
     Defendant._____ )
16

17       Defendant, Alice McMann, hereby answers the first (or whatever) set of

18   interrogatories propounded by plaintiffs.

19   (Type your answers in the numerical order in which they were requested; don't repeat the question you are

20   answering.)

21       I declare under penalty of perjury the foregoing is true and correct.

22   Signed at Sunnyvale, California November 3, 19__.

23

24   _____

25   Alice McMann

26

27

28
```

3. Request for Production of Documents and Other Items

If you are sent a Request for Production, produce the item before or at the time specified. If you can't comply on time, write to your opponent giving a date and time that you can comply with. If you don't have the documents or items asked for, again, write your opponent and explain. If you don't believe the request is within the proper scope of discovery (admissible as evidence or is reasonably calculated to lead to admissible evidence), send a letter explaining why you object.

4. Request for Admissions

Requests for Admissions are frequently used by a lawyer attempting to set you up for a Motion for Summary Judgment (see Chapter 11), so be very careful in reviewing the requests and be sure to answer on time. Next to each statement, write one of the following notations:

Admit. For each statement where you agree with absolutely everything said, write "admit" next to it. If you admit a statement, the other side won't have to prove it in court. Thus, admit only those statements you can't argue about. If you honestly don't know if a statement is true or if you agree with only part of it, don't admit it.

Deny. Write "deny" near each statement in which you deny all or part of what was said. For instance, if a statement says "In June, Defendant refused to sign a paper modifying the contract" and you deny it, say so. If part of it is true, answer something like "The statement is only partly true. I refused to sign the paper on June 7 and June 20, but I offered to sign it June 28." If you deny something that the other party later shows that you should have admitted, the judge

may award him the cost of whatever he had to go through to prove it.

Deny on information and belief. If you are not sure what the truth is, but you believe the plaintiff's statement is probably more false than true, write "deny on information and belief." For instance, if the plaintiff has alleged that the accident happened at night, but you think—and aren't completely sure—it was late on a winter afternoon, use this designation.

Deny because no information. If you have no idea whether or not the allegation in a statement is true, for example, a statement saying that the plaintiff was on the job performing his duties as a delivery person, write "deny because no information."

Completed the form using the sample in Section 2, above, for answering interrogatories.

E. Less Used Methods of Discovery

As mentioned above, two less frequently used methods of discovery are available in Municipal Court. They are:

Request for physical examination. A request by one party that the other party be examined by a doctor if his health is an issue.[5] The request can be for a physical or mental exam. Although medical examinations are not used much in Municipal Court—the examination is expensive and not worth the cost unless an injury claim appears suspicious—cooperate with

---

[5]The rules regarding mental and physical examinations are found at Code of Civil Procedure § 2032. Be sure to read them carefully if you receive a notice requesting your presence at a doctor's office to be examined.

any reasonable request. If your leg broke during an accident, the defendant is entitled to have his doctor take a look at your leg. If you claim severe mental distress as a result of the accident, the defendant can request that you be examined by a psychiatrist, psychologist or similar medical professional.

Anything you say to the doctor during the examination can be used against you in the case. No matter how friendly the doctor may seem, you should not treat the doctor as your friend. She was hired by the other side to explore anything suspicious about your injury claim. You are allowed to have a tape recorder present during the examination and you are entitled to a copy of the resulting report.

Witness list. A request by one party to the other to turn over the list of witnesses, including expert witnesses (see Chapter 13, Section A, for information on expert witnesses), that party plans to use at trial.[6] The request won't come—or shouldn't be made—until you have received a trial date from the court. Witness lists are designed for use in big cases and are rarely used in Municipal Court. Other ways of getting the same information is covered in Chapter 13.

F. Failing to Respond to a Discovery or Case Questionnaire Request

It's possible that the other side won't respond to your discovery request or Case Questionnaire. Many lawyers are not familiar with using the Case Questionnaire and may ignore the requirement to answer it. If you get no response,

your first step is to send the other side (or his lawyer, if he has one) a letter demanding compliance. This is because law requires you to informally try, in good faith, to resolve any discovery dispute by letter or telephone. A court can impose penalties if one of you fails to try.

A sample letter is included below.

Sample Letter Demanding Compliance with Discovery Request or Case Questionnaire

Gregory Dailey
Dailey and Weakly
2323 Mason Street
Santa Barbara, CA

July 5, 19__

Re: Vincent vs. Higgins, Municipal Court Case # 497 233

Dear Mr. Dailey:

I am the plaintiff in the above-referred case. Pursuant to Code of Civil Procedure § 93, your client, Ms. Higgins, was served with a Case Questionnaire when she was served with the Summons and Complaint on May 21, 19__, 45 days ago. Although you have filed an Answer on her behalf, you have not responded to the Questionnaire.

This letter is notify you that unless I receive your response by July 12, 19__, I will file a motion in court to obtain compliance and sanctions as provided by Code of Civil Procedure §§ 93 (e) and 2034.

Yours very truly,

Sandra Vincent

---

[6]Witness lists are covered in Code of Civil Procedure § 2034.

If you still don't receive a response to your discovery request or Case Questionnaire, and you want to force the issue, you will have to file a Motion To Compel a (Further) Response with the court.[7]

One of my favorite judges spends a lot of time hearing these discovery disputes in what is known as a Law and Motion Department of the court. She describes the average motion to compel as "a sandbox fight between well-dressed lawyers who act like children." She thinks the lawyers need a playground director, not a judge. And the poor client (who may be much poorer by the end) has frequently paid $175 an hour for lawyers to think up questions other lawyers are sure to object to. If the dispute goes to court, the client also pays for the lawyer to sit around a courtroom waiting to fight in the sandbox.

If you still want to file your motion, call the clerk's office. Tell the clerk that you plan to file a Motion To Compel a Response to a Case Questionnaire or to your discovery. Ask the clerk what day and time, and in what department of the court, you should schedule your motion for a hearing by a judge. Ask if there is a fee to file a motion. Then, using numbered pleading paper, type up the motion like the samples below.

Have a friend serve the papers by mail. (See Chapter 7, Section E.)

Many times, in response to your filing a motion, the other side will offer to comply if you will drop the motion. Don't agree to drop the motion until you receive an adequate response. If the court will permit it, you can agree to post-pone (continue) the hearing on your motion to a later date, but you should not commit on promises of future compliance.

If the dispute goes to a hearing, dress appropriately and be sure to arrive at court on time. What is known as business attire is best if you have it, but going to court is not an event for which you should buy new clothes. Municipal Court is known as "the people's court" and whatever you wear to work is perfectly acceptable.

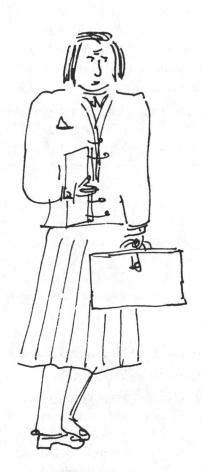

---

[7]This motion is authorized by Code of Civil Procedure § 93(e) (Case Questionnaire) and Code of Civil Procedure § 2030(k) (discovery). If the other side only partially answered your questions, the motion is to compel a further response.

Sample Motion To Compel Response to Case Questionnaire

```
 1  ANDREW CHU
    44 West Ellison Avenue
 2  Chico, CA 95000
    916-555-8989
 3
    Plaintiff In Pro Per
 4

 5

 6

 7

 8                     MUNICIPAL COURT OF CALIFORNIA

 9                          COUNTY OF BUTTE

10

11  ANDREW CHU,                    )         Case No. 3847562
                                   )
12  Plaintiff,                     )         NOTICE OF MOTION AND MOTION
                                   )         TO COMPEL RESPONSE TO
13  vs.                            )         CASE QUESTIONNAIRE
                                   )
14  MAUREEN TAKAHASHI,             )
                                   )
15  Defendant._____   )

16
        Notice is hereby given that at 9 a.m. on November 23, 19__, (be sure this
17
    date is at least 20 days after the date you will mail this notice) in Department __ of the above court,
18
    plaintiff will move pursuant to C.C.P. § 93(e) that sanctions be imposed
19
    against defendant for failing to file a [completed] Case Questionnaire as
20
    required by § 93.
21
        This motion will be based upon the fact that plaintiff served his Case
22
    Questionnaire on defendant on September 2, 19__, that defendant filed an Answer
23
    to plaintiff's Complaint on October 3, 19__ but defendant has not filed his
24
    Case Questionnaire [or defendant has provided incomplete answers to questions:
25
    (list number of each incomplete question and why answer is incomplete)]. Sanctions are requested.
26
    Date:_____
27

28  _____
    Andrew Chu
```

Sample Motion To Compel Response to Discovery

1 ANDREW CHU
   44 West Ellison Avenue
2 Chico, CA 95000
   916-555-8989
3
   Plaintiff In Pro Per
4

5

6

7

8   MUNICIPAL COURT OF CALIFORNIA

9   COUNTY OF BUTTE

10

11 ANDREW CHU,   )   Case No. 3847562
)
12 Plaintiff,   )   NOTICE OF MOTION AND MOTION
)   TO COMPEL RESPONSE TO
13 vs.   )   INTERROGATORIES [OR REQUEST
)   FOR PRODUCTION OF DOCUMENTS
14 MAUREEN TAKAHASHI,   )   OR REQUEST FOR ADMISSIONS]
)
15 Defendant._____)

16   Notice is hereby given that at 9 a.m. on November 23, 19__, in Department __

17 of the above court, plaintiff will move pursuant to C.C.P. § 2030(k) that

18 sanctions be imposed against defendant for failing to (completely) respond to

19 plaintiff's interrogatories (or Request for Production of Documents or Request

20 for Admissions).

21   This motion will be based upon the fact that plaintiff served his interroga-

22 tories (or Request for Production of Documents or Request for Admissions) on

23 defendant on September 2, 19__ and that defendant has not served any response

24 [or defendant has provided incomplete answers to questions: *(list number of each*

25 *incomplete question and why answer is incomplete)*]. Sanctions are requested.

26
    Date:_____
27

28 _____
    Andrew Chu

Bring a copy of the Case Questionnaire, discovery question or admission that has not been responded to, the letter you sent and the papers you filed (Notice of Motion and Motion to Compel a (Further) Response, and the Proof of Service by Mail). If the judge isn't yet in the courtroom when you arrive, check in with the courtroom clerk who sits near the judge's bench.

When the judge announces your case, stand before one of the tables in front of the judge. When the judge asks you to speak, simply explain what has happened: You served the Case Questionnaire or discovery request, the other side did not respond within the time required, you attempted to get the other side to comply by sending a letter, and the other side still has not responded.

Tell the judge how much time you've spent on writing the letter, preparing the motion and appearing in court. Explain that if you were a lawyer, you'd ask for $175 an hour for that time, but because you are a pro per, you'd like an award of sanctions of $60 an hour.

The judge will usually issue his ruling while you are in court. If the judge orders the other side to comply (usually within a certain amount of time) and you still get no response, re-read §§ 93 or 2030 of the Code of Civil Procedure. The other side may be uncooperative just because you are a pro per and may think that you will be unable to cope with his obnoxious behavior. Consider consulting an attorney for possible limited assistance.

If You Didn't Comply With a Discovery Request

If you've failed to comply with discovery—for example, you left in the middle of a deposition because you were being harassed—and the other side files a Motion to Compel you to respond, you should go to court on the day of the hearing and explain to the judge what happened.

G. Discovering Doe Defendants

During discovery, you may find out the name of a defendant you have been identifying as a Doe. Converting Doe defendants to real defendants involves a fair amount of paperwork and can delay your trial date. Thus, you won't want to convert unless it will add something of value to your case. Value might be that:

- the defendant has substantial assets to contribute toward paying a judgment or settlement you obtain

- as a party to the case (not just a possible witness), he must appear at, and participate in, discovery and the trial without your having to serve a subpoena on him

If you decide to turn a Doe defendant into a real defendant, these are the steps to take:

1. Photocopy the Amendment to Complaint form found in the Appendix. Fill in your name, address and phone number in the upper left corner, the county in which the court is located and the name of the case. In the first blank, type in Doe One (or whatever Doe you are using). In the second blank, type the name of the person you are adding as a defendant. Sign your name where it says "Signature of Plaintiff." Ignore the

rest of the form. File it with the court and obtain an file-stamped copy for your records.

2. Make a copy of the Summons issued by the court when you first filed your case. On the bottom of the copy, following the "Notice to the Person Served," check the second box. After the word "(specify)" write "Doe One" or whatever Doe is applicable.

3. Copy this altered Summons. Have it, a copy of the Complaint, your Case Questionnaire and a blank copy of the Case Questionnaire personally served on this defendant as described in Chapter 7. Even if you forgot to serve a Case Questionnaire on the original defendants you served, you can do it now when serving a newly identified Doe defendant.

This Doe defendant is now a real defendant, has 30 days to file an Answer and 45 days to file his Case Questionnaire.

chapter 11

THE OPPOSITION GETS NASTY: SUMMARY JUDGMENT AND OTHER MOTIONS

A lawsuit doesn't have to take very long. As you know by now, the plaintiff files a Complaint, the defendant has 30 days to respond and then the matter can be set for trial. Under the fast track rules of many courts, this can all happen in about two to six months. But few cases are resolved that quickly. One or both parties may want to conduct some discovery. (See Chapter 10.) Or one side may play the litigation game and file some motions.

Motions, which are formal requests to the court to take some action, are the bread and butter of many attorneys. In fact, so many lawyers file motions that, in most California counties, one judge is designated the "law and motion" judge. All this judge does, day after day, is hear motions.

Many motions have nothing to do with the merits of the case. For example, in response to a Complaint, a defendant may file—instead of an Answer—a Motion To Strike, Motion To Quash or Demurrer. These are motions complaining about something the plaintiff put in the Complaint, or the method used to serve the papers on the defendant. Usually, all they really do is delay the inevitable—the filing of an Answer by the defendant. Later on in a case, attorneys file motions to avoid disclosing—or to compel the disclosure of—certain information in discovery. Attorneys also file motions to keep certain evidence out of a trial.

A few motions, however, do address the merits of the case. That is, if you lose the motion, you lose the case, or major issues in the case. Such motions are covered by this chapter.

⚠ Don't file these motions yourself. Not only do they involve another layer of procedural complexity, but you can normally get what you want faster and cheaper by going to trial. For this reason, this chapter covers defending—not filing—motions.

Demand for Bill of Particulars

If you're the plaintiff, your lawsuit is for an unpaid bill based on an open account you've had with the defendant and you did not attach a copy of the account to your Complaint, the defendant can serve you with a Demand for a Bill of Particulars.[1] In this document, the defendant is asking you to send him a proof of the account.

Responding is simple. Within ten days of when you receive the demand, you must prepare, on numbered pleading paper, and send to the defendant—you don't have to file it with the court—a "Response to Demand for Bill of Particulars." Attach a copy of your bill to a form like the sample below. If your normal bill does not include a detailed list of charges showing when and for how much you furnished goods or services, prepare such a bill now. Attach it to the form below.

---

[1]Code of Civil Procedure § 454.

Sample Response to Demand for Bill of Particulars

```
1    ALICE MCMANN
     98 Morton Road
2    Sunnyvale, CA 95000
     408-555-8989
3
     Plaintiff In Pro Per
4

5

6

7

8                   MUNICIPAL COURT OF CALIFORNIA

9                     COUNTY OF SANTA CLARA

10

11   ALICE MCMANN,              )        Case No. SC-90909
                                )
12   Plaintiff,                 )        RESPONSE TO DEMAND FOR
                                )        BILL OF PARTICULARS
13   vs.                        )
                                )
14   DREW SORENSEN,             )
                                )
15   Defendant._____  )

16

17       Attached is plaintiff's Bill of Particulars.

18   Dated: November 3, 19__.

19

20   _____

21   Alice McMann

22

23

24

25

26

27

28
```

A. Motion for Summary Judgment

Like discovery, the Motion for Summary Judgment is another legal reform invented with the best of intentions, but now has run amok because of lawyer excesses.

The motion was designed to weed out weak lawsuits early on so that parties wouldn't have to spend time and money to get ready for an expensive trial. Sadly, because of the way lawyers have bent the process, the cost of preparing or defending such a motion in a complex case can wind up costing as much as a trial. This doesn't seem to bother some lawyers, who happily prepare gargantuan motions that sometimes amount to several pounds of paper.

Most judges dislike reading complex Motions for Summary Judgment filed by large law firms employing legions of young lawyers who prepare them. A judge must search through what is often 50 pages of documents to decide a very technical legal question. And more often than not, the judge denies the motion.

How does all of this relate to your little Municipal Court action? When used against a pro per in Municipal Court, a Motion for Summary Judgment is rarely a good faith effort to get rid of a frivolous lawsuit. It is likely to be much more akin to the neighborhood bully putting his best moves on the new kid on the block to test him out.

If you were a pro per trying to win a lawsuit without the help of this book, you might well lose your case at this stage. As a Municipal Court judge, I saw entirely too many of these motions brought against pro pers who had no idea of how to respond. But if you follow the procedures I set out here, you can normally beat

this sort of motion and perhaps in the process educate your opponent that you can't be scared into giving up your case.

To understand how a Motion for Summary Judgment works, you must know that in a trial, two kinds of issues are resolved—issues of fact and issues of law. An issue of fact is one that can (or cannot) be verified by a witness, including yourself—such as the color of a traffic light at the the time of an accident. In a jury trial, only the jury can decide factual issues.

Issues of law are different. They are for the judge and only the judge to decide, even in a jury trial. Issues of law arise when lawyers try to persuade a judge that based on statutes and cases, the law means one thing or another. An example of an issue of law is the duty of a driver who approaches an intersection as a traffic light turns yellow.

In a Motion for Summary Judgment, the moving party—the party bringing the Motion—asks the judge to:

- declare that there are no important issues of fact in dispute

- review the legal issues

- decide the issues of law so as to make the moving party the winner

> **Example 1:** Rick sues Mindy for colliding with his car in an intersection. Mindy's lawyer files a Motion for Summary Judgment, claiming that because Mindy was to Rick's right and because the law gives the right of way to the driver most to the right when two cars approach an intersection at the same time, no issues of fact remain and she should win. Rick raises an issue of fact—he claims he was halfway through the intersection and therefore had the right of way. The judge denies the motion.

> **Example 2:** Molly and Paula disputed Paula's building of a fence for Molly. Molly never paid and Paula sued. Molly filed a Motion for Summary Judgment saying "I agreed to pay plaintiff $800 to build a new fence in my yard. She never finished the job, so I owe her nothing." In Paula's opposition she asserted "I built the fence to specifications and finished the job." The judge denied the Motion for Summary Judgment because Paula established that there was an issue of fact in dispute.

In responding to a Motion for Summary Judgment, you must show that the factual dispute involves a significant ("controlling") fact in the case, not a minor detail. For instance, the plaintiff claims he was sitting at the intersection of Fifth and Market Streets, waiting for the light to change, when you roared up behind him in a red Porsche and crashed into his car. If your opposition states "My Porsche was not red, it was orange," you have failed to show that there is a dispute over a controlling issue of fact. You'd lose the motion and the case.

If you had said, "I was proceeding through the green light in a westerly direction on Market Street, when plaintiff approached from the south, violated a red light and struck my car," you'd have created a dispute over a controlling issue of fact and the motion should be denied.

Beating the other side's Motion for Summary Judgment does not mean you've won the case. It just means that, like Indiana Jones, you have survived another peril and can go forward to trial.

Once you understand the difference between issues of fact and law, you should familiarize yourself with the relatively complex statute that governs summary judgment motions.[2] A few Municipal Courts have added local rules that make filing such a motion even more complicated. Ask the clerk if your court has special rules on summary judgment motions. Most Municipal Courts don't, but more and more courts are trying to regulate its use.

Once you look at the state law and any local rules, check the timing of the motion.

- It may not be filed with the court earlier than 60 days after you have filed your Complaint (if you're the plaintiff) or Answer (if you're the defendant).

- It cannot be scheduled for hearing within 30 days of the trial.

- If the papers are sent to you by mail (normally they are), they must have been mailed at least 33 days before the scheduled hearing.

---

[2]It is contained in Code of Civil Procedure § 437c.

1. Review the Papers You Receive

If a Motion for Summary Judgment is filed against you, the opposing lawyer should send you:

1. a Notice of Motion, telling you when and where the motion will be heard by a judge

2. a Statement of Undisputed Material Facts

3. any written declarations made by a party or witness to support the motion

4. any answers to interrogatories, admissions of facts or portions of depositions which your opponent will rely on to

Items 1, 3 and 4 are not complicated and you should understand them just by reading them. Item 2 should look something like this:

Separate Statement of Undisputed Material Facts
In Support of Defendant Dawson's Motion For Summary Judgment

Undisputed Material Facts	Supporting Evidence
1. Plaintiff Prior and Defendant Dawson agreed that Prior would construct a front porch for Dawson in exchange for $8,500. It was agreed construction would be completed by March 11, 199__.	Agreed in Plaintiff Prior's Complaint, paragraph III. Copy of contract attached as Exhibit 1.
2. Dawson and Prior agreed to plans for the work.	Declaration of Dawson (attached as Exhibit 2), paragraph 8. Plans attached as Exhibit 3.
3. Prior stopped all work March 9, 199__ and contends that she has completed the work satisfactorily.	Deposition of Prior, (attached as Exhibit 4), page 34, lines 10–23.
4. The work does not comply with the plans.	Declaration of Angelo Russo, City Building Inspector, (attached as Exhibit 5), page 1, lines 19–23.
5. It will cost Dawson $2,500 to have the work completed by a competent contractor.	Declaration of Russo, Exhibit 5, page 4, lines 2–23.

As you can see, this Statement is a summary of the position of the moving party (the defendant here) attempting to show the judge that there is no factual issue to be decided by the court. Because (if you follow my advice) you will not be filing a Motion for Summary Judgment, you need not worry about preparing this Statement.

2. Prepare Your Opposition to the Summary Judgment Motion

At least 14 days before the hearing date, you must serve on the moving party three items:

1. an Opposition to Motion for Summary Judgment

2. a Separate Statement of Disputed and Undisputed Facts in Opposition to Motion for Summary Judgment

3. any declarations, answers to interrogatories, admissions or other material you will rely upon in your opposition

A sample Opposition to Motion for Summary Judgment and a Separate Statement Of Disputed and Undisputed Facts are below. Yours should read something like these, but of course should reflect the facts of your case.

If the motion was filed in bad faith or for the purpose of delay, the court can award you monetary sanctions (a fine). If you believe you're dealing with a bully who is just attempting to exploit your status as a pro per, be sure to ask for sanctions. If you spent money getting the advice of a lawyer to help you oppose the motion, ask for those fees also. Don't request sanctions unless it's clear that there's little chance the motion would have been granted as long as you filed some opposition.

Sample Opposition to Motion for Summary Judgment

```
 1   BLAZE PRIOR
     444 Dry Creek Road
 2   Palm Desert, CA 91999
     619-555-2285
 3
     Plaintiff In Pro Per
 4

 5

 6

 7

 8                    MUNICIPAL COURT OF CALIFORNIA

 9                      COUNTY OF RIVERSIDE

10

11   BLAZE PRIOR,              )         Case No. 844-3994-2
                               )
12   Plaintiff,                )         OPPOSITION TO MOTION FOR
                               )         SUMMARY JUDGMENT
13   vs.                       )
                               )
14   PHILIP DAWSON, DBA        )
     DESERT VIEW               )
15   RESTAURANT,               )         Hearing: Sept. 5, 19__
                               )         Department 23
16   Defendant._____)
```

17   Plaintiff, Blaze Prior, opposes Defendant's Motion for Summary Judgment· set

18 for hearing as indicated above and requests that the motion be denied on the

19 following grounds:

20   1. The motion was not filed according to the time schedule provided by Code

21 of Civil Procedure Section 437c. *[Use if the motion was filed earlier than 60 days after you filed the*

22 *Complaint (if you're plaintiff) or Answer (if you're defendant), if you were not given at least 28 days notice of the*

23 *hearing (33 if the papers were served by mail) or if the hearing date is not at least 30 days before the date of the trial.]*

24   2. The moving party's motion is not supported by a Separate Statement of

25 Undisputed Facts which sets forth the basis for such motion plainly and

26 concisely. *[Use if the moving party has not filed a plain and concise Separate Statement of Undisputed*

27 *Facts similar to the one presented above in Section 1.]*

28   3. The supporting declaration of Building Inspector Angelo Russo for such

motion is based upon evidence which would not be admissible at a trial and does not show affirmatively that the declarant is competent to testify. *[Use if your opponent is relying on hearsay or other inadmissible evidence. Chapter 13, Section A, covers inadmissible evidence.]*

4. As demonstrated by plaintiff's attached declaration, facts essential to justify opposition to the motion exist but cannot be presented at this time. *[Use if you feel confident you could produce facts in opposition to the motion if you had more time to investigate or do discovery, but that for good reason, you have not yet been able to develop those facts. Good reasons might be that you've recently been hospitalized or need a month to raise enough money to take your opponent's deposition.]*

5. The motion is based upon the declaration of a witness who was the sole witness to a material fact relied upon by the moving party. *[Use if the motion is based on the declaration of only one person who has the ability to control the outcome of the case by his or her statement. The court is not bound to deny the motion on this ground, but can in its discretion.]*

Plaintiff requests sanctions be imposed upon defendant for filing this motion in bad faith and for purpose of delay. In support of the request, plaintiff points out that defendant must have realized that in attaching only his own declaration, it would be highly unlikely for the court to grant the motion and further, that defendant was relying upon plaintiff's pro per status to result in his inability to successfully oppose such a motion.

Plaintiff has spent 23 hours researching and preparing this opposition and therefore requests sanctions of $460. In addition, plaintiff has incurred $175 consulting an attorney and $55 to have these documents typed.

Executed at Palm Springs, California, August 20, 19__. I declare under penalty of perjury the factual statements contained above are true and correct.

_____
Blaze Prior

Sample Separate Statement of Disputed and Undisputed Facts

```
 1 ┃ BLAZE PRIOR
   ┃ 444 Dry Creek Road
 2 ┃ Palm Desert, CA 91999
   ┃ 619-555-2285
 3 ┃
   ┃ Plaintiff In Pro Per
 4 ┃
   ┃
 5 ┃
   ┃
 6 ┃
   ┃
 7 ┃
   ┃
 8 ┃                    MUNICIPAL COURT OF CALIFORNIA
   ┃
 9 ┃                       COUNTY OF RIVERSIDE
   ┃
10 ┃
   ┃
11 ┃ BLAZE PRIOR,                   )        CASE NO. 844-3994-2
   ┃                                )
12 ┃ Plaintiff,                     )        SEPARATE STATEMENT OF
   ┃                                )        DISPUTED AND UNDISPUTED
13 ┃ vs.                            )        FACTS OF PLAINTIFF IN
   ┃                                )        OPPOSITION TO MOTION FOR
14 ┃ PHILIP DAWSON, DBA             )        SUMMARY JUDGMENT
   ┃ DESERT VIEW                    )
15 ┃ RESTAURANT,                    )
   ┃                                )
16 ┃ Defendant._____  )
```

17   Plaintiff Prior submits this separate statement of undisputed and disputed

18 facts in opposition to Defendant's Motion for Summary Judgment:

19   DEDENDANT'S MATERIAL FACTS: PLAINTIFF'S MATERIAL FACTS AND
                                                    SUPPORTING EVIDENCE:
20

21   1. Prior and Dawson agreed that   Undisputed.
         Prior would construct a front porch
         for Dawson in exchange for $8,500.
22   It was agreed construction would be
         completed by March 11, 19__.
23

24   2. Prior and Dawson agreed to plans   Undisputed.
         for the work.

25   3. Prior stopped all work March 9,   Undisputed.
         19__ and contends that she
26   completed the work satisfactorily.

27   4. The work does not comply with the Disputed. Declaration of Steve Felt,
         plans.   (attached as Exhibit C), page 2,
28   lines 1-25 (*See Section C, below for help on*
                                            declarations.)

1	5. It will cost Dawson $2,500 to	Disputed. Prior contends that work
2	have the work completed by a competent contractor.	was done satisfactorily; this is irrelevant.

Executed at Palm Springs, California, August 20, 19__. I declare under penalty of perjury the factual statements contained above are true and correct.

_____

Blaze Prior

Here the plaintiff has agreed to items which are not disputed, objected that the declaration of the Building Inspector is not admissible and presented the declaration of Felt, which says that the work was done satisfactorily. The declaration of Felt should be enough to defeat the motion by itself because it demonstrates there is an issue of fact in the case—whether or not the porch was done satisfactorily.

3. Prepare Your Supporting Declarations

In your opposition, you might rely on declarations or statements made in answers to interrogatories, depositions or the Case Questionnaire. A declaration must state clearly that it is made from personal knowledge of the declarant, produce evidence admissible under the rules of evidence (see Chapter 13, Section A) and state that the declarant "is competent to testify to the matter stated therein." Below is a sample.

Your papers in opposition must be filed at the court at least 14 days before the hearing and mailed or personally served on your opponent at the same time. (See Chapter 7.) The person who serves the papers must file a Proof of Service with the court. Your opponent may file a reply to your opposition at least five days before the hearing, but you don't have to respond in writing to that reply.

Lawyers and Their Compliance With The Law

I spend a lot of time in this chapter explaining how to comply with laws and legal procedures. In some cases I suggest you read tedious code sections that have deadlines and requirements that are very specific.

When you get your first motion or declaration from a lawyer that doesn't seem to even begin to comply with the law I told you to obey, you're going to wonder if we are all operating by the same rules.

We are, and I have been telling you what the rules require. But some lawyers don't seem to read the rules or care about complying with them. They just go on slapping together a motion and filing it, hoping their opponent won't object or that the judge will somehow excuse their noncompliance.

Don't despair. The party that follows the rules is usually rewarded. Sloppy lawyers disturb judges and embarrass the lawyers who do things right. If your opponent is a lawyer who dresses expensively, acts pompously and doesn't follow the law, tell the court at the hearing that you object to the papers filed by the opposition for their failure to comply with the rules. Ask the court for sanctions. You have the right to have your opponent follow the same rules you do.

In some large courts, the judges read over the papers and make "tentative decisions." The day before the hearing, the clerk records the decisions on an answering machine tape for you to call and listen to. If you or your opponent still want to argue the matter before the judge, you must notify the court and the other side per rules adopted by the court. If neither of you requests a hearing, the tentative decision becomes the permanent decision. Call the court clerk in advance of the hearing and ask if the court uses a "tentative decision" tape recording.

Sample Declaration in Support of Opposition to Motion for Summary Judgment

1 BLAZE PRIOR
  444 Dry Creek Road
2 Palm Desert, CA 91999
  619-555-2285
3
  Plaintiff In Pro Per
4

5

6

7

8   MUNICIPAL COURT OF CALIFORNIA

9   COUNTY OF RIVERSIDE

10

11 BLAZE PRIOR,   )   Case No. 844-3994-2
)
12 Plaintiff,   )   DECLARATION OF STEVE FELT IN
)   SUPPORT OF OPPOSITION TO
13 vs.   )   MOTION FOR SUMMARY JUDGMENT
)
14 PHILIP DAWSON, DBA   )
   DESERT VIEW   )
15 RESTAURANT,   )
)
16 Defendant. _____   )

17 Steve Felt declares as follows:

18   The following facts are matters of my own personal knowledge and, if sworn,

19 I could testify competently to them in court.

20   I am a contractor licensed by the State of California and have done general

21 construction work including remodeling for 17 years in the Palm Springs area.

22   On July 17, 19__ I was contacted by Plaintiff, who I did not know before

23 that date, and was asked to examine certain plans for a porch construction job

24 and then to inspect the construction work at 895 Lawton Street, Palm Desert,

25 California.

26   I am very familiar with construction plans and use them daily in my work. I

27 carefully looked at the plans (attached to this declaration as Exhibit A) on

28 July 18, 19__. On July 19, 19__, I visited 895 Lawton Street, Palm Desert and

inspected what appeared to be a newly constructed front porch of a restaurant. I found each item specified as a repair, replacement or new construction on the plans to have been done in a superior workmanlike manner. In my opinion, the work specified in the plans has been completed.

Executed in Palm Springs, California, August 10, 19___. I declare under penalty of perjury the foregoing is true and correct.

_____
Steve Felt

When appearing in court on a Motion for Summary Judgment, arrive a little early and check the bulletin board in front of the court to make sure your case is listed there. It is always possible that your motion has been transferred to a different judge in another courtroom because of the exigencies of the day. If so, head for that courtroom.

Once you're in the correct court, check in with the clerk when the judge is not on the bench. If court is in session when you arrive, do not go up to clerk until there is a recess. Once you've checked in (or are waiting to check in), take a seat. Don't leave the room without the clerk's okay.

When your case is called, walk to the table and stand before the one labelled "plaintiff" or "defendant" depending on what you are. The judge will usually call on the moving party to talk first. You can sit down, and be sure not to interrupt your opponent while she's talking.

When you are called upon to reply, point out that your papers counter what the moving party has said. If the judge seems to be siding with your opponent (horrors!) and you see what additional declarations could help, ask the judge for 10 days to file additional declarations. Point out that you are in pro per because of the high cost of hiring a lawyer, that Section 437c of the Code of Civil Procedure is very complicated and that you have done the best you could under the circumstances. Most of such pitches will succeed if you make it clear to the judge what you would expect your new declarations to say and why they should carry the day.

If the judge seems to be siding with you, be sure to remind her that you have requested sanctions against the other side for having filed a frivolous motion.

B. Motion for Summary Adjudication of Issues

A Motion for Summary Adjudication of Issues is the child of the Motion for Summary Judgment. In it the moving party wants the judge to resolve certain, but not all, legal issues. He realizes that a Motion for Summary Judgment will not succeed, but he thinks the case will be simpler if one or two issues are decided before trial.

In a case between a homeowner and a plumber over a less-than-perfect repair job, for example, the plumber (defendant) might file a Motion for Summary Adjudication to determine whether a written invoice he left on the job site, or a later phone conversation quoting a price, determined his fee.

A Motion for Summary Adjudication is often made when a case involves a substantial amount of money. The motion, however, is rarely made in Municipal Court because, even if the moving party wins, he still must prepare and pay for a trial. If your opponent does file a Motion for a Summary Adjudication, you respond in the exact same way you respond to a

Motion for Summary Judgment. (See Section A, above.)

C. Motion for Judgment on the Pleadings

In a Motion for Judgment on the Pleadings, the other side asks the court to:

- look at the Complaint and Answer
- assume everything alleged in both papers is true
- grant judgment for the moving party without a trial because one party left something important out of the Complaint or Answer

If you used the pre-printed Judicial Council forms, a Motion for Judgment on the Pleadings will fail. If you constructed a Complaint or Answer from one of the form books I recommended, the motion is still likely to fail, provided you followed the author's directions. A Motion for Judgment on the Pleadings is rarely filed and even more rarely granted. If your opposition tries to scare you with one, simply show up in court and point out you followed all of the instructions in filling in your forms. The judge will normally need little else to dispatch it.

D. Other Motions: Demurrers, Motions To Quash and Motions To Strike

Motions regarding discovery matters are covered in Chapter 10. Motions before a jury trial to keep certain evidence out are covered in Chapter 15. These and the motions covered in Sections A, B and C, above, are the major motions filed in Municipal Court.

Once in a great while, however, your opponent may file a Demurrer, Motion To Quash or Motion To Strike. They are normally filed by a defendant to simply slow down or harass the plaintiff. Because they are fairly rare, I'll cover them quickly.

Demurrer. There is only one type of Demurrer—a General Demurrer—permitted in Municipal Court. In it, the defendant asserts that the plaintiff has failed to allege all of the elements necessary to state a potentially successful legal theory of recovery (called a Cause of Action). One reason I've urged you to use the printed Complaint forms in Chapter 5 is that they were designed to include all of the elements necessary to state a Cause of Action for which they apply. It is difficult to imagine a successful General Demurrer against one of these forms.

In a Demurrer, the moving party must state what you left out of your Complaint. Read it over and decide if the objection has any merit. If it does and you could correct the Complaint easily, before the hearing retype the Complaint. Simply retitle it on the first page "First Amended Complaint." Make the corrections and file it with the clerk, following the steps in Chapter 6. Have a friend serve it by mail on the defendant. (See Chapter 7.) You're allowed to file one Amended Complaint without the court's permission.[3] When the judge sees that you have amended your Complaint voluntarily, she'll deny (overrule) the Demurrer.

---

[3]Code of Civil Procedure Section 472.

Motion To Strike. In Municipal Court, a Motion To Strike is allowed only to attack the "prayer" portion of a Complaint.[4] The prayer is where you tell the court how much money (or what other relief) you are asking for. If your opponent believes you've asked for something the court can't give, she could file a Motion To Strike. But most Motions To Strike are rarely filed and then usually as a delaying tactic. If you used the printed forms in this book, a Motion To Strike should not succeed. If you have drafted your own Complaint and asked for some form of esoteric relief (an injunction against the governor), however, the motion may fly.

Motion To Quash. A Motion To Quash normally attacks the method used to served the Summons and Complaint on the defendant. If the defendant is around and the plaintiff can have him re-served, this is a pretty silly motion.

If the defendant files a Motion To Quash, you have two choices:

1. Hire a professional process server (see Chapter 7) and serve him over again; or

2. File a declaration with the court explaining how the service took place and ask the judge to declare it valid. If you used a professional server, she can probably prepare the declaration for you and, for a fee, come to court on the hearing day to answer any questions the judge may have.

Motions To Quash are used occasionally to object to a court's jurisdiction over a particular defendant, such as an out-of-state corporation with no offices in California that claims not to do business here. If the defendant files such a motion, you'll need the help of a lawyer. (See Chapter 17.)

---

[4]Code of Civil Procedure Section 92.

chapter 12

THE MEMO TO SET FOR TRIAL AND ARBITRATION

Whether you're a plaintiff or defendant, you are very likely tired of playing lawyer. You probably want to wrap up this adventure and get on with your life. The way to start the final phase of the lawsuit is to ask the court to give you a trial date. You do this by filing a form called a Memorandum To Set Case For Trial ("Memo to Set") with the clerk. Each county has its own form, which you can get from the court clerk. If you're the plaintiff, also ask if the court has a form called "Plaintiff's Election To Arbitrate." A typical Memo to Set is below.

You cannot file a Memo to Set until all defendants (and cross-defendants) have filed an Answer to the Complaint or Cross-Complaint. Some crafty defendants try to stall a case by filing a Cross-Complaint against someone other than the original plaintiff and then never serving it. The idea is to prevent the plaintiff from filing a Memo to Set while an unanswered Cross-Complaint exists. This strategy won't work.[1]

Fast track rules in many courts require an even speedier resolution. In addition, you shouldn't file the Memo to Set until you've received a response to your Case Questionnaire and answers to any interrogatories you've sent out. Otherwise, you may get a trial date before you are ready.

Your court's fast track rules may require that the Memo to Set be filed within a certain number of days after the defendant files her answer. In Los Angeles, for example, you must file the Memo to Set within 165 days of when you filed the Complaint. Otherwise, you may be ordered to appear before a judge and explain the delay.

---

[1]Rule 507 of the Rules of Court states that if a third-party Cross-Complaint has been on file for six months and not been answered, you can still set a trial date.

A. Completing the Memo to Set

 A sample completed Memo to Set for Alameda County is below. Before you start typing up your Memo to Set, make several copies in case you have to start over.

By now, the top of the form should look familiar. Copy the information off the Complaint. Although some courts' forms differ slightly, they ask for the same general information. Complete it using these guidelines:

Nature of the case. Don't write "strong" or "dead bang." The court wants a general description of the type of dispute involved, such as "auto accident," "slip and fall," "breach of contract" or "failure to repay a personal loan." Don't worry about the exact wording.

Name, Address and Telephone No. of Attorney(s)	Space Below for Use of Court Clerk Only
Mark Taylor 777 Highway 80 Emeryville, CA 94600 415-555-3334	

Attorney(s) for plaintiff in pro per

MUNICIPAL COURT FOR THE OAKLAND-PIEDMONT-EMERYVILLE JUDICIAL DISTRICT
COUNTY OF ALAMEDA, STATE OF CALIFORNIA

Mark Taylor

_____
Plaintiff(s)

vs.

Miles Pheeney

_____
Defendant(s)

(Abbreviated Title)

No. _____ 3340005 _____

MEMORANDUM TO SET CASE FOR TRIAL

I hereby represent to the court that this case is at issue, and request that it be set for trial.

Nature of the case: __auto accident__

Jury trial __is not__ demanded. Reporter __is__ requested. Time necessary for trial: __½ day__
(is or is not)   (is or is not)   (Estimate carefully)

This case __is not__ entitled to legal preference is setting. _____
(is or is not)   (If so, state reasons)

The following dates are NOT acceptable to me: __September 4-7, September 17-22, October 3__
__October 19-23, November 11__

Names, addresses and telephone numbers of attorneys for other parties, or of parties appearing in person:

Dated __August 14, 1992__   _____
(Note: Must be signed by attorney or party requesting setting)

DECLARATION OF SERVICE BY MAIL

My __business__ address is __1800 University Ave, Piedmont, California__
(business/residence)

I am, and was at the time herein mentioned mailing took place, __employed__
(a resident/employed)

in the County where said mailing occurrred, over the age of eighteen years and not a party to the above-entitled cause.

On __August 14, 1992__ I served the foregoing document by depositing a copy thereof, enclosed in separate, sealed envelope, with the postage thereon fully prepaid, in the United States mail at __Piedmont__
(city or postal area)

_____, County of __Alameda__ _____, California, each of which envelopes were addressed respectively as follows: Miles Pheeney
3 Ashby Ave.
Emeryville, CA 94666

Executed on __August 14, 1992__, at __Piedmont__, California.
(date)   (city)

I declare under penalty of perjury that the foregoing is true and correct.

_____
(Signature of Declarant)

This space for use of court clerk only

The above-entitled case has been set for trial in MASTER CALENDAR Department

Entered on calendar by _____

on _____ at _____ M. | Entered in register by _____

214-010 (Rev. 1/86)

MEMORANDUM TO SET CASE FOR TRIAL

Rules for the Municipal Courts, Rule 507
Also see local court rule.

Jury trial. The form asks if you want a jury (as opposed to judge) trial. Believe me, answer "no." It's hard enough presenting a case effectively to a judge alone. Selecting and then convincing 12 jurors that you are right is very difficult—not to mention nerve-wracking—for a person without experience. You'll have to learn nearly double the number of rules and procedures. Some of the papers you will need to prepare are quite complex for experienced lawyers; they're far more difficult for a person who has never faced the terminology or procedures involved.

Unfortunately, you may have no choice about having a jury trial. Either party can request one—as long as he pays the jury fee—even on a case that is a $500 fender bender.

Reporter requested. A court reporter records the entire trial and then prepares a transcript. Call the clerk's office and ask if there is a charge for a reporter for a civil trial. If there isn't, go ahead and request one.

If there is, and you can't afford the reporter, you'll be fairly safe in proceeding without one—having or not having a reporter won't influence the judge's decision. The main purpose of requesting a reporter is to protect your right to appeal to the Superior Court. (See Chapter 16.) Without a court reporter, an appeal is much more difficult. But few Municipal Court cases are worth appealing. There is also the incidental benefit of keeping everyone on good behavior because the what's said in the courtroom is taken down verbatim.

Length of trial. This is difficult for anyone to estimate and you are not expected to be precise. If you anticipate that just you and the other side will testify, put "one hour." If you expect a total of three or four witness (for both sides) to testify, type "one-half day." If five to eight wit-

nesses will give testimony, state "one day." Anything more than that, type "one day plus."

Preferential setting. Some cases are entitled to preference. That means that those cases are scheduled for trial before other cases. Put "yes" to this request if you are over 70 and in poor health or you are terminally ill, and unlikely to live more than six months.[2]

Pre-trial conference. The Memo to Set may ask if you want a pre-trial conference. A pre-trial conference is an informal meeting between the parties and a judge to try to settle the case or to at least work out trial procedures. A pre-trial conference is not the same thing as arbitration. (Arbitration in covered in Sections B-D, below.)

Although you are not guaranteed to get a pre-trial conference, if the form asks, you should nevertheless request one. Many are handled by an impartial person, such as a judge, commissioner or volunteer lawyer. If the court sets one up, you'll receive a notice giving you the date, time and location.

Once you fill out the Memo to Set, make two copies. Have a friend serve it by mail on your opponent's lawyer (or your opponent, if he too is a pro per). (See Chapter 7, Section E.) If your opponent disagrees with anything you said in your Memo, such as the length of time or waiving of the jury trial, he can file a counter Memo.

---

[2]This is authorized by Code of Civil Procedure §§ 36(a) and (d).

B. Requesting Judicial Arbitration

Your best chance of reaching a fair resolution of your case is through a settlement. Your second best chance is through the Municipal Court judicial arbitration program. The program operates under the supervision of the Municipal Courts to resolve small and medium-sized lawsuits without a trial. Each county has the option of participating or not, and almost all do.

To Find Out if Your Court Has Judicial Arbitration

 To find out if your court participates in the judicial arbitration program, call the clerk's office and ask. Most clerks in small courts know the answer. In large courts, however, you may have to ask around. The people most likely to know are the clerk who sets civil cases for trial or the division chief.

If your court doesn't offer judicial arbitration, skip ahead to Chapter 13.

Ironically, judicial arbitration involves using a lawyer to help you resolve your lawsuit. But the lawyer doesn't represent you. Instead, as a public service, he serves as the arbitrator (getting paid a relatively small fee per arbitration by the county).

In judicial arbitration, you present a short, informal version of a trial to a knowledgeable lawyer. He tells you what he thinks your case would be worth at a full-blown court trial. Each side can accept or reject the arbitrator's opinion. If a side rejects the opinion, however, that side could be substantially penalized. (This penalty system is described in Section D, below.) A very

high percentage of small and medium-sized cases never go beyond judicial arbitration.

If you are the plaintiff and want to use judicial arbitration, you must file either a Stipulation To Arbitrate or a Plaintiff's Election To Arbitrate when you file the Memo to Set. Some courts provide printed forms. If your court doesn't, use something like the sample, below. If you submit a joint form, you'll get to arbitration more quickly than if only one party submits the form, because the court will skip the pre-trial conference and send the case directly to arbitration.

If you are a defendant, you may not want to bother with arbitration. This is because plaintiffs forced into arbitration against their will frequently reject the award and elect to have a trial once the arbitration is over. If you are a defendant and want arbitration, ask the plaintiff to agree to it. If she agrees, prepare a joint Election To Arbitrate form and file it with the court. If the plaintiff won't agree, you'll have to wait until the pre-trial conference and ask the judge to order arbitration.

Within no more than 30 days of when you file a joint Election To Arbitrate, the arbitration administrator should send you a list of proposed arbitrators. If, instead of a Joint Election, you filed a Plaintiff's Election To Arbitrate, some courts will ignore the plain wording of the law that requires the case to proceed to arbitration.[3] Instead, the court schedules a settlement conference (See Chapter 13, Section I) with a judge or volunteer lawyer. If the settlement conference is scheduled for within 60 days, go along with it. If it's much later, you can complain to the presiding judge by letter, pointing out the law.

---

[3]California Rules of Court Sections 1601 and 1605.

Sample Election to Arbitrate

```
 1 │ ANDREW CHU
   │ 44 West Ellison Avenue
 2 │ Chico, CA 95000
   │ 916-555-8989
 3 │
   │ Plaintiff In Pro Per
 4 │
 5 │
 6 │
 7 │
 8 │           MUNICIPAL COURT OF CALIFORNIA
 9 │               COUNTY OF BUTTE
10 │
11 │ ANDREW CHU,               )      Case No. 3847562
   │                           )
12 │ Plaintiff,                )      [  ] PLAINTIFF'S
   │                           )      [  ] JOINT
13 │ vs.                       )
   │                           )      ELECTION TO ARBITRATE
14 │ MAUREEN TAKAHASHI,        )
   │                           )
15 │ Defendant. _____)
16 │     The undersigned elect to arbitrate this case and request the court to assign
17 │ it pursuant to California Rules of Court 1600 et seq.
18 │
19 │ _____
   │ Plaintiff
20 │
21 │ _____
   │ Defendant
22 │
   │ (Both sign if both agree to arbitrate; otherwise, only the party submitting the form should sign it.)
23 │
24 │
25 │
26 │
27 │
28 │
```

Special Schedule for Vehicle Accident Cases

In every Municipal Court with mandatory arbitration, a motor vehicle accident case must be submitted to arbitration within 120 days of when the defendant files an Answer.[4] This is an attempt by the Legislature to get accident cases moving quickly. If you are a plaintiff and you haven't been assigned to arbitration within that time, speak to the clerk in charge of the civil division.

If a settlement conference doesn't settle the case, tell the judge that you are very anxious to proceed to arbitration. If necessary, point out Code of Civil Procedure § 1141.10, which states that the legislature believes small civil claims—anything under $25,000—are resolved best through arbitration and urges the courts to encourage arbitration. Courts are supposed to follow legislative policies. But not all judges do, and if the settlement conference judge still re-

---

[4]Code of Civil Procedure § 1141.11(d).

fuses, there is nothing practical you can do about it.

If you are sent a list of proposed arbitrators, it will contain the names of three or four people. You are directed to strike one of the names (this person will no longer be considered) and return the list to the arbitration office. You probably won't know anyone and listed and may have trouble deciding who to strike. Many plaintiffs are advised to strike the name of a lawyer who defends insurance companies. But in my experience, a lawyer familiar with the other side's position can be sympathetic and make a fair decision, so I wouldn't proceed on this basis alone.

Getting Information About Potential Arbitrators

Many courts have arbitrators' resumes on file for you to look at. The file contains biographical info such as law school attended, awards received and jobs held. These may or may not be helpful. You can also look up arbitrators in a lawyer directory called *Martindale-Hubbell*, found in most law libraries. My general advice, however, is not to worry about who the arbitrator will be. Most do a good job and try hard to be fair.

When you get the list of arbitrators, your opponent will receive the same list. Each of you may strike one name and return the form. After the administrator gets both forms, he'll send you a notice naming the person who has been selected to hear your case. Under no circumstances should you communicate with the arbitrator or anyone on the list of potential arbitrators except to arrange a hearing date.

Soon after she is selected, the arbitrator will contact you to set the date (usually 35-60 days after the date she was appointed) and location (probably her law office) of the hearing. The arbitrator must notify the court administrator of the date and place of the hearing within 15 days of being appointed. Once the date is set, either side or the arbitrator can postpone it to accommodate a calendar conflict, but if the hearing hasn't taken place within 90 days of when the arbitrator was assigned, she must return the case to the arbitration administrator for reassignment.

The person most likely to have a calendar conflict will be your opponent's lawyer, who may claim to be so busy with other cases that he can't get to this one for months. Litigation often involves date changes, and lawyers normally cooperate with one another. Judges want parties to work out scheduling conflicts, so be cooperative—the next conflict could be yours. But there's a limit—don't accommodate an attorney who wants to delay the hearing excessively, such as beyond 90 days. Let the arbitrator know you want it soon—as provided by law. If your opponent's lawyer and the arbitrator keep delaying, contact the arbitration administrator.

If your opponent's lawyer delays the case beyond 90 days and the case is returned to the administrator, you can file a motion for sanctions against the lawyer.[5] To do so, call the clerk's office. Tell the clerk that you plan to file a motion for sanctions for delaying an arbitration hearing. Ask the clerk what day and time, and in what department of the court, you should schedule your motion for a hearing by a judge.

---

[5] Code of Civil Procedure § 128.5. You may hesitate to file such a motion, figuring a judge won't penalize an attorney who regularly appears in his court. But lawyers have been fined large sums. See *580 Folsom Associates v. Prometheus Development Co.*, 223 Cal.App.3d 1 (1990) and *Salowitz Organization, Inc. v. Traditional Industries*, 219 Cal.App.3d 797 (1990). The law encourages judges to treat motions in this situation favorably.

Then, using pleading paper, type the motion and supporting declaration using the samples below.

C. Preparing for the Arbitration Hearing

To prepare for the arbitration hearing, you need to decide what evidence you will present. Be sure to read Chapter 13; it covers organizing your material for an arbitration hearing or trial. Although you will prepare for the hearing in essentially the same way you'd prepare for a trial, the arbitration hearing itself is much less formal.

As you read Chapter 13, pay close attention to Section F. That material guides you in preparing a chart of your evidence. In the left column of your chart, you will list all the facts in the Complaint that you (or your opponent, if you're the defendant) will have to prove during the hearing. In the right column, you'll list how you (or your opponent) will prove each fact. In a trial, you'd almost always use live witnesses. In an arbitration, however, you want to present all evidence—except the most crucial—in some way other than live witnesses. This will save a lot of time and make the arbitrator happy.

The following evidence can be presented at a judicial arbitration in lieu of live witnesses:[6]

- expert witnesses' written reports (expert witnesses are discussed in Chapter 13, Section A)

- medical records and bills

---

[6] California Rule of Court 1613(b).

Sample Motion for Sanctions

1 ANDREW CHU
  44 West Ellison Avenue
2 Chico, CA 95000
  916-555-8989
3
  Plaintiff In Pro Per
4

5

6

7

8   MUNICIPAL COURT OF CALIFORNIA

9   COUNTY OF BUTTE

10

11 ANDREW CHU,   )   Case No. 3847562
)
12 Plaintiff,   )   NOTICE OF MOTION AND
)   MOTION FOR SANCTIONS
13 vs.   )
)
14 MAUREEN TAKAHASHI,   )
)
15 Defendant._____   )

16

17   Notice is hereby given that at 9 a.m. on November 23, 19__, in Department __

18 of the above court, plaintiff will move pursuant to C.C.P. § 128.5 that

19 sanctions be imposed against defendant's attorney, Bryan Deelay, for failing to

20 cooperate in scheduling a judicial arbitration hearing within 90 days of the

21 date the case was assigned to an arbitrator as required by Rule of Court 1605.

22   This motion will be based upon the fact that Mr. Deelay has failed to

23 cooperate with the arbitrator in setting a date for arbitration. When the

24 arbitrator finally selected a date (October 1, 19__), Mr. Deelay failed to

25 attend.

26 Date:_____

27

   _____
28 Andrew Chu

- evidence showing loss of income (from employer)

- property damage repair bills or estimates, accompanied by a statement indicating whether or not the property was repaired, and if it was, whether it was repaired in full or in part; you must also attach a copy of the bill showing the items repaired and the amount paid

- other bills and invoices

- police reports; however, the arbitrator can't consider any opinion about who was at fault for an accident expressed in a police report

- purchase orders

- checks

- written contracts

- documents prepared and maintained in the ordinary course of business; this would include ledgers, books of account, profit and loss statements and the like

- written statements (declarations) of witnesses

- depositions

If you can't get some evidence into the hearing through one of these devices, you will probably have to bring a live witness to testify.

After you decide what physical evidence you will present, you must write a letter to the opposing side listing—and attaching copies of—all the evidence you will use at the hearing. The letter and attached items of evidence must be hand delivered to the opposing side at least 20 days before the arbitration (25 days if mailed). If you leave out any information, or forget to attach a copy, you won't be able to use the evidence at the hearing, so be thorough. Overlist, if necessary. If you list an item and then don't use it, you won't be penalized. A sample letter is below.

Sample Letter Listing Evidence

Gregory Dailey
Dailey and Weakly
2323 Mason Street
Santa Barbara, CA

July 5, 19__

Re: Vincent vs. Higgins,
Municipal Court Case # 497233

Dear Mr. Dailey:

Under California Rule of Court 1613, I intend to offer the following documentary material (copies are attached) into evidence at the arbitration hearing set for August 1, 19__.

1. The following medical and hospital reports, records and bills:

- bill from Washington Hospital dated January 8, 19__;

- report from Barbara Lazarus, M.D. dated February 2, 19__; and

- bill from Imaging of the World, Inc. for X-rays dated January 9, 19__.

2. Declaration of Ken Rosen, my employer, dated June 17, 19__, showing loss of income.

3. Property damage repair estimate dated March 22, 19__ from Goodie's Garage. Repairs have been made in part. See item 4 below.

4. Invoice from Goodie's Garage dated April 3, 19__.

5. Police report from Officer O'Dell dated December 5, 19__.

6. Declarations under penalty of perjury of Sadie Foster and Martha Conroy dated June 17, 19__.

I also intend to offer into evidence defendant's Case Questionnaire dated July 2, 19__ and his answers to interrogatories, also dated July 2, 19__.

Yours very truly,

Sandra Vincent

Sample Declaration in Support of Motion for Sanctions

1 | ANDREW CHU
44 West Ellison Avenue
2 | Chico, CA 95000
916-555-8989
3 |
Plaintiff In Pro Per
4 |
5 |
6 |
7 |
8 | MUNICIPAL COURT OF CALIFORNIA
9 | COUNTY OF BUTTE
10 |
11 | ANDREW CHU,   )   Case No. 3847562
)
12 | Plaintiff,   )   DECLARATION IN SUPPORT OF
)   MOTION FOR SANCTIONS
13 | vs.   )
)
14 | MAUREEN TAKAHASHI,   )
)
15 | Defendant. _____   )
16 |
     Andrew Chew declares:
17 |
18 | This case was assigned to arbitration on August 15, 19__. On August 25, the
19 | arbitrator assigned to the case, Charles Fair, wrote to each party asking them
20 | to agree to hold the hearing on one of three possible dates, all within the fol-
21 | lowing 60 days.
22 | When Mr. Deelay failed to respond, Mr. Fair wrote each party (a copy of the
23 | letter is attached to this declaration and marked as Exhibit 1) setting the
24 | arbitration hearing for 9 a.m. on October 1, 19__. I was present at the
25 | scheduled time, however, Mr. Deelay never appeared or sent any message that he
26 | would not appear. Mr. Fair telephoned Mr. Deelay and I listened to the
27 | conversation on Mr. Fair's speaker phone. Mr. Deelay told Mr. Fair that other
28 | work made it impossible for him to attend the hearing and that he could not set

1   it for "at least three months."

2   I request sanctions for my preparation for the hearing (11 hours) and for

3   attending the hearing, including transit time (3 hours). I suggest that $30 an

4   hour is an appropriate charge for my time.

5   I declare under penalty of perjury that the foregoing is true and correct.

6   Executed at Oroville, California on November 10, 19__.

7

8   Andrew Chu

Your opponent should deliver to you a similar letter at least 20 (25 if mailed) days before the hearing. If she doesn't, she can't offer any evidence except live witnesses at the arbitration.

If you object to any evidence (other than declarations) your opponent plans to submit, you must subpoena the applicable person (such as a doctor who wrote a medical report) to appear at the arbitration. You do this by getting a subpoena from the court clerk. Fill it out, listing the date and location of the arbitration and the name of the person you want to appear at the hearing. (See Chapter 13, Section E.)

To prevent declarations from being used, deliver a letter to your opponent at least 10 days (15 days if mailed) before the hearing stating that you demand that the witness be present in person pursuant to California Rule of Court 1613(b)(2).

It's unlikely you'll want to force the other side into bringing a live witness rather than documentary evidence or a declaration. If you demand that your opponent bring inconsequential witnesses, everyone else connected with the hearing will roll their eyes upward. ("Here's another crazy pro per trying to make a federal case out of a fender bender.")

Probably, the only reason you'd want a live witness is if the documentary evidence or written declaration is greatly exaggerated and you have no witness or evidence to show otherwise. For example, if your opponent's car was damaged slightly in the accident and she has submitted a bill showing repairs to the transmission, you may need to ask the mechanic if the transmission could have been damaged previously. But before relying on your opponent's witness, try hard to get your own evidence, especially a live witness. If your opponent's witness isn't at the hearing to refute your witness, you'll have the upper hand.

Of course, if your opponent's witness is wildly lying, consider having him come to the hearing just so the arbitrator can see him. Before sending a letter asking that he attend, talk to him yourself. Is he believable? Will he impress the arbitrator? If yes, leave him home. If you can come up with some tough questions he won't be able to wiggle out of, however, make him show up. Then, before you attend the hearing, have a mock hearing with your Sounding Board and make sure your tough questions are really tough.

Discovery and Judicial Arbitration

One major advantage to judicial arbitration for a pro per is that discovery (formal methods used to gather evidence—see Chapter 10) must be completed at least 15 days before the arbitration hearing. Most pro pers do little or no discovery. The attorney on the other side, however, may try to wear you out with a lot of discovery, and the cutoff date could save you from being over-discovered. If your opponent schedules a deposition or attempts other discovery within the 15-day period, write him a letter stating that under California Rule of Court 1612, you refuse to comply.

D. Attending the Arbitration Hearing

As the arbitration hearing approaches, you may be getting nervous. The key to a successful arbitration is to be prepared, and to spend some time trying to anticipate what your opponent might say. This is a perfect opportunity for your Sounding Board to play devil's advocate with you.

On the day of the arbitration hearing, be on time and dress like yourself. If you're a painter who has sued a homeowner for failing to pay, the arbitrator may better understand where you are coming from if you wear your painting overalls than if you show up in the one suit you own and wear to weddings and funerals.

The arbitrator will bring you, your opponent, your opponent's lawyer and any witnesses into a room. Everyone usually sits around a table. If your opponent doesn't show up, the arbitrator will nevertheless proceed and you should consider making a motion in court for sanctions (see Section B, above) if (and when) your opponent rejects the arbitrator's decision. You will have to go to court, as the arbitrator does not have the power to impose sanctions.

The arbitrator might have a tape recorder, but isn't required to tape the proceedings. No one else can record the hearing. The arbitrator usually starts things off by having all of the people who will testify swear to tell the truth. When it comes to your turn, raise your right hand. After the oath has been recited, answer clearly "Yes, I do."

Next, the arbitrator will probably ask the plaintiff to tell him about the case. If you're the plaintiff, you should have rehearsed this. Start at the beginning and proceed chronologically. Talk in the first person. When you reach a place where a document or statement of a witness is relevant, hand it to the arbitrator. Your exhibits should be indexed and at your fingertips—nothing will undermine your self-confidence as much as hunting through a stack of papers for the third time in search of an elusive ambulance bill.

For an example of how to start your case, See the declaration in Chapter 9, Section A.2.b.1. Use it to outline your presentation. You might add a few details, if the incident involved was complicated, but don't get too specific. Your aim here is to get the basic scenario established.

After the plaintiff introduces the case, the arbitrator may ask some questions. She may give the defendant a chance to ask the plaintiff questions or summarize his own case. If you (whether you are the plaintiff or defendant) have witnesses, be sure the arbitrator understands who you have and on what subject they will testify. To guide your witnesses through their testimony, the arbitrator may ask questions or tell you to do so.

Arbitration hearings are informal and short—usually under two hours. The absence of a courtroom and jury minimizes grandstanding. Few, if any, witnesses testify. The arbitrator needs only the important facts, and few Municipal Court cases are complex. Also, remember that the arbitrator is paid a minimal fee no matter how long the hearing takes, so she'll move it along.

If the arbitrator—or more likely your opponent's lawyer—mouths off about doing things more lawyer-like, point to Code of Civil Procedure § 1141.10. It provides that judicial arbitration hearings are to be simple, economical and informal, and that the parties are to be given the maximum opportunity to participate directly in the resolution of their dispute. Don't be too heavy-handed, but protect yourself.

Be Attuned to the Arbitrator's Clues

As a judge who hears lawyers and pro pers present cases every day, I see many people ignore the clues I give about what I find important. This mistake often happens because the presentation has been over-rehearsed to the point of inflexibility. If you say something, and the arbitrator perks up saying "tell me more about that," don't reply with "I'll get back to that later; now I want to cover something else." The ultimate objective in the hearing is to convince the arbitrator to rule in your favor. Inflexibility will only work against you.

E. The Arbitration Decision

It's unlikely that the arbitrator will give you a decision at the end of the arbitration hearing. The arbitration rules give her 10 days to file a decision (called an "award") with the clerk and send each party a copy. You and your opponent then have 30 days (from the date the award was filed with the clerk—or given in writing at the end of the hearing) to reject the decision and request a trial. If neither of you requests a trial, the award becomes a judgment of the court and your case is over. Of course, if you are awarded damages, you still have to collect.

If you lose, you may be tempted to reject the award and request a trial. Except in unusual cases, don't do this. If you have a trial and do the same or worse than you did in the arbitration, you must pay the arbitrator's fee (frequently $150). You must also pay your opponent's court costs, such as filing fees, fees paid

to process servers, deposition costs and—this is the big one—money paid to expert witnesses (see Chapter 13, Section A) since the time of the arbitration.[7] These costs can amount to thousands of dollars, especially if your opponent has several experts testify at the trial.

In researching this book, I reviewed every case in which one party rejected the arbitrator's award and went to trial for a three-year period in one California county. In over 80% of the cases, the party who requested the trial did the same or worse the second time. These people lost their battle and then, after spending more energy and money to fight a second time, shot themselves in the foot.

There will be a rare case in which you have a good ground for rejecting the arbitrator's award and having a trial. Before assuming that your case falls into that category, have a serious discussion with your Sounding Board or even a lawyer. If you still want to pursue a trial, you must file a Request for Trial De Novo After Judicial Arbitration form with the clerk. (A sample is below.) Remember—it must be filed within 30 days after the arbitrator filed the award with the clerk.

---

[7]Code of Civil Procedure § 1141.21(a).

Sample Request for Trial De Novo

```
 1   ANDREW CHU
     44 West Ellison Avenue
 2   Chico, CA 95000
     916-555-8989
 3
     Plaintiff In Pro Per
 4

 5

 6

 7

 8                      MUNICIPAL COURT OF CALIFORNIA

 9                          COUNTY OF BUTTE

10

11   ANDREW CHU,                    )         Case No. 3847562
                                    )
12   Plaintiff,                     )         REQUEST FOR TRIAL DE NOVO
                                    )         AFTER JUDICIAL ARBITRATION
13   vs.                            )
                                    )
14   MAUREEN TAKAHASHI,             )
                                    )
15   Defendant._____ )

16
        The undersigned hereby requests a Trial De Novo After Judicial Arbitration
17
     and waives a jury for that trial.
18

19   Date:_____

20

21   Andrew Chu
     _____

22

23

24

25

26

27

28
```

Have a friend serve by mail the Request for a Trial De Novo on your opponent. (See Chapter 7, Section E.) You'll need to file the Request and the Proof of Service by Mail with the court clerk, not the arbitration administrator.

After you file your Request, the clerk must put your case back on the list of cases awaiting trial at the same spot it would have been had there been no arbitration. Not all clerks know this. To protect yourself, ask to speak to the trial setting clerk when your file your Request. If the clerk asks you to submit a new Memo to Set (see Section A, above), do it. You don't have to under the law, but it's not worth fighting about.

Unless you somehow settle the case soon, you're headed for a trial. It's time to again ask yourself if you want a lawyer to take over. I'm not saying you should, but you should consider the possibility. Even if you don't hand the case over to a lawyer, you may want to buy an hour of a lawyer's time to have her review your case, your evidence and the arbitrator's award.

chapter 13

PREPARING FOR A TRIAL OR ARBITRATION HEARING

In a Small Claims Court dispute, presenting your evidence is simple: you stand up and tell the judge what happened. Unfortunately, presenting evidence in a Municipal Court case is quite a bit more complicated. The process is governed by hundreds of rules developed by lawyers, judges and legislatures over the years. Although you don't need to know all the rules, you will have to learn some of them.

These are three overriding principles that you must understand:

1.   The plaintiff must prove every important fact stated in her Complaint. Unless the plaintiff does this, the defendant can just sit back and do nothing.

The Plaintiff's Burden of Proof

The plaintiff must prove each important fact by "a preponderance of the evidence." A preponderance means that at least 51% of all the evidence supports the plaintiff's side. If the evidence is exactly even, neither side has established a preponderance and the plaintiff looses. This is what is meant by "the burden of proof."

---

2.   The rules of evidence (described below) control how the plaintiff must prove the facts of her case. The most basic rule—the hearsay rule—requires that people with firsthand knowledge can only testify about given events. Thus, the head electrician can't testify about what the other electricians told him happened on the job. Each electrician who actually saw what happened must testify.

3.   Don't assume the judge (or arbitrator or jury) knows any important fact. For example, if your case involves an accident on an important freeway in your area, don't assume the judge

knows the locations of the off ramps. Some judges don't drive. Be ready to bring a map to court. By the same token, don't assume the judge knows that plumbers charge about $20 an hour for their time. The plumber will have to testify. Of course, certain common facts (such as Monday following Sunday) need no proof. But don't assume too much.

A. A Short Course In the Rules of Evidence

To understand what kinds of evidence will be accepted in court or arbitration, you must have a general understanding of the rules of evidence. Understanding these rules will not only help you to put on your case, but it will also help you to object if your opponent presents inappropriate evidence in his portion of the trial. If you don't object to inappropriate evidence, the judge will allow the evidence to be presented. Except in very rare cases, the judge will not make an objection for you.

The rules of evidence are the subject of an excruciating course in law school and a major concentration on the bar examination. Nevertheless, many lawyers never really grasp them, and you cannot be expected to. Below I give you the basic rules, which should suffice, especially if your trial is before a judge who is reasonably sensitive to the challenges facing pro pers.

Your first introduction to the rules of evidence will no doubt come when your opponent objects to a question you pose to a witness. If your opponent objects, the witness should stop talking to let the judge rule on the objection. If the judge says that the objection is "sustained," it means the question is bad, the objection correct and the witness shouldn't answer. If the judge say the objection is "overruled," the question was fine, the objection invalid and the witness should answer.

Some objectionable questions can be rephrased to not violate the rules of evidence. If you don't understand why your question was no good, politely ask the judge to explain her ruling. Although judges are supposed to assume the role of a neutral baseball umpire calling the balls and strikes—and are not supposed to coach—most judges want cases resolved on the merits, not on technicalities. Many will provide limited help to pro pers in introducing relevant evidence and dealing with lawyers' objections.

If you offer evidence that violates a rule of evidence, you can expect your opponent to object. In preparing your case for the trial, don't rely on evidence that violates these rules. Just because a judge may help you around a technical problem doesn't mean she will let you present evidence that is clearly inadmissible.

These are the rules of evidence, presented in the words of the applicable objections. Be sure you understand them.

Irrelevant. Evidence is irrelevant if it does not prove or disprove any disputed fact necessary to determine the case. There is one exception, however: Some evidence that is irrelevant to the outcome of the case but goes to the believability of a witness is allowed in. For example, if a witness to your automobile accident told you at the scene of the accident that he saw the whole thing and you had a green light, your opponent can introduce evidence that the witness was convicted of a felony several years ago or has a poor reputation for truth in the local community.

Leading question. A leading question is one that suggests the answer you want given. ("Isn't it true, Mr. Carlton, that you've never been to Mendocino County?") With a few exceptions, you may not ask leading questions of witnesses you call. You may, however, ask leading questions of your opponent's witnesses. A question that does not suggest a particular answer is not leading. ("Did you or did you not just return from Mendocino County?") Nor is a question focusing on a particular incident. ("Turning to Tuesday, July 3, did you see anything unusual as you drove to work that day?")

Acceptable non-leading questions include:

- "Did you feel nauseated the next day?"
- "What happened next?"
- "Was the car coming towards you on the right or the left?"
- "What did you tell Mr. Carlton when he said the computer wouldn't work?"

Not responsive. A witness must answer the question asked, not a question he wishes you had asked. If an answer is not responsive and you object, the judge should order the answer stricken—which means that everyone is supposed to forget the witness ever said it.

How to Object

Here are a few ways to state some common objections:

"Objection, the question calls for irrelevant evidence."

"Objection, the question is leading and suggestive."

"Objection, the answer is not responsive to the question and I ask that it be stricken."

"Objection, the question calls for an opinion."

"Objection, the question calls for hearsay."

"Objection, the question is unintelligible (or vague or ambiguous)."

"Objection, the question is argumentative."

"Objection, counsel is harassing the witness."

Opinion. Unless a witness has been "qualified" as an expert—he gives testimony describing his special education or experience—she cannot give an opinion when she testifies. For example, a non-expert cannot give an opinion regarding the speed of a car or the reasonable cost of its repair. If you want to offer opinion testimony, ask the witness first what training or experience he has had in the area. The say to the judge "I request permission to question this witness as an expert on _____."

There is one exception to this opinion rule: A non-expert can give an opinion in areas of common experience, such as sobriety, age and race.

Hearsay. This is the most complicated rule of evidence. Yet, at its most basic level, it is quite

simple: Testimony can only be given by a first-hand witness. For example, your testimony that Bob told you he saw the red car run into the green car is hearsay. Bob's testimony that he saw the red car run into the green car is not. As a general rule, hearsay is not admissible. But, alas, there are several exceptions to the hearsay rule. Here are the ones you are likely to need:

1. A statement offered not to prove the truth of its contents is not hearsay. Your testimony "Bob told me he forgot to close the gate" is hearsay if you're trying to show who closed the gate or whether or not the gate was open. But if you want to show that Bob didn't have laryngitis (and that is a relevant issue in the case), then your testimony of what Bob said is not hearsay.

2. Photographs, contracts and street signs brought into court are not considered hearsay because those objects speak for themselves.

3. Business records, such as bills, letters, business records and police reports, brought to court by the person who keeps the business's records are an exception to the hearsay rule. There are a few shortcuts you can use to present business records at a trial or arbitration. See Section G, below (for a trial) and Chapter 12, Section C (for an arbitration hearing).

4. Statements a party previously made which damage that party's own case are considered an admission and may be offered in court as an exception to the hearsay rule. For example, if Lucy exclaims "I'm so sorry I hit you—I was changing radio stations" right after your accident with her, and now denies she ever said it, you can offer it as evidence.

Justifications for the hearsay rule have been offered for years, but none is satisfactory. The common reason given today is that hearsay isn't allowed because the person who made the statement can't be cross-examined. But even prior hearsay statements by a witness present in the courtroom are not admissible—so that's not the real reason. I guess no one really knows why we have the hearsay rule, which is why we have developed so many exceptions.

Don't worry if you're unclear about all the hearsay exceptions. Few people understand them all. I have otherwise rational friends who can debate their peculiarities at parties. You can rely on most judges to know something about the subject and to rule correctly. When your opponent presents some evidence that sounds like hearsay, say "Objection, hearsay." If your opponent objects similarly to something your witness (or you) says, say "Your honor, I am not trained in the law; I submit the issue to you."

B. Statement of Witnesses and Evidence

As noted in Chapter 12, you will receive a notice from the court giving you your trial date. Receipt of this notice should trigger your preparation of a Request for Statement of Witnesses and Evidence form, if you're preparing for a trial—the form is not used in arbitration hearings. On this form, you ask your opponent to list the witnesses and evidence he plans to use at the trial. A copy of this form is in the Appendix.

 After you fill out the form, have a friend serve it by mail on your opponent between 30 and 45 days prior to trial date. (See Chapter 7, Section E.) Your trial date may be getting close, so watch this deadline closely.[1] If there's more than one opponent, be sure to send each one a form. Expect to receive a request yourself. When you get it, you must fill it out and list your witnesses (including declarations) and the evidence you plan to use. You don't have to list yourself or your opponent, as either party can call herself or the other side at the trial. Your opponent must do the same.

A completed sample reply is below.

Have your friend mail back the completed form within 25 days of when you received it in the mail (20 days if it was hand delivered to you). Your opponent must do the same. Although the request and response are not filed with the clerk's office, have your friend fill out

---

[1] Code of Civil Procedure §§ 96 and 97 provide the 30- to 45-day range. And the 30 to 45 days are before the date *first* set by the court for trial. If the court postpones your trial to a later date, you can't use the new date as a basis for sending a Request for Statement of Witnesses and Evidence.

another Proof of Service. (See Chapter 7, Section E.)

If you ignore the form (or your opponent does) or don't respond on time, you cannot offer any documents other than those obtained by formal discovery. (See Chapter 10.) Nor can you present any witnesses other than yourself and your opponent, except a witness whose testimony will impeach another witness. Impeachment testimony shows that at an earlier date, the witness made a statement contrary to what he is now saying.

Your opponent's response will help you plan for the trial, as you now have some idea of what witnesses he'll call and what documents he'll rely on. He is not obliged to call all of the witnesses he lists and may try to scare you with a long list of people he has no intention of bringing. If you want someone on his list as your own witness, serve a subpoena on that person. (See Section E, below.)

C. Live Witnesses or Written Declarations?

If you and/or your opponent will be the only witness(es) you plan to have testify at the arbitration hearing or trial, skip ahead to Section D.

One of the best examples of modernization of our usually-slow legal system is that written statements of witnesses—called declarations— are now admissible in arbitration hearings and Municipal Court trials. (Examples are in Section D, below.) Until quite recently, witnesses always had to be present to give live testimony.

But just because you *can* substitute a written statement for a live witness doesn't mean you necessarily *should*. As a general rule, you should lean toward having all but relatively unimportant witnesses appear live at a trial, while except in unusual situations, you should use written declarations in arbitration hearings. But these rules are not absolute. In both cases, you've got to weigh the advantages and disadvantages of each. You'll want to consider the following:

Persuasiveness. A witness whose testimony will be extremely supportive of your side—for example, a person who didn't know any of the parties (and thus has no motive to lie) and saw a traffic accident from a spot on the sidewalk—should testify in person if possible. She is likely to be much more persuasive in person than on paper. If a witness will testify to routine facts—such as a billing clerk from your doctor's office who would testify about your medical bill—save time, money and hassle by using a declaration instead of his personal testimony.

Sample Reply to Request for Statement of Witnesses and Evidence

1 LAWRENCE BOOTY
   12 Kings Highway
2 Petaluma, CA 93001
   707-555-8989
3
   Plaintiff In Pro Per
4

5

6

7

8   MUNICIPAL COURT OF CALIFORNIA

9   COUNTY OF SONOMA

10

11 LAWRENCE BOOTY,   )   Case No. 809-SC-1992
)
12 Plaintiff,   )   REPLY TO REQUEST FOR
)   STATEMENT OF WITNESSES
13 vs.   )   AND EVIDENCE
)
14 MYER KIM,   )
)
15 Defendant._____)

16

17   Plaintiff intends to call the following witnesses at the time of trial:

18   1. Tom Olson, Olson's Garage, 3409 Cedar Street, Petaluma.

19   2. Lisa Navarro, M.D., 4534 Battery Street, Santa Rosa.

20   3. Declaration of Herbert Kwong, M.D., 2889 5th Avenue, New York, New York.

21   Plaintiff intends to offer the following physical evidence at the time of

22 trial:

23   1. Toyota tire taken from right front of defendant's vehicle.

24   2. Large piece of sheet metal removed from that tire.

25   Plaintiff intends to offer the following documentary evidence at the time of

26 trial (copies are attached):

27   1. Medical records of Dr. Navarro's treatment of plaintiff and bills for

28 that treatment.

2. Medical records of Dr. Kwong's treatment of plaintiff and bills for that treatment.

3. Tow records from Olson's Garage regarding the subject of this lawsuit.

Dated: _____

_____
Lawrence Booty

Cost. Doctors, other experts and police officers must be paid by you if you ask (or subpoena) them to testify. They frequently charge by the hour, so this can be a large expense. This is particularly true if the expert has to wait in the hall a while before she is called to give her testimony. Depending on your budget, you may or may not want to pay the fee.

If you have to bring a doctor, dentist or similar professional to testify, tell the judge before the trial begins and try to arrange a time when the judge will agree to stop whatever else is going on and have your witness testify "out of order."

Inconvenience. Don't seriously inconvenience someone and require him to be present. For example, if a witness to your accident is an airline pilot who will probably be 40,000 feet above ground when your case is heard, a written declaration should suffice. Keep your trial in perspective. While it is of great importance to you, it is not the most important event in the modern world. Of course, if you feel you can only present your trial if the live witness is present, tell him why you need him and try to keep his waiting to a minimum.

D. Using Written Declarations

To use written testimony at an arbitration hearing, you simply prepare a declaration under penalty of perjury and deliver it to your opponent(s) at least 20 days before the hearing. If your opponent wants the witness to testify in person, she must deliver such a demand within 10 days after you serve the declaration. Otherwise, the statement will be admissible as long as it does not violate the rules of evidence.

(See Section A, above.) All this is covered in Chapter 12, Section C.

Preparing written testimony for use at a trial is similar to preparing it for an arbitration hearing.[2] First, you must prepare what is called "a declaration under penalty of perjury" for each witness who will submit a statement. Contact the witness, discuss the possible testimony and agree on what should be said.

For instance, a declaration from your doctor should include a description of your injuries, a description of the doctor's treatment, the amount of his bill, the reasonableness of the bill and your future prognosis. Write a draft and make sure the witness agrees to it. If so, type it up and have him sign it.

A sample declaration is below; be sure to use legal paper.

Make at least one copy of each declaration. Keep the originals and have your friend (who by now is well known at the post office) send one copy of each to your opponent at least 30 days before the trial date. Enclose a letter like the sample below. Make sure your friend fills out a Proof of Service. (See Chapter 7, Section E.)

[2]Code of Civil Procedure § 98 covers written testimony at Municipal Court trials.

Sample Letter Accompanying Declarations

Martin Canseco, Esq.
Henderson, LaRussa and Canseco
1800 Forrest Road, Suite 1311
Gilroy, CA

March 9, 19__

Re: Pines vs. McMurtry and Rivera, Case # 56-2323

Dear Mr. Canseco:

I am the plaintiff in the above-referred case. The attached declaration of Lee Anderson, M.D. is served on you pursuant to Code of Civil Procedure § 98. Dr. Anderson's current address is 3400 Medical Row, Pacific Grove, California. Dr. Anderson will be available there for a reasonable period of time during the 20 days immediately prior to trial.

Yours very truly,

Judy Pines

If your opponent wants a witness's live testimony instead of the declaration—presumably to unleash a withering cross-examination—he must serve a subpoena on the witness to bring her to court. If your opponent doesn't serve a subpoena, the declaration becomes evidence as if the witness was sitting on the witness stand.

That means that if any part of the declaration is hearsay or otherwise not admissible, it doesn't become admissible just because it's in the form of a declaration.

Note on expert witnesses. If you use a written declaration for an expert witness (see Section A, above) to give an opinion, you will have to "qualify" the expert. That simply means you will have to present her credentials. The first paragraph in the above sample declaration qualifies the expert.

If your opponent serves a subpoena on your expert, who is now forced to come to the trial, you may wonder who pays the expert's fee. The answer is unclear, but you ought to argue as forcefully as you can that your opponent should.

Note on custodians of records. Allowing testimony by written declaration is particularly helpful if you need to bring records into court. The live witness wouldn't add much and using a written statement will speed up the trial. A sample is below.

This declaration satisfies two important elements of the case: the injury charges and the reasonableness of those charges. For a declaration from an auto repair person, substitute something like the following for the first two paragraphs in the above sample declaration (custodian of records):

"I am the owner of the Automotive Body Repair Shop, 8935 Fifth Street, Los Angeles, California. I have been in the business of body and fender work for 11 years and have attended numerous classes conducted by manufacturers in this field. I have repaired hundreds of cars damaged in accidents and believe that I am very knowledgeable about my work.

Sample Declaration (Expert Witness)

1 JUDY PINES
   166 Euclid Street
2 Monterey, CA 93001
   408-555-8989
3
   Plaintiff In Pro Per
4

5

6

7

8   MUNICIPAL COURT OF CALIFORNIA

9   COUNTY OF MONTEREY

10

11 JUDY PINES,   )   Case No. 56-2323
)
12 Plaintiff,   )   DECLARATION UNDER PENALTY
)   OF PERJURY
13 vs.   )
)
14 DANIEL MCMURTRY and   )
    CARLOS RIVERA,   )
15   )
    Defendants.   )
16

17 Lee Anderson declares:

18   I am a physician licensed by the State of California with a specialty in

19 internal and sports medicine. I have maintained an active practice in this

20 field in Monterey County since 1977. My resume describing my education and ex-

21 perience is attached to this declaration and marked Exhibit A.

22   I first had occasion to treat Judy Pines on July 3, 19__ when she was

23 brought to the Monterey Peninsula Hospital Emergency Room, where I was on duty.

24 She appeared to have severely injured her left hand and was in a great deal of

25 pain.

26   I gave her medication for her pain and had her hand X-rayed. The bones in

27 her left index finger, middle finger and ring finger were broken. I set the

28 breaks, applied splints, gave her more pain medication and sent her home with

    instructions for care.

1   I saw Ms. Pines four more times over the succeeding two months for treatment

2 of her broken fingers. Four weeks after her first visit she had a reasonable

3 amount of movement in her fingers. By eight weeks after the injury, I believe

4 she had fully recovered.

5   My charges for my medical services were $1055, which I believe to be

6 reasonable and customary in this community.

7   I declare under penalty of perjury that the foregoing is true and correct.

8 Executed at Pacific Grove, California on December 12, 19__.

9

10 _____

    Lee Anderson, M.D.

11

12

13

14

15

16

17

18

19

20

21

22

23

24

25

26

27

28

Sample Declaration (Custodian of Records)

1 | LAWRENCE BOOTY
12 Kings Highway
2 | Petaluma, CA 93001
707-555-8989
3
Plaintiff In Pro Per
4

5

6

7

8 | MUNICIPAL COURT OF CALIFORNIA

9 | COUNTY OF SONOMA

10

11 | LAWRENCE BOOTY,   )   Case No. 809-SC-1992
)
12 | Plaintiff,   )   DECLARATION UNDER PENALTY
)   OF PERJURY
13 | vs.   )
)
14 | MYER KIM,   )
)
15 | Defendant. _____   )

16

17 | Paul Goldberg declares:

18 | I am the head of the records section at Civic Center Hospital in Santa Rosa.

19 | The patient records of the hospital are under my supervision and control.

20 | Attached to this declaration are the records of the hospital's treatment of

21 | Lawrence Booty for the period between September 3, 19__ and September 24, 19__.

22 | The charges listed are the normal and customary charges for the listed services

23 | in this community.

24 | Executed at Santa Rosa, California on January 4, 19__. I declare under

25 | penalty of perjury that the foregoing is true and correct.

26

27 | _____
Paul Goldberg

28

"The plaintiff had his 1990 Chevrolet towed to my shop on September 2, 19__. It had extensive body damage on the right side of the car. The attached bill shows the work that was done to repair the damage under my supervision. All of the work appeared to me to be necessary to repair the damage to the car in a recent collision. The bill also shows my charges for the repair of the automobile, which have been paid. I believe the charges are reasonable under the standards of what is normally charged in Los Angeles for similar work by competent persons."

E. Having Witnesses Attend a Trial or Arbitration Hearing

By now you may have decided that you want a witness to attend the trial or hearing, not to merely write a declaration. You have two options for getting the witness to the hearing or trial:

• ask

• serve a subpoena

Any witness "friendly" to your case—that is, someone who will give testimony in your favor—should initially be asked. If the witness is a family member or close friend who will show up when asked, you need not do anything else. If, however, the person is less than reliable, is someone who you don't really know (a person who witnessed as accident) or is a witness friendly to your opponent, you will want to serve a subpoena.

Serving a subpoena has a few advantages. A forgetful witness is likely to remember the trial date if served with a subpoena. If the witness doesn't show up, the judge or arbitrator is more likely to postpone ("continue") the trial or hearing rather than proceed without the person's testimony if you served a subpoena. And a subpoena can provide the necessary excuse for an employed witness to get some time off from work to testify.

Most people have little idea what a subpoena actually is. It's a one-page form issued by the court, but filled out by you, requiring a witness to attend a trial or arbitration.[3] You get a subpoena from the court clerk, which will be blank except for the clerk's signature and the court's official seal.

Filling out the subpoena takes little work. (A completed sample is below.) Cross out the reference to your attorney. Then type in the witness's name, the address of the court house or arbitration hearing (be sure to include the room number or department) and the time she must appear. Put down the time the trial or hearing is scheduled to begin. If the trial or hearing will last more than one day, however, let your witness know that she need not attend until the day she will actually give her testimony.[4]

If you want the witness to bring any documents, and the witness is either likely to forget or is not a "friendly" witness, you need to check the duces tecum box on the subpoena. You must also draft a declaration listing the precise documents you want the witness to bring and the reason each document is needed for the trial, and state that in your opinion these items are in the witness's possession or control.

[3]Subpoenas are also used to require a witness to attend a deposition. See Chapter 10.
[4]Code of Civil Procedure § 1985.1.

982(a)(15)

ATTORNEY OR PARTY WITHOUT ATTORNEY *(Name and Address)*: Jamie Garcia 82 Southwest Drive San Mateo, CA 94404	TELEPHONE NO. 415-555-2044	FOR COURT USE ONLY

ATTORNEY FOR *(Name)*: plaintiff in pro per

NAME OF COURT: San Mateo County Municipal Court
STREET ADDRESS: Central Branch
MAILING ADDRESS: 800 North Humboldt Street
CITY AND ZIP CODE: San Mateo, CA 94401
BRANCH NAME:

PLAINTIFF/PETITIONER: Jamie Garcia, dba Flour Power

DEFENDANT/RESPONDENT: Anne Warren, individually and dba Anne's Pie Shop

CIVIL SUBPENA ☐ Duces Tecum	CASE NUMBER: 555934

THE PEOPLE OF THE STATE OF CALIFORNIA, TO *(name)*:

Fiona Richey

1. **YOU ARE ORDERED TO APPEAR AS A WITNESS** in this action as follows unless you make a special agreement with the person named in item 3:

   a. Date: March 6, 1992   Time: 9 am   Dept./Div.: 17   Room.:
   b. Address: 800 North Humboldt St.
      San Mateo, CA 94401

2. AND YOU ARE
   a. [X] ordered to appear in person.
   b. [ ] not required to appear in person if you produce a true, legible, and durable copy of the records described in the accompanying affidavit as follows: (1) place the **copy** of the records in an envelope (or other wrapper) and seal it; (2) attach a copy of this subpena to the envelope or write on the envelope the case name and number, name of the witness and date and time from item 1 above; (3) place this first envelope in an outer envelope or wrapper, seal it, and mail it to the clerk of the court at the address in item 1.
   c. [ ] ordered to appear in person and to produce the records described in the accompanying affidavit. The personal attendance of the custodian of records or other qualified witness and the production of the **original** records is required by this subpena. The procedure authorized pursuant to subdivision (b) of section 1560, and sections 1561 and 1562, of the Evidence Code will not be deemed sufficient compliance with this subpena.

3. **IF YOU HAVE ANY QUESTIONS ABOUT WITNESS FEES OR THE TIME OR DATE FOR YOU TO APPEAR, OR IF YOU WANT TO BE CERTAIN THAT YOUR PRESENCE IS REQUIRED, CONTACT THE ATTORNEY REQUESTING THIS SUBPENA, NAMED ABOVE, OR THE FOLLOWING PERSON, BEFORE THE DATE ON WHICH YOU ARE TO APPEAR:**
   a. Name: Jamie Garcia   b. Telephone number: 415-555-2044

4. **Witness Fees:** You are entitled to witness fees and mileage actually traveled both ways, as provided by law, if you request them at the time of service. You may request them before your scheduled appearance from the person named in item 3.

5. You are ordered to appear in this civil matter in your capacity as a peace officer or other person described in Government Code section 68097.1.
   Date: Clerk, by _____ , Deputy

   ┌───┐
   │ DISOBEDIENCE OF THIS SUBPENA MAY BE PUNISHED AS CONTEMPT BY THIS COURT. YOU WILL ALSO BE LIABLE FOR THE SUM │
   │ OF FIVE HUNDRED DOLLARS AND ALL DAMAGES RESULTING FROM YOUR FAILURE TO OBEY. │
   └───┘

Date issued:

....
(TYPE OR PRINT NAME)   ▶

                                                    _____
                                                    (SIGNATURE OF PERSON ISSUING SUBPENA)

                                                    _____
                                                    (TITLE)

(See reverse for proof of service)

Form Adopted by Rule 982
Judicial Council of California   **CIVIL SUBPENA**   Code of Civil Procedure, §§ 1985, 1986, 1987
982(a)(15) [Rev. July 1, 1987]

Sample Declaration (Supporting a Subpoena Duces Tecum)

```
 1   JUDY PINES
     166 Euclid Street
 2   Monterey, CA 93001
     408-555-8989
 3
     Plaintiff In Pro Per
 4

 5

 6

 7

 8                    MUNICIPAL COURT OF CALIFORNIA

 9                       COUNTY OF MONTEREY

10

11   JUDY PINES,                    )        Case No. 56-2323
                                    )
12   Plaintiff,                     )        DECLARATION UNDER PENALTY
                                    )        OF PERJURY
13   vs.                            )
                                    )
14   DANIEL MCMURTRY and            )
     CARLOS RIVERA,                 )
15                                  )
     Defendants._____   )
16

17   Judy Pines declares:

18      Audrey Good is the custodian of the records of Lee Anderson, M.D. and has

19   the records of my treatment by Dr. Anderson in her possession and control. I

20   wish that all records for that treatment from July 3, 19__ to September 30, 19__

21   be produced in court for the trial. These documents show the extent of my

22   injury that resulted from the accident that is the subject of this lawsuit,

23   the treatment by Dr. Anderson and his fees, and thus are clearly relevant.

24      I declare under penalty of perjury that the foregoing is true and correct.

25   Executed at Monterey, California on January 10, 19__.

26

27   _____
     Judy Pines
28
```

Your subpoena or subpoena duces tecum must be personally served on the witness. Serving by mail is not sufficient. See Chapter 7 for instructions on how to personally serve someone.

F. Making a Chart of Your Evidence

To make sure you know exactly what you (or your opponent, if you are the defendant) will have to prove at the trial or hearing and what evidence you (or your opponent) will present to prove each point, I suggest you make a two-column chart of your case. Do this whether you are the plaintiff or defendant. Begin with the Com-plaint. In the left column, list each fact the plaintiff will have to prove.

If you are the plaintiff (or a cross-complainant), list in the right column exactly what evidence you will use to prove the corresponding fact. Review Section A, above, to be sure your evidence is admissible. If you are the defendant (or a cross-defendant), note in the right column the facts asserted in the Complaint (or Cross-Complaint) that you will challenge and what evidence you'll use to do so. If you raised affirmative defenses in your Answer, list them in the left column and the evidence you'll use to prove them in the right.

The sample below is for a case in which you're suing your brother-in-law for failing to pay back money you loaned him.

Facts in Complaint	Evidence
4/12/90—loaned $10,000 to Harold	My testimony. Also Yvonne Reilly who lives Long Beach can confirm; she was in next room
Terms of loan—$250 per month with 9% interest	Note on back of envelope initialed by Harold
Harold paid for six months	Admitted in his answer
Harold made no more payments	My testimony; copies of his bank records sub-poenaed from bank.
Harold owes me $11,978 plus costs	Declaration from Roger Hamilton, C.P.A.

G.   Making a Trial Binder

About a month before the date of your trial or arbitration hearing, you should make a trial binder. This basically consists of a loose-leaf notebook containing all documents you need to bring to the trial or hearing. Tab each major document filed with the court, each item of discovery and each item of evidence. Your binder might include the following:

- Complaint

- Answer

- Plaintiff's Case Questionnaire

- Defendant's Case Questionnaire

- Interrogatories sent by plaintiff and defendant's answers

- Interrogatories sent by defendant and plaintiff's answers

- Copy of April 12, 1990 contract and amendments to the contract

- Letters between the parties before the lawsuit was filed

- Letters between parties after the lawsuit was filed

- Outline of your opening statement (see Chapter 14)

- Declaration of Roger Hamilton, C.P.A.

- Matters to be covered in plaintiff's testimony

- Questions to ask witness Yvonne Reilly

- Questions to ask defendant on cross-examination

- Closing argument

H. Drafting Questions To Ask Your Witnesses

 One important part of preparing for your trial or arbitration hearing is designing questions to ask your witnesses. For help in doing this, I'd suggest you look at either *Trials* or *Proof of Facts*, multi-volume sets published by American Jurisprudence and available in law libraries. These books are written for use anywhere in the United States, so you may have to make some adjustments when using them in California.

Although *Trials* and *Proof of Facts* are written for lawyers, they are relatively simple to use. Turn to either publication's General Index and look up your type of case. You'll see references to hundreds of articles. Many articles include a list of suggested questions. Many questions won't be relevant to your case. You can obviously discard those. For example, if no one was speeding in your auto accident, don't include questions asking the witness to describe how fast a car was going at various sites. Adapt these questions to your case—don't be a slave to them.

You may find it helpful to write out each question you expect to ask. You want to establish why your witness was present and what she saw. If possible, elicit the information so that it is told chronologically. Here are a list of questions you might ask a witness to a traffic accident:

- Ms. Dillingham, do you customarily drive down Interstate 53 at about 2 a.m. in the morning?

- Where are you coming from and where are you going at that hour?

- Were you driving south down Interstate 53 at about 2 a.m. February 14 of last year? (Your opponent could object to this question as being leading, but most judges allow you to ask one or two leading questions to set the scene.)

- Where were you on Interstate 53 at that time?

- Was there anyone else in your car?

- Who?

- Did you see a brown Ford automobile driving on Interstate 53 at that time?

- What did you see the brown Ford do?

- Did you later see me at the scene of the accident?

- Did you notice anything unusual about me?

- What?

Take your witness through enough questions to tell the full story.

I. Attending a Settlement Conference

 If your case is on its way to an arbitration hearing (not a trial) read Chapter 12, not this section, if you haven't already done so.

Some courts hold a settlement conference before a trial. If your court does, you'll receive a notice from the clerk telling you when and where to appear for such a conference. Because over 90% of cases settle before trial, courts try to speed up the settlement process by forcing you to come to meet with a judge to talk turkey. The judge may be the judge scheduled to hear the trial, a different judge or a volunteer lawyer who helps the court.

Settlement conferences are informal proceedings normally held in a judge's office (which, for some strange historical reason, is called the judge's "chambers"). The settlement conference notice may state that you must file a Settlement Conference Statement before the conference itself. If the notice doesn't say what needs to be in the Statement, check your local rules. The Statement gives the judge a chance to familiarize himself with your case. Be sure to comply with any requirement of filing a Statement. If you don't, the judge may fine you.

Judges' settlement styles vary widely, but be prepared to outline the strengths of your case and to handle some probing (and at times unfriendly) questions from the judge about your case's weaknesses. Have in mind your bottom line—the figure you'd accept in settlement—and a higher (or lower if you're the defendant) figure you plan to open with.

The judge may ask to speak to each party separately. Most judges keep what you say in these meetings confidential. That's a sign of a good settlement judge—someone who is trustworthy and whose advice people follow. Of course, because you don't come to court regularly, you'll have to operate on a certain amount of blind faith. After all, if you can't trust a judge, whom can you trust? Don't answer that question.

But not all judges keep things confidential, so ask what will stay in the room and what will be told to your opponent. And let the judge know what you want. For example, if you reveal your absolute bottom line amount to the judge, make it clear that you don't want your opponent told the amount unless the judge is confident your opponent will pay (or accept) that amount.

Can Settlement Figures Come Out During a Trial?

Don't be afraid to make a settlement offer out of fear that the amount you are willing to compromise for will be used against you at the trial. By law, settlement offers are not admissible during a trial.

During the settlement conference, the judge should evaluate the strengths and weaknesses of your case and give you some indication of what he thinks of your chance of success at the trial. The judge may also suggest a settlement figure—possibly far less than what you expected (or far more, if you're a defendant). Nevertheless, consider it seriously.

Some judges dislike doing settlement conferences and provide very little help in arriving at a resolution. Some judges zealously try to settle cases, almost without regard to their true value. Such a judge might think that in your

inexperience you'll accept less than your case is worth (or will pay more than you should). If the judge's suggestion seems too low—and the judge doesn't give you a satisfactory explanation why—let the judge know you're not interested in settling for that amount.

If you reach a settlement, the judge will "put it on the record" so that the plaintiff can enforce it if the defendant later changes her mind. The judge normally does this by bringing the clerk or court reporter into his office and stating the terms of the settlement, such as "Defendant will pay plaintiff $10,000 in ten monthly installments of $1,000. Payments are to made on the first day of each month beginning June 1, 19__ and ending on March 1, 19__." If you want some time to think about the settlement, tell that to the judge and ask for a second conference in a few days. Then talk things over with your Sounding Board.

The judge may ask you to make several decisions at the conference, such as:

- Are you willing to go to arbitration instead of a trial? (Answer yes.)

- If the other side demands a jury trial, will you accept fewer than 12 jurors? (Answer yes—six or eight will be fine.)

- Will you accept a pro tem (temporary) judge in place of a regular judge? (Yes.)

TRIAL BEFORE A JUDGE

Most Municipal Court cases that don't settle are tried before a judge with no jury. Only a few Municipal Court cases are heard by a judge and jury together. If yours is a jury trial, skip ahead to the Chapter 15, *Trial Before a Jury*, before reading this chapter.

The day has arrived for your trial. You've prepared your evidence, your witnesses are ready to testify and you want to get this matter over with. It's time to grab your trial binder and head for the courtroom.

Court houses usually contain several different courtrooms. To find the one where you need to go, look at the Notice of Trial you received from the court. It will direct you to appear in a certain courtroom—called a "department." This may be a court that sends cases to other courtrooms where trials are conducted (the first judge is called either the "master calendar" judge or the "presiding" judge), or it may be the actual courtroom where your trial will be (the judge is called the "trial" judge).

When you find the courtroom, check the court schedule—called a "calendar"—on the bulletin board outside, or possibly inside, of your courtroom. If it's not there, ask the uniformed marshal in the courtroom or the clerk in the room where you filed your papers for help.

When you've confirmed you're in the right courtroom, wait until the court is in recess—the judge is not on the bench—and approach the clerk sitting in the front of the courtroom. Show her your Notice of Trial. She will make a note that you are present. This is called "checking in." If the judge doesn't take a recess and you don't get a chance to check in, don't get concerned; your case will still be announced ("called" in legalese) by the judge or clerk.

Courtrooms can be very busy. You may have to wait around for a while. You can use your waiting time to hold any last minute settlement discussions with your opponent—even the morning of trial is not too late to settle a case. In fact, so many cases settle on the day of trial that on a given day, courts often schedule two or three times as many trials as there are judges available. If fewer cases than expected settle, however, the court will have to reschedule some of the cases.

Eventually, the judge will "call your case." If you've reached a settlement, let the judge know. Otherwise, the judge is likely to ask you to estimate how long your trial will last. Explain that because you are a pro per, it is difficult for you to make such an estimate. Tell the judge how many witness you plan to call and state that you will do all you can to expedite the matter.

If you are in the courtroom with the master calendar judge, he may ask you to step into his office to try and settle the case, he may assign the case to another judge or he may tell you that there's no judge available. In the latter situation, you may be instructed to wait, come back in a few hours or come back in a few days.

A. Sizing Up the Judge

Once you reach the courtroom with the trial judge, spend some time sizing her up. Is she patient? Does she treat any other pro pers with respect? Take note of any quirks. It's possible that the judge is actually a lawyer hired by the court to handle certain cases. These lawyers are called "commissioners" if this is their regular job, or "judges pro tem" if they volunteer to serve as judges only occasionally.

No matter what kind of judge is scheduled to hear your case, you can remove that judge from your case if you don't want her to decide it. But exercise this right sparingly.

1. Commissioners

Commissioners are usually competent and will handle the case very similarly to a judge. If you're assigned a commissioner, you'll be asked to sign an agreement stating that the commissioner is acceptable. As stated above, sign unless you know that the particular commissioner is unfair or incompetent. Refusing the commissioner often means a substantial delay in getting to trial. And the judge you wind up with may be no better.

2. Judges Pro Tem

If you're assigned a judge pro tem, again, you'll be asked to sign an agreement stating that the judge pro tem is acceptable. Whether or not to accept a judge pro tem is not as clear cut as with a commissioner. While many judges pro tem are capable, experienced and fair, some are none of these things. I have seen several judges pro tem who seem to think that small or medium-sized cases are of little importance. Some are big-time trial lawyers who are not familiar with the legal rules that apply to your type of case.

If you know in advance of your trial date that a particular judge pro tem will hear your case, go watch the pro tem handle other cases. If you don't, you'll have to rely on your intuition in deciding whether or not to accept the pro tem. If you are in a hurry to resolve your case, you may want to accept the pro tem unless it is clear she is unfair or incompetent. If you don't accept

him, it could be weeks or possibly even months before you get assigned to a judge. And in some counties, where drug cases consume all the regular judges, you'll only be assigned another pro tem.

3. Regular Judges

You have the right to one removal ("challenge") of a trial judge assigned to your case.[1] Once you've exercised this right, you cannot remove another judge assigned to replace the first one. Removing a particular judge from hearing your case isn't all that easy. Figuring out who to challenge, who the new judge will be and whether the new judge will be better or worse, can be quite complex. It is usually not worth it unless you've determined that a particular judge is awful, or especially awful to pro pers.

The rules for challenging a judge differ depending on when the judge is assigned to your case.

a. Judge Assigned Before the Trial Date

In some counties, you will receive a notice from the court before the trial naming the trial judge or the department where the trial will be. If you get such a notice, call the court and find out the next time the judge in that department will hear a case. If you can, visit the court that day and watch the judge in action.

If you decide the judge is too tough on pro pers or otherwise unacceptable, you must file a Peremptory Challenge Motion at least five days before the trial. A sample is below.

---

[1]Code of Civil Procedure § 170.6.

Sample Peremptory Challenge

```
 1 │  JUDY PINES
    │  166 Euclid Street
 2 │  Monterey, CA 93001
    │  408-555-8989
 3 │
    │  Plaintiff In Pro Per
 4 │
    │
 5 │
    │
 6 │
    │
 7 │
    │
 8 │                    MUNICIPAL COURT OF CALIFORNIA
    │
 9 │                          COUNTY OF MONTEREY
    │
10 │
    │
11 │  JUDY PINES,                    )            Case No. 56-2323
    │                                )
12 │  Plaintiff,                     )            PEREMPTORY CHALLENGE
    │                                )
13 │  vs.                            )
    │                                )
14 │  DANIEL MCMURTRY and            )
    │  CARLOS RIVERA,                )
15 │                                )
    │  Defendants.                   )
16 │
    │
17 │  Judy Pines, declares:
    │
18 │      I am the plaintiff to the within action. Judge Ernest Angler before whom the
    │
19 │  trial in this case is pending is prejudiced against my interest so that I
    │
20 │  believe that I cannot have a fair and impartial trial before him.
    │
21 │      I declare under penalty of perjury that the foregoing is true and correct.
    │
22 │  Executed on June 4, 19__ at Carmel, California.
    │
23 │
    │
24 │  Judy Pines
    │
25 │
    │
26 │
    │
27 │
    │
28 │
```

Once your form is prepared, you must file it with the office of the court clerk (where you filed your Complaint or Answer) and deliver a copy to clerk in the courtroom of the trial judge you are challenging, at least five days before the trial. If you follow this procedure carefully, your challenge will be granted automatically.

b. Judge Assigned the Day of Trial

In many counties, especially larger ones, you won't know the judge's identity until the day of your trial. If you have the chance to observe him and don't like what you see, you can challenge him when he is assigned. When your case is called, stand up and state that you wish challenge the trial judge. The clerk will administer an oath, where you swear to tell the truth. After taking the oath, state "I believe Judge Angler is prejudiced against my interest so that I cannot have a fair and impartial trial before him."

Then sit down and wait for another assignment. You may have to wait several hours or even days before you get assigned to another judge.

B. Rules of Courtroom Etiquette

Going to court can be scary for anyone who has never been there before. A handy and basic paperback on courtroom etiquette is *The First Trial*, by Goldberg (Nutshell Series, West Publishing Co.). It's not written specifically for California and is designed for someone who has recently completed law school. Nevertheless, it has some helpful advice. These rules can also serve as guidelines.

1. Call the judge "Your Honor" or, if you wish, the more global term "the Court." While there is nothing inherently wrong with calling the judge "Judge" or "Judge Ford," it's a bit jarring and usually not done.

2. Be on time. If an emergency occurs and you're going to be late or absent, call the courtroom directly, or the court clerk's office if you don't have the courtroom phone number. Once you're in court, be back on time after a recess or lunch break.

3. Be courteous to everyone, particularly the clerk, the court reporter and the marshall. Don't make insulting, sarcastic or angry remarks about your opponent.

4. Address your opponent, opponent's lawyer and all witnesses as "Mr." or "Ms." and their last name. Never use their first name.

5. Don't sit on the courtroom railings or try to use the court's telephones. There should be a public phone in the hall.

6. Don't be overly fussy about your attire. It's best to dress as you usually do. If yours is a

business dispute, wear your normal business clothing. If you're a construction worker who wasn't paid for work you did, however, there's nothing wrong with wearing clean work clothes.

7. Stay behind the table where you are seated (called the "counsel table") except when handing something to the clerk or a witness, or when you need to point to an item on the exhibit board. Don't walk between the counsel table and where the judge sits unless the construction of the courtroom makes it necessary.

8. Stand when you are speaking. A possible exception is when you are making an objection or a statement of only a few words.

9. Address all objections, statements and arguments to the judge, prefacing your remarks with "your honor" or "the court," not to your opponent's lawyer or a witness.

10. Don't interrupt the judge. No matter how wrong you think the she is, don't argue when she talks. If the other side objects to one of your questions, don't ask another one until the judge rules on the objection.

11. If the judge rules that an objection is "sustained," it means the objection is allowed and your statement or question is stricken. Continue to argue the matter at your own peril. If you ask to say a few more things about the matter, most judges won't let you.

12. Tell your witnesses not to discuss their testimony with any other witnesses.

13. When you are asking questions or watching your opponent ask questions, don't nod your head or grimace. Act as though everything is going just as your expected it would.

C. The Trial Begins

The proceedings begin when the trial judge or clerk calls out the name of your case. When this happens, walk up to the long table in front of the judge, remain standing and state your name. If the table doesn't have signs identifying the plaintiff's and defendant's sides, the plaintiff should stand on the side closer to the witness box.

What happens next depends on how the judge runs a courtroom. Hear are the most likely scenarios:

• The judge, ever hopeful of saving time by arranging a settlement, will take the parties (and any attorneys) into her office for a few minutes to find out what the case is all about and perhaps suggest a settlement.

• The judge will ask the plaintiff to make an opening statement—some brief remarks that outline how the plaintiff plans to proceed.

• The judge will ask the plaintiff to "call your first witness." A judge who does this wants you to know that her court is busy and she wants to get down to business.

Even if the judge holds a settlement conference or tells the plaintiff to call the first witness, each party has the right to make an opening statement. If the judge doesn't offer the chance, and you want to make such a statement, you can ask to.

If you just had a settlement conference with the judge and ask to make an opening statement, the judge may say no, feeling that it's a waste of time. Even if there was no conference, the judge, especially in a short trial, may prefer that you get right to the evidence. At this early stage of the trial, skip the opening statement and don't make waves. Remember—this judge will determine the outcome of your case. If you appear difficult to deal with, the judge may subconsciously be prejudiced (despite her best intentions) against you.

If the judge allows opening statements, the plaintiff goes first. Give a short explanation of who your witnesses will be and what each is expected to say. End by stating that after all the evidence is presented, you believe Her Honor (the judge) will conclude you're entitled to an award of whatever amount you are seeking.

The defendant, too, should give a short explanation of his witnesses and their testimony. He should end by stating that after the evidence is given, he believes Her Honor will conclude that the plaintiff is entitled to nothing and that he is entitled to the costs of his lawsuit.

To help you prepare, put an outline of your opening statement in your trial binder. (See Chapter 13, Section G.) Here's an example of a plaintiff's opening statement in a contract case:

"My name is Jean Harvey. I am representing myself in this case against the Computers Forever Corporation, which runs a store at 8905 Sixth Street in this city. I will have two witnesses in my case—myself and Francis Felix.

"I will testify that I bought a Fidelity 22 computer at the defendant's store on June 15th of last year after discussing my needs with Marcia Randolph, a store clerk. I told Ms. Randolph that I needed to purchase a dependable computer to run the seven different software programs I use, and which will be compatible with the computer systems my customers use.

"Ms. Randolph recommended the Fidelity 22 system and I paid the defendant store $8,250 for a complete system. I will testify that the sys-

tem broke down frequently and had trouble running most of my programs.

"Mr. Felix teaches computer science at the local community college and is an expert in computer utilization. He will testify that the Fidelity 22 system is an undependable IBM clone manufactured by a now-out-of-business offshore company. Mr. Felix will state that while the system can run simple IBM software, it's primary problem is its inability to run sophisticated desk top publishing programs such as the ones I carefully explained to Ms. Randolph that I use.

"At the conclusion of the case, I will ask Your Honor to award me the $8,250 I spent on this useless system and $4,345 for the work I will show I lost because of its inadequacy. Thank you."

D. Plaintiff's Case

After any opening statement from the defendant (or if the judge ordered that the opening statements be skipped), the plaintiff begins the case. (Some defendants choose not to give their opening statement until the end of the plaintiff's entire case.) Be sure to have your trial binder in hand.

1. Presenting Witnesses

Before you call your first witness, state: "Your Honor, I move to have all witnesses excluded from the courtroom." The judge will grant your motion and announce that all persons who expect to be witnesses in the trial must leave the courtroom. This request is designed to protect against a later witness changing his testimony to conform to an earlier witness.

Look around and see who stays. If anyone in the courtroom (with the exception of the defendant) is later called as a witness by your opponent, you will want to point out that that person should not be allowed to testify because he did not obey the judge's order to leave the courtroom.

Now you are ready to call your first witness. Simply state "Plaintiff calls (name of your first) as a witness." Often your best first witness will be yourself, in which case say "Plaintiff calls herself as a witness." The witness goes to the witness stand and is sworn to tell the truth by the clerk. Then you begin asking questions, which should be in your trial binder. Start out by asking his name (unless the clerk already has done so) and home address or occupation if either is relevant to the case.

If you call yourself first, you get the opportunity to outline your case early and fill in details later with other witnesses. You may hesitate to call yourself because you may be unsure how to question yourself. The judge may let you testify in a narrative without questions and answers—just explain what happened more or less chronologically. But this makes it difficult for your opponent (or his lawyer) to object to your testimony. Thus, the judge may insist that you ask yourself a question and then answer it. You can't use a non-lawyer friend to ask the questions.

Once your witness is on the stand, take him through the questions you've prepared until he has told his story. When you are finished, say "No further questions." The judge will turn to your opponent and say "Cross-examine."

How to Elicit Testimony

When you're standing in front of the judge asking questions, you may be tempted to skip the questions and just tell the judge what the case is all about. Don't. Evidence (other than documents) must come to the judge by way of questions and answers. (See Chapter 13, Section H, for examples of questions to ask.) If you're surprised by a witness's answer to a question, don't argue with him or make a speech to the judge about how the witness is lying.

Also, avoid the practice of burying your nose in your trial binder and never looking up to see how the judge or a witness reacts.

Now the defendant gets to cross-examine the witness. (See Section E, below.) The plaintiff's job is to listen carefully and object to improper questions. An objection should be made immediately—don't let the witness answer the question. You object by saying "Objection, the question calls for an opinion [calls for hearsay, is leading or whatever]." Then stop. The judge may ask you or your opponent for more information. Then she'll rule. "Sustained" means you win and the question is stricken. "Overruled" means you lose and the witness must answer.

After the defendant finishes the cross-examination, the judge will ask the plaintiff if she has anything on "redirect." Redirect is an opportunity for the plaintiff to ask more questions of the witness that relate specifically to something that came up in the cross-examination. You can't bring up a new issue or clarify something the witness said when you first examined him, unless the defendant asked about it in the cross-examination. If nothing important came up that you feel needs rebutting, simply say, "No questions."

Example: Mark, a plaintiff's witness, testifies that he saw an accident. On cross-examination by the defendant, he says he isn't 100% sure it was the way he just described. On redirect, Carl the plaintiff wants to convince the judge that Mark *was* sure or almost sure of what he saw. Carl elicits from Mark the details of where he was standing, his unobstructed view and his clear memory of that day. Carl doesn't ask Mark why he said he wasn't absolutely sure on cross-examination. Carl has made his point.

If the plaintiff asks questions on redirect, the defendant can ask questions in response. This back and forth rebuttal will go on until one party passes or the judge looses patience.

If you have any written declarations—statements from absent witnesses—to submit (see Chapter 13, Section D), after your live witnesses have testified say something like "Your Honor, pursuant to Section 98 of the Code of Civil Procedure, on June 3 I served on Mr. Dane [the defendant or his lawyer] declarations of Dr. Rudolph Dimes and Ms. Patricia Gonzalez. I also served the notice required by that section. I ask that the declarations be admitted in evidence." Then hand the declaration to the clerk

and a copy of it to your opponent. There should be no objection to this procedure.

2. Presenting Documents or Objects

To introduce documents (other than declarations) and other physical objects into evidence, you need a witness to identify the object, testify to its authenticity and connect it up to the case. Here are the steps to take:

Step 1. Show the object—or give a copy of it—to your opponent. The best time to do this is before you call your first witness. Say to your opponent "This is a copy of a letter I want to offer in evidence. I'm showing it to you now to save time later."

Step 2. When the witness who will identify the object reaches that portion of his testimony, hand the item to the clerk and say, "I'd like to have this document (or object) marked for identification." The clerk will attach a letter or number ID tag. Open your trial binder to your sheet marked exhibits and record the number or letter that has been given. Then put down a brief description of the item. Later you can refer to the item simply by its exhibit number or letter.

Step 3. Hand the item to the witness and say "Mr. Smyth, I am handing you Plaintiff's Exhibit 4. Can you tell me what that is?" The witness then replies, "Yes, it is a bill I gave you last March for the repair of your 1989 Mazda RX7" or "Yes, it is the letter I received from the defendant around Christmas last year." Then turn to the judge and say, "Your Honor, I offer Plaintiff's Exhibit 4 into evidence."

Your opponent can object to the introduction of this evidence by claiming it is irrelevant, hearsay or otherwise inadmissible. (See Chapter 13, Section A.) The judge then rules that it is either admitted or not. If it's admitted, you can refer to it during the case and the judge can consider it in making the decision. If it is not admitted, you can't refer to it and the judge can't consider it.

3. After Presenting the Evidence

After the plaintiff's witnesses have testified and he has introduced his declarations and physical evidence, the plaintiff should say "I rest my case." This means that he has no more witnesses at this time.

4. Responding to the Defendant's Motions

After the plaintiff rests her case, the defendant—if he believes the plaintiff has not proven a crucial element of her case—can ask the judge, by way of a motion, for immediate judgment in the defendant's favor. These motions are infrequently granted, but can be dangerous for a pro per plaintiff.

If the defendant makes such a motion (sometimes called a Motion for Non-Suit), control your desire to panic. Listen carefully to what the defendant claims you left out and if the judge seems sympathetic to the defendant's request, ask for permission to reopen your case to supply the missing evidence—if you can. If the judge grants your request, your best bet often is to put yourself back on the witness stand and introduce what's missing.

If you don't feel you need to offer more evidence (or you have no more), open your binder to the chart of your evidence. Identify each aspect of your case that you needed to prove and explain to the judge how you've proven

each. If the judge agrees, he'll deny the defendant's motion. If the judge grants the defendant's motion, state that under Code of Civil Procedure § 632 you are entitled to a written statement of the judge's reason for granting the motion and that you are requesting such a statement. (No need to be Mr. Nice Guy at this point!)

E. Defendant's Case

After the plaintiff rests, the defendant puts on his case. This is much the same as what the plaintiff just did. The defendant may call witnesses, present written declarations and introduce physical objects. If you're the defendant you should read Sections C and D, above. What applies to plaintiffs applies equally to defendants. Here are a few other points to consider:

Opening statement. The defendant can make his opening statement right after the plaintiff makes her opening statement or after the plaintiff concludes her presentation and rests her case. Unless you have surprise evidence the plaintiff doesn't expect, make your opening statement right away. This way the judge will know your theory while she is listening to the plaintiff.

Presenting witnesses. You may be your most important and best witness. If so, take the witness stand to lead off your case. Remember that you must prove any affirmative defense you raised in your answer. (See Chapter 8.)

Motion for judgment when the plaintiff rests. If the plaintiff hasn't proven one of the elements of her case, you can ask for judgment when she rests. Say, "Your honor, defendant moves for judgment under Code of Civil

Procedure § 631.8." Then state why. For example, if you are being sued for damaging someone's car, you might say "Plaintiff has not produced any evidence showing that I owned or was driving the car that struck her car." If the judge wants to hear more, she will tell you.

Concerns About Cross-Examination

Both the plaintiff and defendant are entitled to cross-examine any witness called by the other. Don't cross-examine a witness just for the sake of cross-examination. Have some attainable goal in mind. If you cross-examine a strong defense witness without achieving something, all you have done is let her repeat what she said on direct examination.

 If your opponent is relying on an obvious lie to contest your case, you may want to read up on successful methods of cross-examination. A good reference is *Effective Direct and Cross-Examination*, by Brockett and Keker. This book is published by the California Continuing Education of the Bar (CEB). Also, *Trials*, a multi-volume set published by American Jurisprudence, can be helpful. (See Chapter 13, Section H, for a discussion on *Trials*.) Both of these books should be at your local law library.

F. Plaintiff's Rebuttal

After the defendant rests his case—called his witnesses and introduced declarations and physical objects—the plaintiff can call a new witness or recall a previous witness to rebut (answer) something that came up during the defendant's case. Don't do this just to have a witness repeat what was said before. Use rebuttal to raise an issue you would have brought up earlier had you

known what the defendant's witnesses would say.

G. Closing Arguments

Each side is entitled to make a final speech to the judge summarizing the important evidence. This is called a closing argument. Plaintiff goes first. Then the defendant gives his closing argument. After the defendant finishes, the plaintiff can rebut anything the defendant says.

Before the trial begins, you should prepare an outline of a closing argument and put it in your Trial Binder. Most judges take a short recess after all the witnesses have testified to give the parties a little time to prepare their closing arguments. During the recess, you can revise your closing argument based on evidence presented during the trial. If you were able to take verbatim notes of any important testimony given during the trial, try to work some of that language into your closing argument.

If the judge wants you to jump right into your closing argument without taking a break, you can ask for a short (ten minutes or so) recess to review your notes and revise the closing statement you had planned to make. But a recess is discretionary with the judge and if the judge refuses, you will have to press ahead and do the best you can.

Although you will probably want to summarize the evidence, in a trial that has lasted only a few hours the judge will probably have a pretty good recollection of what the important testimony was. Don't waste everyone's time going over the whole case as if the judge just walked into the room. A plaintiff might say something like this:

"Your Honor, you have heard the evidence and I am confident you understand why it has been necessary for me to bring this lawsuit and go through these unfamiliar legal procedures to get to this moment. If my inexperience and unfamiliarity with court procedures has caused problems, I apologize.

"Your Honor, of all the testimony given today, I thought the most important was that of Mr. Jara, the plumber who inspected the job after the defendant, Mr. Warren, had finished. Mr. Jara testified, and I think I got his exact words here, 'I would have been ashamed to have left a repair job in that sort of condition.' Mr. Jara said that elbow joints were improperly installed and were the cause of my damage.

"Your Honor, I am asking for damages in the sum of $7,459 plus my court costs in the amount of $136. My damages are composed of [break down the components]. If you have any questions, I will be happy to attempt to answer them. Thank you for the opportunity to put on this trial today."

If you're a pro per defendant, keep in mind that the plaintiff has two chances to summarize his case while you have only one. You can't rebut the plaintiff's rebuttal. Thus, be complete when it is your turn. You would argue something as follows:

"Your Honor, you have heard the evidence and I am confident you understand why it has been necessary for me to defend this lawsuit and go through these unfamiliar legal procedures to get to this moment. If my inexperience and unfamiliarity with court procedures has caused problems, I apologize.

"Your Honor, the plaintiff called my shop and asked for an emergency repair. When we stopped her leak, as Mr. Warren testified, he

called her at her office and told her what we had done. He said, 'There may be other problems further on down the pipe, but it would take me another hour or two to check it out.' She said she couldn't afford that work right now. What more could we do under the circumstances? I think we acted very responsibly. I ask for judgment for the defendant."

Then the plaintiff might offer the following rebuttal:

"Your Honor, I realize Mr. Warren claims to have called me and asked if I wanted more work done. But when pressed, Mr. Warren said he was not absolutely sure he had called me. He said he knew he didn't use the kitchen telephone, and he could not recall what phone he did use. As I testified, however, I do remember the details of this debacle very carefully. I am sure he did not call me. If he had called me, I would have authorized the work, given that I had over a thousand dollars in the bank and would not have left a leaking pipe in my basement. Thank you again."

The judge may ask questions during the closing arguments, especially if he has concerns with some part of the case. Although it can be stressful, treat it as the most important part of the trial and answer as directly and thoroughly as possible.

H. Judgment

The judgment, of course, is the ultimate moment you are waiting for. It may seem anticlimactic after preparing for, and conducting, a trial. And what's worse, you may have to wait for the judgment. When the closing arguments have ended, the judge may do one of three things: announce the decision immediately, take a short recess (30 minutes or so) before announcing a decision or "take the matter under submission." The latter means that the judge needs a few days to make a decision and you'll be informed by mail.

If you win and are either told in court or sent the decision in the mail—the courtroom clerk may prepare a written form containing the actual judgment or you may be expected to prepare it. Once you know you have won, contact the clerk's office and ask who prepares the judgment. If you're required to prepare it, the clerk's office should have a form you can use.

Usually the day the judge signs the judgment (or the day after), the clerk (where you filed your papers) "enters the judgment." This means that the clerk notes the judgment in a record book—called the "register of actions" or the "judgment book"—kept in the clerk's office and sends you a "Notice of Entry of Judgment." Within ten days of when the clerk enters the judgment, you must file a form (called a "cost bill") stating your legal costs—filing fee, process server fees, deposition costs, statutory witness fees (not experts) and court reporter fees. The form is available from the clerk.

TRIAL BEFORE A JURY

I have served as judge for several pro per jury trials in Municipal Court. I didn't enjoy it and no one else did either.

Not the jurors: "I thought juries were used only for important cases. This case is pretty small, and nobody seems to know what they are doing. What am I doing here?"

Not the attorney for the other side: "If I'm not careful, I will end up making the jury sympathetic for the pro per. I'm supposed to be a lawyer, but I feel more like a baby sitter."

Not the pro per: "I knew it wouldn't be like television, but this is ridiculous and way more complicated than it needs to be. The judge keeps asking me to make decisions—I just wish he'd tell me what my choices were."

What all of this adds up to is one simple rule—avoid a jury trial if it is at all possible.

A. If Your Opponent Requests a Jury Trial

Unfortunately you don't always have the choice of avoiding a jury trial. Your opponent might request one in a misguided effort to discourage you from proceeding with your lawsuit. Or she may think you will never master the required procedures and will fall apart when forced to face 12 of your peers.

If your opponent requests a jury trial, you have three options:

• Reconsider your decision not to use a lawyer. Few lawyers relish taking over a case just to do the trial, but if you're persistent and willing to pay several hundred dollars an hour for their time, you'll find someone.

• Make another effort to settle, especially if you rejected a decent settlement offer in the past.

• Proceed as planned. This chapter will guide you through the procedure. I won't make you an expert in a few pages, but I can show you how to make the jury feel empathetic to a pro per, which may yield a good result.

In general, you should freely acknowledge to the judge and jury that conducting a jury trial is difficult and unfamiliar for you. In addition, many successful pro pers find the opportunity to let the jury know they didn't request a jury trial—their opponent did.

Finally, you want to place as much of the responsibility as possible on the judge to take the actions necessary for you to get a fair trial. Most judges will understand that you did not create the need for a jury. As long as you don't pretend to possess a level of expertise you don't have, the judge is likely to give you a hand.

A jury trial is more formal than a trial before a judge. A judge can't help you through the rough spots as easily as the judge can if there was no jury. If the jury sees a judge advising you, the jury may conclude that the judge wants you to win and be influenced accordingly.

Motions In Limine

Before the trial actually starts, the judge will probably hold a conference to explore last-minute settlement possibilities and to plan the trial. While you're in the meeting, your opponent may orally make some "motions in limine." This archaic terms translates roughly as motions at the threshold of the trial. Normally such a motion is used to address problems either party anticipates will arise during the trial.

For example, if your opponent's lawyer was hired by an insurance company, he won't want you to state that fact in front of the jury and will make a motion asking the judge to order you not to do so. Don't bother opposing the motion. The judge will grant it—so be careful of what you say once the trial starts.

Your opponent's lawyer will probably also make a motion to prevent you from introducing evidence he feels is so prejudicial that the jury should not be allowed to see it. For example, he may say "Your Honor, the photo the plaintiff wants to introduce showing his injury at the scene of the accident is so bloody that it will inflame the jury. I ask that it be excluded."

You probably won't be able to anticipate the other side's motions and you surely won't know the law that applies. Here is where you apply a basic "trust the judge" approach. Tell the judge you believe you should be allowed to use all evidence that supports your case, that the photo (or other evidence) is important to show your injuries, but that you will rely on the judge to decide what is right in the situation.

When your opponent is finished making his motions in limine, be sure you understand all of the judge's rulings clearly. You don't want to introduce evidence or say something during the trial that the judge has excluded.

B. Jury Selection

If your opponent requests a jury trial, you're going to have to help select the actual jurors. When you are in the judge's office before the start of the trial (to discuss settlement and motions in limine), the judge should explain how he plans to handle jury selection. If he doesn't, ask. Until recently, most judges used juries of 12. But now, many judges ask the parties to agree to eight. You should agree. It will shorten the process. With 12 person juries, a minimum of nine must agree on a verdict. With eight jurors, six must agree.

Jury selection begins with the judge's clerk reading the names of a number of potential jurors, who leave the audience area and sit in the jury box. The judge makes some remarks and introduces the parties and any lawyers to the potential jurors. First impressions are important. When you are introduced, rise, smile and nod to the people in the jury box and then the people in the audience.

The object of jury selection is to choose people who can decide the case without being influenced by pre-existing prejudice or sympathy. Your aim is to find 12 (or eight, if so agreed) people who appear not to dislike you and who sound as though they can be fair. You do this by asking questions and excusing ("challenging") potential jurors you don't like. Unfortunately, many lawyers believe it's their role to find jurors predisposed to their client's side. These lawyers sometimes question and challenge for hours. Don't get sucked into this. Jurors hate it and frequently get an early bad impression of a lawyer who overdoes it.

Questioning of potential jurors begins with the judge. Then each side is allowed to ask questions. The judge may restrict the amount of time or the number of questions, but you must be given the chance to ask questions that might indicate some prejudice from a potential juror. These are the methods the judge may use:

Traditional. The 12 (or eight) potential jurors are seated in the box. The judge questions each of them, one at a time. After the judge is done asking questions of all of them, the plaintiff questions potential Juror One and the defendant questions potential Juror One. Then the plaintiff questions potential Juror Two and the defendant questions potential Juror Two. The process is repeated until all potential jurors are questioned.

Traditional with a twist. Same as above, but after the judge has questioned all potential jurors, the plaintiff does the same thing followed by the defendant who takes her turn.

Packs. Same as above, except that in addition to the potential jurors in the box, the judge seats six (called a "six-pack"), 12 or any other number of potential jurors in the front rows of the audience. As seats open up in the jury box (when a party exercises a challenge), these potential jurors fill them.

When the questioning of the potential jurors begins, be prepared to track their relevant answers. Before the trial, divide a large sheet of paper into 12 (or eight) squares, each one representing a different jury seat. If the judge uses a six- or 12-pack, add more squares. (See diagram, below.)

Juror 6	Juror 5	Juror 4	Juror 3	Juror 2	Juror 1
Juror 12	Juror 11	Juror 10	Juror 9	Juror 8	Juror 7

As each potential juror takes a seat, write his or her name in the square corresponding to the seat he or she sits in. If the potential juror is later removed, cross out the name and write in the replacement. If he or she says something you don't like, note in the box that you might want to challenge the person. Or, if the person seems particularly fair or good for you, make an appropriate note.

Your case is likely to be fairly routine and the average jury panel will give you a fair hearing. In fact, accepting the first panel of 12 (or eight) that sits down can be a good strategy for a pro per. I've seen pro pers stand up, and rather than ask questions of each potential juror, simply say "I would have been satisfied to have a trial before a judge alone, but my opponent requested a jury trial. I have only one question for the jury: will anyone hold it against me because I can't talk and act like a lawyer?"

C. Challenging Jurors

There are two kinds of juror challenges: challenges for cause and peremptory challenges. Challenges for cause are for people who have a problem such as a limited grasp of English, prior knowledge of the case or the parties, or an admitted prejudice that will make it difficult for them to be fair. Sometimes these people will be excused by the judge without your saying anything. Other times, you'll have to challenge the person yourself, specifying why you think the person should be excused.

Peremptory challenges are different. They are made by you without any explanation. You can challenge anyone you don't feel right about, but you are limited to six peremptory challenges in a 12-person jury. In an 8-person jury, the judge will probably cut your peremptory challenges to four.

Example 1: A potential juror whose spouse was injured as a pedestrian in a crosswalk says in answer to a question that she thinks she can be fair. But if you are a driver being sued for having struck a pedestrian in a crosswalk, you should challenge her when the time comes. As impartial as she might want to be, she probably resents the driver who hit her husband and she may unconsciously take it out on you.

Example 2: A potential juror answers a question posed by the judge by saying his uncle is a plumber. You can say: "Juror Three, Mr. Edgars—you said that your uncle is a plumber. As you know, I am suing a plumber. How close are you to this uncle?" If he says he is fairly close, ask "will that cause you at all to be prejudiced against me?" Listen carefully to the answer. If you have any question about his ability to be fair and impartial, challenge him at the appropriate time.

After the judge and parties are done asking questions, the judge will probably ask if you have any challenges for cause. Most of these will have been taken care of by the judge. But if the judge missed one, say "I challenge juror number __ for cause." You can make an unlimited number of challenges for cause, but you must explain your reason. If the potential juror admits to not being able to be fair, say "the juror has a state of mind which is likely to lead her to be prejudiced against me."

Once challenges for cause are done with, the judge will ask if you have any peremptory challenges. If you do, simply say "plaintiff (or defendant) thanks and excuses juror number __." If you don't wish to challenge anyone, say "plaintiff (or defendant) passes." Your opponent also will be given an opportunity to challenge, and if he passes too, the challenging of these jurors is over. If your opponent exercises a challenge, you get another chance to challenge a juror if you wish.

If a potential juror is challenged, a person from the audience (or the six-pack) is called as a replacement. These replacements are questioned and challenged in the same manner as described above. If the trial will take more than one day, the judge may decide to pick one or two alternate jurors in case a regular juror becomes ill. The alternates are questioned and challenged similarly. You have unlimited challenges for cause and one peremptory challenge for each alternate seat to be filled.

Jury selection ends when 12 (or eight) jurors and any alternates are seated and both sides have either passed or exercised all their peremptory challenges. Once jurors and alternates are selected, the clerk administers an oath in which they swear to do their job.

D. Preparing Jury Instructions

When a trial is over but before the jurors retire to the jury room to reach a decision ("deliberate"), the judge reads them some instructions on the law to guide them in their work. These are called "jury instructions." They:

• explain the law that applies in the case

• direct the jurors to apply that law to the facts of the case they just heard

• explain general legal principles

• outline the deliberation process

The judge's presentation of the jury instructions usually takes about 15 minutes. The jury often take the instructions very seriously. Jurors usually believe in the judicial system and in following rules. I have seen more than a few cases in which the jurors come into court profoundly disturbed by the verdict they are about to render, but convinced they must to it "because that is the law the judge read us and we have sworn to uphold the law." Other jurors struggle to avoid applying instructions they feel are unfair.

 The judge does not manufacture the instructions out of thin air. At the beginning of the trial, the judge will usually ask each party to submit a written set of instructions that party wants the judge to read. The parties get the instructions primarily from a book called *California Jury Instructions, Civil* (called "BAJI" because it was first published as the *Book of Approved Jury Instructions*).

BAJI is available in all California law libraries, so you should have little problem finding it. The problem will be in putting it to meaningful use. BAJI is so complex that you are likely to find its contents more frustrating than enlightening.

That said, how can you come up with useful jury instructions? You have two alternatives:

1. Hire a lawyer to prepare jury instructions for you. For a lawyer to learn something about your case and then search BAJI and other sources to develop a decent set of instructions will involve at least two to three hours of time. If you intend to find a lawyer who will do this, make the arrangements several weeks before your trial date so the lawyer has the time to do the work before the trial.

2. Rely on the judge to construct evenhanded jury instructions without contributions from you. If you follow this plan, when you meet before the trial begins, tell the judge that you:

• haven't hired a lawyer because the amount involved does not justify the expense

• had hoped for a trial by the judge alone, but that the other side requested a jury trial

• realize you are expected to produce instructions, but that it is beyond your abilities

• will accept whatever instructions the judge deems appropriate

The judge may ask you if you understand that higher (appellate) courts have ruled a trial judge is not required to prepare jury instructions for a party who does not do so on his own. Tell the judge that you understand, but that you also believe that the 1979 California Supreme Court case, *Agarwal vs. Johnson,* 25 Cal.3d 951, puts some responsibility on the court regarding jury instructions. Then leave it at that. With a little luck, the judge will give you a hand and present some instructions that are reasonably fair.

E. The Trial

The basic outline of a jury trial is the same as a trial before a judge. Each side makes an opening statement, presents evidence, introduces documents, cross-examines the other side's witnesses and makes a closing argument. If you haven't already done so, read Chapter 14. I only supplement that material here.

1. Opening Statement

Your opening statement in a jury trial is more important than in a judge trial. It is the jury's first real opportunity to hear from you, and you should make the most of it. The jurors will be inclined to identify with you, not the lawyer representing your opponent. By being friendly and frank when telling them what the case is about and why they are being asked to resolve your dispute, you can build a rapport.

In your opening statement, you'll want to outline your case. You should state what you think the testimony will be and what you expect the jury to do after they have heard the evidence, but you cannot argue the case or attempt to persuade the jury. If you start arguing, your opponent is likely to object and the judge may admonish you.

If you are the plaintiff, conclude your opening statement by saying something like "once you have heard all of the evidence I will ask you to return a verdict for me in the amount of $17,800." If you are a defendant, conclude with "once you have heard from all of the witnesses, I will ask that you return a verdict finding for me and awarding the plaintiff nothing."

2. Presenting Evidence and Making Objections

The chief difference between a jury trial and trial before a judge is that in a jury trial you need to be especially careful to object to improper questions before a witness blurts out something the jury should not hear. While you can expect a judge to ignore an improper statement made by a witness, you can't expect a jury to do so. If a witness gives an answer before you object, the fact that you eventually win your objection may be irrelevant.

If you hear a question that calls for hearsay or other inadmissible evidence, don't be shy. Loudly, state "objection." The witness should stop talking. If he doesn't, interrupt him and ask the judge to tell him to stop talking until the judge rules on the objection.

The judge may rule on your objection without your having to specify why you are objecting. But don't count on it. Some judges will ask you what your objection is. If your judge does, explain it as best you can: "the question calls for an answer that is hearsay" or "the question is leading."

3. Closing Argument

In your closing argument, you're given wide latitude to persuade the jury you are right, as long as your argument is based upon evidence presented during the trial. You can't refer to what someone "probably would have said had he been here" or talk about "facts" you believe to be true unless they were established during the trial.

If you're uncertain about whether or not you can say something in your closing argument, during a recess before the closing arguments begin, ask the judge.

Many pro pers find it helpful to begin their closing argument by explaining to the jury that they have done their best under the circumstances, but that they feel like a fish out of water doing battle against a highly trained lawyer on the other side. If you follow such a statement with a cogent recapitulation of the evidence, it may be quite effective with the jury, especially if your opponent's lawyer has been stuffy.

F. Jury Deliberations

After the closing arguments, the judge will read the jury instructions. (Some judges read the instructions before the closing arguments.) Then the judge's clerk swears the marshal to keep the jury private and to bring the jurors back when they have reached a verdict. Stand as the jury leaves the courtroom. Do not attempt to communicate with the jurors or do anything—other than smile confidently—as they walk out.

You are expected to stay close by while the jury deliberates. The jurors may want to come back into the court and ask a question of the judge or hear some of the evidence re-read. If you need to leave the courtroom for more than a few minutes, tell the judge's clerk where you will be.

When the jury reaches a decision (verdict), the jurors are brought back to the courtroom. The head juror (foreperson) hands a written verdict to the marshal, who hands it to the judge. The judge makes sure it is in proper form, and then hands it to the clerk who reads it aloud. The judge then asks if anyone wants the individual jurors polled. Don't bother. Jurors never change their vote. If either side says yes, the clerk asks each juror if he or she agrees with the verdict. The winner needs three-quarters (nine of 12 or six of eight).

The judge will probably thank the jurors and make a speech about how important their service has been. Then he will announce that court is recessed, and, unless he has directed you otherwise, you are free to talk to the jurors. They can refuse to talk to you, however, so don't badger them if they want to be left alone.

chapter 16

AFTER THE TRIAL

The trial is over. You survived. If you struggled to follow the directions in this book, you may even have received compliments from the clerk about how "professional" you were. But what if, despite all of that, you lost—the judge or jury ruled in favor of your opponent? You may think it's over. That's not necessarily true. If you believe that the judge or jury made a serious mistake either before or during the trial, you can make a motion for a new trial or file an appeal to a higher court. If you won the case, of course your opponent has the right to ask for a new trial or to appeal.

Appealing or requesting a new trial are complicated, time consuming and beyond the ability of all but the most determined pro per. They require legal research, legal writing and the preparation of a formal brief. This chapter only describes the two procedures briefly. If you want to pursue either one, you'll need to hire a lawyer right away or, for the next several months, make a career out of fighting your case.

A. Requesting a New Trial

You request a new trial by filing a Motion for New Trial with the trial judge. In it, you ask the judge to throw out everything that happened at the trial and to start over. The judge may grant the motion if you show that any of the following

materially affected your rights and the outcome of the case:[1]

- an irregularity in the proceedings of the court, jury or your opponent, or an order of the court, prevented you from having a fair trial

- misconduct by the jury, such as talking to a party during the trial, unauthorized viewing of the scene of the accident or incident or doing any other independent research during the trial

- an accident or surprise at the trial, which ordinary prudence could not have guarded against

- newly found evidence which could not have been discovered and produced during the trial

- excessive or inadequate damages

- insufficient evidence to justify the decision— after a jury trial, this allows the judge to overrule the jury if the judge believes the verdict was clearly wrong

- an error in applying the law

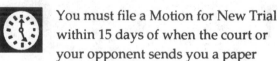 You must file a Motion for New Trial within 15 days of when the court or your opponent sends you a paper called a Notice of Entry of Judgment. The counting of the 15 days starts the day after the Notice was mailed. After a party files a Motion for New Trial, the other party has 10 days to file a response.

As hopeful as it may sound, a Motion for New Trial is granted infrequently. A judge who heard the case without a jury seldom grants one because, in essence, the judge would be admit-

---

[1]Code of Civil Procedure § 657.

ting that he made a major mistake during the trial. After a jury trial, the judge usually will grant a Motion for a New Trial only if he feels the jury was way off base in its decision.

If your opponent files a Motion for a New Trial, carefully read the papers filed in support of the Motion. If they are so full of legalese that they are incoherent, consider hiring a lawyer for the limited job of defending your victory.

 If your opponent has simply written a diatribe about how unfair the result is, you can probably file a your own response. An excellent source for drafting a response to a Motion for a New Trial is *Cal Practice* (Bancroft Whitney), Chapter 54. In either case, you must file a response within ten days. The court will then set a hearing date. If the judge doesn't ruled on the motion within 60 days of when it was filed, it is deemed denied.

B. Appealing

Frequently, when the media covers a big trial, the loser (or her lawyer) promises to appeal to a higher court and is "confident that the decision will be overturned." This is conventional lawyer talk. In truth, few cases are appealed and even fewer are reversed. This is because an appellate court can reverse a decision only if the trial judge made a serious mistake in applying the law. A factual finding by a jury—or by a judge— normally cannot be reversed. Most Municipal Court judges have handled hundreds of vehicle accident and contract cases and make very few errors.

If your case was held before a pro tem (volunteer lawyer) judge, not a regular judge,

however, you may have a better chance of winning an appeal. Although pro tems may be fine lawyers, they haven't attended the many training programs offered to California judges and are somewhat more likely to make legal errors that could result in a reversal.

To appeal a Municipal Court decision, you must file a paper called a Notice of Appeal with the Municipal Court clerk's office within 30 days of when the you are sent the Notice of Entry of Judgment. You must also pay a filing fee, of around $50. If you are not sent a Notice, you must file your Notice of Appeal within 90 days after the judgment is actually entered (noted in the official court books by the court clerk). After your Notice is filed, the case will be transferred to the Superior Court's Appellate Division for review.

 Within ten days of filing your notice of appeal, you must file several other documents with the court identifying the papers, other than a reporter's transcript, you plan to rely on to prove your appeal.[2] If you're going to appeal, you'll need to make an early appointment with a lawyer and present your case in an orderly and clear fashion. If you want to represent yourself in the appeal, you'll have your work cut out for you, but you can get some help from *Cal Practice* (Bancroft Whitney), Chapter 61.

In reviewing the case, the Appellate Court reads only the court reporter's transcript of what happened at the trial. The Appellate Court does not see or judge the credibility of the witnesses.

---

[2]California Rules of Court 124-130.

In essence, the Appellate Court must accept the judge or jury's belief of one witness and disbelief of another.

If your opponent appeals after you win the case, again consider hiring a lawyer. Unfortunately, even if you win the appeal, you'll have to pay the lawyer's fee yourself. Thus, talk to a few lawyers who specialize in appeals to find their cost. Compare the cost to the seriousness of the "error" raised by your opponent. If you're convinced it's a weak argument, you may want to go it alone—that is, not hire a lawyer.

Before defending an appeal on your own, take a look at the *California Civil Appellate Practice* (2d Edition), published by the California Continuing Education of the Bar (CEB). Most Superior Court Appellate Divisions have law clerks who study appeals, so it is likely that even if you don't have a lawyer, your opponent's argument will be scrutinized fairly carefully.

chapter 17

FINDING A GOOD LAWYER

I've probably read every book published in the U.S. in the last 10 years discussing how to choose a lawyer. I've certainly tried to. And I've concluded that there is no sure-fire way to find a good attorney.

That's not to say there aren't good lawyers in California—there are many. Unfortunately, however, there are a substantial number who do an inadequate job on even a simple case. And using the selection methods recommended by, for example, a bar association to find a lawyer, could easily land you in the office of someone who will do a poor job.

Before explaining how to find a lawyer, let's first eliminate the types of lawyers your are not looking for:

- the expensive, flamboyant lawyer who gets his name in the newspaper a lot. He'd probably charge you a bundle (up to $250 an hour) and pass your case on to a recent law school graduate who works for him.

- the associate or partner at a giant law firm that represents big businesses. These lawyers charge $200-$400 an hour and few know much about simple cases or keeping costs down.

- the lawyer who won't tell you how she plans to handle your case and wants to make all decisions herself. These lawyers are annoyed—and intimidated—by clients who know anything about the law. What they want is a passive client who doesn't ask a lot of questions and pays the bill on time each month.

What you do want is a dedicated, smart and skilled lawyer who regularly handles small and medium-sized cases. The lawyer should understand that you prefer to handle your case as a pro per whenever possible. He should be willing to charge you a reasonable rate to consult as difficulties arise. If the case turns so complex that you change your mind about going pro per, the lawyer should be willing to take it over.

The best referrals to such lawyers will probably come from an independent paralegal listed in the Yellow Pages under "Paralegals" or "Typing Services." You also may be able to find help by calling the National Association of

Independent Paralegals at 800-542-0034. These businesses help people complete and file court papers, but cannot give legal advice. Almost daily they refer their clients to lawyers and get feedback on the lawyers' work.

Some people recommend that you ask friends and relatives for names of lawyers they've used and liked. The problem with this approach, however, is that your friends and relatives don't necessarily know if they got the best possible result at a reasonable price. They know if the lawyer treated them decently and returned their phone calls, which is important—but only a part of the picture! Maybe the case was such a winner that even the most incompetent lawyer couldn't have lost it. Maybe the result obtained was only a fraction of what the case was worth.

Other people recommend using a lawyer referral program run by a county bar association or commercial network. I don't. These programs usually take the names of any lawyer who has passed the bar examination and agrees to follow certain (minimal) rules. Similarly, I'd suggest steering clear of the advertised nationwide legal clinics that claim to be reasonably priced. Their fees are very similar to other lawyers and they have a tremendous amount of lawyer turnover.

Other people suggest asking a lawyer who specializes in a field of law different from the area where you need help—such as asking a divorce lawyer for the name of a personal injury lawyer. This isn't a bad idea—lawyers often know competent attorneys in other fields—but it can be dangerous. Instead of referring you to the best lawyer for your case, you may be given the name of a law school friend or brother-in-law who just opened his own law office. And many lawyers pay a referral fee of as much as a third

of what they collect to the lawyer who sent them the case. This obviously can have an impact on who they recommend.

Once you get the names of some lawyers, your most important job it to talk to them person. Call and ask for a brief interview. You may have to pay a small fee for the lawyer's time, but many don't charge for an initial consultation. Be ready to explain your case and exactly what services you want from the lawyer. Note how the lawyer responds to your pro per efforts.

Remember, having read this book you know far more about the legal process than the average person. Does the lawyer seem comfortable with that? Does the lawyer give you clear, concise answers to your questions—or does the lawyer want to maintain an aura of mystery about the legal system? Pay attention to your own intuition.

Once, when I was practicing law, a scientist called me and said he had selected five possible lawyers to handle his case. He wanted to meet with me for 30 minutes to ask me some questions and decide whether or not to hire me. I was intrigued and asked him to come in. During the 30 minutes, he asked good questions about how I worked on a case, how I felt about settlements—as opposed to taking every case to trial, my billing practices and the like. I was impressed with his involvement in his case. It was the only time in my 15 years of practice that anyone did this.

Once you choose a lawyer, be sure to get a written agreement outlining exactly what the lawyer promises to do and what you're expected to pay. If appropriate, include something stating the maximum fee you are willing to pay unless you agree in writing otherwise.

APPENDIX FORMS

Request for Dismissal

Complaint—Personal Injury, Property Damage, Wrongful Death

Motor Vehicle Cause of Action

Premise Liability Cause of Action

General Negligence Cause of Action

Intentional Tort Cause of Action

Exemplary Damages Attachment

Contract Complaint

Breach of Contract Cause of Action

Common Counts Cause of Action

Breach of Warranty—Merchantability Cause of Action

Breach of Warranty—Fitness Cause of Action

Summons

Case Questionnaire

Proof of Service by Mail

Answer—Personal Injury, Property Damage, Wrongful Death

Answer—Contract

Cross-Complaint—Personal Injury, Property Damage, Wrongful Death

Request for Entry of Default

Interrogatories

Request for Admissions

Amemdment to Complaint

Request for Statement of Witnesses and Evidence

Sheet of Pleading Paper

Name, Address and Telephone No. of Attorney(s)

Space Below for Use of Court Clerk Only

Attorney(s) for ....

............................COURT OF CALIFORNIA, COUNTY OF...................
(SUPERIOR, MUNICIPAL, or JUSTICE)

....
(Name of Municipal or Justice Court District or of branch court, if any)

Plaintiff(s):

Defendant(s):

(Abbreviated Title)

CASE NUMBER

REQUEST FOR DISMISSAL
TYPE OF ACTION

☐ Personal Injury, Property Damage and Wrongful Death:
    ☐ Motor Vehicle   ☐ Other
☐ Domestic Relations   ☐ Eminent Domain
☐ Other: (Specify) ....

TO THE CLERK: Please dismiss this action as follows: (Check applicable boxes.)
1. ☐ With prejudice   ☐ Without prejudice
2. ☐ Entire action   ☐ Complaint only   ☐ Petition only   ☐ Cross-complaint only
    ☐ Other: (Specify)*

Dated: ....
*If dismissal requested is of specified parties only, of specified causes of action only or of specified cross-complaints only, so state and identify the parties, causes of action or cross-complaints to be dismissed.

Attorney(s) for ....

(Type or print attorney(s) name(s))

TO THE CLERK: Consent to the above dismissal is hereby given.**

Dated: ....
**When a cross-complaint (or Response (Marriage) seeking affirmative relief) is on file, the attorney(s) for the cross-complainant (respondent) must sign this consent when required by CCP 581(1), (2) or (5).

Attorney(s) for ....

(Type or print attorney(s) name(s))

(To be completed by clerk)
☐ Dismissal entered as requested on ....
☐ Dismissal entered on ....as to only ....
☐ Dismissal not entered as requested for the following reason(s), and attorney(s) notified on ....

_____, Clerk

Dated..   By_____, Deputy

Form Adopted by Rule 982 of
The Judicial Council of California
Revised Effective July 1, 1972

REQUEST FOR DISMISSAL

CCP 581, etc.;
Cal. Rules of Court,
Rule 1233

ATTORNEY OR PARTY WITHOUT ATTORNEY (NAME AND ADDRESS):   TELEPHONE: FOR COURT USE ONLY

ATTORNEY FOR (NAME)

Insert name of court, judicial district or branch court, if any, and post office and street address:

PLAINTIFF:

DEFENDANT:

☐ DOES 1 TO _____

COMPLAINT—Personal Injury, Property Damage, Wrongful Death   CASE NUMBER:

☐ **MOTOR VEHICLE**   ☐ OTHER *(specify):*
    ☐ **Property Damage**   ☐ **Wrongful Death**
    ☐ **Personal Injury**   ☐ **Other Damages** *(specify):*

---

1. This pleading, including attachments and exhibits, consists of the following number of pages: _____

2. a. Each plaintiff named above is a competent adult
    ☐ **Except** plaintiff *(name):*
        ☐ a corporation qualified to do business in California
        ☐ an unincorporated entity *(describe):*
        ☐ a public entity *(describe):*
        ☐ a minor   ☐ an adult
            ☐ for whom a guardian or conservator of the estate or a guardian ad litem has been appointed
            ☐ other *(specify):*
        ☐ other *(specify):*

    ☐ **Except** plaintiff *(name):*
        ☐ a corporation qualified to do business in California
        ☐ an unincorporated entity *(describe):*
        ☐ a public entity *(describe):*
        ☐ a minor   ☐ an adult
            ☐ for whom a guardian or conservator of the estate or a guardian ad litem has been appointed
            ☐ other *(specify):*
        ☐ other *(specify):*

  b. ☐ Plaintiff *(name):*
      is doing business under the fictitious name of *(specify):*

      and has complied with the fictitious business name laws.
  c. ☐ Information about additional plaintiffs who are not competent adults is shown in Complaint—
      Attachment 2c.   (Continued)

Form Approved by the
Judicial Council of California
Effective January 1, 1982
Rule 982.1(1)

**COMPLAINT—Personal Injury, Property Damage,
Wrongful Death**

CCP 425.12 C-87

3. a. Each defendant named above is a natural person
   ☐ **Except** defendant *(name):*   ☐ **Except** defendant *(name):*

   ☐ a business organization, form unknown   ☐ a business organization, form unknown
   ☐ a corporation   ☐ a corporation
   ☐ an unincorporated entity *(describe):*   ☐ an unincorporated entity *(describe):*

   ☐ a public entity *(describe):*   ☐ a public entity *(describe):*

   ☐ other *(specify):*   ☐ other *(specify):*

   ☐ **Except** defendant *(name):*   ☐ **Except** defendant *(name):*

   ☐ a business organization, form unknown   ☐ a business organization, form unknown
   ☐ a corporation   ☐ a corporation
   ☐ an unincorporated entity *(describe):*   ☐ an unincorporated entity *(describe):*

   ☐ a public entity *(describe):*   ☐ a public entity *(describe):*

   ☐ other *(specify):*   ☐ other *(specify):*

   b. The true names and capacities of defendants sued as Does are unknown to plaintiff.

   c. ☐ Information about additional defendants who are not natural persons is contained in Complaint—
      Attachment 3c.
   d. ☐ Defendants who are joined pursuant to Code of Civil Procedure section 382 are *(names):*

4. ☐ Plaintiff is required to comply with a claims statute, **and**
   a. ☐ plaintiff has complied with applicable claims statutes, **or**
   b. ☐ plaintiff is excused from complying because *(specify):*

5. This court is the proper court because
   ☐ at least one defendant now resides in its jurisdictional area.
   ☐ the principal place of business of a corporation or unincorporated association is in its jurisdictional area.
   ☐ injury to person or damage to personal property occurred in its jurisdictional area.
   ☐ other *(specify)*

6. ☐ The following paragraphs of this complaint are alleged on information and belief *(specify paragraph numbers):*

7. ☐ The damages claimed for wrongful death and the relationships of plaintiff to the deceased are
☐ listed in Complaint—Attachment 7 ☐ as follows:

8. Plaintiff has suffered
☐ wage loss
☐ hospital and medical expenses
☐ property damage
☐ other damage (specify):

☐ loss of use of property
☐ general damage
☐ loss of earning capacity

9. Relief sought in this complaint is within the jurisdiction of this court.

10. PLAINTIFF PRAYS
For judgment for costs of suit; for such relief as is fair, just, and equitable; and for
☐ compensatory damages
☐ **(Superior Court)** according to proof.

☐ **(Municipal and Justice Court)** in the amount of $_____
☐ other (specify):

11. The following causes of action are attached and the statements above apply to each: (Each complaint must have
one or more causes of action attached.)
☐ Motor Vehicle
☐ General Negligence
☐ Intentional Tort
☐ Products Liability
☐ Premises Liability
☐ Other (specify):

. . . .
(Type or print name)   (Signature of plaintiff or attorney)

_____ **CAUSE OF ACTION—Motor Vehicle**   **Page** _____
(number)

ATTACHMENT TO ☐ Complaint   ☐ Cross-Complaint

(Use a separate cause of action form for each cause of action.)

Plaintiff *(name):*

MV-1. Plaintiff alleges the acts of defendants were negligent; the acts were the legal (proximate) cause of injuries and damages to plaintiff; the acts occurred
on *(date):*
at *(place):*

MV-2. DEFENDANTS
    a. ☐ The defendants who operated a motor vehicle are *(names):*

      ☐ Does _____ to _____
    b. ☐ The defendants who employed the persons who operated a motor vehicle in the course of their employment are *(names):*

      ☐ Does _____ to _____
    c. ☐ The defendants who owned the motor vehicle which was operated with their permission are *(names):*

      ☐ Does _____ to _____
    d. ☐ The defendants who entrusted the motor vehicle are *(names):*

      ☐ Does _____ to _____
    e. ☐ The defendants who were the agents and employees of the other defendants and acted within the scope of the agency were *(names):*

      ☐ Does _____ to _____
    f. ☐ The defendants who are liable to plaintiffs for other reasons and the reasons for the liability are
      ☐ listed in Attachment MV-2f ☐ as follows:

      ☐ Does _____ to _____

Form Approved by the
Judicial Council of California
Effective January 1, 1982
Rule 982.1(2)   **CAUSE OF ACTION—Motor Vehicle**   CCP 425.12 C-88

_____ **CAUSE OF ACTION—Premises Liability**   Page _____
(number)

ATTACHMENT TO ☐ Complaint   ☐ Cross-Complaint

(Use a separate cause of action form for each cause of action.)

Prem.L-1. Plaintiff *(name):*
alleges the acts of defendants were the legal (proximate) cause of damages to plaintiff.
On *(date):*   plaintiff was injured on the following premises in the following

fashion *(description of premises and circumstances of injury):*

Prem.L-2.   ☐ **Count One—Negligence** The defendants who negligently owned, maintained, managed and operated
the described premises were *(names):*

☐ Does _____ to _____

Prem.L-3.   ☐ **Count Two—Willful Failure to Warn** [Civil Code section 846] The defendant owners who willfully
or maliciously failed to guard or warn against a dangerous condition, use, structure, or activity were
(names):

☐ Does _____ to _____
Plaintiff, a recreational user, was ☐ an invited guest ☐ a paying guest.

Prem.L-4.   ☐ **Count Three—Dangerous Condition of Public Property** The defendants who owned public property
on which a dangerous condition existed were *(names):*

☐ Does _____ to _____
a. ☐ The defendant public entity had ☐ actual ☐ constructive notice of the existence of the
dangerous condition in sufficient time prior to the injury to have corrected it.
b. ☐ The condition was created by employees of the defendant public entity.

Prem.L-5. a. ☐ **Allegations about Other Defendants** The defendants who were the agents and employees of the
other defendants and acted within the scope of the agency were *(names):*

☐ Does _____ to _____
b. ☐ The defendants who are liable to plaintiffs for other reasons and the reasons for their liability are
☐ described in attachment Prem.L-5.b ☐ as follows *(names):*

Form Approved by the
Judicial Council of California
Effective January 1, 1982
Rule 982.1(5)
CAUSE OF ACTION—Premises Liability   CCP 425.12

C-91

_____ **CAUSE OF ACTION—General Negligence**   Page _____
(number)

ATTACHMENT TO ☐ Complaint   ☐ Cross-Complaint

(Use a separate cause of action form for each cause of action.)

GN-1. Plaintiff *(name):*

       alleges that defendant *(name):*

              ☐ Does _____ to _____

       was the legal (proximate) cause of damages to plaintiff. By the following acts or omissions to act, defendant
       negligently caused the damage to plaintiff
       on *(date):*
       at *(place):*

       (description of reasons for liability):

Form Approved by the
Judicial Council of California
Effective January 1, 1982
Rule 982.1(3)

CAUSE OF ACTION—General Negligence

CCP 425.12   C-89

_____ **CAUSE OF ACTION—Intentional Tort**   Page _____
(number)

ATTACHMENT TO ☐ Complaint   ☐ Cross-Complaint

(Use a separate cause of action form for each cause of action.)

IT-1.   Plaintiff *(name):*

alleges that defendant *(name):*

☐ Does _____ to _____

was the legal (proximate) cause of damages to plaintiff. By the following acts or omissions to act, defendant intentionally caused the damage to plaintiff
on *(date):*
at *(place):*

(description of reasons for liability):

Exemplary Damages Attachment

Page _____

ATTACHMENT TO ☐ Complaint ☐ Cross-Complaint

EX-1. As additional damages against defendant (name):

Plaintiff alleges defendant was guilty of
☐ malice
☐ fraud
☐ oppression
as defined in Civil Code section 3294, and plaintiff should recover, in addition to actual damages, damages to make an example of and to punish defendant.

EX-2. The facts supporting plaintiff's claim are as follows:

EX-3. The amount of exemplary damages sought is
    a. ☐ not shown, pursuant to Code of Civil Procedure section 425.10.
    b. ☐ $

Form Approved by the
Judicial Council of California
Effective January 1, 1982
Rule 982 1(13)

Exemplary Damages Attachment

CCP 425.12

ATTORNEY OR PARTY WITHOUT ATTORNEY (NAME AND ADDRESS):	TELEPHONE:	FOR COURT USE ONLY
ATTORNEY FOR (NAME):		

Insert name of court, judicial district or branch court, if any, and post office and street address:

PLAINTIFF:

DEFENDANT:

☐ DOES 1 TO _____

CONTRACT ☐ COMPLAINT ☐ CROSS-COMPLAINT	CASE NUMBER:

1. This pleading, including attachments and exhibits, consists of the following number of pages: _____

2. a. Each plaintiff named above is a competent adult
   ☐ **Except** plaintiff *(name):*

      ☐ a corporation qualified to do business in California
      ☐ an unincorporated entity *(describe):*
      ☐ other *(specify):*

   b. ☐ Plaintiff *(name):*
      ☐ has complied with the fictitious business name laws and is doing business under the fictitious name of *(specify):*
      ☐ has complied with all licensing requirements as a licensed *(specify):*

   c. ☐ Information about additional plaintiffs who are not competent adults is shown in Complaint—Attachment 2c.

3. a. Each defendant named above is a natural person
   ☐ **Except** defendant *(name):*   ☐ **Except** defendant *(name):*

      ☐ a business organization, form unknown   ☐ a business organization, form unknown
      ☐ a corporation   ☐ a corporation
      ☐ an unincorporated entity *(describe):*   ☐ an unincorporated entity *(describe):*

      ☐ a public entity *(describe):*   ☐ a public entity *(describe):*

      ☐ other *(specify):*   ☐ other *(specify):*

   b. The true names and capacities of defendants sued as Does are unknown to plaintiff.
   c. ☐ Information about additional defendants who are not natural persons is contained in Complaint—Attachment 3c.
   d. ☐ Defendants who are joined pursuant to Code of Civil Procedure section 382 are *(names):*

(Continued)

If this form is used as a cross-complaint, plaintiff means cross-complainant and defendant means cross-defendant.

Form Approved by the
Judicial Council of California
Effective January 1, 1982
Rule 982.1(20)

COMPLAINT—Contract

CCP 425.12   C-96

COMPLAINT—Contract

4. ☐ Plaintiff is required to comply with a claims statute, and
    a. ☐ plaintiff has complied with applicable claims statutes, or
    b. ☐ plaintiff is excused from complying because *(specify):*

5. ☐ This action is subject to ☐ Civil Code section 1812.10 ☐ Civil Code section 2984.4.

6. This action is filed in this ☐ county ☐ judicial district because
    a. ☐ a defendant entered into the contract here.
    b. ☐ a defendant lived here when the contract was entered into.
    c. ☐ a defendant lives here now.
    d. ☐ the contract was to be performed here.
    e. ☐ a defendant is a corporation or unincorporated association and its principal place of business is here.
    f. ☐ real property that is the subject of this action is located here.
    g. ☐ other *(specify):*

7. ☐ The following paragraphs of this pleading are alleged on information and belief *(specify paragraph numbers):*

8. ☐ Other:

9. The following causes of action are attached and the statements above apply to each: *(Each complaint must have one or more causes of action attached.)*
    ☐ Breach of Contract   ☐ Common Counts
    ☐ Other *(specify):*

10. PLAINTIFF PRAYS
    For judgment for costs of suit; for such relief as is fair, just, and equitable; and for
    ☐ damages of $_____
    ☐ interest on the damages ☐ according to proof ☐ at the rate of _____ percent per year
    from *(date):*
    ☐ attorney fees ☐ of $_____ ☐ according to proof.
    ☐ other *(specify):*

. . . .

_____   _____
(Type or print name)   (Signature of plaintiff or attorney)

(If you wish to verify this pleading, affix a verification.)

CAUSE OF ACTION—Breach of Contract   Page _____

_____ _____ _____
(number)

ATTACHMENT TO   ☐ Complaint   ☐ Cross-Complaint

(Use a separate cause of action form for each cause of action.)

BC-1. Plaintiff *(name):*

       alleges that on or about *(date):*
       a ☐ written ☐ oral ☐ other *(specify):*
       agreement was made between *(name parties to agreement):*

       ☐ A copy of the agreement is attached as Exhibit A, **or**
       ☐ The essential terms of the agreement ☐ are stated in Attachment BC-1 ☐ are as follows *(specify):*

BC-2. On or about *(dates):*
       defendant breached the agreement by ☐ the acts specified in Attachment BC-2 ☐ the following acts
       (specify):

BC-3. Plaintiff has performed all obligations to defendant except those obligations plaintiff was prevented or
       excused from performing.

BC-4. Plaintiff suffered damages legally (proximately) caused by defendant's breach of the agreement
       ☐ as stated in Attachment BC-4 ☐ as follows *(specify):*

BC-5. ☐ Plaintiff is entitled to attorney fees by an agreement or a statute
          ☐ of $
          ☐ according to proof.

BC-6. ☐ Other:

Form Approved by the
Judicial Council of California
Effective January 1, 1982
Rule 982.1(21)   **CAUSE OF ACTION—Breach of Contract**   CCP 425.12   C-97

_____ **CAUSE OF ACTION—Common Counts**   Page _____
(number)

ATTACHMENT TO ☐ Complaint ☐ Cross-Complaint

(Use a separate cause of action form for each cause of action.)

CC-1. Plaintiff *(name):*

alleges that defendant *(name):*

became indebted to ☐ plaintiff ☐ other *(name):*

a. ☐ within the last four years
    (1) ☐ on an open book account for money due.
    (2) ☐ because an account was stated in writing by and between plaintiff and defendant in which it
        was agreed that defendant was indebted to plaintiff.

b. ☐ within the last ☐ two years ☐ four years
    (1) ☐ for money had and received by defendant for the use and benefit of plaintiff.
    (2) ☐ for work, labor, services and materials rendered at the special instance and request of defendant
        and for which defendant promised to pay plaintiff
        ☐ the sum of $
        ☐ the reasonable value.
    (3) ☐ for goods, wares, and merchandise sold and delivered to defendant and for which defendant
        promised to pay plaintiff
        ☐ the sum of $
        ☐ the reasonable value.
    (4) ☐ for money lent by plaintiff to defendant at defendant's request.
    (5) ☐ for money paid, laid out, and expended to or for defendant at defendant's special instance and
        request.
    (6) ☐ other *(specify):*

CC-2. $, which is the reasonable value, is due and unpaid despite plaintiff's demand,
    plus prejudgment interest ☐ according to proof ☐ at the rate of _____ percent per year
    from *(date):*

CC-3. ☐ Plaintiff is entitled to attorney fees by an agreement or a statute
        ☐ of $
        ☐ according to proof.

CC.4. ☐ Other:

Form Approved by the
Judicial Council of California
Effective January 1, 1982
Rule 982.1(22)

CAUSE OF ACTION—Common Counts   CCP 425.12   C-98

_____ CAUSE OF ACTION—Breach of Warranty (Merchantability)   Page____
(number)

ATTACHMENT TO   ☐ Complaint   ☐ Cross-Complaint

BWM-1.   Plaintiff *(name):*

alleges that on or about *(date):*
defendant(s) *(seller):*

sold plaintiff *(quantity and description of goods):*

at retail and plaintiff bought such goods from defendant(s) for a price of *(amount):* $_____.
☐ A true copy of a memorandum or contract regarding this sale is attached to this Cause of Action as Exhibit BWM-1.

BWM-2.   ☐ On or about *(date):*
defendant(s) *(manufacturer):*

manufactured such goods for the purpose of their eventual sale to retail buyers.

BWM-3.   ☐ On or about *(date):*
defendant(s) *(distributor):*

acquired such goods from defendant(s) manufacturer and distributed them to defendant(s) seller for eventual retail sale to consumers.

BWM-4.   ☐ In the process, defendant(s) *(name):*

appended to such goods a written warranty which is attached to this Cause of Action as Exhibit BWM-4.

BWM-5.   Such retail sale to plaintiff was accompanied separately and individually by the implied warranty that such goods were merchantable by defendant(s) *(name):*

CAUSE OF ACTION—Breach of Warranty (Merchantability) (continued)   Page _____

BWM-6.   Defendant(s) breached their respective warranties implied in the sale in that *(describe):*

As a result of the breach by defendant(s), plaintiff did not receive merchantable goods as impliedly warranted by defendant(s).

BWM-7.   Plaintiff discovered such breach of warranty on or about *(date):*

a. ☐ On or about *(date):*
plaintiff notified defendant(s) *(name):*

☐ By letter, a true copy of which is attached to this Cause of Action as Exhibit BWM-7.

☐ Other *(describe):*

BWM-8.   As a legal result of such breach of the warranty of merchantability by defendant(s), plaintiff has been damaged in the amount $_____.

_____ **CAUSE OF ACTION**—Breach of Warranty (Fitness)   Page____
(number)

ATTACHMENT TO   ☐ Complaint   ☐ Cross-Complaint

BWF-1   Plaintiff *(name)*:

alleges that on or about *(date)*:
plaintiff required *(quantity and description of goods)*:

for the particular purpose of *(describe)*:

To select and furnish suitable goods for such purpose, plaintiff relied on the skill and judgment of defendant(s) (name):

BWF-2.   On or about *(date)*
defendant(s) sold to plaintiff *(quantity and description of goods sold)*:

and plaintiff bought such goods from defendant(s), in such reliance, for the amount of *(price paid)*: $_____.
☐ A true copy of the memorandum or contract of the sale is attached to this Cause of Action as Exhibit BWF-2.

BWF-3.   At the time of the retail sale of such goods, defendant(s) had reason to know the particular purpose for which the goods were required because plaintiff expressly communicated such purposes to defendant(s). Defendant(s) further knew plaintiff was relying on the skill and judgment of defendant(s) to select and furnish suitable goods; thus there was an implied warranty that the goods were fit for such purpose.

BWF-4.   Defendant(s) breached such warranty in that plaintiff did not receive suitable goods and such goods were not fit for the particular purpose for which they were required in that *(describe failure):*

BWF-5.   Plaintiff discovered such breach of warranty on or about *(date):*

    a. ☐ On or about *(date):*

    plaintiff notified defendant(s) *(name):*

      ☐ By letter, a true copy of which is attached to this Cause of Action as Exhibit BWF-5.

      ☐ Other *(describe):*

BWF-6.   As a result of such breach of warranty of fitness by defendant(s), plaintiff has been damaged in the amount of $_____.

SUMMONS
(CITACION JUDICIAL)

NOTICE TO DEFENDANT: *(Aviso a Acusado)*

YOU ARE BEING SUED BY PLAINTIFF:
(A Ud. le está demandando)

You have *30 CALENDAR DAYS* after this summons is served on you to file a typewritten response at this court.	*Después de que le entreguen esta citación judicial usted tiene un plazo de 30 DIAS CALENDARIOS para presentar una respuesta escrita a máquina en esta corte.*
A letter or phone call will not protect you; your typewritten response must be in proper legal form if you want the court to hear your case.	*Una carta o una llamada telefónica no le ofrecerá protección; su respuesta escrita a máquina tiene que cumplir con las formalidades legales apropiadas si usted quiere que la corte escuche su caso.*
If you do not file your response on time, you may lose the case, and your wages, money and property may be taken without further warning from the court.	*Si usted no presenta su respuesta a tiempo, puede perder el caso, y le pueden quitar su salario, su dinero y otras cosas de su propiedad sin aviso adicional por parte de la corte.*
There are other legal requirements. You may want to call an attorney right away. If you do not know an attorney, you may call an attorney referral service or a legal aid office (listed in the phone book).	*Existen otros requisitos legales. Puede que usted quiera llamar a un abogado inmediatamente. Si no conoce a un abogado, puede llamar a un servicio de referencia de abogados o a una oficina de ayuda legal (vea el directorio telefónico).*

CASE NUMBER: *(Numero del Caso)*

The name and address of the court is: *(El nombre y dirección de la corte es)*

The name, address, and telephone number of plaintiff's attorney, or plaintiff without an attorney, is:
(El nombre, la dirección y el número de teléfono del abogado del demandante, o del demandante que no tiene abogado, es)

DATE: _____ Clerk, by _____, Deputy
(Fecha) *(Actuario)* *(Delegado)*

[SEAL]

NOTICE TO THE PERSON SERVED: You are served
1. ☐ as an individual defendant.
2. ☐ as the person sued under the fictitious name of *(specify)*:
3. ☐ on behalf of *(specify)*:

    under: ☐ CCP 416.10 (corporation) ☐ CCP 416.60 (minor)
           ☐ CCP 416.20 (defunct corporation) ☐ CCP 416.70 (conservatee)
           ☐ CCP 416.40 (association or partnership) ☐ CCP 416.90 (individual)
           ☐ other:
4. ☐ by personal delivery on *(date)*:

Form Adopted by Rule 982
Judicial Council of California
982(a)(9) [Rev. January 1, 1984]

(See reverse for Proof of Service)
SUMMONS

C-53
CCP 412.20

PROOF OF SERVICE — SUMMONS
(Use separate proof of service for each person served)

1. I served the
   a. ☐ summons ☐ complaint ☐ amended summons ☐ amended complaint
      ☐ completed and blank Case Questionnaires ☐ Other *(specify)*:
   b. on defendant *(name)*:

   c. by serving ☐ defendant ☐ other *(name and title or relationship to person served)*:

   d. ☐ by delivery ☐ at home ☐ at business
      (1) date:
      (2) time:
      (3) address:

   e. ☐ by mailing
      (1) date:
      (2) place:

2. Manner of service *(check proper box)*:
   a. ☐ **Personal service.** By personally delivering copies. (CCP 415.10)
   b. ☐ **Substituted service on corporation, unincorporated association (including partnership), or public entity.** By leaving, during usual office hours, copies in the office of the person served with the person who apparently was in charge and thereafter mailing (by first-class mail, postage prepaid) copies to the person served at the place where the copies were left. (CCP 415.20(a))
   c. ☐ **Substituted service on natural person, minor, conservatee, or candidate.** By leaving copies at the dwelling house, usual place of abode, or usual place of business of the person served in the presence of a competent member of the household or a person apparently in charge of the office or place of business, at least 18 years of age, who was informed of the general nature of the papers, and thereafter mailing (by first-class mail, postage prepaid) copies to the person served at the place where the copies were left. (CCP 415.20(b)) *(Attach separate declaration or affidavit stating acts relied on to establish reasonable diligence in first attempting personal service.)*
   d. ☐ **Mail and acknowledgment service.** By mailing (by first-class mail or airmail, postage prepaid) copies to the person served, together with two copies of the form of notice and acknowledgment and a return envelope, postage prepaid, addressed to the sender. (CCP 415.30) *(Attach completed acknowledgment of receipt.)*
   e. ☐ **Certified or registered mail service.** By mailing to an address outside California (by first-class mail, postage prepaid, requiring a return receipt) copies to the person served. (CCP 415.40) *(Attach signed return receipt or other evidence of actual delivery to the person served.)*
   f. ☐ Other *(specify code section)*:
      ☐ additional page is attached.

3. The "Notice to the Person Served" (on the summons) was completed as follows (CCP 412.30, 415.10, and 474):
   a. ☐ as an individual defendant.
   b. ☐ as the person sued under the fictitious name of *(specify)*:
   c. ☐ on behalf of *(specify)*:
      under: ☐ CCP 416.10 (corporation) ☐ CCP 416.60 (minor) ☐ other:
             ☐ CCP 416.20 (defunct corporation) ☐ CCP 416.70 (conservatee)
             ☐ CCP 416.40 (association or partnership) ☐ CCP 416.90 (individual)
   d. ☐ by personal delivery on *(date)*:

4. At the time of service I was at least 18 years of age and not a party to this action.

5. Fee for service: $

6. Person serving:
   a. ☐ California sheriff, marshal, or constable.
   b. ☐ Registered California process server.
   c. ☐ Employee or independent contractor of a registered California process server.
   d. ☐ Not a registered California process server.
   e. ☐ Exempt from registration under Bus. & Prof. Code 22350(b).

   f. Name, address and telephone number and, if applicable, county of registration and number:

I declare under penalty of perjury under the laws of the State of California that the foregoing is true and correct.

(For California sheriff, marshal, or constable use only)
I certify that the foregoing is true and correct.

Date:

Date:

▶ _____
   (SIGNATURE)

▶ _____
   (SIGNATURE)

982(a)(9) [Rev. January 1, 1984]

Name of Court:
State of California, County of

PLAINTIFF:	CASE NUMBER:
DEFENDANT:	

CASE QUESTIONNAIRE

Requesting Party *(name)*:

Responding Party *(name)*:

—INSTRUCTIONS—

1. The purpose of the case questionnaire is to help the parties settle their differences without spending a lot of money. This is accomplished by exchanging information about the case early in the lawsuit. The exchange of case questionnaires may be started only by a plaintiff (or cross-complainant).

2. **Instructions for plaintiffs (and cross-complainants)**

   a. Under Code of Civil Procedure section 93, a plaintiff (or cross-complainant) *may* serve a *completed* case questionnaire and a blank case questionnaire *with the complaint (or cross-complaint)*.

   b. This is the only way you can require defendants (or cross-defendants) to serve you with a completed case questionnaire.

3. **Instructions for defendants (and cross-defendants)**

   a. If you have been served with a completed case questionnaire by a plaintiff (or cross-complainant), then you *must* fill in the blank case questionnaire. Your completed case questionnaire must be served on the requesting plaintiff (or cross-complainant) *with your answer to the complaint* (or cross-complaint).

   b. **THIS IS NOT AN ANSWER OR RESPONSE TO THE COMPLAINT.**

4. **Instructions for all parties**

   a. **ALL QUESTIONS REFER TO THE INCIDENT OR AGREEMENT IN THIS LAWSUIT ONLY.**

   b. Answer each question. If a question is not applicable, answer "NA."

   c. Your answers are not limited to your personal knowledge, but you are required to furnish all information available to you or anyone acting on your behalf, whether you are a plaintiff, defendant, cross-complainant, or cross-defendant.

   d. Type or *legibly* print your answer below each question. If you cannot completely answer a question in the space provided on the case questionnaire, check the "attachment" box and put the number of the question and the complete answer on an attached sheet of paper. You should *not* put part of an answer on the case questionnaire and part on the attachment. You may put more than one answer on each attached page.

   e. When you have completed the case questionnaire, sign the verification and **serve** the original.

   f. You may compel compliance with these requirements under Code of Civil Procedure section 2034.

   g. **DO NOT FILE THIS CASE QUESTIONNAIRE WITH THE COURT.**

(Page one of four)

PLAINTIFF:	CASE NUMBER:
DEFENDANT:	

—QUESTIONS—

1. FOR ALL CASES

    a. State your name and street address.

    b. State your current business name and street address, type of business entity, and your title.

    c. Describe in detail your claims or defenses and the facts on which they are based, giving relevant dates.

       ☐ See attachment for answer number 1c.

    d. State the name, street address, and telephone number of each person who has knowledge of facts relating to this lawsuit and specify his or her area of knowledge.

       ☐ See attachment for answer number 1d.

    e. Describe each document or photograph that relates to the issues or facts. You are encouraged to attach a copy of each. For each that you have described but not attached, state the name, street address, and telephone number of each person who has it.

       ☐ See attachment for answer number 1e.

1. f. Describe each item of physical evidence that relates to the issues and facts, give its location, and state the name, street address, and telephone number of each person who has it.

    ☐ See attachment for answer number 1f.

    g. State the name and street address of each insurance company and the number of each policy that may cover you in whole or part for the damages claimed.

    ☐ See attachment for answer number 1g.

2. FOR PERSONAL INJURY OR PROPERTY DAMAGE CASES
    a. Describe each injury or illness that you received and your present complaints about each.

    ☐ See attachment for answer number 2a.

    b. State the name, street address, and telephone number of each physician, dentist, or other health care provider who treated or examined you, the type of treatment, the dates of treatment, and the charges by each to date.

    ☐ See attachment for answer number 2b.

    c. Itemize the medical expenses you anticipate in the future.

    ☐ See attachment for answer number 2c.

    d. Itemize your loss of income to date, give the name and street address of each source, and show how the loss is computed.

    ☐ See attachment for answer number 2d.

2. e. Itemize the loss of income you anticipate in the future, give the name and street address of each source, and show how the loss is computed.

[ ] See attachment for answer number 2e.

f. Itemize your property damage and state the amount or attach an itemized bill or estimate.

[ ] See attachment for answer number 2f.

g. Describe each other item of damage or cost that you claim and state the amount.

[ ] See attachment for answer number 2g.

3. FOR CASES BASED ON AGREEMENTS

a. In addition to your answer to 1e, state all the terms and give the date of any part of the agreement that is not in writing.

[ ] See attachment for answer number 3a.

b. Describe each item of damage or cost you claim, state the amount, and show how it is computed.

[ ] See attachment for answer number 3b.

VERIFICATION

I declare under penalty of perjury under the laws of the State of California that the foregoing answers are true and correct.

Date:

. . . . ▶ _____

(TYPED OR PRINTED NAME)   (SIGNATURE)

PARTY WITHOUT ATTORNEY *(My Name and Address)*:

MY TELEPHONE NO.:

FOR COURT USE ONLY

NAME OF COURT:

STREET ADDRESS:

MAILING ADDRESS:

CITY AND ZIP CODE:

BRANCH NAME:

PLAINTIFF:

DEFENDANT:

PROOF OF SERVICE BY MAIL
(CCP Sections 1013a, 2015.5)

CASE NUMBER

declare that:

1. At the time of service I was at least 18 years of age and not a party to this legal action.

2. I am a resident of or employed in the county where the mailing occurred.

3. My business or residence address is: _____ .

4. I served copies of the following paper(s) in the manner shown:

    a. Papers served [list exact titles of paper(s)]:

    b. Manner of service: by placing true copies in a sealed envelope addressed to each person whose name and address is given below and:

    ☐ depositing the envelope in the United States Mail with the postage fully prepaid; or

    ☐ (If deposited at a business:) Placing for collection and mailing following ordinary business practices. I am readily familiar with the business practice for collection and processing of correspondence for mailing with the United States Post Office. The correspondence will be deposited with the United States Post office on the same date as the date of deposit (below) in the ordinary course of business.

    (1) Date of Deposit: _____

    (2) Place of Deposit (city & state; business address if deposited at a business) : _____

5. I declare under penalty of perjury under the laws of the State of California that the foregoing is true and correct. Executed on _____ at _____, California.

Print Name: _____   _____

[Signature of Person Who Served Papers]

Name and Address of Each Person to Whom Documents Were Mailed:

☐ _____Additional names and addresses on reverse.

PROOF OF SERVICE BY MAIL

ATTORNEY OR PARTY WITHOUT ATTORNEY (NAME AND ADDRESS):	TELEPHONE:	FOR COURT USE ONLY
ATTORNEY FOR (NAME):		
Insert name of court, judicial district or branch court, if any, and post office and street address:		
PLAINTIFF:		
DEFENDANT:		

ANSWER—Personal Injury, Property Damage, Wrongful Death	CASE NUMBER:
☐ COMPLAINT OF (name): ☐ CROSS-COMPLAINT OF (name):	

1. This pleading, including attachments and exhibits, consists of the following number of pages: _____

DEFENDANT OR CROSS-DEFENDANT (name):

2. ☐ Generally **denies** each allegation of the **unverified** complaint or cross-complaint.

3. a. ☐ DENIES each allegation of the following numbered paragraphs:

   b. ☐ ADMITS each allegation of the following numbered paragraphs:

   c. ☐ DENIES, ON INFORMATION AND BELIEF, each allegation of the following numbered paragraphs:

   d. ☐ DENIES, BECAUSE OF LACK OF SUFFICIENT INFORMATION OR BELIEF TO ANSWER, each allegation of the following numbered paragraphs:

   e. ☐ ADMITS the following allegations and generally denies all other allegations:

(Continued)

Form Approved by the
Judicial Council of California
Effective January 1, 1982
Rule 982.1(15)

ANSWER—Personal Injury, Property Damage, Wrongful Death

CCP 425.12

C-95

ANSWER—Personal Injury, Property Damage, Wrongful Death

f. ☐ DENIES the following allegations and admits all other allegations:

g. ☐ Other (specify):

AFFIRMATIVELY ALLEGES AS A DEFENSE

4. ☐ The comparative fault of plaintiff or cross-complainant (name):
as follows:

5. ☐ The expiration of the Statute of Limitations as follows:

6. ☐ Other (specify):

7. DEFENDANT OR CROSS-DEFENDANT PRAYS
For costs of suit and that plaintiff or cross-complainant take nothing.
☐ Other (specify):

. . . .
(Type or print name)   (Signature of party or attorney)

ATTORNEY OR PARTY WITHOUT ATTORNEY (NAME AND ADDRESS):   TELEPHONE: FOR COURT USE ONLY

ATTORNEY FOR (NAME):

Insert name of court, judicial district or branch court, if any, and post office and street address:

PLAINTIFF:

DEFENDANT:

ANSWER—Contract

CASE NUMBER:

☐ **TO COMPLAINT OF** *(name):*
☐ **TO CROSS-COMPLAINT OF** *(name):*

1. This pleading, including attachments and exhibits, consists of the following number of pages: _____
2. DEFENDANT *(name):*

   answers the complaint or cross-complaint as follows:
3. *Check ONLY ONE of the next two boxes:*
   a. ☐ Defendant generally denies each statement of the complaint or cross-complaint. *(Do not check this box if the verified complaint or cross-complaint demands more than $1,000.)*
   b. ☐ Defendant admits that all of the statements of the complaint or cross-complaint are true EXCEPT:
      (1) Defendant claims the following statements are false *(use paragraph numbers or explain):*

      ☐ Continued on Attachment 3.b.(1).
      (2) Defendant has no information or belief that the following statements are true, so defendant denies them *(use paragraph numbers or explain):*

      ☐ Continued on Attachment 3.b.(2).
                              (Continued)

If this form is used to answer a cross-complaint, plaintiff means cross-complainant and defendant means cross-defendant.

Form Approved by the
Judicial Council of California
Effective January 1, 1982
Rule 982.1(35)

ANSWER—Contract

CCP 425.12

C-1C

ANSWER—Contract

4. ☐ AFFIRMATIVE DEFENSES
Defendant alleges the following additional reasons that plaintiff is not entitled to recover anything:

☐ Continued on Attachment 4.

5. ☐ Other:

6. DEFENDANT PRAYS
    a. that plaintiff take nothing.
    b. ☐ for costs of suit.
    c. ☐ other (specify):

. . . .
_____
(Type or print name)

_____
(Signature of party or attorney)

ATTORNEY OR PARTY WITHOUT ATTORNEY (NAME AND ADDRESS):   TELEPHONE: | FOR COURT USE ONLY

ATTORNEY FOR (NAME)

Insert name of court, judicial district or branch court, if any, and post office and street address.

SHORT TITLE:

CROSS-COMPLAINANT:

CROSS-DEFENDANT:

☐ DOES 1 TO _____

CROSS-COMPLAINT—Personal Injury, Property Damage, Wrongful Death

CASE NUMBER:

☐ **Apportionment of Fault** ☐ **Declaratory Relief**
☐ **Indemnification** ☐ **Other** *(specify):*

1. This pleading, including exhibits and attachments, consists of the following number of pages: _____

CROSS-COMPLAINANT *(name):*

SAYS AGAINST CROSS-DEFENDANT *(name):*

2. ☐ The following causes of action are attached and the statements below apply to each: *(In the attachments plaintiff means cross-complainant and defendant means cross-defendant.)*
     ☐ Motor Vehicle   ☐ Products Liability
     ☐ General Negligence   ☐ Premises Liability
     ☐ Intentional Tort
     ☐ Other *(specify):*

3. a. Each cross-complainant named above is a competent adult
     ☐ **Except** cross-complainant *(name):*

         ☐ a corporation qualified to do business in California
         ☐ an unincorporated entity *(describe):*
         ☐ a public entity *(describe):*
         ☐ a minor   ☐ an adult
            ☐ for whom a guardian or conservator of the estate or a guardian ad litem has been appointed
            ☐ other *(specify):*
         ☐ other *(specify):*

   b. ☐ Information about additional cross-complainants who are not competent adults is contained in Cross-Complaint—Attachment 3b.   (Continued)

Form Approved by the
Judicial Council of California
Effective January 1, 1982
Rule 982 1(14)

CROSS-COMPLAINT— Personal Injury, Property Damage,
Wrongful Death

CCP 425 12   C-94

CROSS-COMPLAINT—Personal Injury, Property Damage, Wrongful Death Page two

4. a. Each cross-defendant named above is a natural person

☐ **Except** cross-defendant *(name)*:   ☐ **Except** cross-defendant *(name)*:

☐ a business organization, form unknown   ☐ a business organization, form unknown
☐ a corporation   ☐ a corporation
☐ an unincorporated entity *(describe)*:   ☐ an unincorporated entity *(describe)*:

☐ a public entity *(describe)*:   ☐ a public entity *(describe)*:

☐ other *(specify)*:   ☐ other *(specify)*:

b. The true names and capacities of cross-defendants sued as Does are unknown to cross-complainant.

c. ☐ Information about additional cross-defendants who are not natural persons is contained in Cross-Complaint—Attachment 4c.

5. ☐ Cross-complainant is required to comply with a claims statute, **and**
a. ☐ has complied with applicable claims statutes, **or**
b. ☐ is excused from complying because *(specify)*:

6. ☐   **Cause of Action—Indemnification**
    (number)

a. I am informed and believe that cross-defendants were the agents, employees, co-venturers, partners, or in some manner agents or principals, or both, for each other and were acting within the course and scope of their agency or employment.

b. The principal action alleges among other things conduct entitling plaintiff to compensatory damages against me. I contend that I am not liable for events and occurrences described in plaintiff's complaint.

c. If I am found in some manner responsible to plaintiff or to anyone else as a result of the incidents and occurrences described in plaintiff's complaint, my liability would be based solely upon a derivative form of liability not resulting from my conduct, but only from an obligation imposed upon me by law; therefore, I would be entitled to complete indemnity from each cross-defendant.

7. ☐   **Cause of Action—Apportionment of Fault**
    (number)

I am informed and believe that each cross-defendant was responsible, in whole or in part, for the injuries, if any, suffered by plaintiff. If I am judged liable to plaintiff, each cross-defendant should be required:

a. to pay a share of plaintiff's judgment which is in proportion to the comparative negligence of that cross-defendant in causing plaintiff's damages and

b. to reimburse me for any payments I make to plaintiff in excess of my proportional share of all cross-defendants' negligence.

CROSS-COMPLAINT— Personal Injury, Property Damage, Wrongful Death (Continued)   Page three

8. ☐ ————————————— . **Cause of Action—Declaratory Relief**
             (number)

An actual controversy exists between the parties concerning their respective rights and duties because cross-complainant contends and cross-defendant disputes ☐ as specified in Cross-Complaint—Attachment 8
☐ as follows:

9. ☐   **Cause of Action—(Specify):**
             (number)

10. CROSS-COMPLAINANT PRAYS
For judgment for costs of suit; for such relief as is fair, just, and equitable; and for
☐ compensatory damages
   ☐ **(Superior Court)** according to proof.
   ☐ **(Municipal and Justice Court)** in the amount of $ ....

☐ total and complete indemnity for any judgments rendered against me.

☐ judgment in a proportionate share from each cross-defendant.

☐ a judicial determination that cross-defendants were the legal cause of any injuries and damages sustained by plaintiff and that cross-defendants indemnify me, either completely or partially, for any sums of money which may be recovered against me by plaintiff.

☐ other (specify):

_____   _____
(Type or print name)   (Signature of cross-complainant or attorney)

**CROSS-COMPLAINT—Personal Injury, Property Damage,
Wrongful Death (Continued)**

Rule 982.1(14) (cont'd)   CCP 425.12   C-94

ATTORNEY OR PARTY WITHOUT ATTORNEY *(Name and Address)*:	TELEPHONE NO.:	FOR COURT USE ONLY

ATTORNEY FOR *(Name)*:

Insert name of court and name of judicial district and branch court, if any:

PLAINTIFF:

DEFENDANT:

REQUEST FOR (Application)	☐ ENTRY OF DEFAULT ☐ CLERK'S JUDGMENT ☐ COURT JUDGMENT	CASE NUMBER:

1. TO THE CLERK: On the complaint or cross-complaint filed
   a. On *(date)*:
   b. By *(name)*:
   c. ☐ Enter default of defendant *(names)*:

   d. ☐ I request a court judgment under CCP 585(b), (c), 989, etc. *(Testimony required. Apply to the clerk for a hearing date, unless the court will enter a judgment on an affidavit under CCP 585(d).)*
   e. ☐ Enter clerk's judgment
      (1) ☐ For restitution of the premises only and issue a writ of execution on the judgment. CCP 1174(c) does not apply. (CCP 1169) ☐ Include in the judgment all tenants, subtenants, named claimants, and other occupants of the premises. The Prejudgment Claim of Right to Possession was served in compliance with CCP 415.46.
      (2) ☐ Under CCP 585(a). *(Complete the declaration under CCP 585.5 on the reverse (item 3).)*
      (3) ☐ For default previously entered on *(date)*:

2. **Judgment to be entered**

	Amount	Credits Acknowledged	Balance
a. Demand of complaint	$	$	$
b. Statement of damages (CCP 425.11) (superior court only)*			
(1) Special	$	$	$
(2) General	$	$	$
c. Interest	$	$	$
d. Costs *(see reverse)*	$	$	$
e. Attorney fees	$	$	$
f. **TOTALS**	$	$	$

   g. **Daily damages** were demanded in complaint at the rate of: $ per day beginning *(date)*:

Date:

▶

. . . .
(TYPE OR PRINT NAME) _____ (SIGNATURE OF PLAINTIFF OR ATTORNEY FOR PLAINTIFF)

* *Personal injury or wrongful death actions only.*

FOR COURT USE ONLY	(1) ☐ Default entered as requested on *(date)*: (2) ☐ Default NOT entered as requested *(state reason)*:

By: _____

(Continued on reverse)

Form Adopted by the
Judicial Council of California
982(a)(6) [Rev. September 30, 1991*]

REQUEST FOR ENTRY OF DEFAULT
(Application to Enter Default)

Code of Civil Procedure, §§ 585-587, 1169

*See note on reverse.

SHORT TITLE:	CASE NUMBER:

3. ☐ **DECLARATION UNDER CCP 585.5** *(Required for clerk's judgment under CCP 585(a))* This action
  a. ☐ is ☐ is not on a contract or installment sale for goods or services subject to CC 1801, etc. (Unruh Act).
  b. ☐ is ☐ is not on a conditional sales contract subject to CC 2981, etc. (Rees-Levering Motor Vehicle Sales and Finance Act).
  c. ☐ is ☐ is not on an obligation for goods, services, loans, or extensions of credit subject to CCP 395(b).

4. **DECLARATION OF MAILING (CCP 587)** A copy of this Request for Entry of Default was
  a. ☐ **not mailed** to the following defendants whose addresses are **unknown** to plaintiff or plaintiff's attorney *(names)*:

  b. ☐ **mailed** first-class, postage prepaid, in a sealed envelope addressed to each defendant's attorney of record or, if none, to
    each defendant's last known address as follows:
    (1) Mailed on *(date)*:   (2) To *(specify names and addresses shown on the envelopes)*:

    I declare under penalty of perjury under the laws of the State of California that the foregoing items 3 and 4 are true and correct.
Date:

....   ▶ _____
    (TYPE OR PRINT NAME)   (SIGNATURE OF DECLARANT)

5. **MEMORANDUM OF COSTS** *(Required if judgment requested)* **Costs and Disbursements** are as follows (CCP 1033.5):
  a. Clerk's filing fees . . . . $
  b. Process server's fees . . . . $
  c. Other *(specify)*: . . . . $
  d. . . . . $
  e. **TOTAL** . . . . $ ══════════
  f. ☐ Costs and disbursements are waived.

    I am the attorney, agent, or party who claims these costs. To the best of my knowledge and belief this memorandum of costs
is correct and these costs were necessarily incurred in this case.

    I declare under penalty of perjury under the laws of the State of California that the foregoing is true and correct.
Date:

....   ▶ _____
    (TYPE OR PRINT NAME)   (SIGNATURE OF DECLARANT)

6. ☐ **DECLARATION OF NONMILITARY STATUS** *(Required for a judgment)* No defendant named in item 1c of the application
    is in the military service so as to be entitled to the benefits of the Soldiers' and Sailors' Civil Relief Act of 1940 (50 U.S.C.
    Appen. § 501 et seq.).

    I declare under penalty of perjury under the laws of the State of California that the foregoing is true and correct.
Date:

....   ▶ _____
    (TYPE OR PRINT NAME)   (SIGNATURE OF DECLARANT)

NOTE: Continued use of form 982(a)(6) (Rev. July 1, 1988) is authorized until June 30, 1992, *except* in unlawful detainer proceedings.

ATTORNEY OR PARTY WITHOUT ATTORNEY *(Name and Address)*:	TELEPHONE NO.:

ATTORNEY FOR *(Name)*

NAME OF COURT AND JUDICIAL DISTRICT AND BRANCH COURT, IF ANY:

SHORT TITLE OF CASE:

FORM INTERROGATORIES	CASE NUMBER:
Asking Party:	
Answering Party:	
Set No.:	

Sec. 1. Instructions to All Parties

(a) These are general instructions. *For time limitations, requirements for service on other parties, and other details, see Code of Civil Procedure section 2030 and the cases construing it.*

(b) These interrogatories do not change existing law relating to interrogatories nor do they affect an answering party's right to assert any privilege or objection.

Sec. 2. Instructions to the Asking Party

(a) These interrogatories are designed for optional use in the superior courts only. A separate set of interrogatories, Form Interrogatories—Economic Litigation, which have no subparts, are designed for optional use in municipal and justice courts. However, they also may be used in superior courts. See Code of Civil Procedure section 94.

(b) Check the box next to each interrogatory that you want the answering party to answer. Use care in choosing those interrogatories that are applicable to the case.

(c) The interrogatories in section 16.0, Defendant's Contentions—Personal Injury, should not be used until the defendant has had a reasonable opportunity to conduct an investigation or discovery of plaintiff's injuries and damages.

(d) Additional interrogatories may be attached.

Sec. 3. Instructions to the Answering Party

(a) In superior court actions, an answer or other appropriate response must be given to each interrogatory checked by the asking party.

(b) As a general rule, within 30 days after you are served with these interrogatories, you must serve your responses on the asking party and serve copies of your responses on all other parties to the action who have appeared. See Code of Civil Procedure section 2030 for details.

(c) Each answer must be as complete and straightforward as the information reasonably available to you permits. If an interrogatory cannot be answered completely, answer it to the extent possible.

(d) If you do not have enough personal knowledge to fully answer an interrogatory, say so, but make a reasonable and good faith effort to get the information by asking other persons or organizations, unless the information is equally available to the asking party.

(e) Whenever an interrogatory may be answered by referring to a document, the document may be attached as an exhibit to the response and referred to in the response. If the document has more than one page, refer to the page and section where the answer to the interrogatory can be found.

(f) Whenever an address and telephone number for the same person are requested in more than one interrogatory, you are required to furnish them in answering only the first interrogatory asking for that information.

(g) Your answers to these interrogatories must be verified, dated, and signed. You may wish to use the following form *at the end of your answers:*

"I declare under penalty of perjury under the laws of the State of California that the foregoing answers are true and correct.

_____   _____
(DATE)   (SIGNATURE)

Sec. 4. Definitions

Words in **BOLDFACE CAPITALS** in these interrogatories are defined as follows:

(a) **INCIDENT** includes the circumstances and events surrounding the alleged accident, injury, or other occurrence or breach of contract giving rise to this action or proceeding.

(b) **YOU OR ANYONE ACTING ON YOUR BEHALF** includes you, your agents, your employees, your insurance companies, their agents, their employees, your attorneys, your accountants, your investigators, and anyone else acting on your behalf.

(Continued)

Page 1 of 8

Form Approved by the
Judicial Council of California
FI-120 [Rev. July 1, 1987]

FORM INTERROGATORIES

CCP 2030, 2033.5
Post-Record Catalog #FI-120

(c) **PERSON** includes a natural person, firm, association, organization, partnership, business, trust, corporation, or public entity.

(d) **DOCUMENT** means a writing, as defined in Evidence Code section 250, and includes the original or a copy of handwriting, typewriting, printing, photostating, photographing, and every other means of recording upon any tangible thing and form of communicating or representation, including letters, words, pictures, sounds, or symbols, or combinations of them.

(e) **HEALTH CARE PROVIDER** includes any **PERSON** referred to in Code of Civil Procedure section 667.7(e)(3).

(f) **ADDRESS** means the street address, including the city, state, and zip code.

Sec. 5. Interrogatories

The following interrogatories have been approved by the Judicial Council under section 2033.5 of the Code of Civil Procedure:

CONTENTS

1.0 Identity of Persons Answering These Interrogatories

1.1 State the name, **ADDRESS**, telephone number, and relationship to you of each **PERSON** who prepared or assisted in the preparation of the responses to these interrogatories. (Do not identify anyone who simply typed or reproduced the responses.)

2.0 General Background Information — Individual

[ ] 2.1 State:
(a) your name;
(b) every name you have used in the past;
(c) the dates you used each name.

[ ] 2.2 State the date and place of your birth.

[ ] 2.3 At the time of the **INCIDENT**, did you have a driver's license? If so, state:
(a) the state or other issuing entity;
(b) the license number and type;
(c) the date of issuance;
(d) all restrictions.

[ ] 2.4 At the time of the **INCIDENT**, did you have any other permit or license for the operation of a motor vehicle? If so, state:
(a) the state or other issuing entity;
(b) the license number and type;
(c) the date of issuance;
(d) all restrictions.

[ ] 2.5 State:
(a) your present residence **ADDRESS**;
(b) your residence **ADDRESSES** for the last five years;
(c) the dates you lived at each **ADDRESS**.

[ ] 2.6 State:
(a) the name, **ADDRESS**, and telephone number of your present employer or place of self-employment;
(b) the name, **ADDRESS**, dates of employment, job title, and nature of work for each employer or self-employment you have had from five years before the **INCIDENT** until today.

[ ] 2.7 State:
(a) the name and **ADDRESS** of each school or other academic or vocational institution you have attended beginning with high school;
(b) the dates you attended;
(c) the highest grade level you have completed;
(d) the degrees received.

[ ] 2.8 Have you ever been convicted of a felony? If so, for each conviction state:
(a) the city and state where you were convicted;
(b) the date of conviction;
(c) the offense;
(d) the court and case number.

[ ] 2.9 Can you speak English with ease? If not, what language and dialect do you normally use?

[ ] 2.10 Can you read and write English with ease? If not, what language and dialect do you normally use?

[ ] 2.11 At the time of the **INCIDENT** were you acting as an agent or employee for any **PERSON**? If so, state:
(a) the name, **ADDRESS**, and telephone number of that **PERSON**;
(b) a description of your duties.

[ ] 2.12 At the time of the **INCIDENT** did you or any other person have any physical, emotional, or mental disability or condition that may have contributed to the occurrence of the **INCIDENT**? If so, for each person state:
(a) the name, **ADDRESS**, and telephone number.

(b) the nature of the disability or condition;

(c) the manner in which the disability or condition contributed to the occurrence of the **INCIDENT**.

☐ 2.13 Within 24 hours before the **INCIDENT** did you or any person involved in the **INCIDENT** use or take any of the following substances: alcoholic beverage, marijuana, or other drug or medication of any kind (prescription or not)? If so, for each person state:

(a) the name, **ADDRESS**, and telephone number;

(b) the nature or description of each substance;

(c) the quantity of each substance used or taken;

(d) the date and time of day when each substance was used or taken;

(e) the **ADDRESS** where each substance was used or taken;

(f) the name, **ADDRESS**, and telephone number of each person who was present when each substance was used or taken;

(g) the name, **ADDRESS**, and telephone number of any **HEALTH CARE PROVIDER** that prescribed or furnished the substance and the condition for which it was prescribed or furnished.

3.0 General Background Information — Business Entity

☐ 3.1 Are you a corporation? If so, state:

(a) the name stated in the current articles of incorporation;

(b) all other names used by the corporation during the past ten years and the dates each was used;

(c) the date and place of incorporation;

(d) the **ADDRESS** of the principal place of business;

(e) whether you are qualified to do business in California.

☐ 3.2 Are you a partnership? If so, state:

(a) the current partnership name;

(b) all other names used by the partnership during the past ten years and the dates each was used;

(c) whether you are a limited partnership and, if so, under the laws of what jurisdiction;

(d) the name and **ADDRESS** of each general partner;

(e) the **ADDRESS** of the principal place of business.

☐ 3.3 Are you a joint venture? If so, state:

(a) the current joint venture name;

(b) all other names used by the joint venture during the past ten years and the dates each was used;

(c) the name and **ADDRESS** of each joint venturer;

(d) the **ADDRESS** of the principal place of business.

☐ 3.4 Are you an unincorporated association? If so, state:

(a) the current unincorporated association name;

(b) all other names used by the unincorporated association during the past ten years and the dates each was used;

(c) the **ADDRESS** of the principal place of business.

☐ 3.5 Have you done business under a fictitious name during the past ten years? If so, for each fictitious name state:

(a) the name;

(b) the dates each was used;

(c) the state and county of each fictitious name filing;

(d) the **ADDRESS** of the principal place of business.

☐ 3.6 Within the past five years has any public entity registered or licensed your businesses? If so, for each license or registration:

(a) identify the license or registration;

(b) state the name of the public entity;

(c) state the dates of issuance and expiration.

4.0 Insurance

☐ 4.1 At the time of the **INCIDENT**, was there in effect any policy of insurance through which you were or might be insured in any manner (for example, primary, pro-rata, or excess liability coverage or medical expense coverage) for the damages, claims, or actions that have arisen out of the **INCIDENT**? If so, for each policy state:

(a) the kind of coverage;

(b) the name and **ADDRESS** of the insurance company;

(c) the name, **ADDRESS**, and telephone number of each named insured;

(d) the policy number;

(e) the limits of coverage for each type of coverage contained in the policy;

(f) whether any reservation of rights or controversy or coverage dispute exists between you and the insurance company;

(g) the name, **ADDRESS**, and telephone number of the custodian of the policy.

☐ 4.2 Are you self-insured under any statute for the damages, claims, or actions that have arisen out of the **INCIDENT**? If so, specify the statute.

5.0 [Reserved]

6.0 Physical, Mental, or Emotional Injuries

☐ 6.1 Do you attribute any physical, mental, or emotional injuries to the **INCIDENT**? If your answer is "no," do not answer interrogatories 6.2 through 6.7.

☐ 6.2 Identify each injury you attribute to the **INCIDENT** and the area of your body affected.

☐ 6.3 Do you still have any complaints that you attribute to the **INCIDENT**? If so, for each complaint state:

(a) a description;

(b) whether the complaint is subsiding, remaining the same, or becoming worse;

(c) the frequency and duration.

☐ 6.4 Did you receive any consultation or examination (except from expert witnesses covered by Code of Civil Procedure, § 2034) or treatment from a **HEALTH CARE PROVIDER** for any injury you attribute to the **INCIDENT**? If so, for each **HEALTH CARE PROVIDER** state:

(a) the name, **ADDRESS**, and telephone number;

(b) the type of consultation, examination, or treatment provided;

(c) the dates you received consultation, examination, or treatment;

(d) the charges to date.

6.5 Have you taken any medication, prescribed or not, as a result of injuries that you attribute to the **INCIDENT**? If so, for each medication state:

(a) the name;

(b) the **PERSON** who prescribed or furnished it;

(c) the date prescribed or furnished;

(d) the dates you began and stopped taking it;

(e) the cost to date.

6.6 Are there any other medical services not previously listed (for example, ambulance, nursing, prosthetics)? If so, for each service state:

(a) the nature;

(b) the date;

(c) the cost;

(d) the name, **ADDRESS**, and telephone number of each provider.

6.7 Has any **HEALTH CARE PROVIDER** advised that you may require future or additional treatment for any injuries that you attribute to the **INCIDENT**? If so, for each injury state:

(a) the name and **ADDRESS** of each **HEALTH CARE PROVIDER**;

(b) the complaints for which the treatment was advised;

(c) the nature, duration, and estimated cost of the treatment.

7.0 Property Damage

7.1 Do you attribute any loss of or damage to a vehicle or other property to the **INCIDENT**? If so, for each item of property:

(a) describe the property;

(b) describe the nature and location of the damage to the property;

(c) state the amount of damage you are claiming for each item of property and how the amount was calculated;

(d) if the property was sold, state the name, **ADDRESS**, and telephone number of the seller, the date of sale, and the sale price.

7.2 Has a written estimate or evaluation been made for any item of property referred to in your answer to the preceeding interrogatory? If so, for each estimate or evaluation state:

(a) the name, **ADDRESS**, and telephone number of the **PERSON** who prepared it and the date prepared;

(b) the name, **ADDRESS**, and telephone number of each **PERSON** who has a copy;

(c) the amount of damage stated.

7.3 Has any item of property referred to in your answer to interrogatory 7.1 been repaired? If so, for each item state:

(a) the date repaired;

(b) a description of the repair;

(c) the repair cost;

(d) the name, **ADDRESS**, and telephone number of the **PERSON** who repaired it;

(e) the name, **ADDRESS**, and telephone number of the **PERSON** who paid for the repair.

8.0 Loss of Income or Earning Capacity

8.1 Do you attribute any loss of income or earning capacity to the **INCIDENT**? If your answer is ''no,'' do not answer interrogatories 8.2 through 8.8.

8.2 State:

(a) the nature of your work;

(b) your job title at the time of the **INCIDENT**;

(c) the date your employment began.

8.3 State the last date before the **INCIDENT** that you worked for compensation.

8.4 State your monthly income at the time of the **INCIDENT** and how the amount was calculated.

8.5 State the date you returned to work at each place of employment following the **INCIDENT**.

8.6 State the dates you did not work and for which you lost income.

8.7 State the total income you have lost to date as a result of the **INCIDENT** and how the amount was calculated.

8.8 Will you lose income in the future as a result of the **INCIDENT**? If so, state:

(a) the facts upon which you base this contention;

(b) an estimate of the amount;

(c) an estimate of how long you will be unable to work;

(d) how the claim for future income is calculated.

9.0 Other Damages

9.1 Are there any other damages that you attribute to the **INCIDENT**? If so, for each item of damage state:

(a) the nature;

(b) the date it occurred;

(c) the amount;

(d) the name, **ADDRESS**, and telephone number of each **PERSON** to whom an obligation was incurred.

9.2 Do any **DOCUMENTS** support the existence or amount of any item of damages claimed in interrogatory 9.1? If so, state the name, **ADDRESS**, and telephone number of the **PERSON** who has each **DOCUMENT**.

10.0 Medical History

10.1 At any time before the **INCIDENT** did you have complaints or injuries that involved the same part of your body claimed to have been injured in the **INCIDENT**? If so, for each state:

(a) a description;

(b) the dates it began and ended;

(c) the name, **ADDRESS**, and telephone number of each **HEALTH CARE PROVIDER** whom you consulted or who examined or treated you.

☐ **10.2** List all physical, mental, and emotional disabilities you had immediately before the **INCIDENT**. (You may omit mental or emotional disabilities unless you attribute any mental or emotional injury to the **INCIDENT**.)

☐ **10.3** At any time after the **INCIDENT**, did you sustain injuries of the kind for which you are now claiming damages. If so, for each incident state:
(a) the date and the place it occurred;
(b) the name, **ADDRESS**, and telephone number of any other **PERSON** involved;
(c) the nature of any injuries you sustained;
(d) the name, **ADDRESS**, and telephone number of each **HEALTH CARE PROVIDER** that you consulted or who examined or treated you;
(e) the nature of the treatment and its duration.

11.0 Other Claims and Previous Claims

☐ **11.1** Except for this action, in the last ten years have you filed an action or made a written claim or demand for compensation for your personal injuries? If so, for each action, claim, or demand state:
(a) the date, time, and place and location of the **INCIDENT** (closest street **ADDRESS** or intersection);
(b) the name, **ADDRESS**, and telephone number of each **PERSON** against whom the claim was made or action filed;
(c) the court, names of the parties, and case number of any action filed;
(d) the name, **ADDRESS**, and telephone number of any attorney representing you;
(e) whether the claim or action has been resolved or is pending.

☐ **11.2** In the last ten years have you made a written claim or demand for worker's compensation benefits? If so, for each claim or demand state:
(a) the date, time, and place of the **INCIDENT** giving rise to the claim;
(b) the name, **ADDRESS**, and telephone number of your employer at the time of the injury;
(c) the name, **ADDRESS**, and telephone number of the worker's compensation insurer and the claim number;
(d) the period of time during which you received worker's compenstation benefits;
(e) a description of the injury;
(f) the name, **ADDRESS**, and telephone number of any **HEALTH CARE PROVIDER** that provided services;
(g) the case number at the Worker's Compensation Appeals Board.

12.0 Investigation — General

☐ **12.1** State the name, **ADDRESS**, and telephone number of each individual:
(a) who witnessed the **INCIDENT** or the events occurring immediately before or after the **INCIDENT**;
(b) who made any statement at the scene of the **INCIDENT**;
(c) who heard any statements made about the **INCIDENT** by any individual at the scene;

(d) who **YOU OR ANYONE ACTING ON YOUR BEHALF** claim has knowledge of the **INCIDENT** (except for expert witnesses covered by Code of Civil Procedure, § 2034).

☐ **12.2** Have **YOU OR ANYONE ACTING ON YOUR BEHALF** interviewed any individual concerning the **INCIDENT**? If so, for each individual state:
(a) the name, **ADDRESS**, and telephone number of the individual interviewed;
(b) the date of the interview;
(c) the name, **ADDRESS**, and telephone number of the **PERSON** who conducted the interview.

☐ **12.3** Have **YOU OR ANYONE ACTING ON YOUR BEHALF** obtained a written or recorded statement from any individual concerning the **INCIDENT**? If so, for each statement state:
(a) the name, **ADDRESS**, and telephone number of the individual from whom the statement was obtained;
(b) the name, **ADDRESS**, and telephone number of the individual who obtained the statement;
(c) the date the statement was obtained;
(d) the name, **ADDRESS**, and telephone number of each **PERSON** who has the original statement or a copy.

☐ **12.4** Do **YOU OR ANYONE ACTING ON YOUR BEHALF** know of any photographs, films, or videotapes depicting any place, object, or individual concerning the **INCIDENT** or plaintiff's injuries? If so, state:
(a) the number of photographs or feet of film or videotape;
(b) the places, objects, or persons photographed, filmed, or videotaped;
(c) the date the photographs, films, or videotapes were taken;
(d) the name, **ADDRESS**, and telephone number of the individual taking the photographs, films, or videotapes;
(e) the name, **ADDRESS**, and telephone number of each **PERSON** who has the original or a copy.

☐ **12.5** Do **YOU OR ANYONE ACTING ON YOUR BEHALF** know of any diagram, reproduction, or model of any place or thing (except for items developed by expert witnesses covered by Code of Civil Procedure, § 2034) concerning the **INCIDENT**? If so, for each item state:
(a) the type (i.e., diagram, reproduction, or model);
(b) the subject matter;
(c) the name, **ADDRESS**, and telephone number of each **PERSON** who has it.

☐ **12.6** Was a report made by any **PERSON** concerning the **INCIDENT**? If so, state:
(a) the name, title, identification number, and employer of the **PERSON** who made the report;
(b) the date and type of report made;
(c) the name, **ADDRESS**, and telephone number of the **PERSON** for whom the report was made.

☐ **12.7** Have **YOU OR ANYONE ACTING ON YOUR BEHALF** inspected the scene of the **INCIDENT**? If so, for each inspection state:

(a) the name, **ADDRESS**, and telephone number of the individual making the inspection (except for expert witnesses covered by Code of Civil Procedure, § 2034);

(b) the date of the inspection.

13.0 Investigation — Surveillance

13.1 Have **YOU OR ANYONE ACTING ON YOUR BEHALF** conducted surveillance of any individual involved in the **INCIDENT** or any party to this action? If so, for each surveillance state:

(a) the name, **ADDRESS**, and telephone number of the individual or party;

(b) the time, date, and place of the surveillance;

(c) the name, **ADDRESS**, and telephone number of the individual who conducted the surveillance.

13.2 Has a written report been prepared on the surveillance? If so, for each written report state:

(a) the title;

(b) the date;

(c) the name, **ADDRESS**, and telephone number of the individual who prepared the report;

(d) the name, **ADDRESS**, and telephone number of each **PERSON** who has the original or a copy.

14.0 Statutory or Regulatory Violations

14.1 Do **YOU OR ANYONE ACTING ON YOUR BEHALF** contend that any **PERSON** involved in the **INCIDENT** violated any statute, ordinance, or regulation and that the violation was a legal (proximate) cause of the **INCIDENT**? If so, identify each **PERSON** and the statute, ordinance, or regulation.

14.2 Was any **PERSON** cited or charged with a violation of any statute, ordinance, or regulation as a result of this **INCIDENT**? If so, for each **PERSON** state:

(a) the name, **ADDRESS**, and telephone number of the **PERSON**;

(b) the statute, ordinance, or regulation allegedly violated;

(c) whether the **PERSON** entered a plea in response to the citation or charge and, if so, the plea entered;

(d) the name and **ADDRESS** of the court or administrative agency, names of the parties, and case number.

15.0 Special or Affirmative Defenses

15.1 Identify each denial of a material allegation and each special or affirmative defense in your pleadings and for each:

(a) state all facts upon which you base the denial or special or affirmative defense;

(b) state the names, **ADDRESSES**, and telephone numbers of all **PERSONS** who have knowledge of those facts;

(c) identify all **DOCUMENTS** and other tangible things which support your denial or special or affirmative defense, and state the name, **ADDRESS**, and telephone number of the **PERSON** who has each **DOCUMENT**.

16.0 Defendant's Contentions — Personal Injury

[See Instruction 2(c)]

16.1 Do you contend that any **PERSON**, other than you or plaintiff, contributed to the occurrence of the **INCIDENT** or the injuries or damages claimed by plaintiff? If so, for each **PERSON**:

(a) state the name, **ADDRESS**, and telephone number of the **PERSON**;

(b) state all facts upon which you base your contention;

(c) state the names, **ADDRESSES**, and telephone numbers of all **PERSONS** who have knowledge of the facts;

(d) identify all **DOCUMENTS** and other tangible things that support your contention and state the name, **ADDRESS**, and telephone number of the **PERSON** who has each **DOCUMENT** or thing.

16.2 Do you contend that plaintiff was not injured in the **INCIDENT**? If so:

(a) state all facts upon which you base your contention;

(b) state the names, **ADDRESSES**, and telephone numbers of all **PERSONS** who have knowledge of the facts;

(c) identify all **DOCUMENTS** and other tangible things that support your contention and state the name, **ADDRESS**, and telephone number of the **PERSON** who has each **DOCUMENT** or thing.

16.3 Do you contend that the injuries or the extent of the injuries claimed by plaintiff as disclosed in discovery proceedings thus far in this case were not caused by the **INCIDENT**? If so, for each injury:

(a) identify it;

(b) state all facts upon which you base your contention;

(c) state the names, **ADDRESSES**, and telephone numbers of all **PERSONS** who have knowledge of the facts;

(d) identify all **DOCUMENTS** and other tangible things that support your contention and state the name, **ADDRESS**, and telephone number of the **PERSON** who has each **DOCUMENT** or thing.

16.4 Do you contend that any of the services furnished by any **HEALTH CARE PROVIDER** claimed by plaintiff in discovery proceedings thus far in this case were not due to the **INCIDENT**? If so:

(a) identify each service;

(b) state all facts upon which you base your contention;

(c) state the names, **ADDRESSES**, and telephone numbers of all **PERSONS** who have knowledge of the facts;

(d) identify all **DOCUMENTS** and other tangible things that support your contention and state the name, **ADDRESS**, and telephone number of the **PERSON** who has each **DOCUMENT** or thing.

16.5 Do you contend that any of the costs of services furnished by any **HEALTH CARE PROVIDER** claimed as damages by plaintiff in discovery proceedings thus far in this case were unreasonable? If so:

(a) identify each cost;

(b) state all facts upon which you base your contention;

(c) state the names, **ADDRESSES**, and telephone numbers of all **PERSONS** who have knowledge of the facts;

(d) identify all **DOCUMENTS** and other tangible things that support your contention and state the name, **ADDRESS**, and telephone number of the **PERSON** who has each **DOCUMENT** or thing.

16.6 Do you contend that any part of the loss of earnings or income claimed by plaintiff in discovery proceedings thus far in this case was unreasonable or was not caused by the **INCIDENT**? If so:

(a) identify each part of the loss;

(b) state all facts upon which you base your contention;

(c) state the names, **ADDRESSES**, and telephone numbers of all **PERSONS** who have knowledge of the facts;

(d) identify all **DOCUMENTS** and other tangible things that support your contention and state the name, **ADDRESS**, and telephone number of the **PERSON** who has each **DOCUMENT** or thing.

16.7 Do you contend that any of the property damage claimed by plaintiff in discovery proceedings thus far in this case was not caused by the **INCIDENT**? If so:

(a) identify each item of property damage;

(b) state all facts upon which you base your contention;

(c) state the names, **ADDRESSES**, and telephone numbers of all **PERSONS** who have knowledge of the facts;

(d) identify all **DOCUMENTS** and other tangible things that support your contention and state the name, **ADDRESS**, and telephone number of the **PERSON** who has each **DOCUMENT** or thing.

16.8 Do you contend that any of the costs of repairing the property damage claimed by plaintiff in discovery proceedings thus far in this case were unreasonable? If so:

(a) identify each cost item;

(b) state all facts upon which you base your contention;

(c) state the names, **ADDRESSES**, and telephone numbers of all **PERSONS** who have knowledge of the facts;

(d) identify all **DOCUMENTS** and other tangible things that support your contention and state the name, **ADDRESS**, and telephone number of the **PERSON** who has each **DOCUMENT** or thing.

16.9 Do **YOU OR ANYONE ACTING ON YOUR BEHALF** have any **DOCUMENT** (for example, insurance bureau index reports) concerning claims for personal injuries made before or after the **INCIDENT** by a plaintiff in this case? If so, for each plaintiff state:

(a) the source of each **DOCUMENT**;

(b) the date each claim arose;

(c) the nature of each claim;

(d) the name, **ADDRESS**, and telephone number of the **PERSON** who has each **DOCUMENT**.

16.10 Do **YOU OR ANYONE ACTING ON YOUR BEHALF** have any **DOCUMENT** concerning the past or present physical, mental, or emotional condition of any plaintiff in this case from a **HEALTH CARE PROVIDER** not previously identified (except for expert witnesses covered by Code of Civil Procedure, § 2034)? If so, for each plaintiff state:

(a) the name, **ADDRESS**, and telephone number of each **HEALTH CARE PROVIDER**;

(b) a description of each **DOCUMENT**;

(c) the name, **ADDRESS**, and telephone number of the **PERSON** who has each **DOCUMENT**.

17.0 Responses to Request for Admissions

17.1 Is your response to each request for admission served with these interrogatories an unqualified admission? If not, for each response that is not an unqualified admission:

(a) state the number of the request;

(b) state all facts upon which you base your response;

(c) state the names, **ADDRESSES**, and telephone numbers of all **PERSONS** who have knowledge of those facts;

(d) identify all **DOCUMENTS** and other tangible things that support your response and state the name, **ADDRESS**, and telephone number of the **PERSON** who has each **DOCUMENT** or thing.

20.0 How the Incident Occurred — Motor Vehicle

20.1 State the date, time, and place of the **INCIDENT** (closest street **ADDRESS** or intersection).

20.2 For each vehicle involved in the **INCIDENT**, state:

(a) the year, make, model, and license number;

(b) the name, **ADDRESS**, and telephone number of the driver;

(c) the name, **ADDRESS**, and telephone number of each occupant other than the driver;

(d) the name, **ADDRESS**, and telephone number of each registered owner;

(e) the name, **ADDRESS**, and telephone number of each lessee;

(f) the name, **ADDRESS**, and telephone number of each owner other than the registered owner or lien holder;

(g) the name of each owner who gave permission or consent to the driver to operate the vehicle.

20.3 State the **ADDRESS** and location where your trip began, and the **ADDRESS** and location of your destination.

20.4 Describe the route that you followed from the beginning of your trip to the location of the **INCIDENT**, and state the location of each stop, other than routine traffic stops, during the trip leading up to the **INCIDENT**.

20.5 State the name of the street or roadway, the lane of travel, and the direction of travel of each vehicle involved in the **INCIDENT** for the 500 feet of travel before the **INCIDENT**.

20.6 Did the **INCIDENT** occur at an intersection? If so, describe all traffic control devices, signals, or signs at the intersection.

20.7 Was there a traffic signal facing you at the time of the **INCIDENT**? If so, state:
(a) your location when you first saw it;
(b) the color;
(c) the number of seconds it had been that color;
(d) whether the color changed between the time you first saw it and the **INCIDENT**.

20.8 State how the **INCIDENT** occurred, giving the speed, direction, and location of each vehicle involved:
(a) just before the **INCIDENT**;
(b) at the time of the **INCIDENT**;
(c) just after the **INCIDENT**.

20.9 Do you have information that a malfunction or defect in a vehicle caused the **INCIDENT**? If so:
(a) identify the vehicle;
(b) identify each malfunction or defect;
(c) state the name, **ADDRESS**, and telephone number of each **PERSON** who is a witness to or has information about each malfunction or defect;
(d) state the name, **ADDRESS**, and telephone number of each **PERSON** who has custody of each defective part.

20.10 Do you have information that any malfunction or defect in a vehicle contributed to the injuries sustained in the **INCIDENT**? If so:
(a) identify the vehicle;
(b) identify each malfunction or defect;
(c) state the name, **ADDRESS**, and telephone number of each **PERSON** who is a witness to or has information about each malfunction or defect;
(d) state the name, **ADDRESS**, and telephone number of each **PERSON** who has custody of each defective part.

20.11 State the name, **ADDRESS**, and telephone number of each owner and each **PERSON** who has had possession since the **INCIDENT** of each vehicle involved in the **INCIDENT**.

50.0 Contract

50.1 For each agreement alleged in the pleadings:
(a) identify all **DOCUMENTS** that are part of the agreement and for each state the name, **ADDRESS**, and telephone number of each **PERSON** who has the **DOCUMENT**;
(b) state each part of the agreement not in writing, the name, **ADDRESS**, and telephone number of each **PERSON** agreeing to that provision, and the date that part of the agreement was made;
(c) identify all **DOCUMENTS** that evidence each part of the agreement not in writing and for each state the name, **ADDRESS**, and telephone number of each **PERSON** who has the **DOCUMENT**;
(d) identify all **DOCUMENTS** that are part of each modification to the agreement, and for each state the name, **ADDRESS**, and telephone number of each **PERSON** who has the **DOCUMENT**;
(e) state each modification not in writing, the date, and the name, **ADDRESS**, and telephone number of each **PERSON** agreeing to the modification, and the date the modification was made;
(f) identify all **DOCUMENTS** that evidence each modification of the agreement not in writing and for each state the name, **ADDRESS**, and telephone number of each **PERSON** who has the **DOCUMENT**.

50.2 Was there a breach of any agreement alleged in the pleadings? If so, for each breach describe and give the date of every act or omission that you claim is the breach of the agreement.

50.3 Was performance of any agreement alleged in the pleadings excused? If so, identify each agreement excused and state why performance was excused.

50.4 Was any agreement alleged in the pleadings terminated by mutual agreement, release, accord and satisfaction, or novation? If so, identify each agreement terminated and state why it was terminated including dates.

50.5 Is any agreement alleged in the pleadings unenforceable? If so, identify each unenforceable agreement and state why it is unenforceable.

50.6 Is any agreement alleged in the pleadings ambiguous? If so, identify each ambiguous agreement and state why it is ambiguous.

REQUEST FOR ADMISSIONS

[ ] **Truth of Facts** [ ] **Genuineness of Documents**

Requesting Party:

Responding Party:

Set No.:

You are requested to admit within thirty days after service of this Request for Admissions that

A. [ ] each of the following facts is true *(number each fact consecutively)*:

[ ] continued on Attachment A.

B. [ ] the original of each of the following documents, copies of which are attached, is genuine *(number each document consecutively)*:

[ ] continued on Attachment B.

▶

. . . .

    (TYPE OR PRINT NAME)   (SIGNATURE OF PARTY OR ATTORNEY)

AMENDMENT TO COMPLAINT

PARTY WITHOUT ATTORNEY (My Name and Address):

MY TELEPHONE NO.:

FOR COURT USE ONLY

NAME OF COURT:

STREET ADDRESS:

MAILING ADDRESS:

CITY AND ZIP CODE:

BRANCH NAME:

PLAINTIFF:

DEFENDANT:

AMENDMENT TO COMPLAINT
(CCP Section 474)

CASE NUMBER

When plaintiff filed the Complaint in this case, plaintiff was ignorant of the true name of a defendant and therefore plaintiff designated that defendant in the Complaint by the fictitious name: _____ .

Plaintiff has since discovered that the true name of that defendant is: _____ .

Plaintiff hereby amends his/her Complaint by the inserting the true name of that defendant in place of the previously designated fictitious name wherever it appears in the Complaint.

_____
Signature of Plaintiff

_____

Proper cause appearing, plaintiff is hereby allowed to file the above amendment to the Complaint.

Date: _____   _____
COURT COMMISSIONER OF _____ COUNTY

AMENDMENT TO COMPLAINT

— DO NOT FILE WITH THE COURT —

ATTORNEY OR PARTY WITHOUT ATTORNEY (Name and Address):	TELEPHONE NO.:

ATTORNEY FOR (Name)

NAME OF COURT
STREET ADDRESS
MAILING ADDRESS
CITY AND ZIP CODE
BRANCH NAME

PLAINTIFF:

DEFENDANT:

REQUEST FOR STATEMENT OF WITNESSES AND EVIDENCE	CASE NUMBER:

Requesting Party *(name):*

Responding Party *(name):*

Under Code of Civil Procedure section 96, you are requested to serve on the undersigned, within 20 days, a statement of:

1. The names and street addresses of witnesses you intend to call at trial (except for any individual who is a party to this action).

2. A description of each document that you intend to offer at trial. Attach a copy of each document available to you.

3. A description of each photograph and other physical evidence you intend to offer at trial.

Witnesses and evidence that will be used only for impeachment need not be included.

YOU WILL NOT BE PERMITTED TO CALL ANY WITNESS OR INTRODUCE ANY EVIDENCE NOT INCLUDED IN YOUR RESPONSE TO THIS REQUEST, EXCEPT AS OTHERWISE PROVIDED BY LAW.

Date:

▶

_____
(TYPED OR PRINTED NAME)

_____
(SIGNATURE OF PARTY OR ATTORNEY)

1

2

3

4

5

6

7

8

9

10

11

12

13

14

15

16

17

18

19

20

21

22

23

24

25

26

27

28

CATALOG

ESTATE PLANNING & PROBATE

Plan Your Estate With a Living Trust
Attorney Denis Clifford
National 1st Edition
This book covers every significant aspect of estate planning and gives detailed specific, instructions for preparing a living trust, a document that lets your family avoid expensive and lengthy probate court proceedings after your death. *Plan Your Estate* includes all the tear-out forms and step-by-step instructions to let you prepare an estate plan designed for your special needs.
$19.95/NEST

Nolo's Simple Will Book
Attorney Denis Clifford
National 2nd Edition
It's easy to write a legally valid will using this book. The instructions and forms enable people to draft a will for all needs, including naming a personal guardian for minor children, leaving property to minor children or young adults and updating a will when necessary. Good in all states except Louisiana.
$17.95/SWIL

The Power of Attorney Book
Attorney Denis Clifford
National 4th Edition
Who will take care of your affairs, and make your financial and medical decisions if you can't? With this book you can appoint someone you trust to carry out your wishes and stipulate exactly what kind of care you want or don't want. Includes Durable Power of Attorney and Living Will Forms.
$19.95/POA

How to Probate an Estate
Julia Nissley
California 6th Edition
If you find yourself responsible for winding up the legal and financial affairs of a deceased family member or friend, you can often save costly attorneys' fees by handling the probate process yourself. This book shows you the simple procedures you can use to transfer assets that don't require probate, including property held in joint tenancy or living trusts or as community property.
$34.95/PAE

The Conservatorship Book
Lisa Goldoftas & Attorney Carolyn Farren
California 1st Edition
When a family member or close relative becomes incapacitated due to illness or age, it may be necessary to name a conservator for taking charge of their medical and financial affairs. *The Conservatorship Book* will help you determine when and what kind of conservatorship is necessary. The book comes with complete instructions and all the forms necessary to file conservatorship documents, appear in court, be appointed conservator and end a conservatorship when it is no longer necessary.
$24.95/CON

LEGAL REFORM

Legal Breakdown: 40 Ways to Fix Our Legal System
Nolo Press Editors and Staff
National 1st Edition
Legal Breakdown presents 40 common sense proposals to make our legal system fairer, faster, cheaper and more accessible. It explains such things as why we should abolish probate, take divorce out of court, treat jurors better and give them more power, and make a host of other fundamental changes.
$8.95/LEG

GOING TO COURT

Everybody's Guide to Small Claims Court
Attorney Ralph Warner
National 5th Edition
California 9th Edition
These books will help you decide if you should sue in small claims court, show you how to file and serve papers, tell you what to bring to court and how to collect a judgment.
National $15.95/NSCC
California $14.95/ CSCC

Fight Your Ticket
Attorney David Brown
California 4th Edition
This book shows you how to fight an unfair traffic ticket—when you're stopped, at arraignment, at trial and on appeal.
$17.95/FYT

Collect Your Court Judgment
Gini Graham Scott, Attorney Stephen Elias & Lisa Goldoftas
California 2nd Edition
This book contains step-by-step instructions and all the forms you need to collect a court judgment from the debtor's bank accounts, wages, business receipts, real estate or other assets.
$19.95/JUDG

How to Change Your Name
Attorneys David Loeb & David Brown
California 5th Edition
This book explains how to change your name legally and provides all the necessary court forms with detailed instructions on how to fill them out.
$19.95/NAME

The Criminal Records Book
Attorney Warren Siegel
California 3rd Edition
This book shows you step-by-step how to seal criminal records, dismiss convictions, destroy marijuana records and reduce felony convictions.
$19.95/CRIM

MONEY MATTERS

Barbara Kaufman's Consumer Action Guide
Barbara Kaufman
California 1st Edition
This practical handbook is filled with information on hundreds of consumer topics. Barbara Kaufman, the Bay Area's award-winning host and producer of KCBS Radio's *Call for Action*, gives consumers access to their legal rights, providing addresses and phone numbers of where to complain where things to wrong, and providing resources if more help is necessary.
$14.95/CAG

Money Troubles: Legal Strategies to Cope With Your Debts
Attorney Robin Leonard
National 1st Edition
Are you behind on your credit card bills or loan payments? If you are, then *Money Troubles* is exactly what you need. Covering everything from knowing what your rights are—and asserting them to helping you evaluate your individual situation, this practical, straightforward book is for anyone who needs help understanding and dealing with the complex and often scary topic of debts.
$16.95/MT

How to File for Bankruptcy
Attorneys Stephen Elias, Albin Renauer & Robin Leonard
National 3rd Edition
Trying to decide whether or not filing for bankruptcy makes sense? *How to File for Bankruptcy* contains an overview of the process and all the forms plus step-by-step instructions on the procedures to follow.
$24.95/HFB

Simple Contracts for Personal Use
Attorney Stephen Elias & Marcia Stewart
National 2nd Edition
This book contains clearly written legal form contracts to buy and sell property, borrow and lend money, store and lend personal property, release others from personal liability, or pay a contractor to do home repairs. Includes agreements to arrange child care and contract with caterers, photographers and other service providers for special events.
$16.95/CONT

FAMILY MATTERS

The Living Together Kit
Attorneys Toni Ihara & Ralph Warner
National 6th Edition
The Living Together Kit is a detailed guide designed to help the increasing number of unmarried couples living together understand the laws that affect them. Sample agreements and instructions are included.
$17.95/LTK

A Legal Guide for Lesbian and Gay Couples
Attorneys Hayden Curry & Denis Clifford
National 6th Edition
Laws designed to regulate and protect unmarried couples don't apply to lesbian and gay couples. This book shows you step-by-step how to write a living-together contract, plan for medical emergencies, and plan your estates. Includes forms, sample agreements and lists of both national lesbian and gay legal organizations, and AIDS organizations.
$17.95/LG

The Guardianship Book
Lisa Goldoftas & Attorney David Brown
California 1st Edition
The Guardianship Book provides step-by-step instructions and the forms needed to obtain a legal guardianship without a lawyer.
$19.95/GB

How to Do Your Own Divorce
Attorney Charles Sherman
(Texas Ed. by Sherman & Simons)
California 17th Edition & Texas 4th Edition
These books contain all the forms and instructions you need to do your divorce without a lawyer.
California $18.95/CDIV
Texas $17.95/TDIV

Practical Divorce Solutions
Attorney Charles Sherman
California 2nd Edition
This book is a valuable guide to the emotional aspects of divorce as well as an overview of the legal and financial decisions that must be made.
$12.95/PDS

California Marriage & Divorce Law
Attorneys Ralph Warner, Toni Ihara & Stephen Elias
California 11th Edition
This book explains community property, pre-nuptial contracts, foreign marriages, buying a house, getting a divorce, dividing property, and more.
$19.95/MARR

How to Adopt Your Stepchild in California
Frank Zagone & Attorney Mary Randolph
California 3rd Edition
There are many emotional, financial and legal reasons to adopt a stepchild, but among the most pressing legal reasons is the need to avoid confusion over inheritance or guardianship. This book provides sample forms and step-by-step instructions for completing a simple uncontested adoption by a stepparent
$19.95/ADOP

BUSINESS

How to Write a Business Plan
Mike McKeever
National 3rd Edition
If you're thinking of starting a business or raising money to expand an existing one, this book will show you how to write the business plan and loan package necessary to finance your business and make it work.
$17.95/SBS

Marketing Without Advertising
Michael Phillips & Salli Rasberry
National 1st Edition
This book outlines practical steps for building and expanding a small business without spending a lot of money on advertising.
$14.00/MWAD

The Partnership Book
Attorneys Denis Clifford & Ralph Warner
National 4th Edition
This book shows you step-by-step how to write a solid partnership agreement that meets your needs. It covers initial contributions to the business, wages, profit-sharing, buy-outs, death or retirement of a partner and disputes.
$24.95/PART

How to Form Your Own Nonprofit Corporation
Attorney Anthony Mancuso
National 1st Edition
This book explains the legal formalities involved and provides detailed information on the differences in the law among 50 states. It also contains forms for the Articles, Bylaws and Minutes you need, along with complete instructions for obtaining federal 501 (c) (3) tax exemptions and qualifying for public charity status.
$24.95/NNP

The California Nonprofit Corporation Handbook
Attorney Anthony Mancuso
California 6th Edition
This book shows you step-by-step how to form and operate a nonprofit corporation in California. It includes the latest corporate and tax law changes, and the forms for the Articles, Bylaws and Minutes.
$29.95/NON

How to Form Your Own Corporation
Attorney Anthony Mancuso
California 7th Edition
New York 2nd Edition
Texas 4th Edition
Florida 3rd Edition
These books contain the forms, instructions and tax information you need to incorporate a small business yourself and save hundreds of dollars in lawyers' fees.
California $29.95/CCOR
New York $24.95/NYCO
Texas $24.95/TCOR
Florida $24.95/FLCO

The California Professional Corporation Handbook
Attorney Anthony Mancuso
California 4th Edition
Health care professionals, lawyers, accountants and members of certain other professions must fulfill special requirements when forming a corporation in California. This book contains up-to-date tax information plus all the forms and instructions necessary to form a California professional corporation.
$34.95/PROF

The Independent Paralegal's Handbook
Attorney Ralph Warner
National 2nd Edition
The Independent Paralegal's Handbook provides legal and business guidelines for those who want to take routine legal work out of the law office and offer it for a reasonable fee in an independent business.
$19.95/ PARA

Getting Started as an Independent Paralegal
(Two Audio Tapes)
Attorney Ralph Warner
National 1st Edition
Approximately three hours in all, these tapes are a carefully edited version of a seminar given by Nolo Press founder Ralph Warner. They are designed to be used with *The Independent Paralegal's Handbook.*
$44.95/GSIP

PATENT, COPYRIGHT & TRADEMARK

Patent It Yourself
Attorney David Pressman
National 3rd Edition
From the patent search to the actual application, this book covers everything from use and licensing, successful marketing and how to deal with infringement.
$34.95/PAT

The Inventor's Notebook
Fred Grissom & Attorney David Pressman
National 1st Edition
This book helps you document the process of successful independent inventing by providing forms, instructions, references to relevant areas of patent law, a bibliography of legal and non-legal aids and more.
$19.95/INOT

How to Copyright Software
Attorney M.J. Salone
National 3rd Edition
This book tells you how to register your copyright for maximum protection and discusses who owns a copyright on software developed by more than one person.
$39.95/COPY

THE NEIGHBORHOOD

Neighbor Law:
Fences, Trees, Boundaries & Noise
Attorney Cora Jordan
National 1st Edition
Neighbor Law answers common questions about the subjects that most often trigger disputes between neighbors: trees, fences, boundaries and noise. It explains how to find the law and resolve disputes without a nasty lawsuit.
$14.95/NEI

Dog Law
Attorney Mary Randolph
National 1st Edition
Dog Law is a practical guide to the laws that affect dog owners and their neighbors. You'll find answers to common questions on such topics as biting, barking, veterinarians and more.
$12.95/DOG

HOMEOWNERS

How to Buy a House in California
Attorney Ralph Warner, Ira Serkes &
George Devine
California 1st Edition
This book shows you how to find a house, work with a real estate agent, make an offer and negotiate intelligently. Includes information on all types of mortgages as well as private financing options.
$18.95/BHCA

For Sale By Owner
George Devine
California 1st Edition
For Sale By Owner provides essential information about pricing your house, marketing it, writing a contract and going through escrow.
$24.95/FSBO

The Deeds Book
Attorney Mary Randolph
California 1st Edition
If you own real estate, you'll need to sign a new deed when you transfer the property or put it in trust as part of your estate planning. This book shows you how to find the right kind of deed, complete the tear-out forms and record them in the county recorder's public records.
$15.95/DEED

Homestead Your House
Attorneys Ralph Warner, Charles Sherman & Toni Ihara
California 7th Edition
This book shows you how to file a Declaration of Homestead and includes complete instructions and tear-out forms.
$9.95/HOME

LANDLORDS & TENANTS

The Landlord's Law Book: Vol. 1, Rights & Responsibilities
Attorneys David Brown & Ralph Warner
California 3rd Edition
This book contains information on deposits, leases and rental agreements, inspections (tenant's privacy rights), habitability (rent withholding), ending a tenancy, liability and rent control.
$29.95/LBRT

The Landlord's Law Book: Vol. 2, Evictions
Attorney David Brown
California 3rd Edition
Updated for 1991, this book will show you step-by-step how to go to court and get an eviction for a tenant who won't pay rent—and won't leave. Contains all the tear-out forms and necessary instructions.
$29.95/LBEV

Tenant's Rights
Attorneys Myron Moskovitz & Ralph Warner
California 11th Edition
This book explains the best way to handle your relationship both your landlord and your legal rights when you find yourself in disagreement. A special section on rent control cities is included.
$15.95/CTEN

OLDER AMERICANS

Elder Care: Choosing & Financing Long-Term Care
Attorney Joseph Matthews
National 1st Edition
This book will guide you in choosing and paying for long-term care, alerting you to practical concerns and explaining laws that may affect your decisions.
$16.95/ELD

Social Security, Medicare & Pensions
Attorney Joseph Matthews with Dorothy Matthews Berman
National 5th Edition
This book contains invaluable guidance through the current maze of rights and benefits for those 55 and over, including Medicare, Medicaid and Social Security retirement and disability benefits and age discrimination protections.
$15.95/SOA

JUST FOR FUN

29 Reasons Not to Go to Law School
Attorneys Ralph Warner & Toni Ihara
National 3rd Edition
Filled with humor and piercing observations, this book can save you three years, $70,000 and your sanity.
$9.95/29R

Devil's Advocates: The Unnatural History of Lawyers
by Andrew & Jonathan Roth
National 1st Edition
This book is a painless and hilarious education, tracing the legal profession. Careful attention is given to the world's worst lawyers, most preposterous cases and most ludicrous courtroom strategies.
$12.95/DA

Poetic Justice: The Funniest, Meanest Things Ever Said About Lawyers
Edited by Jonathan & Andrew Roth
National 1st Edition
A great gift for anyone in the legal profession who has managed to maintain a sense of humor.
$8.95/PJ

RESEARCH & REFERENCE

Legal Research: How to Find and Understand the Law
Attorney Stephen Elias
National 2nd Edition
A valuable tool on its own or as a companion to just about every other Nolo book. This book gives easy-to-use, step-by-step instructions on how to find legal information.
$14.95/LRES

Family Law Dictionary
Attorneys Robin Leonard & Stephen Elias
National 2nd Edition
Finally, a legal dictionary that's written in plain English, not "legalese"! *The Family Law Dictionary* is designed to help the nonlawyer who has a question or problem involving family law—marriage, divorce, adoption or living together.
$13.95/FLD

Patent, Copyright & Trademark: The Intellectual Property Law Dictionary
Attorney Stephen Elias
National 2nd Edition
This book explains the terms associated with trade secrets, copyrights, trademarks, patents and contracts.
$15.95/IPLD

Legal Research Made Easy: A Roadmap Through the Law Library Maze
2-1/2 hr. videotape and 40-page manual
Nolo Press/Legal Star Communications
If you're a law student, paralegal or librarian—or just want to look up the law for yourself—this video is for you. University of California law professor Bob Berring explains how to use all the basic legal research tools in your local law library with an easy-to-follow six-step research plan and a sense of humor.
$89.95/LRME

SOFTWARE

WillMaker
Nolo Press/Legisoft
National 4th Edition
This easy-to-use software program lets you prepare and update a legal will—safely, privately and without the expense of a lawyer. Leading you step-by-step in a question-and-answer format, *WillMaker* builds a will around your answers, taking into account your state of residence. *WillMaker* comes with a 200-page legal manual which provides the legal background necessary to make sound choices. Good in all states except Louisiana.
IBM PC
(3-1/2 & 5-1/4 disks included) $69.95/WI4
MACINTOSH $69.95/WM4

For the Record
Carol Pladsen & Attorney Ralph Warner
National 2nd Edition
For the Record program provides a single place to keep a complete inventory of all your important legal, financial, personal and family records. It can compute your net worth and also create inventories of all insured property to protect your assets in the event of fire or theft. Includes a 200-page manual filled with practical and legal advice.
IBM PC
(3-1/2 & 5-1/4 disks included) $59.95/FRI2
MACINTOSH $59.95/FRM2

California Incorporator
Attorney Anthony Mancuso/Legisoft
California 1st Edition
Answer the questions on the screen and this software program will print out the 35-40 pages of documents you need to make your California corporation legal. Comes with a 200-page manual which explains the incorporation process.
IBM PC
(3-1/2 & 5-1/4 disks included) $129.00/INCI

The California Nonprofit Corporation Handbook
(computer edition)
Attorney Anthony Mancuso
California 1st Edition
This book/software package shows you step-by-step how to form and operate a nonprofit corporation in California. Included on disk are the forms for the Articles, Bylaws and Minutes.
IBM PC 5-1/4 $69.95/NPI
IBM PC 3-1/2 $69.95/NP3I
MACINTOSH $69.95/NPM

How to Form Your Own New York Corporation & How to Form Your Own Texas Corporation
Computer Editions
Attorney Anthony Mancuso
These book/software packages contain the instructions and tax information and forms you need to incorporate a small business and save hundreds of dollars in lawyers' fees. All organizational forms are on disk. Both come with a 250-page manual.

New York 1st Edition
IBM PC 5-1/4 $69.95/NYCI
IBM PC 3-1/2 $69.95/NYC3I
MACINTOSH $69.95/NYCM

Texas 1st Edition
IBM PC 5-1/4 $69.95/TCI
IBM PC 3-1/2 $69.95/TC3I
MACINTOSH $69.95/TCM

VISIT OUR STORE

If you live in the Bay Area, be sure to visit the Nolo Press Bookstore on the corner of 9th & Parker Streets in West Berkeley. You'll find our complete line of books and software—new and "damaged"—all at a discount. We also have t-shirts, posters and a selection of business and legal self-help books from other publishers.

HOURS

Monday to Friday	10 a.m. to 5 p.m.
Thursdays	Until 6 p.m
Saturdays	10 a.m. to 4:30 p.m.
Sundays	10 a.m. to 3 p.m.

950 Parker St., Berkeley, California 94710

ORDER FORM

Name _____

Address (UPS to street address, Priority Mail to P.O. boxes)

Catalog Code	Quantity	Item	Unit price	Total
		Subtotal		
		Sales tax (California residents only)		
		Shipping & handling		
		2nd day UPS		
		TOTAL		
		PRICES SUBJECT TO CHANGE		

SALES TAX
California residents add your local tax:
7 1/4%, 7 3/4%, or 8-1/4%

SHIPPING & HANDLING
$4.00   1 item
$5.00   2-3 items
+$.50   each additional item
Allow 2-3 weeks for delivery

IN A HURRY?
UPS 2nd day delivery is available:
Add $5.00 (contiguous states) or
$8.00 (Alaska & Hawaii) to your regular shipping and handling charges

FOR FASTER SERVICE, USE YOUR CREDIT CARD AND OUR TOLL-FREE NUMBERS:
Monday-Friday, 7 a.m. to 5 p.m. Pacific Time

US & CA outside 415 & 510 area code	1 (800) 992-6656
CA (inside 510 area code)	549-1976
General Information	1 (510) 549-1976
Fax us your order	1 (510) 548-5902

METHOD OF PAYMENT
☐ Check enclosed
☐ VISA   ☐ Mastercard   ☐ Discover Card   ☐ American Express

Account #   Expiration Date
_____

Signature Authorizing
_____

Phone

HFB

N O L O   P R E S S   /   9 5 0   P A R K E R   S T R E E T   /   B E R K E L E Y   C A   9 4 7 1 0

UPDATE SERVICE

RECYCLE YOUR OUT-OF-DATE BOOKS AND
GET 25% OFF YOUR NEXT PURCHASE!

It's important to have the most current legal information. Because laws and legal procedures change often, we update our books regularly. To help keep you up-to-date, we are extending this special offer: Send or bring us the title portion of the cover of any old Nolo book and we'll give you a 25% discount off the retail price of any new Nolo book! You'll find current prices and an order form at the back of this book. Generally speaking, any book more than two years old is of questionable value. Books more than four or five years old are usually a menace. This offer is to individuals only.

OUT-OF-DATE = DANGEROUS

FREE NOLO NEWS SUBSCRIPTION

When you register, we'll send you our quarterly newspaper, the *Nolo News,* free for two years. (U.S. addresses only.) Here's what you'll get in every issue:

INFORMATIVE ARTICLES

Written by Nolo editors, articles provide practical legal information on issues you encounter in everyday life: family law, wills, debts, consumer rights, and much more.

UPDATE SERVICE

The *Nolo News* keeps you informed of legal changes that affect any Nolo book and software program.

BOOK AND SOFTWARE REVIEWS

We're always looking for good legal and consumer books and software from other publishers. When we find them, we review them and offer them in our mail order catalog.

ANSWERS TO YOUR LEGAL QUESTIONS

Our readers are always challenging us with good questions on a variety of legal issues. So in each issue, "Auntie Nolo" gives sage advice and sound information.

COMPLETE NOLO PRESS CATALOG

The *Nolo News* contains an up-to-the-minute catalog of all Nolo books and software, which you can order using our toll-free "800" order line. And you can see at a glance if you're using an out-of-date version of a Nolo product.

LAWYER JOKES

Nolo's famous lawyer joke column continually gets the goat of the legal establishment. If we print a joke you send in, you'll get a $20 Nolo gift certificate.

We promise *never* to give your name and address to any other organization.

Your Registration Card

Complete and Mail Today

Everybody's Guide to Municipal Court   Registration Card

We'd like to know what you think! Please take a moment to fill out and return this postage paid card for a free two-year subscription to the *Nolo News.* If you already receive the *Nolo News,* we'll extend your subscription.

Name _____ Ph.(   ) _____

Address _____

City _____ State _____ Zip _____

Where did you hear about this book? _____

For what purpose did you use this book? _____

Did you consult a lawyer?		Yes	No		Not Applicable		
Was it easy for you to use this book?	(very easy)	5	4	3	2	1	(very difficult)
Did you find this book helpful?	(very)	5	4	3	2	1	(not at all)

Comments _____
_____
_____
_____
_____
_____

THANK YOU   MUNI

[Nolo books are]..."written in plain language, free of legal mumbo jumbo, and spiced with witty personal observations."

—ASSOCIATED PRESS

"Well-produced and slickly written, the [Nolo] books are designed to take the mystery out of seemingly involved procedures, carefully avoiding legalese and leading the reader step-by-step through such everyday legal problems as filling out forms, making up contracts, and even how to behave in court."

—SAN FRANCISCO EXAMINER

"...Nolo publications...guide people simply through the how, when, where and why of law."

—WASHINGTON POST

"Increasingly, people who are not lawyers are performing tasks usually regarded as legal work... And consumers, using books like Nolo's, do routine legal work themselves."

—NEW YORK TIMES

"...All of [Nolo's] books are easy-to-understand, are updated regularly, provide pull-out forms...and are often quite moving in their sense of compassion for the struggles of the lay reader."

—SAN FRANCISCO CHRONICLE